Cinema is a dominant force in the lives of many people living in Asia, a continent that has a number of distinguished national film industries. A concept central to much of Asian film production is melodrama. This path-breaking study examines the importance of melodrama in the film traditions of Japan, India, China, Indonesia, the Philippines, and Australia. Exploring with theoretical sophistication the various ways that melodrama operates, the essays contained in this volume shed light on the different traditions of Asian cinema, as well as on the wider cultural discourse in which they participate.

MELODRAMA AND ASIAN CINEMA

CAMBRIDGE
STUDIES
IN FILM

GENERAL EDITORS

Henry Breitrose, *Stanford University*
William Rothman, *University of Miami*

ADVISORY BOARD

Dudley Andrew, *University of Iowa*
Anthony Smith, *Magdalen College, Oxford*
Colin Young, *National Film School*

OTHER BOOKS IN THE SERIES

Film and Phenomenology, by Allan Casebier
Chinese Cinema: Culture and Politics since 1949, by Paul Clark
The Gorgon's Gaze: German Cinema, Expressionism and the Image of Horror,
by Paul Coates
Nonindifferent Nature: Film and the Structure of Things, by Sergei Eisenstein
(trans. Herbert Marshall)
Constructivism in Film: The Man with the Movie Camera, by Vlada Petric
Renoir on Renoir: Interviews, Essays, and Remarks, by Jean Renoir (trans.
Carol Volk)
The Taste for Beauty, by Eric Rohmer (trans. Carol Volk)
The "I" of the Camera: Essays in Film Criticism, History, and Aesthetics, by
William Rothman
The British Documentary Film Movement, 1926–1946, by Paul Swann
Metaphor and Film, by Trevor Whittock

MELODRAMA AND ASIAN CINEMA

Edited by
WIMAL DISSANAYAKE
East–West Center
Institute of Culture and Communication

CAMBRIDGE UNIVERSITY PRESS
Cambridge, New York, Melbourne, Madrid, Cape Town, Singapore, São Paulo

Cambridge University Press
The Edinburgh Building, Cambridge CB2 2RU, UK

Published in the United States of America by Cambridge University Press, New York

www.cambridge.org
Information on this title: www.cambridge.org/9780521414654

© Cambridge University Press 1993

First published 1993
This digitally printed first paperback version 2005

A catalogue record for this publication is available from the British Library

Library of Congress Cataloguing in Publication data
Melodrama and Asian cinema / Wimal Dissanayake, editor.
p.   cm.
ISBN 0-521-41465-2
1. Motion pictures – Asian.   2. Melodrama in motion pictures.
I. Dissanayake, Wimal.
PN1993.5.A75M45   1993
791.43'095 – dc20   92-23862

ISBN-13 978-0-521-41465-4 hardback
ISBN-10 0-521-41465-2 hardback

ISBN-13 978-0-521-61208-1 paperback
ISBN-10 0-521-61208-X paperback

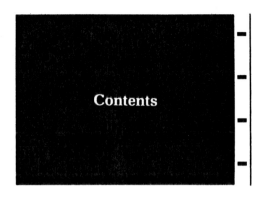

Contents

Contributors

Susan Dermody is a member of the Faculty of Humanities at the University of Technology, Sydney, Australia. She and Elizabeth Jacka coauthored the two-volume study *The Screening of Australia*.

Wimal Dissanayake is the assistant director of the Institute of Culture and Communication, East–West Center, and the head of its film program. He is the author of several books including *Cinema and Cultural Identity* and *Sholay – A Cultural Reading*. He is the editor of the *East–West Film Journal*.

Teresita A. Herrera is in the Department of Political Science, University of Hawaii. One of her areas of scholarly interest is cinema in the Philippines and questions of culture and nationhood.

E. Ann Kaplan is professor of English and director of the Humanities Institute at the State University of New York at Stony Brook. She has written widely on women in film, cultural studies, and television. Among her books are *Women and Film, Psychoanalysis and Cinema*, and most recently *Motherhood and Representation: The Mother in Popular Culture and Melodrama*.

Ma Ning holds a doctorate in film studies from Monash University, Australia. He is a well-known scholar of Chinese cinema, and one of his main areas of interest is Chinese melodrama.

Scott Nygren is associate professor of film studies in the Department of English at the University of Florida. He has previously published in such journals as *Wide Angle, Journal of Film and Video, Jump Cut*, and *East–West Film Journal*. He is currently writing a book on Japanese cinema.

William Rothman is a well-known film scholar who now teaches at the University of Miami. He is the author of *Hitchcock: The Murderous Gaze* and *The "I" of the Camera: Essays in Film Criticism, History, and Aesthetics*.

Catherine Russell is assistant professor of film studies at Concordia University, Montreal, Canada. The relationship between cinema and cultural discourse is one of her domains of scholarly interest.

Krishna Sen teachers in the School of Humanities at Murdoch University, Perth, Australia. She is an editor of the quarterly magazine *Inside Indonesia*. Her book on Indonesian cinema is due to be published in early 1993.

Maureen Turim is professor of film studies in the English Department at the University of Florida. Her most recent book is *Flashback in Film: Memory and History*. Her articles have appeared in numerous journals and anthologies.

Yuejin Wang is a Ph.D. candidate in the Department of Fine Arts, Harvard University. He has published articles in journals such as *Framework, Wide Angle, East–West Film Journal*, and *Public Culture*. He is a highly regarded scholar of Chinese cinema.

Paul Willemen is an influential film commentator based in London. He is a former editor of the British film journal *Framework* and has done pioneering work on film and melodrama. He is a coeditor of *Questions of Third Cinema*.

Mitsuhiro Yoshimoto teaches in the Department of Asian Languages and Literature and in the comparative literature program at the University of Iowa. He is currently working on two projects: the problematic of the body in the age of new capitalist empires and the origins of modern Japanese art.

Acknowledgments

For over a decade I have been coordinating the East–West Center's annual film symposium, which brings to the Center distinguished film scholars working on Asian cinema and comparative poetics of cinema. It has been a truly rewarding educational experience for me to interact with these fine minds. Many of the papers gathered in this volume were first presented at the symposium on melodrama held in 1989. First of all I wish to thank all the contributors to this volume. Bill Rothman took a great interest in this project from the very beginning. I would like to express my deep sense of gratitude to Bill Rothman and Kitty Morgan for their friendship and wise counsel over the years. My wife Doreen and my daughter Niru helped me in numerous ways in the preparation of this manuscript. It has been a pleasure to work with the staff and editors of the Cambridge University Press. Their efficiency and professionalism are exemplary.

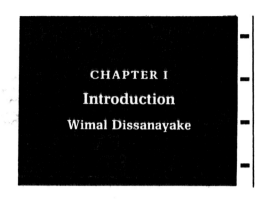

"Melodrama" comes from the Greek word *melos,* meaning song and originally denoted a stage play accompanied by music. According to the early nineteenth-century use of the term, melodrama meant a romantic and sentimental play that contained songs and music deemed appropriate for enhancing the situations presented on stage. It is generally believed that the French writer Jean Jacques Rousseau first used the term *melodrame* in this sense. "Pygmalion," with liberetto by Rousseau, was first performed in Lyon in 1770, and is considered the first melodrama in the West. From France, the term spread to other European cultures. In later times, music ceased to be an integral part of melodrama, and the term came to signify a form of drama characterized by sensationalism, emotional intensity, hyperbole, strong action, violence, rhetorical excesses, moral polarities, brutal villainy and its ultimate elimination, and the triumph of good. The words melodrama and melodramatic, which were originally applied to stage plays, later came to be used to describe and evaluate aspects of literature and film.

Until very recent times, the term melodrama was used pejoratively to typify inferior works of art that subscribed to an aesthetic of hyperbole, and which were given to sensationalism and the crude manipulation of the audiences' emotions (Brooks 1976). However, the past fifteen years or so has seen a distinct rehabilitation of the term within film studies with the reexamination of such issues as the nature of representation in cinema and the role of ideology and female subjectivity in films. Melodrama is now primarily employed not as a term of derogation or disparagement but as a neutral term that characterizes certain genres of film. Many contemporary film scholars and critics have begun to explore the nature, structure, and significance of melodramas and the complex ways in which they draw spectators into the orbit of narration. Melodrama has come to be recognized as containing subversive potential for exposing bourgeois ideology and an enabling vision to map the dialectic between ideology and desire.

1

The objective of this short essay is to call attention to this terminological and evaluative metamorphosis and to underscore the importance of melodrama in our appreciation of Asian cinema. In this regard I wish to focus on what I think are three important aspects related to film and melodrama. The first is that melodrama tends to give prominence to the experiences, emotions, and activities of women. Melodramas bring to the fore facets of women's experiences that are submerged in other genres and provide a forum for the expression of repressed feminine voices (Gledhill 1987). Melodramas may not have succeeded totally in breaking loose of the shackles of patriarchy, but they constitute an important moment in the development of the consciousness of women – hence the current interest in them by serious students of cinema.

Second, with the spread of postmodernist thinking, more and more film theorists and critics are abandoning the received categories of high art and low art, elitist aesthetics and popular entertainment, and are beginning to pay more attention to fundamental issues of representation, the role of ideology, and cultural construction. As a consequence, women's romances, crime thrillers, rock 'n' roll music, slasher films, comics, and television soap operas are receiving the kind of scrutiny that was once reserved for the canonized works of Eliot and Joyce and Kafka. Hence it is hardly surprising that melodramas, which form a vital segment of popular entertainment, should receive careful and sympathetic attention. A consequence has been the exposure of the complex and subtle working of ideology in melodramas and the cultural contradictions inherent in them. In works of art subscribing to a credo of realism, whether they be literature or film – and realism represents one stylistic antithesis of melodrama – the ubiquitous working of ideology is concealed and "naturalized." But melodramas, with their strong action, emotional intensities, and rhetorical excesses, assume an antirealistic orientation. The excesses and extremes in melodrama become signifiers of the alienation of their characters and useful openings through which we can discern the play of ideology.

Third, melodramas are important because of the ways they illuminate the deeper structures of diverse cultures. Thus far I have been discussing melodrama within the context of Western cultural discourse. But it is crucial to bear in mind that melodrama also constitutes an important area of creative expression in many Asian cultures. All cultural artifacts are products of specific histories and cultural formations, and melodramas exemplify in concrete ways the diverse casts of mind, shapes of emotion, vocabularies of expression, imaginative logics, and priorities of valuation of different cultures. Art in any society cannot be understood in aesthetic terms alone but needs to be related to other domains of social activity; concomitantly, melodramas gain in depth and definition when examined in relation to the fabric of life and cultural contours of the society from which they emerge. By examining the processes of creation and modes of reception of film melodramas in different Asian countries, we can move closer to the cultural wellsprings of human creativity. Let us, for example, consider the notion of villainy, which is central to melodrama. The way this notion is conceptualized in Western melodramas is significantly different from the ways in which it is formulated in, say, the melodramas of Raj Kapoor (India) or Lino Brocka (Philippines). In most Asian societies melodrama has a distinguished history considerably different from its history in the West and is intimately linked to myth, ritual, religious practices, and ceremonies. In this regard, it is well to remember the words of the anthropologist Clifford Geertz, who observed that it is out of participation in the general system of symbolic forms we call culture that participation in the particular we call art, which is in fact but a sector of culture, is possible, and a theory of art is therefore simultaneously a theory of culture (Geertz 1983). The implications of this observation for the cross-cultural study of melodrama are profound and far-reaching.

Although we may use the term melodrama to characterize some types of Asian cinema, it is well to remind ourselves that none of the Asian languages has a synonym for this word. Such terms as we find in modern usage are recent coinages based on the English word. For example, in many of the South Asian languages terms such as *bhavathishaya natya* (drama with excessive emotion) and *adbhuta rasa pradhana sukhanta nataka* (dramas with happy endings in which the emotion of strangeness is uppermost), which are used to designate the term melodrama, are clearly of recent vintage. Classical India possessed a very rich dramatic literature, much of which could be categorized as melodrama. Some of the theoretical treatises composed on drama that were in India are among the finest in the world, but the concept of melodrama does not figure in them. Ancient scholars categorized drama into ten groups based on the structure of the drama, the nature of the protagonist, and the character of the aesthetic emotion generated. The idea of melodrama as we currently understand the term seems to cut across and pervade all ten types of drama.

Although there is no term for melodrama in the classical vocabularies, Asian scholars and critics of cinema are increasingly using this Western term to effect finer discriminations. As a consequence of the impact of the West, literature, drama, and cinema (which is directly an outgrowth of Western influence) have undergone profound transformations. Consequently, newer discriminations need to be made in relation to genre, experience, and sensibility, and the concept of melodrama is proving handy. As we seek to employ this term for conceptual clarification, we need to constantly keep in mind that melo-drama in Asia connotes different sets of associations from those obtaining in the West.

For example, the concept of suffering is pivotal to the discourse of film melodrama in Asian cultures. We need to bear in mind the fact that most Asian cultures valorize human suffering as a pervasive fact of life and that salvation is a liberatory experience emanating from the insights into the nature and ineluctability of human suffering. Hence the metaphysical understanding of suffering becomes the condition of possibility for participating in the meaning of life. Suffering and the ensuing pathos are commonly found in Western melodrama as well; however, their place in and significance to Asian film melodramas are considerably different (Dissanayake and Sahai 1991).

In Asian melodrama, as in Western melodrama, the family figures very prominently. However, there are significant differences regarding the presuppositions of family as they are thematized in Asian melodra-mas. In Western melodramas, by and large, it is the individual in the context of the family that is of interest to the filmmaker, whereas in Asian melodrama it is the family as a unit that generates the most in-terest. To phrase it differently, in Western melodramas it is the indi-vidual self in relation to family that is explored, whereas in Asian melodramas it is the familial self that is the focus of interest.

A study of melodrama in relation to Asian cinema enables us to un-derstand better the dynamics of modernization taking place in Asia. It helps us to appreciate some vital dimensions of social modernization in terms of cultural differences. As a consequence, the dialectic be-tween social existence and cultural production gains in depth and def-inition. For example, Paul Willemen, in his insightful analysis in this volume of the popular Indian melodrama, *Andaz,* argues that the film presents the tensions and contradictions involved in the adoption of precapitalist social relations to a capitalist environment, while "forget-ting" that the Indian bourgeosie is itself a colonial legacy.

An examination of the ways that culturally determined icons and symbols, music and dance, organization of space and time, and so on figure in Asian melodrama serves to deepen our understanding of the interplay of social relations and cultural production in diverse socie-ties and lifeworlds. Moreover, the mechanisms through which audi-ences construct subjectivities vis-à-vis melodramatic film summon up deep-seated cultural psychologies. Both in Western and Asian melod-ramas, questions of interpersonal relations, moral meanings, and the workings of good and evil are depicted in accordance with a poetics of hyperbole. However, the ways these are portrayed in the respective cin-emas, the diverse ways they are framed and textually produced, illumi-nate underlying cultural differences. For example, as Peter Brooks points out, the characters in melodrama generally assume essential psychic features of father, mother, and child (Brooks 1976). The way these characters are depicted in Indian melodramas has the distinct cultural imprint of Indian society and tradition.

Asian melodramas represent a confluence of tradition and modernity, Eastern and Western sensibilities, voices of past and present. Cinema as an art form was introduced to Asia from the West but was very quickly indigenized (Dissanayake 1988). For example, Indian film melodramas deploy a creatively invigorating interplay among Western form, classical Indian theater, folk plays, and the more modern Parsi theater. To understand the cultural discourse surrounding Asian melodrama, one has to understand the significance of such sedimentations. The essays gathered in this volume further such a project. Films are cultural expressions in which the artistic, industrial, technological, economic, and political dimensions are inextricably linked. When analyzing films, whether they be comedies or melodramas or any other genre, historical context, political imagination, theoretical method, and textural analysis should come into a productive union, as the essays in this volume exemplify.

The essay by E. Ann Kaplan deals with questions of subjectivity and ideology and the relevance of theories of Western melodrama to modern Chinese cinema. In her chapter, Kaplan examines four Chinese films in relation to the problems posed by cross-cultural analysis. The challenge, as she sees it, is to undertake cross-cultural research in ways that avoid defamiliarizing the foreign text, appropriating it, subordinating it to the Western discourses, or domesticating it into dominant Western theoretical paradigms. Hence, this essay sets the stage for the ensuing chapters.

In the next essay, Ma Ning examines Chinese family melodrama of the early 1980s against the conceptual backdrop of symbolic representation and symbolic violence. In view of the fact that family holds such a position of centrality in Chinese society, it is not surprising that family melodrama is one of the most pervasive and powerful forms of symbolic expression in China. Ma Ning indicates how, given the vital interface between politics and aesthetics in socialist countries, the Chinese family melodrama, which constitutes a significant form of social representation, responded promptly to the vital changes in Communist Party policies. The essay goes on to point out how the films' adoption of traditionally Chinese modes of perception and a patriarchal logic that both informs and conditions the viewers' understanding of social realities prepare the viewer/subject for social change even as the asymmetrical power relations of domination and exploitation are perpetuated.

The essay by William Rothman deals with the Chinese film *The*

Goddess, made in the 1930s. The author makes a convincing case for the need to reexamine this outstanding film, which he claims is worthy of comparison with the greatest American, French, Soviet, German, or Japanese silent films. In comparing and contrasting *The Goddess* with American film melodramas as exemplified by *Blonde Venus,* the essay attempts to grasp what, if anything, is specifically "Chinese" about this film.

The next essay, by Yuejin Wang, one of the longest in the collection, deals with melodrama as historical understanding. The author is of the conviction that history and melodrama seek to create and recreate the other after its own image, to fashion the other into a simulacrum of itself. He explores this thesis by comparing Chinese and Western films in relation to Chinese history and to modern theories of art and culture.

In his essay, Mitsuhiro Yoshimoto discusses melodrama, postmodernism, and Japanese cinema. Pointing out that a purely formal investigation of melodrama in the postwar Japanese cinema offers few useful insights, he advocates the necessity of examining melodrama against the background of social and political changes. Morever, he asserts that, although the studies of Hollywood melodrama of the 1950s are important, they cannot be taken as a direct model for the analysis of the melodramatic form found in postwar Japanese cinema because of the clear divergences between the social and cultural matrixes that gave rise to them.

In the next essay, devoted to a discussion of Kon Ichikawa's film, *An Actor's Revenge,* Scott Nygren considers the film as the site of contestatory discourses of power and gender identification precipitated by a play of seemingly contradictory theatrical and cinematic styles. He argues that the film foregrounds melodrama as a style that uneasily pivots between traditional Kabuki theater and Western cinematic realism, and analyzes implications of this fact on gender relationships as portrayed in the film.

Catherine Russell's essay focuses on the melodramas of Ozu and Mizoguchi, arguing that Japanese ethnography has a particular ideological cast and that there is an identifiable melodramatic structure to the Japanese notion of national identity.

Maureen Turim, in "Psyches, ideologies and melodrama: The United States and Japan," compares the ways in which the Americans and Japanese have assimilated an originally European melodramatic tradition.

In the first of the book's two essays on Indian melodramas, Paul Willemen analyzes the film *Andaz.* Willemen's essay underlines the urgency of considering the different ways that what is designated as melodrama operates within Western and non-Western social formations and historicities. In the second, Wimal Dissanayake discusses the concepts of evil and social order and how they constitute an evolving dialectic within three of the most popular films ever made in India.

The next essay in the volume, by Krishna Sen, addresses the politics of melodrama in Indonesian cinema. Like many of the chapters, Sen's calls attention to significant similarities and dissimilarities between Hollywood and Asian melodramas. She makes the point that in the 1970s there was a significant shift in Indonesian cinema away from a predominantly historical and nationalist textural structure and that this shift can partially be explained by the social and political transformations that took place during this period. She goes on to examine the concrete interplay between politics and film melodrama in Indonesia.

From Indonesia we move to the neighboring Philippines. In their chapter titled "Power, pleasure, and desire: The female body in Filipino melodrama," Teresita A. Herrera and Wimal Dissanayake demonstrate the close relation, in Filipino film melodramas, between the symbolic constitution of womanhood in the filmic enunciation and the films' discourse on the human body.

The next essay is on Australian melodrama. Culturally speaking, Australia is not an Asian country. However, no doubt spurred by the influx of Asian immigrants, Australian culture has made strenuous efforts to identify with Asia. In "The register of nightmare: Melodrama as it disappears in Australian film," Susan Dermody introduces us to the complex world of Australian melodrama. Admitting to the ambivalence initially experienced by so many film scholars who seek to examine melodrama, the author finds herself lamenting that, although there are melodramatic aspects to almost all current Australian films and television programs, full-fledged melodramas are comparatively rare in Australian culture.

Concluding the volume is an "Overview" by William Rothman, which attempts to put Western film study's recent embrace of Asian cinema – as witnessed by the present collection of essays – into historical perspective, and provocatively addresses the question of whether, in embracing Asian cinema the way it has done, the field has adequately acknowledged specifically Asian ways of thinking.

References

Brooks, Peter (1976). *The Melodramatic Imagination: Balzac, Henry James, Melodrama, and the Mode of Excess.* New Haven: Yale University Press.
Dissanayake, Wimal (1988). *Cinema and Cultural Identity: Reflections on Films from Japan, India and China.* New York: University Press of America.

Dissanayake, Wimal, and Malti Sahai (1991). *Sholay – A Cultural Reading.*
   New Delhi: Wiley Eastern Limited.
Geertz, Clifford (1983). *Local Knowledge.* New York: Basic Books.
Gledhill, Christine, ed. (1987). *Home Is Where the Heart Is: Studies in Melo-
   drama and the Woman's Film.* London: BFI Publishing.

CHAPTER II

Melodrama / subjectivity / ideology: Western melodrama theories and their relevance to recent Chinese cinema

E. Ann Kaplan

As I have argued elsewhere (Kaplan 1989), cross-cultural analysis is difficult: It is fraught with danger. We are either forced to read works produced by the Other through the constraints of our own frameworks/ theories/ideologies; or to adopt what we believe to be the position of the Other – to submerge our position in that of the imagined Other. Yet, cross-cultural work appears increasingly essential in an era when secure national identities are being eroded in the wake of multiple immigrations and other boundary confusions. The challenge is to undertake cross-cultural research in ways that avoid defamiliarizing the alien text, appropriating or "managing" it, with the result of making it subordinate to the imaginary Western "master" discourses; or, worse still, "domesticating" it into dominant Western critical paradigms (see Zhang n.d.). Arguably, since all texts conceal their multiple and shifting meanings, it is conceivable that cross-cultural work (from many directions, incidentally: North American–Chinese interchange represents only two of the desirable exchanges) might uncover strands of a text's multiple meanings different from those found by critics in the originating culture.

I hope to contribute to theories of cross-cultural analysis through the limited project of seeing how far certain European and North American theories of melodrama may illuminate select Chinese films of the 1980s. I cannot pretend to a knowledge of Chinese language, culture, and history it would take years to gain: The aim is to get close to some alien texts rather than leaving them "over there" by seeing what understandings can emerge from entering such texts via theories developed for reading films in my own culture. The hoped-for end is mutually beneficial intercultural exchange, if anything like that is possible given the obvious differential between China and America as world powers.

Texts from a culture other than the critic's may be approached using one of two main kinds of discourse, that is, aesthetic and political. The aesthetic discourse may take two forms, either humanist/individualist or focused on genre. The political discourse may take many forms, including economic, ideological, and institutional concerns. The danger of the first approach, used alone, is eliding the specificity of cultural differences under a universalizing, humanist discourse which then masks oppressive, intercultural relations (e.g., colonialism, hierarchical power relations based on class, sex, and race). The danger of the second approach is eliding the specificity of the level of representation, subjectivity, the cultural imaginary.

In order to avoid the dangers inherent in either approach used alone, I here attempt to combine an aesthetic *genre* approach, focusing on how *subjectivity* is represented (but avoiding humanist/individualist traps), with attention to political/economic/ideological discourses, which focus on why certain representations emerge at a specific time, on whose possible interests specific images serve, on the institutional constraints on image production.

I have chosen melodrama as the most suitable genre for illuminating select Chinese films of the 1980s, for bringing them "close." This genre's theoretical parameters, as these have been worked out in European/North American[1] literary and film research, seem to best suit the sphere in representation occupied by the Chinese films I discuss. This sphere may loosely be called that of the "domestic," entailing the level of love/sex, marriage/motherhood, jealousy, loss, murder or other violence; infidelity, preoedipal/oedipal relations. Other qualities have to do with (a) exaggeration/excess; (b) allegorical or stereotypical good versus evil forces; (c) the individual shown as at the mercy of forces beyond his or her control – that seem to waft the figure in directions he or she did not produce. Significantly, dramas (or other forms with such features) are to be found in early modes in many nations, including China: Often, these modes (like the Chinese opera) involve the use of standardized makeup, which literalizes what became less obvious in much Western melodrama – namely, precisely melodrama's interest in fixed types representing generalized emotions and situations. They also literalize (through circus, folk, and song elements) the retention of the popular, again hidden in late Western melodrama.

The two melodrama discourses can be distinguished. The first aesthetic melodrama discourse is mainly interested in the cultural repression of unconscious desire (sexual, oedipal), whereas the second political one concerns repressed social prohibitions to do with, in particular, class and race. Both theories rely on a notion of melodrama fulfilling a function of expressing what cannot be said; or, in Gledhill's (1987, 38) words, acknowledging "demands inadmissible in the codes of social, psychological or political discourse." But theories differ in whether they are concerned with repression within the human individual (implying a humanist perspective), or within the "self" now seen rather as a "subject," with all that shift in terminology implies. ("Subjectivity" here connotes a theoretical paradigm in which the self no longer exists as an entity that persists through time, space, and language, but which is rather constructed through signifying practices, in particular contexts, particular time/space/history relations.)

But the question immediately arises: To what extent does the domestic level of things, which melodrama addresses, connote the same meanings in different cultures? Wouldn't the dramatically contrasting organization of domestic relations cross-culturally prohibit easy comparison?

An aesthetic (humanist/individualist) perspective might solve this dilemma by showing that cross-culturally, much art is partly the result of some unresolved encounter with the Real that presses for rearticulation, for closure through representation. People (partly) make art for this reason, and they (partly) desire to consume art for the same reason. There are obviously many ways in which to re-present or "construct" the encounter with the Real: Modes in early cultures often use mythic, religious, or, at any rate, ritualistic forms for dealing with such encounters with the Real. But, in the modern period (dating in Europe and North America from the Industrial Revolution and the inception of the modern nuclear family) it seems that cross-culturally certain aesthetic modes, ones we call "melodramatic" (as outlined here), appeal to the largest number of people.

But the problem is the generality of the position. Within different cultures, and even in the same culture in different historical periods, the various melodramatic styles and enunciative positions (governed by class, race, gender, nationality, even if unconsciously) each bear the marks of specific ideologies. Using the term "melodrama" loosely, the genre has a long history in many cultures: European/North American traditions can date the mode back to the Greeks and to the particular combination of *melos* (music) and drama that the Greeks used. Much has been written about the alteration from Aeschylean, to Sophoclean, and finally to Euripidean tragedy, with the latter altering earlier tragic forms to initiate the melodrama mode that later European/North American cultures came to imitate.

But modern European/North American melodrama emerges in the eighteenth century, for specific political/ideological/economic reasons. The genre coincides with the rise of the new bourgeois class during the first Industrial Revolution. According to Peter Brooks (1976), the drive for melodrama in this period was a drive for moral meaning in a post-Enlightenment world in which prior religious and transcendent values no longer gave significance to people's lives. Melodrama was to provide the clear moral meaning missing in the bourgeoisie's daily, lived experience. Hence, the interest of this class in the fixed dramatic types (heroine–villain–hero) and in repetition of the struggle between archetypally good and evil forces. Nevertheless, in the modern period (unlike melodrama in other cultures), in Europe and North America the genre used realism. This was because, in order to consolidate its power, the bourgeoisie desired art that mirrored its institutional modes, forms, rituals, making them seem natural, nonideological, "given." ("Realism," as a style, however, changed historically as social codes and constructs changed, so as to synchronize with the audience's constructs of "reality" in any one period. It is not a fixed style, therefore.)

Given my concern here with film, it is important to note that melodrama takes on new life in the twentieth century with the invention of film and with the development of the classical Hollywood film industry, which quickly became internationalized. The literature on melodrama in film and television criticism is too large and complex for me to summarize adequately here (see Gledhill 1987). Let me note merely that interest in melodrama arose in the second wave of film research in connection with attention to the subversive potential in Sirk's 1950s melodramas. These films seemed to open up space prohibited by the so-called Classical Realist Film text, which was (in the theory) restricted to oppressive patriarchal norms. The largely male critics engaged in this work focused more on broadly defined bourgeois ideology about the family in general than on the films' specifically *female* address. In remedying the failure to deal with female address, feminists pointed out the specific relevance of particularly the 1930s and 1940s melodrama modes to women. Feminists have been exploring ways in which the genre (a) permitted the articulation of unconscious female needs, desires, and frustrations and (b) allowed for female figures to be subjects of narratives (and at the center of the plot) rather than objects of male desire.[2]

But if traces of the Frankfurt School, elitist (modernist) cultural position remains in the theorizing by male critics, there is a parallel danger in uncritical acceptance of any materials that women enjoy because to do otherwise entails abhorring the "feminine." Tania Modleski flirts with this danger in her criticism of male theorists for privileging melodramas that seemed critical of the status quo over those that were clearly not (Modleski, 1988). The debate highlights problems endemic to this sort of study: how to describe *differences* among kinds of text without getting caught in the binarisms inherent in European/ North American culture and language – polarities that always denigrate the emotional/irrational/kinesthetic/domestic level of things (associated with the "feminine") in favor of the intellect/reason/culture/ public sphere (associated with the masculine).

I do not want to eliminate the importance of Brechtian "distanciation" theories or Althusserian notions of the operation of ideology, but aim rather to construct a theoretical apparatus such that they can be applied without "denigrating" femininity, or indeed locking the "feminine" into the binary opposite (i.e., emotion, the irrational) of male intellect and reason. I thus distinguish between domestic melodramas that seem *complicit* with dominant, patriarchal ideology (calling these "women's *melodramas*") and those that contain elements that *resist* dominant ideology (calling these "women's *films*").

Because I have elsewhere developed this distinction at some length (Kaplan 1983; 1990) I will not elaborate. Sufficient for my purposes in relation to the Chinese films of the 1980s to be discussed is the notion that "complicit" women's melodramas are ultimately enunciated from a patriarchal position, even if the narrative makes a woman central. These complicit narratives satisfy certain needs generated by being female in patriarchy, such as the desire for the possibility of reexperiencing, through identification with characters sufficiently (on the surface) like ourselves, unsatisfactory encounters with the Real. That is, women want narratives that provide meaning through completing what was not completed for them, as in romance narratives, for example, of the rich-boy-finds-poor-girl type; or narratives that reenact unpleasurable losses (of child, lover, wealth, and so forth) but turn out better than they did for spectators' own lives; or finally, from the psychoanalytic perspective, narratives that allow spectators to reexperience their deepest fears (of death, murder, entrapment, violation) in the safe confines of the imaginary sphere of art, where nothing can really now harm them.

While these films repeat patriarchal constraints on women, as Mulvey has pointed out, there is something important about them. As she puts it, "in the absence of any coherent culture of oppression, the simple fact of recognition has aesthetic importance: there is a dizzy satisfaction in witnessing the way that sexual difference under patriarchy is fraught, explosive, and erupts dramatically into violence within its own stomping ground, the family" (Mulvey 1976–7, 52).

The resisting elements in the woman's films lie in their positioning a female desire, a female subjectivity as theoretically possible, even if it cannot be achieved within existing frameworks. Whereas the woman's melodrama is still an oedipal narrative (the story of how man comes to be man), the woman's film raises the question of what it means to be *female*. A few films even go so far as to ask what it might mean to be female outside of the patriarchal definition; they ask what learning to be *woman* might offer in addition to heterosexual coupling and motherhood.

On another level, issues of class address, of the relationship between subject and state, and of melodrama's categorization as "low"

culture need to be taken into account as part of a broader consideration of *ideology* underlying melodrama. If male critics have tended to
neglect the specificities of gender in dealing with melodrama, female
critics have tended to neglect ideology. Both groups have perhaps not
paid sufficient attention to the fact that, in Gledhill's words, "melodrama touches the socio-political only at that point where it triggers
the psychic" (Gledhill 1987, 37). The importance of this will become
clear in exploring the relevance (or not) of some of these theories to
specific Chinese films. In order to engage such an exploration, I have
chosen two postliberation, so-called fourth-generation films, Huang
Jianzhong's *A Good Woman (Liangjia funü)* and Xie Fei's *The Girl
from Hunan (Xiangnü xiaoxiao)*, for close comparison and contrast. I
set both films against, on the one hand, Xie Jin's *The Legend of Tianyun Mountain (Tianyunshan chuanqi*, 1979; third generation) and Hu
Mei's *Army Nurse (Nüer lou*, 1986; fifth generation) so as to exemplify
the diversity of developments in relation to Chinese films of the 1980s,
as seen from the self-conscious perspective of European/North American theories of melodrama, of subjectivity and desire, discussed previously, and (in conclusion) of the relevance of the modernism/
postmodernism trajectory. I hope both to problematize the theories
themselves *and* to illuminate the films under discussion by focusing
particularly on the construction of female (and male) subjectivity and
their representation vis-à-vis the state. A main aim is to explore the
relevance of melodrama theory to Chinese cinema of the 1980s. If the
films *are* melodramas, then some questions are: How far do construc-
tions use the (limited) subversive potentialities of the European/North
American woman's film? How far do the woman's melodrama's complicit possibilities prevail? Are some texts politically subversive while
complicit in relation to gender, and vice versa?

All the films to be mentioned were produced during what seems, in
light of the tragic events of 1989 in Tiananmen Square, to have been a
brief moment of political relaxation after the tense and rigidly ideological period of the Cultural Revolution. This fact (i.e., that the films
now seem to have been a brief anomaly) makes it more important than
ever to understand what they indicate about changes taking place in
China in the early 1980s, which partly brought about the violence of
the crackdown. Third-, fourth-, and fifth-generation films need situating within the context of earlier Chinese film legacies, such as the hu-
manist/leftist social realist tradition of the so-called Golden Age 1930s
and 1940s; the revolutionary, propagandistic tradition of the Cultural
Revolution; and finally, the idealist, romantic/melodramatic 1950s tradition. They also need situating in the context of European and North
American film influences. China has traditionally always had much
cultural intercourse with Europe, so that its aesthetic traditions devel-

oped in connection with other aesthetic modes. Although there was a twenty-year or so period during the most dogmatic postliberation years when links with Europe and North America were weakened, as soon as full cultural intercourse could resume, it did. So European and North American films have functioned as strong influences on the generations in question, and this influence needs to be taken into account as well as more specifically "Chinese" traditions.

It is, then, not impossible to posit direct influence from European/ North American film melodrama on representations of subjectivity in the films in question, or to find them fulfilling functions European and North American theorists have assigned to the form. Yet a problem emerges that has to be addressed before discussing subjectivity: It is important that European/North American melodrama arose at a time when the bourgeois class needed to differentiate itself from both the working and aristocratic classes. In contemporary China, on the other hand, the films emerge within a nation dominated by the Communist Party's ideology of classlessness – of the equality of all united under one state government, one political party. How then can the films be "melodrama"?

Although the class situation is not analogous to those in Europe and North America, some films of the 1980s do serve a subversive function analogous to that in European/North American melodrama in terms of the need for articulation of social, political, and psychological discourses not permitted in China at the time – a need to construct meaning and significance in a context where those available through the Communist Party and the state had been discredited by people's experiences over the recent decades (particularly in the Cultural Revolution). As Esther Yau (1988) has pointed out, the construction of a generalized subject (going back at least to the 1949 liberation) becomes a traumatic cultural dislocation that film directors in the early 1980s were trying to comprehend and to move beyond. But, more important, the directors represent an effort at definition and restoration of Chinese identity made possible by the period of relative political openness beginning at the end of the 1970s. This openness left a gap for reinserting in representation subjective experiences that had broad appeal (i.e., that were not "personal," idiosyncratic, or even "individual" in the usual senses). The films aim to construct or imagine selves other than those available within dominant discourses. The degree to which such selves do, or do not, rely on European/North American concepts of the "free" individual is something that will be explored in film analyses. But, regardless of the kind of "self" at issue, all the films show concern with the *relationship of subject to the state* in a way different from that in European/North American films and film theory. However, the differences in the way this relationship is constituted vary from film to film, as does also the issue of each film's speaking position. The distinction I made between women's *films* and women's *melodramas* in Europe and North America may then be useful here.

Made in 1979, Xie Jin's *The Legend of Tianyun Mountain* marks a decisive break with the propagandistic tradition of the "cultural revolution" (in which films still attacked the old, evil imperialist society and focused on decadence) and prepares for the fourth- and fifth-generation films. Set in 1979, the film offers a severe critique of both the "cultural revolution" and of the earlier Anti-Rightist campaign. One of its heroines is the new communist youth – energetic, hardworking, and committed to correcting the party's recent errors. The two main messages of the film are (I) that the party must not commit the error of condemning good party members because of a slight difference over immediate strategy and (2) that party leaders must not allow personal revenge to affect their need to be just. The film retains a view of the subject as in the service of the state; problems between subject and state happened because the state made a wrong judgment, not because the *relationship between subject and state was wrong.* The film insists that the "happy" woman is the one committed to work for the state: or, to put it in psychoanalytic terms, the one who takes the state as her object of desire or who displaces sexual desire into working for the state.

But the film nevertheless makes use of earlier melodramatic traditions in the story of the older heroine (who is central in the main story), against whom the energetic communist figure (central in the framing story) is pitted. (The tension between the dramatically opposed cinematic strategies within the same film results in a disorienting experience for the North American spectator, although arguably not so for Chinese viewers who have lived within the contradictory cinematic traditions upon which the film draws.) The narrative of the older heroine's passionate love affair with a comrade who later joins the "rightist" group, her heartrending, love-versus-ambition choice to stay with him and be ostracized or to marry into party circles, her resulting unhappy marriage, and so forth are all told in flashback sequences similar to those in many classical Hollywood melodramas. The spectator is drawn into the narrative via techniques of identification with desire and loss in a manner similar to Hollywood strategies.

Nevertheless, the film's melodramatic modes work to support dominant party ideology in its late 1970s, reformed mode. In this sense, the film is a complicit woman's melodrama: Its narrative does not question dominant codes, as do narratives in *A Good Woman* and *Army Nurse*, which I would put in the resisting "woman's film" category; nor does it offer a cynical (subtextual) reading, as in *Girl from Hunan.*

In terms of the subject–state relationship, and ⟨
eral, Huang Jianzhong's *A Good Woman* (1985) is
one hand, its background frame continues the dir⟨
film (i.e., giving a positive view of the nascent Comm
now in a far less heavy-handed manner); but on the
the usual oedipal narrative, focusing rather on how
into *woman*. It here differs from Xie Fei's *A Girl fron   ...an* (1986),
which comments on woman's patriarchal positioning.

Woman was made from a script by Li Kuanding, rather than being
made (like *Hunan*) directly from Shen Congwen's 1929 short story,
"Xiaoxiao," about forced rural child-marriage. If Li used the story, he
nevertheless alters things so that the narrative is set in 1948. This enables him to include the figure of the party cadre, who comes to the
village on the verge of the 1949 liberation in order to "modernize" the
people and so to improve their lives. The film, then, takes a political
stance in support of the Communist Party, at least in its immediate
preliberation form. The cadre befriends the heroine, Xingxian, and,
quietly, shows her that she can leave her appalling situation. The
cadre, in fact, makes possible an official divorce for Xingxian, who has
fallen in love with Kaibing, an itinerant farm worker. In this film then,
the state (or state-to-be) is beneficent in helping the heroine to escape
from the backward, oppressive, and rigid rural codes that hem her in.

But unlike Xie Jin's *Tianyun, Woman* does not ignore or undervalue
female subjectivity and sexual desire. On the contrary, portraying the
emergence of such desire is an important part of its project. It also
does not deny or belittle the strong emotional bonds that develop between Xingxian and her child-husband. The heroine is indeed a "good
woman" in the sense of her sensitivity to the pain of others, her kindness, her willingness to help out and to obey the local rules as far as
she can.

Woman importantly reinserts individual interest as viable. Hitherto,
as Chris Berry (1989, 8–41) has noted, individual interest had been
negatively coded in films, which entailed negativity toward any focus
on sexual difference. The newer 1980s films challenged these codes by
daring to insert male and female desire, thus altering the negative coding of individual interest. The viewing subject is invited to identify
with a heroine whose desire is made impossible by her obligations to
the state or to social customs. One can see this as the Chinese adopting once again an ideology of individualism (challenged by the liberation) that particularly the United States and West European nations
still heavily rely upon, but which some American feminists have in
turn challenged. Interest in such an ideology of individual subjectivity
must be set against the costs of the prior construction of the generalized self mentioned earlier: Such a self usually has repressive conse-

ces, particularly for women and ethnic minorities, and in the case China was largely patriarchal and Han.

Good Woman was far less popular than *Hunan*, presumably because it refuses many of the melodramatic pleasures of the latter film,[4] and functions more within the didactic tradition, as we have seen. Through the figure of the party cadre sent out to the countryside to challenge (and, it is hoped, eradicate) ancient customs like forced marriage, the film explores sexual institutions on the eve of the liberation, and it shows how such institutions construct especially female sexuality. The film's credit sequence (written by Li Kuanding) is deliberately "educational." It details the limited, repressive roles that women have traditionally occupied in China: "Women are the most respected people in China," we learn, "but they are the most pitiable." Further, the credit sequence notes that women's roles are inscribed in Chinese characters: Over an old sculpture of a woman, we read: "Woman Kneeling, ca. 1600–1100 B.C.: The earliest character for 'woman' is a woman kneeling on the ground, her hands crossed on her chest." The different female roles are not only shown in letters, but also through Chinese art. Each work is dated, approximately, and the sequence moves chronologically towards A.D. 1948, when the film takes place. Representations include women kneeling, sweeping, breast feeding, praying (for a son), giving birth, having feet bound, hulling rice, turning a millstone, being married, being punished for adultery, and mourning. As Kim Kerbis notes, these traditional images show the three faces of Chinese woman's life, namely, (1) biological processes of giving birth and breast feeding; (2) hard female labor (her activity close to slave work); (3) female "culture" (woman acted upon), as in submission to the male (kneeling), to God (praying), and sexually (having feet bound). Because the Chinese characters for the title, "The Good Woman," change constantly, we can assume that these characters themselves tell a tale, without, however, producing any real change in women's actual conditions over the three-thousand-year period.[5]

The narrative is told from the point of view of the young bride, Xingxian, married to a nine-year-old rural boy, Yi Shaowei (Weiwei, as he is called). We are made to see the pathetic situation for both "husband" and "wife" of this sexual mismatch, and the frustration for both of the developmental gap. The film dwells on the developing and genuine tenderness between Xingxian and Weiwei as they live together. The effects are produced to a large extent through the brilliant personal performances of the two actors.

This is not to say that the relationship is not in some way sexualized; the film admits the bodily pleasures the two have and indeed focuses in a sort of comic way on the absent usual marital sexual relationship by playing on the young boy's constant need to pee! This enables the camera to catch the smallness of his organ and the inappropriateness of the child as a lover for the maturing woman. The heroine is positioned as surrogate mother, and the child relies on his real mother, who lives with them.

Good Woman's strategies rely on traditional Chinese painting and literary aesthetics and further on Japanese and New Wave film techniques. This produces at times an intended distance from the narrative close to the Brechtian devices so admired by some European avantgarde filmmakers of various historical moments. Distanciation is enhanced by the deliberate contrast between Xingxian and the mad woman who haunts the community and, indeed, who alone dares openly to be sexual. Because she is mad, and only because of this, the woman (who becomes one kind of alter ego for the heroine – the party cadre is another) has the freedom to create highly sexual sculptures and to roam the terrain at night alone, clearly in a state of high sexual arousal. Through this contrast, the film insists on the pathetic choices open to women in this society – namely, a constraining child marriage or a perverse sexuality outside of the community, produced through the woman's earlier adulterous transgression. She is ostracized and shunned by all, but this has, paradoxically, given her the right to represent the community's repressed sexual desires. Specifically, the mad woman embodies Xingxian's desires, evidenced in her interest in the erotic statue the mad woman carves and which Xingxian buys and buries (significantly) in the rice storage pot (food and sex are equally necessary, it seems).

An intense sexual attraction develops between the heroine and an itinerant worker, Kaibing. But the film does not give us explicit erotic images: The relationship is indicated only in subtle, indirect ways, and we see no actual physical encounter (it is not even clear that the relationship is fully consummated). Nevertheless, the heroine's desire is clearly marked, and her interest in Kaibing seen as equal to his interest in her. However, the film sidesteps the issue of female sexuality, ultimately, in leaving ambiguous at the end where Xingxian is going and whether or not a sexual life will be available to her. She could be going to meet, and marry, Kaibing, or to work with the Communists.

The mad woman is the figure most reminiscent of melodrama in the film. Situated as she is on the fringe of the community, she functions as a warning for the heroine of what her culture might do to her. The mad woman opens up the terrain of excess female sexuality, of female eroticism, particularly in the sequence where the camera closes in on her scalpel grating out the sculpture's vagina. But ultimately the figure is contained via the mediation of the party cadre, who becomes the rational mean between rigid codes hemming in all female sexuality, and the mad woman's dangerous excess. In this way, *Woman* makes a comment on melodrama quite similar to that in *Tianyun*. It marks its place also as beyond melodrama in offering important images of female–female bonding (Xingxian and the party cadre; Xingxian and the mad woman, in a special way; Xingxian and her husband's mother, Wu Niang, and aunt, etc.), and of woman's special kinds of conflict between loyalty to family and needs for self-fulfillment.

Woman's subversiveness then lies more in the portrayal of the heroine than in its overall politics. It is here that it falls into the woman's *film*, as against woman's *melodrama*, category. It perhaps masks its subversion by paying lip service to local (studio) need to avoid offending the Party bureaucracy while presenting in Xingxian a new female Chinese image.

Any subversiveness in *A Girl from Hunan* arises from very different strategies. The film sticks close to the original story, taking place between 1910 and 1926. Like the original, on the surface the film seems merely to insist that ancient customs constrained both men and women (but more particularly women) and to show how these oppressive customs nevertheless perpetuate themselves in a perverse manner, because ultimately everyone (even the original child-bride and husband) gets something out of the customs.

Melodramatic aspects of *Hunan* emerge if we read it as the first wave of male critics read Sirk's 1950s melodramas, that is, as using the melodrama form for social criticism. This reading uncovers a subtext in the film, available to those so situated as to perceive it. Addressing an audience dissatisfied with things in the China in which the film was made, this subtext seeks to expose the frustrations and sufferings of both men and women by constructing a national allegory out of Shen Congwen's story. The narrow, rigid rural community, ruled brutally by its "baron," stands in for the communist state, which also imposes harsh restrictions on individual behavior and constrains people in numerous ways.[6] Like European/North American melodrama, *Hunan* precisely does not offer any solution or alternative; but it does offer clarification, a clear sense of right and wrong, an analysis of people's current sufferings, and a cynical, bitter, ironical reflection on what some may be getting out of the contemporary regime. In Peter Brooks's terms, the film "exteriorises conflict and psychic structures, producing ...what we might call the 'melodrama of psychology'" (Brooks 1976, 35–36). It releases into the public terrain fears, wishes, and desires forbidden social expression.

This explains why the film's characters are less fully developed than those in *Woman*. Melodrama requires symbolized figures, emotions, and happenings in order to function as providing clear moral messages. The woman's film, on the other hand, precisely moves away from melodrama to the degree that it relies on characters who are complex, who have conflicts, and who must create moral meaning for themselves. *Woman,* then, like the woman's film generally, uses the realist style.

Set in the preliberation period (the film moves from 1910 up to 1926, as noted), *Hunan* also deals with a forced child marriage and the teenage heroine's passionate love affair with an itinerant farm worker, Huagou. The film's strategies invite identification with the central female heroine and address specifically female concerns around marriage, motherhood, sexuality, and the family – in short, the domestic; but the heroine's inner conflicts are subordinated to emphasis on the broader village structure. The editing largely adheres to classical Hollywood codes, although there are some cuts more suggestive of recent Japanese or European New Wave films in their use of time and space.

For the most part, the narrative is told from the perspective of the heroine, Xiaoxiao, and we understand the constraints of her position. Female subjectivity is, on a surface level, inscribed in the film. However, because the film is preoccupied with the question of general suffering and frustration in contemporary China, it quite disturbingly wrenches the point of view from the heroine in key sexual scenes, suggesting a classically patriarchal ideology of a young woman's sexual arousal dependent on male initiation. Huagou, the itinerant farmhand working for Xiaoxiao's in-laws, is seen asking his boss for leave to go to town, clearly for sexual gratification. He notes that "the little virgin" is "filling out," and his gaze betrays his desire. Catching the look, Xiaoxiao throws him his food in anger. Xiaoxiao's six-year-old husband, Chunguan, sensing something of what is going on (these child-husbands are sexually precocious given their situation), begins to sing a sexual song, which Huagou picks up and continues, to Xiaoxiao's embarrassment.

This scene is soon followed by one showing Xiaoxiao getting undressed and caressing her maturing body, indicating both her having been aroused by Huagou and her own sexual restlessness. These two scenes set the stage for the seduction, which is hard to read accurately cross-culturally. My own reading cannot help but be influenced by recent European and North American feminist film theories. Taken at its face value, the scene would seem to follow the classical tradition of positioning woman as object of male desire. Finding himself because of an unexpected rain storm in the barn with Xiaoxiao half undressed, changing her wet clothes, Huagou gives rein to the desire he had earlier resisted (one night he is seen quenching his lust via a moonlight swim). Xiaoxiao is at least partly afraid and unwilling: she calls to Chunguan when Huagou sends him off; but before she has time to resist properly, Huagou has violently ripped off her breastcloth and laid her in the straw. Again, following classical Hollywood codes, the camera cuts to nature and to the rain, the passage of intercourse marked by the ceasing of the storm. Equally classically, the heroine is then seen lying satisfied on the straw.

This erotically coded scene would appear to satisfy the spectator's possible fantasies about seduction, even rape, and many people might, I think, admit its pleasures. Such representation of explicit sexuality was unthinkable during the Cultural Revolution, and even in the late 1970s. On this level, then, the graphic depiction of male desire is itself subversive, as is the heroine's explicit stirrings of desire. For women, in addition, the film's pleasures would fit those Laura Mulvey mentioned earlier, in giving female spectators that "dizzy satisfaction in witnessing the way that sexual difference under patriarchy is fraught, explosive, and erupts dramatically into violence within its own stomping ground, the family."

Nevertheless, from a European/North American feminist point of view, which emerged in European and North American societies where graphic sexual images have long been commonplace, the gendered sexual representations in *Hunan* remain a problem in terms of their patriarchal bias. Perhaps equally problematic from a European/North American feminist point of view is the invitation to pleasure in the semierotic surrogate-mother/infant-boy relationship between Xiaoxiao and Chunguan. We see the little boy on the one hand sucking on his real mother's breast (the couple live on the farm belonging to the boy's mother; the marriage is partly to provide the family with the wife's free labor), often with his wife there, while at the same time he parades his power over his wife. The two engage in semierotic play, Xiaoxiao in one scene displacing her sexual arousal by Huagou onto Chunguan through passionate, if nonexplicitly sexual, kissing.

It is hard to avoid finding an appeal to incestuous male fantasy. The film seems to act out an unconscious male fantasy for regression to the infantile state, although Chris Berry has suggested that the film may, like *Red Sorghum*, be addressing contemporary Chinese male unconscious desire for revenge on women's newfound liberation — the communist state insists on parity in the public sphere if not in the home. It is, after all, a parity that contrasts dramatically with the situation in prerevolutionary China.

Hunan, however, as noted, arguably makes a strong subversive statement about contemporary China in its subtext. Through its study of the evils of the old society, in particular its custom of forced marriage, the film implicitly equates the whole system of rural people dominated by oppressive and rigidly enforced ancient social codes, monitored by what amount to local barons, to the communist leadership. The brutality of the adulteress's treatment makes the case vividly, as does also the dilemma that Xiaoxiao puts the family in by getting illicitly pregnant. The film constantly juxtaposes the country to the town, where young women can be students, wear their hair short, leave their arms bear, have sexual relations with, and marry, fellow students, and so forth. Two poignant scenes juxtapose Xiaoxiao and the girl students, and later, her now teen-aged husband is pitted against the students, who ridicule him for having a wife ten years older than he is. These "girl students" represent young contemporary Chinese students interested in the "West" and in modernization. The film's bitterly ironic ending is particularly reminiscent of that in Sirk's *All That Heaven Allows.*

The Girl from Hunan, then, interestingly combines melodramatic conventions akin to Hollywood ones with a sound track and visual style that arguably derives (like certain stylistic elements in *Woman*) from Chinese painting and literary aesthetics. In addition, the film raises the question of recent Chinese film as a sort of "national allegory," to which I have already alluded.

It is difficult to adjudicate the very different filmic projects represented in the two films: one could argue that the first film idealizes both the rural community and the Communist Party, while the second is far more honest both in its cinematic pleasures and in its political cynicism. On the other hand, *Woman* dramatically portrays the coming to independence and sexual awareness of a young woman, to the extent of her actually managing to leave the repressive rural environment at the end, and refusing the masochistic situation of the mad woman. In *Hunan,* by contrast, the heroine first masochistically succumbs to the dominant repressive order and then sadistically awaits her turn to oppress others. If there is a national allegory here, that would prevent the film from being utterly cynical; it would situate it as a warning to refuse such collusion with oppression, to refuse some easy gains for the higher principle. But this reading has to be looked for: It is not there on the surface.

If Hu Mei's *Army Nurse* also raises the question of the degree to which some of the fifth-generation films – particularly those set in some past era – are allegories for commentary on China's contemporary scene, the film itself is clearly allied with the European/North American "woman's film." The only film discussed made by a female director, *Army Nurse* manifests a new self-conscious split between an evident, but socially forbidden eroticism and romantic love and the heroine's explicit interpellation by the state. Like some 1930s and 1940s Hollywood "woman's films" (e.g., *Imitation of Life, Now Voy-*

ager) Army Nurse is a serious and careful study of a young woman's thoughts and feelings about discovering love and sex, and enduring many frustrations.

Without essentializing the female position, it does seem that, as a director, Hu Mei's sensitivities to female desire and female subjectivity are greater than those evident in any of the other films discussed. As against those films, hers makes a clear statement about the role of the contemporary state in legislating female desire; or, to put it differently, in *Army Nurse* the viewer is asked to identify with a heroine whose desire is rendered "impossible" by her obligations to the state.

Set in the years immediately following the Cultural Revolution, this film, like *Woman,* eschews all conventional melodramatic devices, and because of this, the spectator is denied many of the usual cinematic pleasures. The film pursues its study of the heroine's situation by asking us to identify with her, to move through her situations with her, to experience what her life is like, without appeals either to unconscious erotic desire or to political persuasion. The device of the heroine's voice-over narration increases the spectator's close identification with her. In this way, the film arguably offers more resistance to dominant Chinese sexual and political codes than either of the other films discussed. In asserting the heroine's subjectivity, and in making us identify with her sexual desire and its impossibility, the film contains an intensely erotic scene focusing on female desire but without showing the female body: The heroine's desire for one of her male patients (she is a nurse) is graphically and unambiguously imaged as the nurse is bandaging the soldier's wound. The bandaging is eroticized to an almost unbearable degree – the camera cutting between the heroine's face and the man's shoulder with its wound. (The director told me that originally the scene had been much longer – and even more erotic – but the studio leadership insisted on its being cut.) The film makes clear the constraints of the heroine's institutional framing and yet asserts the need for some sort of social responsibility. But nowhere does the film directly address the larger contemporary Chinese situation.

Hu Mei (in an interview I had with her in 1987) suggested that her own and many other films dealing with the frustrations of heroines could be seen as a relatively safe way for Chinese directors to comment on the more general frustrations people endure under communism. Here Hu validated the kind of reading I have done for *Hunan.* But, perhaps ironically, her own film seems more specifically about woman's situation than any of the others discussed here. Presumably, her film could be read on both (or either) level(s), but the careful and in-depth study of the heroine – a study reinforced by the voice-over narration – for me takes precedence.

The endings

Given the double-layered nature of this project – namely, the framing of the discussion of melodrama and recent Chinese films by the larger concern with problematizing cross-cultural research – it is fitting that this chapter should have two endings. First, some conclusions about juxtaposing some European/North American melodrama theories and select Chinese films. What has this illuminated?

The juxtaposition has revealed differences in degrees of subversiveness in the films and their relationship to dominant Chinese ideology. Interestingly, we have seen how different levels of resistance are to be found within *Hunan* (the film closest to woman's melodrama) and within *Army Nurse* (the film most like some Hollywood woman's films). Significant in the use of melodrama in *Hunan* is how explicit the film makes the fact that the heroine's troubles come from constraining *social codes*. In much European and North American melodrama, by contrast, the forces against the heroine are seen as metaphysical, beyond human control, and somehow inherent in humans' existential condition. *Army Nurse,* meanwhile, makes even more explicit the oppressive nature of *party* codes for the female protagonist. The theoretical framework made clear the complicit political stance taken in *Tianyun* and the tactful stance in *Woman*.

The juxtaposition has let us evaluate representations of female sexuality and subjectivity in the various films. We saw that the melodrama genre made possible in *Hunan* daring expression of a sexual discourse hitherto repressed in contemporary China, and for which there was no other language than the visual. By the same token, we saw that both *Army Nurse* and *Woman,* drawing on the woman's film, situated themselves more specifically than the other films in the heroine's point of view. Both showed unusual interest in socially disallowed *female* sexual discourses, but the closeness to the inner world of the heroine in *Army Nurse* was particularly remarkable. *Woman* moves beyond the norm in the figure of the central female character, whose emerging individuality provides the focus of the narrative.

Finally, the theoretical framework made it possible to avoid the high–low polarization of *Woman* and *Hunan.* Intellectual life in China, as in Europe and North America, still contains a bias against texts in the popular/melodrama register. The combination in many national cinemas of the melodramatic theatrical tradition and the mechanically produced image could not fail to be scorned by literary establishments in nations undergoing the first industrial revolution. The high–low art polarity functioned in China, as in Europe and North America, to privilege the written word, but the Chinese opera was a close second in some periods. Cinema's links with opera in China helped cinema to achieve a certain status, but the high–low discourse entered in relation to which films were valued, which not (predictably, the more melodramatic and popular the film genre, the less its value in the eyes of the literary establishment). It would be easy to apply such a polarity to *Hunan* and *Woman* (i.e., to label the former, derogatively, "melodrama," the latter, respectfully, as "New Wave/Alternative Cinema"). A different polarity could likewise be applied to *Tianyun* and *Woman*, with the former being labeled, derogatively, "didactic realism," the latter, again, with praise, "New Wave/Alternate." But such polarities prohibit fully understanding each film's unique project. The framework here has allowed us to see the differing achievements of the various films without making hierarchical judgments.

Second, conclusions in relation to the larger framework that concerns problematizing cross-cultural research: The main question has to do with whether or not analyses such as the present one "domesticate" the alien text by approaching it via European/North American theoretical constructs. The framework has provided this European/North American critic with an entry into texts that I might otherwise have not known what to do with. But what about its use to others, particularly to people from China but not confined to them? How far do such analyses provide a starting point for a cultural interchange – even if, perhaps, a negative one (i.e., that critics claim that the analysis misses the point of the films)? Doesn't such a response provide precisely the ground for the kind of cultural interchange I began by saying seemed necessary in our historical period? Isn't it better that I approach alien texts through cultural constructs that belong to me rather than, in Paul Willemen's words, participating in a cultural "ventriloquism" which eradicates my own backgrounds, skills, and training? Isn't cross-cultural work necessarily a collaborative project, such that we share our various readings, each raise our own kinds of issues, and debate the merits or not of a particular theory for a particular cultural text? A different methodology can transform the object of study – and it may be useful to all of us to have the experience of such transformations.

Notes

1. After much thought, I decided to abandon the term "Western." "Western" suggests an illusory monolithic entity; it also calls up its binary opposite, namely, "Eastern," also an illusory monolithic entity. I played with Western/Non-Western, but this did not avoid the first set of problems. I tried "First" and "Third" World terms, but found these even more problematic. I settled, then, on a certain literalness, that is, to name the countries where most of the

theoretical constructs I here use have been recently reformulated and discussed: Europe (East and West) and North America.

2. There is no room here to detail the enormous amount of work done on melodrama by feminist film theorists. Central essays include those by Laura Mulvey (1976–7; 1990). See also Doane (1982; 1987). Central also to discussions are Teresa de Lauretis's interventions, especially *Alice Doesn't* (1984).

3. As one of the older, fourth-generation directors, Huang Jianzhong worked in the Beijing Studio, where Chen Kaige (later to direct *The Yellow Earth*) was his assistant. After doing this film, Huang went on to make a very experimental film, influenced by the Japanese director, Oshima.

4. Let me comment on audience response, briefly. Never any kind of reliable measure, I understand (from informal discussion with Chris Berry) that relying on audience interviews would not lead anywhere. If in Europe and North America one must always be wary of what people tell you they think about a film, this is even more true in China, where people will be concerned to give what they think might be "the correct line" on a film. Reviews in both cases are a different matter: One can always learn about dominant literary/film discourses from the ways that films are discussed in reviews. Certainly, Chinese reviews of the films under discussion would show something about the establishment party line at the time. Unfortunately, I have not had access to English translations of such reviews. In any case, that sort of discussion lies outside my purposes (which have to do with what might be opened up in the films for a European or North American reader by using some European/North American theories); and the reviews would not account for the popularity that interests me here. Determining the reasons for audience pleasure in a film is precisely what it is hard to get at anywhere. I can only hypothesize that the more open sexuality there is, the more popular a film will be, especially in China, given the bar on such pleasurable images.

5. Kerbis (n.d.) details these opening scenes clearly.

6. This reading is supported by a review of the film in a film publication from the People's Republic of China. Noting that *Hunan* "shows the tenacity of our age-old traditions," the reviewer goes on to say: "Now in the 80s, how much is left of feudalistic thinking in our country?... Now the Four Modernisations will have to overcome the hurtles [*sic*] of bureaucracy, anti-science, anti-human rights, and reactionary forces. We believe that this story about Xiao Xiao will arouse the people's cultural and social consciousness."

References

Berry, Chris (1989). "China's New 'Women's Cinema.'" *Camera Obscura* 18:8–41.

Brooks, Peter (1976). *The Melodramatic Imagination: Balzac, Henry James, Melodrama and the Mode of Excess.* New Haven: Yale University Press.

De Lauretis, Teresa (1984). *Alice Doesn't: Feminism, Semiotics, Cinema.* Bloomington: Indiana University Press.

Doane, Mary Ann (1982). "Film and the Masquerade: Theorizing the Female Spectator." *Screen* 23, 3–4 (September):74–87.

— (1987). *The Desire to Desire: The Woman's Film of the 1940s.* Bloomington: Indiana University Press.

Gledhill, Christine, ed. (1987). *Home Is Where the Heart Is: Studies in Melodrama and the Woman's Film.* London: BFI Publishing.

Kaplan, E. Ann (1983). "Theories of Melodrama: A Feminist Perspective." *Women and Performance* 1, 1:40–48.

— (1989). "Problematizing Cross-Cultural Analysis: The Case of Women in the Recent Chinese Cinema." *Wide Angle* 11, 2:40–50. Reprinted in *Deep Focus* (Bangalore, India).

— (1992). *Motherhood and Representation: The Mother in Popular Culture and Melodrama.* London: Routledge.

Kerbis, Kim (n.d.). "The Good Woman through Western Eyes." Unpublished paper.

Modleski, Tania (1988). *The Woman Who Knew Too Much.* New York: Methuen.

Mulvey, Laura (1976–7). "Notes on Sirk and Melodrama." *Movie* 25–26:53–6.

— (1990). "After-Thoughts on Visual Pleasure and Narrative: Duel in the Sun." Reprinted in *Psychoanalysis and Cinema,* ed. E. Ann Kaplan, 24–35. London: Routledge.

Yau, Esther (1988). Paper on *Sacrificed Youth,* read at the Humanities Institute, SUNY, Stony Brook.

Zhang, Yingjin (n.d.). "The Power(lessness) of the Discourses: Reflections on Recent Western Scholarship in Chinese Cinema." Unpublished paper.

CHAPTER III

Symbolic representation and symbolic violence: Chinese family melodrama of the early 1980s

Ma Ning

Family melodrama has been one of the dominant forms of expression in Chinese cinema since its beginning in the early years of this century. The centrality of the genre in Chinese cinema derives to some extent from the position of the family in Chinese society. The family, rather than the individual or the state, was the most significant social unit in traditional China. In addition to its basic socioeconomic functions, the family constituted a unique social-security system that provided care for its needy and aging members and a religious unit where ancestor worship was performed (Eastman 1988). The Chinese family as a social institution was characterized by a hierarchical power structure, but it also represented a cultural ideal consisting of a set of norms that motivated the individual in his or her social practices.

Although the family pattern in traditional China varied, the extended family system, which was typical of the land-owning gentry class, was the culturally dominant type (Lang 1946). The hierarchical power relations within this patriarchal family system were sanctioned by Confucianism, the dominant ideology of both the state and the family. Of the five moral codes Confucianism prescribed to govern human relationships – ruler–subject, father–son, husband–wife, elder brother–younger brother, friend–friend – three concerned the family. Since the late nineteenth century, as Western capitalism has forced its way into China, this dominant social institution has been increasingly challenged by the emergence of the nuclear family as a new sociocultural norm. The process of interaction between different family systems and cultural ideals coincided with a general sociocultural conflict involving political forces of all persuasions.

Despite the great social transformation of the twentieth century, China today retains much of its traditional past. Although the 1949 communist revolution, with its ideal of creating a classless society, had posed serious challenges to the traditional family and social system, they were, to some extent, undermined by the compromises the Communists had to make in order to gain maximum support from a peasantry deeply rooted in traditional ideologies. Consequently, a modified version of the traditional extended family system came into being after 1949, and the cultural ideal it embodied could be found in various aspects of Chinese political and social life. Together they formed the basis of what is called Chinese patriarchal socialism (Stacey 1983). Social and familial relations in rural China after 1949 were very much regulated by a new political ethical system that was a synthesis of Confucian and communist principles (Madsen 1984).

Since 1979 the greatest impact on this modified version of the traditional extended family and the cultural ideal it embodied has come from the modernization drive, which has inevitably brought with it a different value system. Caught up in this conflict between tradition and modernization, the Chinese family is undergoing a process of restructuring. At this point, it is still difficult to assess the impact on the family of the changes in social and economic circumstances accompanying modernization. One might argue that family planning, especially the one-child policy, a major goal of the modernization drive, could contribute to a reduction in family size and changes in family structure. In fact, however, this impact more often than not is offset by other socioeconomic factors. For instance, the decollectivization of agricultural production enabled the individual peasant family to resume its former role as the basic unit of production and ownership. Labor-intensive, household-based farm production tends to strengthen the traditional big family rather than weaken it.

The number of Western-type nuclear families has increased drastically in the urban areas, although the extended family still can be identified: About 5 percent of the households in Beijing contain three generations or more, including married children (Chen 1985, 198). In the vast rural areas, a modified extended family system remains the norm. Although there is a tendency toward reduction in family size and separation of the large extended household into couple-centered conjugal units in the rural areas, the strong intergenerational relationships among the separated units still tend to hold them tightly together. As a result, the average family is often a compromise: The household is economically divided and separately managed but remains a common ceremonial and ritual whole (Chen 1985, 194).

An examination of changes in cultural ideals and moral values concerning the family in China draws an equally contradictory picture. In people's daily conversations, phrases like the "small cozy family" and "tiny enjoyable nest" to some extent have replaced previous militant, altruistic terms such as the "big revolutionary family" and "noble collective interest" (Chen 1985, 197). On the other hand, a modernized version of the notorious nepotism of prerevolutionary China has re-emerged, ironically, as a social norm in the post-Mao era. Phrases like

"Good connections make good business" and "Better to have a power-ful grandfather than a good education" prevail, although sometimes used ironically.

This confusion in cultural values is also reflected in the official ide-ology of the new party leadership that assumed power around 1979. While reaffirming its adherence to the basic principles of socialism, it argues for the necessity of reforming the ailing economic system in ac-cordance with the Western capitalist model. Party ideologists argue from a developmental approach that the socialist system established in 1949 according to the Soviet model is too "advanced" to be effective, so the party should lead the people "backward" to capitalism first in order to proceed to communism at a later stage.[1] Drastic changes in party policies – such as abandoning class struggle as the major means of social change, privatization of agricultural production, and the rein-troduction of a market economy – can be seen as signs of this "back-ward" movement. All these changes were made under the slogan of "modernization." Thus the conflict between tradition and modernization in the social context of this new period has unmistakable political implications.

The modernization drive, which became the official party policy after the Cultural Revolution (1966–76), can also be seen as a re-sponse to the legitimation crisis that confronted the new regime in the post-Mao era. The 1970s witnessed intense political struggles within the party leadership. If the Cultural Revolution could be interpreted as a power struggle between Mao and the radical group aligned with him, on one side, and the moderate Liu Shaoqi faction, which first articu-lated the "go-backward" theory in the 1950s and the early 1960s, on the other, the end of the Cultural Revolution saw the ascendancy of the latter in the political arena. The subsequent policy changes ushered in by the new leadership, popular as they were, did not go unopposed. Furthermore, the worsening of the economy, the expansion of the bu-reaucratic system, the disintegration of "socialist" morality, and the ever-increasing demand for more freedom and democracy by intellec-tuals and students have precipitated this crisis.

Communist regimes have usually claimed legitimacy on the basis of their appropriation of Marx's teleological view of history as a dialectic movement toward communism through class struggle (Brugger 1985). In the post-Mao China, however, the legitimation crisis faced by the Chinese Communist Party has resulted in the abandonment of "the normative appeals of the earlier years, which in Althusserian language might be seen as the privileging of the ideological instance" or "the coercive appeals involved in the primacy given to class struggle, which Althusserians prefer to call privileging of the political instance" in favor of remunerative appeals as the privileging of the economic instance to "achieve legitimate domination" (Hannan 1985, 122). Delivery of consumer goods through modernization to meet the demands of the people for a better life has become the new telos that legitimates the new regime, although there are indications that a swing back to the former appeals is possible, if the regime believes itself to be seriously threatened.[2]

Given the close link between politics and aesthetics in socialist countries, the Chinese family melodrama, as a vital form of social representation, was quick to respond to significant changes in party policies. Unlike the films made before and during the Cultural Revolution – which are characterized by an indulgence in moral polarization and didacticism, inflated political expression, and melodramatic conflict between stereotyped characters of the opposing classes – the more recent productions concentrate more on changing human relationships within the family, represented in a more realistic fashion with emphasis on mundane details of everyday life. A large number of the melodramatic films deal specifically with the changes that have occurred during the modernization process, especially the economic prosperity of the Chinese peasantry under the new party policy.

The family melodramas of the new period, especially those that deal with family conflict in a rural setting, have enjoyed great popularity as well as wide critical acclaim. *The In-Laws,* for example, won several awards, and ticket sales in both city and country totaled more than 560 million as of the end of 1982 (Berry 1985, 32). The tendency of the genre toward a more realistic style and its capacity to respond to, or rather mediate, the immediate experience of the people caught up in a period of rapid social change have been hailed by Chinese critics as one of the achievements of Chinese cinema in the new period.

In this essay I shall examine some of the key texts of the Chinese family melodrama of the early 1980s that deal specifically with family changes in a rural setting, such as *The In-Laws (Xiyingmen,* Shanghai Studio, 1982), *Country Couple (Xiangyin,* Pearl River Studio, 1984), and *In the Wild Mountains (Yueshan,* Xi'an Studio, 1985). I shall attempt to identify and elucidate those formal mechanisms specific to Chinese family melodrama and how they work in relation to the dominant political and cultural discourses underlying the film representation that legitimate the existing political order with recourse to the normative structure of Chinese culture.

A central concern here is the social inscription of the Chinese family melodrama of the new period and the ideological implications of this inscription: the extent to which the representation of family conflict and its resolution functions as a symbolic reenactment of the general sociopolitical confrontation as well as the complication in China in the early 1980s and the ways in which this representation implicates the viewer in the actual social processes. The emphasis on social inscription is motivated by the conviction that since the communist revolution in 1949 social practice in China has increasingly taken the form of various kinds of political discourse, as the genesis of the Cultural Revolution would make clear. In the cultural realm, symbolic or metaphoric discourse about the social and political issues is expected and accepted at all levels.

This phenomenon is not associated only with the cultural life of contemporary China but is a legacy of Chinese culture as a whole. Since ancient times, Chinese cultural production has tended toward a fusion of history and fiction with emphasis on didacticism (Plaks 1975). This tendency has resulted in the unique formal quality of the Chinese narrative text: the textualization of the context. Consequently, I pay great attention to the complex ways in which Chinese melodramatic films textualize their social context. This context not only covers the extratextual contradictions to which the film texts can be seen as a symbolic response but also the conditions that bear on the actual reception of the film texts.

In dealing with the social inscriptions of the Chinese melodramatic text, one necessarily confronts a critical issue or problematic in the study of melodrama in the West: the interesting but complex correlations that exist between melodrama as a specific ideological project and the historically specific social, cultural, and economic conditions of a given social formation. A number of Western critics (Eckert 1973–4, Kleinhans 1978) have deployed "the concept of displacement to suggest melodrama's mystifying resolution of 'real' social conflicts . . . at the surrogate level of family and personal relations" (Gledhill 1987, 13). This mode of categorization, Gledhill suggests, has its weaknesses, "for it suggests that the 'real' lies in a set of socio-economic relations outside the domestic and personal sphere, to which issues of sexual relations, of fantasy and desire are secondary." An alternative is to approach melodrama as an art form that articulates a specific mode of experience (Elsaesser 1972) or an aesthetic ideology (Rodowick 1987) overdetermined by a set of social, psychic, and formal factors with critical attention concentrated on the internal economy of the melodramatic representation itself.

Although I attempt to incorporate the methodologies of these Western critics, my approach is more in line with the ideas put forward by the French author Pierre Bourdieu in working toward a general theory of practice. A key concept in his theory is the habitus, which he defines as "systems of durable, transposable *dispositions,* structured structures predisposed to function as structuring structures, that is, as principles of the generation and structuring of practices and representations" produced by "the structures constitutive of a particular type of environment (e.g., the material conditions of existence characteristic of a class condition)" (Bourdieu 1977, 72). Or to be more concrete, he elaborates,

the structures characteristic of a determinate type of conditions of existence, through the economic and social necessity which they bring to bear on the relatively autonomous universe of family relationships, or more precisely, through the mediation of the specifically familial manifestations of this external necessity (sexual division of labour, domestic morality, cares, strife, tastes, etc.), produce the structures of the habitus which become in turn the basis of perception and appreciation of all subsequent experience. (Bourdieu 1977, 78)

With the help of this concept of the habitus we are able to understand "the dialectic of the internalization of externality and the externalization of internality" that would give our domestic and personal experience a priority importance in structuring our perception of and interaction with social realities. As the critical project undertaken here is to explore the constitutive role played by the Chinese melodramatic text in perpetuating the existing power structure of the Chinese family and society, I also find helpful Bourdieu's discussion of the habitus in relation to the forms of symbolic violence whose function it is to maintain relations of domination and exploitation in areas of human interaction where notions of domination and exploitation are least expected. His theory also prompts me to look into the specific way in which the Chinese melodramatic text incorporates what I would call the habitual mode of perception of the Chinese peasantry which is produced by and tends to reproduce the conditions (at the same time real and imaginary) of existence characteristic of this social group even when the conditions of its existence are becoming historically irrelevant.

Family conflict and social change

One important characteristic of the Chinese family melodrama of the early 1980s that deals with family conflict in a rural setting is its ability to engage its intended audience at a social as well as personal level. Take *The In-Laws* for instance. Set in East China shortly after the Cultural Revolution, the film gives a detailed account of the process of household division, which, as a structural feature of the Chinese extended family system, is experienced by its individual members at some stage of their lives. The issue is first raised by Qiangying, the wife of the eldest son, Renwen, when the second son of the Chen family gets married. Her main argument is that the mother-in-law, who is the treasurer of the household, discriminates in economic matters, especially favoring the new bride and the unmarried daughter. The incessant quarrels among the family members, especially the females, make a split inevitable. An agreement is reached after a family meeting that the household properties be divided between the two sons, each of whom in return should support one of the two elderly people in the family: the mother and the grandpa. Regarding the latter as a burden to her newly established household, Qiangying mistreats him by asking him to do all sorts of heavy work while feeding him only the crudest meals. When her husband finds out, he slaps her in the face. Enraged, Qiangying pursues him to his workplace and interrupts the work routine by fighting with him. She then leaves home to stay with her father's family. The angry husband follows her there and threatens her with divorce. Fearing that a divorce will deprive her of everything she has, Qiangying returns to ask for forgiveness.

The social significance of the narrative, especially the household division, will become clear when examined in the political context of China in the early 1980s. The family system represented in the film is that of the traditional extended family in its modified form after the revolution. Collective farming in rural areas of China in the form of mutual-aid groups or the people's communes of the 1950s and 1960s is structurally similar to the traditional extended family in its classical form. The strength of the extended family system as a major social institution and cultural ideal lies in its economic efficiency as well as its social cohesion. Large households that contain extended families of several generations form mutual-support networks that help to even out the heavy burden of labor-intensive agricultural production as well as provide welfare services for the needy and the sick. Their advantages are most obvious in cases of social and natural disaster, which are not infrequent in China. Inherent in the cultural ideal associated with the extended family system is the traditional value of providing all the members with enough food from the "common pot" (Chen 1985, 194), which became the cornerstone of Chinese patriarchal socialism under Mao.

Whatever efficiency this form of social organization may have is inevitably dissipated by the huge bureaucratic machine patriarchal socialism has generated. Furthermore, the perennial suspicion that the other members may not cooperate fully in collective endeavors or that some of them may use their power to extract a larger share than they deserve from the "common pot" has made individual members less enthusiastic in the collective-farming variant of the extended family system. The decollectivization policy introduced by the new leadership after Mao was designed to encourage individual initiative and productivity. It has been hailed as a realistic policy based on a reassessment of the needs of the people. To implement this policy, it was necessary to negate the traditional cultural ideal of the family or the state as "a common pot." From this perspective then, the division of the extended family household into separate small households represented in *The In-Laws* can be seen as a metaphor for the general process of privatization advocated by the new leadership in the late 1970s and the early 1980s.

The film also engages the viewer at a more personal level. This is because the dramatic conflict in *The In-Laws* unfolds in a series of conflictual relationships among family members, especially the females, that are regarded as part of the everyday experience and therefore are largely taken for granted by the Chinese audience. Insofar as what is called everyday experience is already a construct of history, ideology, and sociality, the rearticulation of this immediate experience in the family melodrama of the early 1980s warrants further investigation.

The Chinese extended family system is a hierarchical power structure replete with internal conflict (Cohen 1976, Wolf 1970, Stacey 1983). The major threat to the stability of the system is the struggle of the daughters-in-law for a better share of the household resources for their uterine families. As a counterstrategy, the family patriarchy emphasizes fraternal solidarity, sometimes even at the expense of intimacy among marital couples. As such, the strained relationship between spouses in various forms of wife abuse can be seen as the displacement of fraternal conflict within the patriarchal extended family system. Furthermore, due to the strict sexual segregation and sexual division of labor maintained by the patriarchy, antagonism in the extended family system is also displaced onto two almost legendary conflictual relationships among women: enmity between the mother-in-law and the daughter-in-law and enmity between daughters-in-law. In the former case, the mother-in-law, as the delegate of the patriarchy, is not only the supervisor of the daughter-in-law's life and work but also her competitor for the affection and loyalty of the son/husband. In the latter case, the conflict comes from each woman's effort, often encouraged by her husband, to strengthen the financial position of her uterine family in the joint household.

It becomes obvious that what is regarded as merely commonplace experience is conditioned by the structure of the family system and its patriarchal logic. This common experience can also be seen as a product of the habitual mode of perception of the Chinese peasantry, for the patriarchal logic as a practical logic or a polysemic conceptual scheme immanent in both the mode of production characteristic of the Chinese peasantry and its cultural production also plays an active role in domestic politics. The main function of the patriarchal logic in domestic politics, which usually involves family conflicts in terms of generation and gender, is to generate an ideology that "makes woman a principle of division and discord" (Bourdieu 1975, 62). This ideology has its own material basis in the division of labor between the sexes, which "predisposes the woman to be less sensitive to symbolic profits and freer to pursue material profits." In China, politics in everyday life often takes the form of *guanxi,* official or unofficial. This activity bears a certain relationship to what Bourdieu calls investment in symbolic capital, that is, behaviors in line with certain ethical codes (sense of honor, generosity, etc.) that turn interpersonal relationships into a disguised form of power relationship. In the case of contemporary China, although the ethical codes may be different, as they are often a blend of ethical and political principles, the structure remains the same as it functions according to the rule of reciprocity. Thus one might say access to symbolic capital (behavior in line with so-called socialist virtues such as devotion to the collective interest and unselfishness) means access to both formal and informal power.

A closer look at the social status of the major male and female characters represented in the film reveals that gender difference is an important indicator of access to power. Whereas the males are represented as authorities of the family as well as the village community (the eldest son is a cadre, the second son is the production team leader), the females function basically as the labor force within the family or without. This asymmetrical power relation can be clearly seen in the family meeting sequence in which the members sit together to discuss the issue of household division. The sequence begins with a close-up shot of the second son and zooms out to reveal that the eldest son sits right opposite him with the camera set behind him. A reverse shot shows his face wincing when the wife steps on his toes to force him to consent. Here we can see that although Qiangying is represented as the initiator of the family division, she occupies no place within the power structure of the family, as is shown in cinematic codes that organize the family space in terms of an opposition between the eldest son and the second son with the community head as the mediator.

The dramatization of the domestic conflict in this sequence produces a series of displacements that not only identify Qiangying as the source of family discord but also obscure the nature of the household division as well as its social causality. The first shot of the sequence, as an establishing shot, also reveals the seating arrangement of the family members: They are seated according to the two new families to be set up, forming a circle. This seating arrangement is confirmed in the middle of the sequence when the camera pans 360 degrees to reveal the reaction of the other members of the family to her demand. The significance of the seating arrangement can be seen in figure 1.

The position of the community head as the mediator is where the

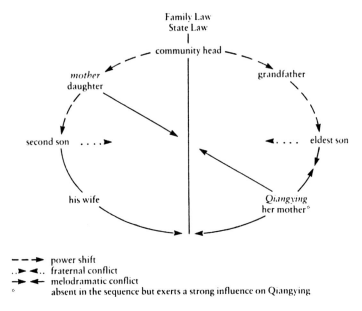

Figure 1. The family seating arrangement and its significance in *The In-Laws*.

axis intersects the circle and divides it into two spheres in which the two sons occupy the central position in relation to other members of the family to be set up. The community head as the mediator (representing the deceased father) is flanked by the mother and the grandfather. This seating arrangement is significant as it reveals the nature of the household division as a process of power transfer that unfolds within this family space. After the division, the center of the power structure within the family shifts to the sons. (This shift, to some extent, may represent the process of the localization of power in China in the post-Mao era, in which the state transfers part of its power to the administrative level of the production unit – in the case of agricultural production, to the individual peasant family.) When the community head gets a positive response from the members of the family to the idea of household division (in this case, the daughter's opinion is not solicited), he turns to the grandfather and the mother for a detailed plan. The camera cuts to the mother when she announces the division plan that specifies that the household properties be divided between the two sons, leaving the daughter in the cold. This is a moment of great emotion. Although the mother acts here as the delegate of the (deceased) patriarch, she is also the victim of the plan as she will fall from her position of power to the powerless position she used to occupy when she was a girl, like the position occupied by the daughter in the Chen family. The music and the facial expressions of both the mother and the daughter who share the same frame add to the pathos of the drama. It is interesting that the division plan, which is based on the traditional family law in terms of its exclusion of women from owning household properties, when challenged by Qiangying (for the wrong reason), is backed up by the state law (the New Marriage Law of 1980) produced by the community head. The melodramatic conflict unfolding in this family space between Qiangying and the rest of the family members, especially the mother and the daughter, produces an emotional structure that identifies Qiangying as the cause of their undue suffering and obscures the whole affair of household division as a restructuring of patriarchal power. As figure 1 shows, despite the dramatized conflict, the two pairs of mother–daughter relationships are mirror images of each other, for both are victims of the patriarchal family system.

What is crucial in this process of power transfer is the reestablishment of the patriarchal authority, which should be understood as the center of a complex network of social relations (Rodowick 1987). Its reestablishment depends upon a total identification on the part of the individual with the established order. The problem of individual identity, which is essential to the establishment of patriarchal power, can be clearly seen in the case of the eldest son and his wife, Qiangying. One is weak in character, not ready to assume the role of the patriarch, whereas the other is obsessed by an excessive desire for power, unwilling simply to assume the subservient role defined by the patriarchy within the traditional family order. The narrative that centers on household division unfolds a melodramatic conflict that perpetuates a series of symbolic divisions and oppositions through which patriarchal authority reestablishes itself. As the real issue at the center of the household division is the transfer of power within the Chinese patriarchy, the weakness in the personality of the eldest son (the legal successor according to traditional Chinese family law) and the excessive desire of Qiangying become the two crucial factors that threaten a smooth transfer of power. As a result, the person who can assume power is the second son. His uncompromising criticism of Qiangying entitles him to the position of the patriarch. This is confirmed in the last sequence of the film by another 360-degree pan shot which shows that the second son precedes the eldest son in the seating arrangement when the reconciled family members from the two households gather for dinner.

Here one cannot help but notice that the process of this power transfer realized in the narrative coincides with the popular representation of the power struggle waged in China after Mao's death. The new leadership headed by Deng Xiaoping defeated the ultraleftist group headed by Mao's widow, Jiangqing (metonymically suggested in the film by Qiangying), and her colleagues and then replaced Mao's "legal" successor, Hua Guofeng. The recourse to the melodramatic conventions of family conflict or court intrigue (often within the confines of the royal family) to represent significant historical and political change is a prominent feature of Chinese cultural production in the post-Mao era.

There are two distinct dimensions to politics in China: a rigid, formal power structure or order that corresponds to the basic social and family order and ever-changing informal power relations between different individuals and social groups (Pye 1985). Significant, or rather observable, political changes more often than not are the results of changes in the informal power relations between individuals and social groups rather than any significant change in the formal power structure of the family or state. Furthermore, the ways in which power circulates in both the public and private spheres are regulated by the economy of the exchange of symbolic capital. The dynamics of this economy become the ultimate concern of Chinese politics and its representation in art works such as the family melodrama.

Power–pleasure nexus

The patriarchal logic inherent in the habitual mode of perception both informs the Chinese representation of political and social change and conditions its practice. To what extent is the patriarchal ideology already implicit in the use of the cinematic codes in Chinese cinema? It has been argued that the classic Hollywood film text operates within a specific paradigm. Within this paradigm, "the place of male figures, the subject place and the place in reference to which the text is ordered are all mapped on top of one another so that maleness, subjectivity, and centered ordering are all hooked up into each other to constitute one phallocentric viewing subject" (Berry 1985, 32–42). Berry argues by way of a detailed analysis of certain shot sequences in films like *Li Shuangshuang* (1962) and *The In-Laws* that Chinese cinema operates within a rather different paradigm in that the place of the viewing subject is usually a privileged one that is not "gender-identified," as the film does not establish the place of the viewing subject in a stable association with the place of any figure in the text, male or female. This Chinese cinematic convention, he suggests, constitutes part of an antiindividual aesthetic, so that when it is associated with one of the figures in individual scenes of a film, this association, contrary to the norms of the Hollywood cinema, only functions to signify moments of transgression, failure, and collapse of harmony. It then becomes quite obvious that in the Chinese cinematic text, as the analysis shows, "it is to the very negative assertion of individual interests that sexual difference is attached."

Berry's argument offers great insight into the workings of the Chinese cinematic text. It also raises interesting questions about subject positioning. For instance, what is the relationship between film audience as engendered social subjects constructed by the patriarchal ideology and the viewing subject of the Chinese cinematic text, which is not gender specific? Or more precisely, to what extent is the habitual mode of perception of the Chinese peasantry and its patriarchal logic embodied in the cinematic structure of the Chinese melodramatic text? To give a tentative answer to these questions, I will examine in some detail the unique mode of address found in the Chinese melodramatic texts such as *The In-Laws*.

Film narration in *The In-Laws* is highly self-conscious. Its mode of address is made explicit in the credit sequence, which opens with a shot that pans from right to left across a lake with mountains in the distance and then zooms in on the Chen village on the lake. In the second shot, the camera continues this movement forward, following some villagers to the gates of the Chen household, where a wedding is taking place. It stays outside the gates and tilts upward to focus on the inscription on the gates, "Xiyingmen" (Happiness Overflowing from the Gates). In the next shot, these Chinese characters are enlarged to become the title of the film. Then the characters for "Happiness" and "within" dwindle into a lefthand corner of the screen while the character for "gates" becomes even larger. Because of the shape of the ideogram, it becomes a frame for the credits and a series of shots introducing the main characters. The camera then continues its forward movement until it is finally positioned between the double gates and goes on to present the drama that is going to take place within the Chen family household. Despite the happy mood conveyed by the music and the tranquil landscape, the viewer is prepared for the trouble that is to come by at least one cue: the dwindling of the characters for "happiness" and "within." However, what is most interesting about the camerawork in this sequence is that the camera is already positioned like a village spectator peeping through the opening of the gates to find out what is going on inside. This camera positioning, which conforms to certain voyeuristic behavior of the peasants, most clearly manifested in the folk custom of listening in to the wedding-night activities of the newly wed couple, is used here to elicit audience interest in the narrative. It might also be said that the position of the viewing subject offered by the text is, to some extent, already gender specific, although, as Berry (1985) carefully points out, the ways in which sexual difference is inscribed in the Chinese cinematic text could be very different from the Western norm.

It should be emphasized that the voyeuristic viewing process this camera positioning activates is overdetermined by social as well as psychical factors. In rural China, family quarrels usually occur in the household courtyard, which is flanked on three sides by buildings and opens to the road on one side. This architectural design is structurally similar to a theater stage. The crowd of villagers drawn to the family quarrel constitutes the audience, whose opinions more often than not influence the way in which the quarrel is resolved. The privileged position the camera occupies in relation to the spectacle of the family conflict is similar to that of the villagers. In fact, the villagers as spectators are inscribed in those quarrel sequences of the film. The significance of this inscription has to be carefully examined, as it will help us understand the kind of viewing process the text attempts to activate as well as the connection between the positioning of the viewing subject and the official ideology of Chinese patriarchal socialism, which is a curious combination of Confucian (patriarchal) and communist (collective) principles.

The villager/spectators inscribed in the rural melodramas of the 1980s bear a close relationship to the real-life audiences of the film (the single largest audience of such films is the peasants), who in their daily lives are witnessing and experiencing significant political and social changes structurally similar to what is happening to the peasant families represented in these films. Just as the new policies rekindled the individualism repressed by the official ideology of patriarchal socialism and the traditional cultural ideal it embodies, the artistic reenactment of this significant political change gives full play to the social and psychical tensions inherent in these peasants.

This can be seen in the first family quarrel sequence of the film, which occurs in the courtyard of the Chen family prior to the household division. In this sequence, the camera is positioned within the courtyard and often occupies the central position, panning and tracking to delineate the relationship between Qiangying and the rest of the family members. Here the villager/spectators gathering at the gates are denied any direct vision. The camera acts as their delegate. Its gaze is centered on Qiangying as she, in the absence of her husband, provokes the anger of the others and thus makes the division inevitable. Here the aggressiveness and self-interest of Qiangying can be seen as the displacement of the desire of the villager/spectators suppressed by the patriarchy in the name of the interest of the joint household or collective enterprise. The spectacle within the courtyard offers great pleasure, as can be seen in the laughter of the spectators inscribed in the film. It might be said that what underlies this cinematic structure is the same patriarchal logic that actually informs the family conflict within the patriarchal extended family. Commonly in such quarrels, the husband encourages the wife to stage a fight while he himself makes an excuse to be absent or simply hides himself behind the gates to enjoy the spectacle and then pockets the gain, leaving the wife to take the blame for the trouble.

A power-pleasure nexus runs through the film text. Laura Mulvey (1975, 311) in her seminal essay entitled, "Visual Pleasure and Narrative Cinema," gives an interesting account of the viewing process activated by the classic Hollywood text based on Freudian psychoanalysis and its reformulation by Jacques Lacan. She argues that due to the castration anxiety experienced by the male subject, two kinds of relationships can be identified between the position occupied by the male viewer and his surrogate in the text and the female image projected by the film narrative: A voyeuristic relationship in which a preoccupation with "the re-enactment of the original trauma (investigating the woman, demystifying her mystery), counterbalanced by the devaluation, punishment or saving of the guilty object" occurs and a fetishistic relationship in which "complete disavowal of castration by the substitution of a fetish object or turning the represented figure itself into a fetish" is at work. Her argument helps to reveal that the power relations activated in the viewing process are as much determined by the unconscious psychological mechanisms as they are by sociological factors.

From her point of view then, the structure of the look in *The In-Laws* can be seen as activating a viewing process in which the place of the viewing subject oscillates between a fetishistic relationship with the leading female character, Qiangying, in which she is transformed into a phallic woman, and a voyeuristic relationship in which she has to be proved the guilty party. The camera, as a delegate of the villager/spectator, focuses on Qiangying in moments of her transgression: the challenge to the patriarchy by openly demanding household division, the usurpation of its power by arranging a marriage for the daughter with the help of another woman in order to get rid of her, the maltreatment of the elderly after the household division, fighting with the husband and hitting a government official by mistake in the process, and finally neglecting her duty toward the children by walking out of the Chen family. In this representation, she is transformed into a phallic woman.

While Qiangying, in her moments of transgression, has given full expression to the repressed desire of the villager/spectator, she also poses a certain threat, in both sociological and psychical terms. As the narrative unfolds, both the husband and the villagers find that things are gradually getting out of control. This threat is reproduced by the cinematic structure of the film. In the fighting sequence, there is an unusual point-of-view shot format that deviates from the standard cinematic structure of the film, which usually requires that the camera adopt an invisible third-person position or rather a privileged position divorced from the literary point of view of any particular figure in the text (Berry 1985). In this shot, the viewer is positioned as the government official who has been slapped in the face by Qiangying and is offered a double vision of the situation through his broken glasses. He is frightened to see now that there are as many of Qiangying as there are her husband, all fighting with each other. For the first time in the narrative, the potency of the viewing subject in his all-encompassing vision is also under threat. Furthermore, the viewer is made aware of the serious consequences of not trying to contain this situation.

As a pivotal point in the cinematic text, the film narrative reorients the viewer toward a predominantly voyeuristic relationship with the leading female character by focusing on the question of whether or not Qiangying would accept the blame for all the trouble and be punished. The second quarrel sequence, which occurs after the household division in the front yard of Qiangying's parents' household, where she is staying after walking out of the Chen family, plays an important role in containing her and brings the narrative to its resolution. Her husband, Renwen, pursues her to the door and demands a divorce, which usually was the legal means to proclaim publicly a woman's guilt in traditional China.

There is an obvious divorce of the camera's gaze and its primary object, Qiangying. Much of its attention is now shifted to her mother, who is trying to prevent the divorce. The camerawork in this sequence also differs from that of the first one in that the camera is positioned alternatively within the courtyard and outside it among the villager/spectators. In this sequence, the point of view of the villager/spectator is foregrounded. Both Qiangying's mother and Renwen appeal to the spectators. The mother accuses Renwen of bullying the women by hitting his wife. Renwen retorts by saying that his act is justified as Qiangying has mistreated the elderly in the family. His appeal to the Confucian moral codes wins the support of the villagers, as is shown in a pan shot of the villager/spectators, who cheer him when he mentions he has hit his wife. The loss of moral support from the village community at large forces Qiangying to return to the Chen family for forgiveness.

The last sequence of the film presents a "happy, large" family (including the daughter's husband-to-be) at dinner in the household courtyard with Qiangying waiting at the table. The camerawork in this sequence, again, is highly self-conscious, featuring such devices as the 360-degree pan and unusual camera angles. Placed as if at the center of the table, the camera pans as Qiangying (who is almost totally excluded from the field of vision) first serves Grandpa, then the mother,

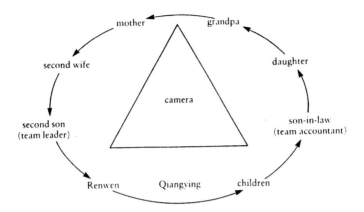

Figure 2. Social space and cinematic codes in *The In-Laws*.

followed by the second son, who is about to eat the food when his wife, Suiying, intervenes and hands the bowl to Renwen, who then passes it to his children. They in turn pass it to their neighbor, the daughter's husband-to-be, and then the daughter, who finally decides to put it in front of Grandpa. In the next shot, the camera is vertically placed high above the table but remains at the center with everyone of the Chen family at the table, including Qiangying smiling into the camera. The social space organized by the cinematic codes used here can be seen in figure 2.

Although the use of the 360-degree pan in the family-meeting sequence manages to convey a sense of conflict by originating from Qiangying when she makes her demand, the pan shot in this sequence is used to signify family unity and harmony by starting from the grandpa and eventually returning to him when patriarchal authority is reestablished through the resolution of the initial conflict. It should be remembered that patriarchal authority does not lie in any particular figure in the family. Rather it should be understood as the center of a complex network of social relations. The panning camera circumscribes the family space as a social space, as it has done in the family-meeting sequence. In this new social space, the family members, in their relationship to the three new family heads (the two sons and the son-in-law), form a triadic relationship that signifies stability and harmony when each leaves to accept his or her defined position within the family instead of an initial binary opposition between the two sons maneuvering for control.

It is also noticeable that the mediating role played by the community authority, whose power cuts across the center of the family space, is now assumed by the camera, which rises from its position at the center of the table to give a bird's-eye view of the whole extended family. The coincidence between the figuration of patriarchal authority as the center of social relations and the position of the camera at the center of the family space and the place of the viewing subject it constructs is very significant. It reveals that the spectacle of a happy, big family with which the film ends can also be seen as an imaginary projection that reassures the viewing subject as well as his representative in the text – the curious villager/spectator – that nothing has really changed after all the trouble, for the camera, representing the law and authority of the patriarchy, is in absolute control, despite moments of failure and transgression.

Tradition and modernization

The changes in party policies since the late 1970s have had far-reaching consequences that cannot be dealt with in any depth here. Suffice it to say that a new socioeconomic order is emerging. The challenges it poses to the existing power structure can be seen in various forms of social unrest and discontent. The impending sociopolitical confrontation as well as the complication are often expressed in the Chinese family melodrama of the new period in terms of a conflict between tradition and modernization. The significance of this rearticulation has to be carefully evaluated.

Here I turn to the film *In the Wild Mountains,* which is among the best family melodramas, including the prize-winning *Life* (1984) and *Old Well* (1987), made by the Xi'an Film Studio, a stronghold of the "rebellious" fifth-generation filmmakers since Wu Tianmin, a renowned filmmaker himself, took charge there in 1983. Unlike other family melodramas made in the same period that celebrate the advent of modernization, these films tend to explore the ambiguities and contradictions inherent in the process of modernization.

The narrative of *In the Wild Mountains* revolves around two couples living in a village in the Qinling Mountains in southern Shaanxi in the early 1980s when agricultural production has been privatized. Like many conservative peasants there, Huihui sticks to the old ways and lives contentedly as his forefathers before him did. His only worry is that his wife, Quilan, cannot bear children for him. On the other hand, Hehe, a young and energetic ex-soldier, is determined to seek prosperity through business ventures. After several failures to establish a successful business, Hehe's conservative wife, Quolan, divorces him on the ground that he has totally neglected his duty as a husband and father. Out of goodwill, Huihui then invites him to live in his household. Quilan becomes attracted to Hehe's new ideas, and Huihui sees in Quolan an opportunity to continue his family tradition. As a result,

Huihui's family also collapses, but in the process two new families are established based on individual choice.

An incompatibility of cultural values plays a crucial role in the respective collapses of the two families. Huihui and Quolan share traditional peasant ideals: close ties to land, belief in traditional farming methods, a big household with many children, and strict observance of traditional ethics. Hehe and Quilan subscribe to the new moral values of individual enterprise: social mobility, freedom, and, most important of all, a belief in the wonders of the marketplace. It is interesting to note the way in which this sociocultural conflict and its resolution are represented in the film.

The climax of the conflict is built up in the middle section of the film, which consists of several strands of actions: Quilan goes to town to meet Hehe, who once worked as a laborer there; Huihui attempts to cope with the explosive situation at home; Quilan suddenly returns and she and Huihui quarrel, which results in divorce. The parallel editing of these scenes establishes a sense of contrast and potential confrontation. It also helps to bring to the foreground the deployment of different cultural codes in the construction of diegetic time and space in both the city and the country scenes.

The city sequence opens significantly in a marketplace, a social space characterized by the process of the exchange of goods and services. Hehe comes to the city to sell his new product for a high profit instead of selling his labor for wages as he used to do. He and Quilan, who has followed him there, tour the shops, in which there is a dazzling display of consumer items, which signifies the material abundance brought about by the new market economy. The use of certain cinematic devices such as rapid change in location helps to convey a sense of social mobility and freedom (they have a chance to meet privately and talk like lovers amid a group of kids playing naked in the water). The ultimate signified here is a new socioeconomic order that defines the characters as individuals who can pursue their own happiness by free choice.

The village scene, on the other hand, is organized in a rather different temporal-spatial framework. The rumor of Quilan's elopement with Hehe spreads very fast in the village. Villagers abandon their work to gather in front of Huihui's household courtyard. The sequencing of the shots suggests a centripetal movement toward Huihui's household. Hehe's home is represented as the center of the social arena. The structure of the look, like the quarrel sequences in *The In-Laws*, projects a theatrical spectacle. In an attempt to win moral support, Huihui, sitting beside the entrance to his home, starts to recount to them his failure as a husband to confine his wife and as a father to ensure his family lineage unbroken. His reference to ancestry and time-honored tradition, shared by the villagers, reveals that the characters live in an eternal past. Also noticeable in the scene is a sense of communal bond. There is no distinction between the private and the public, as all the characters act within the network of traditional ethics, and their identity is defined in relation to the community at large.

The juxtaposition of country and city, tradition and modernization as symbols for different socioeconomic orders contending for domination is a prominent feature of Chinese cultural production in the 1980s and can be found in many films made in the new period. What is interesting about *In the Wild Mountains* and other melodramatic films made in the Xi'an Studio is that this juxtaposition is threaded with contradiction. In the city scene, for example, Hehe rejects Quilan's love and persuades her to return to her husband. In the village scene, Huihui's public appeal does not lead to the punishment of Quilan by the villagers according to traditional family law. The sense of contradiction as well as conflict built up in these sequences is significant, as it tells much about China of the mid-1980s, a transitional period full of contradictions.

In this transitional period, the family, like other social institutions, is in a process of restructuring. And this process can be understood as a response to economic problems. Thus in the narrative of this film, the issue of infertility, in both human and economic terms, is posited as the ultimate cause of family discord. Around this issue unfold the stories of Huihui's effort to restore the dream of a large, happy family with many children and of Hehe's business venture.

Although there are moments in the film when sociopolitical conflicts within Chinese society are revealed, the film as a whole tends to downplay such conflict. The film contains a number of narrative strands: It can be read as a success story reflecting the economic changes in the rural areas of China or as a story of family change reflecting the restructuring of certain social institutions. In either case, the narrative evolves according to its own logic, so that the text in its final resolution overcomes the heterogeneous elements and returns to a status of homogeneity.

The mythic-logic of the dialectic transformation inherent in the ancient Chinese yin-yang or *you-wu* theory plays an important role in the economic success story. Within this cosmological paradigm, fertility in either human or economic terms is understood as a natural transformation of matter. For example, for Huihui, the traditional peasant, human excrement can either be consumed by the pigs, who in turn produce meat for human consumption, or used as fertilizer for wheat growing (indicated in an exchange of dialogue between Huihui and Quilan in one of the scenes). The storage of manure is part of his daily activity and vital to successful farming. What Hehe does is supposedly

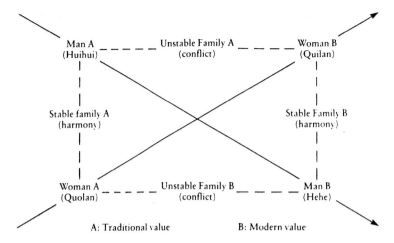

Figure 3. Resolution of family conflict through restructuring in *In the Wild Mountains*.

different since he is interested in business and profit. But ironically, the business he runs is the raising of squirrels, whose excrement he collects, because it is a traditional medical recipe for curing human infertility. The resolution of the problem of infertility raised at the beginning of the film lies in his product: the squirrel excrement that brings him both economic success and a cure for his newly wed but sterile wife. Thus the incompatibility of the old and the new socioeconomic orders metaphorically represented by a conflict in cultural values subscribed to by the two male characters is reconciled for the viewer through the evocation of the mythic-logic of the Chinese culture inherent in the habitual mode of perception of the Chinese peasantry.

In the narrative of the family change, the initial family conflict is resolved by a process of restructuring so that the final recoupling of the incompatible pairs resolves the initial conflict without a total negation of the cultural premises of the other as is illustrated in figure 3. The horizontal coupling is in constant conflict. Only the vertical recoupling produces stability. The family conflict as a conflict between different value systems is resolved by a process of restructuring according to compatible cultural values that generates a stable structure found in families across the value scale.

In this representation, there is an implicit comparison between the two new families and the sociocultural paradigm they represent. This is not only seen in Hehe's miraculous economic success and the cure he holds for female sterility but is also indicated by a shift in the power structure of the family after restructuring: a liberation of woman from the bottom of the hierarchy of the traditional family when she acquires a sense of self-identity and a conscious abandoning of the patriarchal privileges by man in the modern family and the modern state when he discovers his success depends on the marketplace, the precondition of which is freedom and equality. Although the process of restructuring can be seen as another manifestation of the dialectic transformation of the yin-yang, *you-wu* theory, an overvaluation of stability, which has its roots in the traditional moral economy of the peasantry (Scott 1976), is at work here, so that the two families based on different socioeconomic orders can be identified as stable structures, and the potential conflict within each of them does not surface.

Here we can see that while the film representation through a series of implicit comparisons may influence the viewer in favor of the new paradigm, it also functions in certain ways, especially through an appropriation of the habitual mode of perception of the Chinese peasantry, to divert his or her attention from those asymmetrical power relations in terms of gender and class inherent in the Chinese social and economic organizations.

The issue of gender relations is relevant here because the film representation as a social metaphor capitalizes on the ancient custom of wife swapping that existed in the area in which the film is set. The use of this anthropological material points to the narrative function of the women in the text. Lévi-Strauss (1969), in his analysis of kinship systems in primitive societies, pointed out the symbolic status of women in the structure of social organization and language. As exchange objects, they are the means by which men express their relationship with each other. In feminist terminology, the representation of women in the film functions as an empty sign that signifies the two socioeconomic orders subscribed to by the two male characters and the patriarchal logic that underlies each of them, despite the difference in their orientations. In this representation, men are active agents in the creation of social wealth as well as culture, while women are reduced to the status of problems to be solved or properties to be exchanged.

Sexual politics

An examination of the representation of gender relations is important as it also holds the key to an understanding of class relations in Chinese society. Since the 1930s, Chinese filmmakers, especially those who worked within the tradition of the May Fourth movement of 1919,[3] have often used gender relations to represent class relations metonymically in their film practice. This convention has to do with the institution of the Chinese family. The inferior position of women within the traditional family system was reinforced by the institution of marriage which prescribed that the bride should be chosen from a family that was slightly lower in social status. Among members of the land-owning gentry, concubinage was widely practiced. Girls from the lower classes were often purchased to provide sexual services to the master. Thus to undertake a critique of the oppressive nature of the traditional social and family order, Chinese filmmakers, especially those with leftist leanings, often adopted the gender/class paradigm to signify the patterns of domination and exploitation that exist within the traditional family and social system.

In the Chinese family melodrama of the new period, the representation of gender relations within a family context has taken on new connotations. The film *Country Couple*, which is exclusively concerned with the issue of gender inequality, is a case in point. Set in a mountain village in south China in the early 1980s, the film centers on two related families: the Yu and the Tao. The main character, Yu Musheng, runs the ferry for the community, and his wife, Tao Chun, takes care of the household chores. Their relationship is strictly in accordance with the Confucian moral codes, and as such they are praised as an ideal couple by Tao's granduncle but criticized by his granddaughter, Xingzhi. When the film opens, the wife has been sick for sometime. Although Yu knows about her sickness, he never takes it seriously. Whenever she complains about a pain in her stomach, he just gives her some *rendan* (a traditional medicine that supposedly alleviates any kind of pain). Her condition becomes more and more serious, until one day she collapses while working in the field. She is then taken to a hospital by her cousin, Xingzhi. Diagnosed as suffering from cancer, she has only a few months to live. The news gives Yu a shock. He realizes his negligence and starts to do everything he can to help her, including shouldering the household chores. The sudden reversal of roles in the family upsets Tao. She finds it hard to adjust. Meanwhile, Xingzhi and her boyfriend are also trying to work out a new relationship.

The representation of gender inequality in this film functions at two different levels. First of all, it is authorized by the party discourse on modernization as a proper part of a critique of the traditional social order. However, such is the poignancy of the critique that it cannot be totally contained by the political discourse of the Party and is thus open to a reading that will make explicit the asymmetrical power relations in Chinese patriarchal socialism as well.

The film, as a melodramatic narrative, devotes much of its attention to the two principal female characters: Tao Chun and her young cousin, Xingzhi. The construction of these two characters is based on a series of antitheses: dependence versus independence, self-denial ver-

sus aggressiveness, obligation versus desire, tradition versus modernization, and so forth. These antithetical terms constitute the parameters
with which two different moral orders are contrasted. The world in
which the middle-aged couple, Yu and Tao, live is based on a set of
clearly defined traditional values. Within this moral paradigm, the
identity of the wife as an independent individual is almost non-
existent, as can be seen in Tao's catchphrase, "I always follow you,"
by which she is identified as a virtuous woman and an ideal wife by
village elders. This phrase signifies a specific type of relationship between husband and wife prescribed by the traditional ideology of Confucianism: the patron–client relationship. The asymmetrical power
relations of domination and subordination inherent in this relationship are rationalized by the concept of mutual obligation and dependency.

Firmly opposed to this moral order, the cousin, Xingzhi, is trying to
work out a new relationship of partnership and mutual respect with
her boyfriend, Minghan. The tragedy of Tao makes it clear to them that
to follow the Confucian moral codes is anachronistic. The particular
stance Xingzhi adopts is a critical one. She constantly criticizes Yu for
his treatment of his wife and challenges her boyfriend if he shows any
sign of male chauvinism. As part of the discourse on modernization,
her critique centers on the victimization of women by the traditional
moral order.

It is necessary to contextualize the character Xingzhi, who serves in
the narrative as the mouthpiece of the party's modernization policy.
The discourse on women's liberation was predominant during the Cultural Revolution. It was politically suppressed in the post-Mao era because of its association with Jiangqing and the Gang of Four. The
textual strategy aimed at containing excessive female desire within the
bounds of the patriarchy, which has been identified in *The In-Laws*,
illustrates the fate of Chinese feminist discourse quite vividly. The re-
emergence of a pseudofeminist discourse occurred only when it was
recruited by the Party in its modernization drive. There, the reconstruction of female subjectivity and desire is permeated with a discourse of
consumerism that encourages women to participate in mass consumption – the motivation as well as the effect of modernization. When
asked what she really wants, Tao Chun, inspired by the new life-style
of Xingzhi, implies that she would like to be decently dressed up so
that she could go and see the train pulled by a locomotive (symbol of
progress) that brings new ideas as well as consumer goods into this
secluded mountainous region.

This reconstruction of female subjectivity contains other political overtones. For instance, although the discourse on modernization

voiced by Xingzhi in the text challenges the sexual inequality inherent in the traditional moral discourse, it does not in any way question the conventional notion of the sexual division of labor. In the film, the two male characters engage in community work: Yu operates the ferry for the local community, and Minghan runs a oil extraction machine for the commune. The two women, Tao in particular, engage in farming as well as domestic work. Although the contract system is already in force in the film, the distinction between husband's work as communal and wife's work as purely domestic is clearly marked. In the rural context of China, domestic work involves not only household maintenance and child rearing but also animal husbandry and vegetable production on the private plot.

The emphasis on the contribution of the wife works in support of the new party policy on privatization. This is because the representation of the sexual division of labor in this film signifies the sometimes conflictual and sometimes complementary relationship between two different modes of production: communal and private. Since agricultural collectivization in the early 1950s, the issue of the private plot of each peasant household has been hotly debated again and again. The leftists in the party have called it the "capitalist's tail" which must be cut off, whereas the rightists insist that it should be allowed to exist in order to subsidize peasant family income. In *Country Couple,* as in a number of other films, private enterprise is metonymically represented in feminine and domestic terms (partly due to the fact that private enterprise in China in the 1980s is largely confined to family-based, self-employed economic activities), which allows it to appropriate a set of connotations vital to the pathos of the text: productivity and victimization. Indeed, these connotations are traditionally associated with the image of the maternal in family melodrama. The valorization of women's sacrifice, one major convention of the Chinese family melodrama, is often used to evoke public sympathy for the process of privatization, a major policy change in the party's modernization drive. A much clearer example of this tendency is a recent popular melodramatic text, *Hibiscus Town* (1987), in which the leading female protagonist is an entrepreneur whose thriving private business becomes the cause of her suffering during the Cultural Revolution.

However, there is a double edge to this emphasis on the contribution of the wife, for it can also be seen as an endorsement of the ever-stronger demand of the disadvantaged for a larger share of the formal power of the state as well as the family. The unequal distribution of power as well as wealth is effectively disguised by an ideology that makes women a principle of division and discord, which has its material basis in the existence of a mode of production based on the sexual division of labor. In view of this, one might say that the emphasis on the contribution of the wife toward the welfare of the family can be seen as a first step toward challenging it.

In *Country Couple* there are moments when the patriarchal discourse that underwrites the construction of female subjectivity is made explicit. Melodrama can be approached either as a specific cinematic genre specializing in heterosexual and family relations or a pervasive mode across popular culture (Gledhill 1987). Peter Brooks (1976, xiii, 188), in his concern with melodrama as a mode of conception and expression – or, in his words, "as a certain fictional system for making sense of experience" – describes it as "a mode of excess: the postulation of signified in excess of the possibilities of the signifier, which in turn produced an excessive signifier." This excessive mode of the melodramatic expression in *Country Couple*, which lies partly in an elaborate texture of metaphors, parables, and riddles, makes possible a progressive reading of the text.

Central to the meaning of the text is the riddle of a bamboo pole. In one scene when hungry children are waiting for Tao to return from the field to cook for them, the daughter poses the riddle to the younger brother to amuse him: "What is green with leaves at home, but thin and yellow away from home? Dipped under water again and again, it comes up dripping with tears." At this moment, the little boy sees Tao coming back from the field and runs toward her, crying "Mama." The paradigmatic significance of the riddle can be made clear by the following equation.

Narrative Syntagma		Male Subject		Patriarchal Family		"Socialist" State		Traditional Ideology
Subject	•	*Boatman*	•	*Husband*	•	*Ruling Elite*	•	*Patron*
Object	•	His Pole (signifier of the Phallus)	•	Wife	•	The Masses	•	Client

The "intended" signified of the riddle is the bamboo pole, which the husband Yu uses to move the ferryboat across the river. The riddle as a signifying chain actualizes a subject–object relationship. Homologous to the narrative text as a symbolic representation, it also, to some extent, reveals the premises of its patriarchal discourse. In the domestic context in which the riddle is articulated, the signified of the riddle shifts from the bamboo pole to the mother. The introduction of this new signified turns the riddle itself into a metaphor of the husband–wife relationship within the traditional family context. But there is a social dimension to the riddle as well. The image of the boat implied in the riddle is a rather conventional symbol for the state or society as a whole. In the political discourse of the 1960s and the early 1970s, the party leadership was often referred to as a helmsman. Here the riddle, or the narrative for that matter, as a specific syntagma, is also capable of illustrating the homology of asymmetrical power relations in terms of gender and class existing at the level of the state as well as that of the family.

Although the text indicates that there is a significant change in the husband's attitude toward the wife after she is hospitalized, it also suggests that this change is motivated by the realization that he has neglected his duty toward the welfare of his wife in return for her loyalty. Thus the self-criticism he undertakes still operates within the traditional patron–clientage paradigm, which applies not only to the interpersonal relationships within the Chinese family but also to the relationship between the ruling elite within the party and the people in general under patriarchal socialism. The former is supposed to display an almost paternal concern for and responsiveness to the needs of the latter, who in turn should display absolute filial and political loyalty to the former. The reorientation toward economic development indicated by the changes in the party's policies are often interpreted as a genuine response to the needs of the people. But from a political perspective, it can be seen as an attempt to accumulate symbolic capital vital to the exercise of what Bourdieu (1977) calls symbolic violence that functions to shroud the relations of domination in terms of Confucian moral codes such as mutual obligation and dependency. This can be seen clearly in those sequences of the film when Yu decides to buy Tao new clothes as well as agrees to her demand to see the locomotive. He even tries to reverse the roles of husband and wife. In a rather moving sequence when Tao is discharged from the hospital, we see that the daughter presents her with the academic record that needs the signature of the family head. Bitten by remorse, Yu suggests that Tao should sign it. Tao refuses, saying it is not right. It is only when Yu insists that she does finally sign. A close-up shot of her name in Chinese characters accompanied by sentimental music constitutes a strong emotional appeal, signaling that the husband finally recognizes the wife's rightful place within the family. But it is ironic that her action is totally dictated by the husband and therefore her inscription bears the unmistakable mark of the (party and the family) patriarchy.

Conclusion

A political perspective is assumed in this study of the Chinese family melodrama of the early 1980s, which views China's modernization campaign as a strategy adopted by the new leadership to cope with the legitimation crisis it faced in the post-Mao era. Although the new policies made under the slogan of modernization have brought about significant changes in Chinese social and economic life, the basic power structure of Chinese society remains largely unchanged. As is made clear in the above analysis of the three films, this formal power structure remains very much intact because the visible political changes very much result from the recirculation of the informal power relations. This circulation of power in both the public and the domestic spheres continues to be regulated by the economy of the exchange of a specific form of symbolic capital, which is a set of ethical codes based on a curious combination of Confucian and communist principles.

Deeply rooted in the normative structure of Chinese culture, this basic power structure is perpetuated in various forms of social representation and social practice. The Chinese family melodrama as a specific form of social representation provides us with a typical example. By examining in great detail the social inscription of the Chinese family melodrama and the ideological implications of this inscription, this essay not only reveals the extent to which the melodramatic narrative functions as a symbolic response to the general sociopolitical confrontation and the complication as they are transposed into domestic terms but also explores the ways in which the film representation of this conflict exerts a form of symbolic power over its viewers by implicating them in the actual social processes.

This symbolic power lies mainly in the capacity of the text to use the habitual mode of perception of the Chinese along with its patriarchal logic that both informs the viewer's understanding of the social realities and conditions his or her social practice. The adoption of the habitual mode of perception, embodied in various narrative strategies as well as the cinematic structure of the Chinese family melodrama, while preparing the viewer/subject for the process of actual social change, also contributes to the perpetuation of those asymmetrical power relations of domination and exploitation in the Chinese social and political organization that are now beginning to take a new and increasingly modernized guise.

Notes

1. For a detailed analysis of the contradictions inherent in the official ideology of the Chinese Communist Party in the new period see Brugger (1985).
2. The ruthless crackdown on student demonstrations for democracy in 1986 and the recent massacre in Beijing in which thousands of students died clearly show that the Deng regime would always be ready to resort to repres-

sive means to maintain power. The news of the massacre reached me when I was revising this essay. I would therefore like to take this opportunity to strongly condemn the Beijing regime for the atrocities it committed against the Chinese people.
3. The May Fourth movement of 1919 was the first democratic movement in modern Chinese history. Its impact on Chinese social, cultural, and political life cannot be overestimated.

References

Berry, Chris (1985). "Sexual Difference and the Viewing Subject in *Li Shuang-shuang* and *The In-Laws.*" In *Perspectives on Chinese Cinema*, ed. Chris Berry, 32–47. Cornell University East Asian Papers, no. 39. Ithaca, N.Y.: Cornell University.

Bourdieu, Pierre (1977). *Outline of a Theory of Practice.* Cambridge: Cambridge University Press.

Brooks, Peter (1976). *The Melodramatic Imagination: Balzac, Henry James, Melodrama, and the Mode of Excess.* New Haven: Yale University Press.

Brugger, Bill, ed. (1985). *Chinese Marxism in Flux: 1978–84.* London: Croom Helm.

Chen, Xiangming (1985). "The One-Child Population Policy, Modernization, and the Extended Chinese Family." *Journal of Marriage and the Family* 47, 1:183–202.

Cohen, Myron (1976). *House United, House Divided: The Chinese Family in Taiwan.* New York: Columbia University Press.

Eastman, Lloyd (1988). *Family, Fields, and Ancestors: Constancy and Change in China's Social and Economic History, 1550–1949.* New York: Oxford University Press.

Eckert, Charles (1973–4). "The Anatomy of a Proletarian Film: Warner's *Marked Woman.*" *Film Quarterly,* 27, 2. Reprinted in *Movies and Methods: An Anthology*, vol. 2, ed. Bill Nichols, 407–25. Berkeley: University of California Press, 1985.

Elsaesser, Thomas (1972). "Tales of Sound and Fury: Observations on the Family Melodrama." *Monogram* 4:2–15. Reprinted in *Movies and Methods: An Anthology*, vol. 2, ed. Bill Nichols, 165–89. Berkeley: University of California Press, 1985.

Gledhill, Christine (1987). "The Melodramatic Field: An Introduction." In *Home Is Where the Heart is: Studies in Melodrama and the Woman's Film,* ed. Christine Gledhill, 5–38. London: BFI Publishing.

Hannan, Kate (1985). "Economic Reform, Legitimacy, Efficiency and Rationality." In *Chinese Marxism in Flux: 1978–84*, ed. Bill Brugger, 119–41. London: Croom Helm.

Kleinhans, Chuck (1978). "Notes on Melodrama and the Family under Capitalism." *Film Reader* 3:40–7.

Lang, Olga (1946). *Chinese Family and Society.* New Haven: Yale University Press.

Lévi-Strauss, Claude (1969). *The Elementary Structures of Kinship.* Boston: Beacon Press.

Madsen, Richard (1984). *Morality and Power in a Chinese Village.* Berkeley: University of California Press.

Mulvey, Laura (1975). "Visual Pleasure and Narrative Cinema," *Screen 16,* 3:6–18. Reprinted in *Movies and Methods: An Anthology,* vol. 2, ed. Bill Nichols, 303–15. Berkeley: University of California Press, 1985.

Plaks, Andrew (1975). "Towards a Critical Theory of Chinese Narrative." In *Chinese Narrative: Critical and Theoretical Essays,* ed. Andrew Plaks, 309–352. Princeton: Princeton University Press.

Pye, Lucian (1985). *Asian Power and Politics: The Cultural Dimensions of Authority.* Cambridge, Mass.: Harvard University Press.

Rodowick, David (1987). "Madness, Authority and Ideology: The Domestic Melodrama of the 1950s." In *Home Is Where the Heart Is: Studies in Melodrama and the Woman's Film,* ed. Christine Gledhill, 268–80. London: BFI Publishing.

Scott, James (1976). *The Moral Economy of the Peasant.* New Haven: Yale University Press.

Stacey, Judith (1983). *Patriarchy and Socialist Revolution in China.* Berkeley: University of California Press.

Wolf, Margery (1970). "Child Training and the Chinese Family." In *Family and Kinship in Chinese Society,* ed. Maurice Freedman, 37–62. Stanford: Stanford University Press.

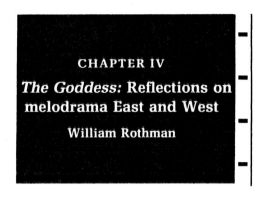

CHAPTER IV

The Goddess: Reflections on
melodrama East and West

William Rothman

No one has a perspicuous picture of the totality of Chinese cinema of the 1920s, 1930s, and 1940s. Many films have been lost, partly because little was done to preserve them after their commercial run, partly because China suffered so much physical destruction during many years of devastating war. After 1949, Chinese films were shown to scholars selectively: Films of a leftist tendency were privileged, others were less readily available. Even Paul Clark, researching his pioneering and invaluable study, viewed almost exclusively the work of "progressive" filmmakers and saw few of the more typical commercial productions of the pre-1949 period.

Students of the American cinema have gradually come to the realization that popular genres *are* serious, at least in their own terms. This realization has led to a kind of critical reassessment that has barely begun in the case of pre-1949 Chinese commercial cinema. The bulk of Chinese popular films remains neglected, and the films that have been studied have primarily been explicated in political and ideological terms, not subjected to criticism intended to address their achievement, and the implications of their achievement, as films. (India is another country whose popular cinema stands in fundamental need of critical reassessment.)

I realize that this chapter will do little to redress this neglect. *The Goddess* is not at all an "ordinary" or "typical" Shanghai product of

In writing this essay, I was able to study only a VHS copy of *The Goddess,* rather poor in quality and unsubtitled to boot. No doubt, I have made errors as a result of not being able to see details that would be plainly visible in a print. No doubt, too, I have made other errors of interpretation that no China specialist would have made. Surely, such errors would have been far more numerous had Wang Yuejin not patiently explained to me relevant elements of the social context that I would not otherwise have comprehended.

The essay benefits greatly from my viewing of the tape with Wang Yuejin and Ellen Draper, and from our subsequent discussion, and from the opportunity I had to speak about the film at the China Institute in New York, for which I am grateful to Nancy Jervis.

the thirties. I know that it is unfashionable to say what I am about to say, but it is nonetheless important for me to say it: I have chosen to write about *The Goddess* because I feel inspired by the film and am convinced that it is a masterpiece, one of the major examples of the worldwide art of silent cinema, worthy of comparison to the greatest American, French, Soviet, German, or Japanese silent films. All students of film, and of China, should know this film and ponder its achievement. In a sense, this is my main thesis, over and above the particular ideas I will advance as I begin to reflect on the film and its relationship to the American melodramas that I find it fruitful to compare with it.

In the twenties and thirties, the audience for American film was all of America (and most of the world). The audience for Chinese film was specifically urban, and predominantly in cities – Shanghai first among them – that were the centers in China of Western trading, where Western goods, fashions, and life-styles were most widespread (at least within certain classes). Until political turmoil forced it to relocate, and then relocate again, China's "Hollywood," the hub of its commercial movie industry, was Shanghai.

In China, film itself was nontraditional; it entered on the wave of Western influence. Thus all Chinese films, even the most "traditional" opera or martial arts films, were reflections of, and reflections on, new ideas and forms of life that were entering China from the West, or, more accurately, were emerging in China in part motivated by China's encounters with the West.

In China, as in Japan and India, film represents a radical discontinuity in traditional culture. But film represents a radical discontinuity in Western, and specifically American, culture as well. Even in the West, and even in America, all films, no matter how "traditional" their cultural sources, were motivated by, and motivated, radically new ideas and forms of life. In America, these ideas and forms of life, however new, had sources within America's own cultural tradition. My belief is that the same was true in China: Chinese film was "Western," but it was also Chinese in its forms and its sources. Nor is it possible to make a sharp distinction between what is Chinese and what is Western, what is "inside" or "outside" the Chinese cultural tradition, just as it is not possible to draw such a line in the case of the West, or of America.

As Stanley Cavell demonstrates in his pioneering work on Hollywood romantic comedies of the thirties and forties, and in his more recent essays on romantic melodramas, the transcendentalism of Emerson and Thoreau is a central source of popular American movie genres. Their roots in American transcendentalism are essential to what makes American films American. But transcendentalism in America, a late American flowering of European romanticism, also is a reflection of, and reflection on, the great impact of the introduction to the West of Asian religion, philosophy, and art. That is, Hollywood romantic comedies and melodramas have "Eastern" as well as "Western" sources. They mark American culture's ongoing conversation with itself, which is also a conversation with China (and with the rest of Asia as well). In the same fashion, Chinese films mark China's conversation with the West, and with America, which is also Chinese culture's ongoing conversation with itself.

Wu Yonggang, the director of *The Goddess*, spent several years in Hollywood before returning to China to work within the Shanghai industry. Clearly, his film has an extreme technical sophistication and self-consciousness that invites comparison with that of the Hollywood director who obviously deeply influenced and inspired him: Josef von Sternberg. Like *Blonde Venus*, the von Sternberg melodrama that is especially closely related to it, *The Goddess* evidences a complete mastery of the forms and techniques that constitute the "classical" style, a style we sometimes identify with Hollywood but which is also international.

To be sure, *The Goddess* has stylistic idiosyncrasies, such as the occasional use of rapid pans in place of edits to effect transitions from framing to framing. (Is this a gesture peculiar to *The Goddess*, or is it characteristic of all Wu Yonggang's films, or of Chinese cinema, or a branch of Chinese cinema, in this period?) Yet the film places itself squarely within the mainstream of the classical film tradition. Judged as an example of this international style, Indian films of the thirties all seem lacking (what this means is that this is not an appropriate way to judge them). But *The Goddess*, like any of the great Japanese films of the period by directors like Ozu, Mizoguchi, and Naruse, is different. Judged as an example of the classical style, it is impeccable and extremely sophisticated in its direction; the acting is sublime; the story is moving and deep.

This assessment does not make *The Goddess* any less "Chinese." Noel Burch argues, to quite perverse effect (and David Bordwell is inclined to go along with him to a large extent) that the "Japaneseness" of a Japanese film can only be a function of its systematically violating "Western codes," especially of editing, as if Japanese films that do not violate Western editing codes cannot possibly also uphold Japanese aesthetic traditions, or revise them from the inside. But Japanese filmmakers have proved themselves capable of employing "Western codes" no less idiomatically than American or European filmmakers (even if they have sometimes revised them in the process), and have equally made the conventions of classical cinema their own without betraying their Japaneseness. Then why think of these conventions as exclusively Western, alien to Japan (or China, or India)?

Once Asia cedes classical style to the West, lamentable consequences follow, as, for example, when Satyajit Ray's filmmaking practice is shunned by aspiring Indian filmmakers, who criticize him for employing a "language" that is Western, not Indian, although he is obviously as much at home in this ostensibly Western "language," as capable of being himself – and his is a most distinctively Bengali self – as any American or European.

The point was appreciated by all filmmakers of the "Golden Age": Classical cinema is an international medium in which traditional cultural difference can be expressed, perhaps even *cannot but* be expressed. It represents a radically new perspective, paradigmatic of the first half of the twentieth century (as television is paradigmatic of the second half), in which cultural difference can be acknowledged and – is this a paradox? – thereby transcended.

If *The Goddess* evidences a mastery of classical style in general, it is equally masterful in its employment of the specific forms and strategies of a particular genre that, likewise, we sometimes identify with Hollywood but which is also international: the romantic melodrama that Stanley Cavell so evocatively names "the melodrama of the unknown woman." This genre encompasses such American exemplars as *Camille, Stella Dallas, Gaslight, Now Voyager,* and *Letter from an Unknown Woman.* Again, the great example directed by von Sternberg is *Blonde Venus* – like *The Goddess,* a film about a mother reduced to prostitution by her commitment to raising her young son.

Cavell traces the close logical relationship between the melodrama of the unknown woman and the genre of romantic comedy he calls "the comedy of remarriage." In American comedies like *It Happened One Night, The Awful Truth, The Philadelphia Story,* or *Adam's Rib,* a woman finds her voice, is fulfilled, through the attainment of a new kind of marriage, one characterized as a conversation between equals, the whole process also being interpreted as one of her education, and interpreted as well as a political allegory about the fulfillment of the American dream of creating a new America, an ideal human community, a utopia.

The melodramas of the unknown woman, too, center on a woman's quest for selfhood, but in this genre the woman attains – or fails to attain – fulfillment not through an ideal marriage, which is for one reason or another barred to her, but on her own, or only with the help of the world of women, forsaking or transcending marriage. These films do not glorify a woman's suffering, her victimization, as is conventionally supposed. Like the remarriage comedies, they are dedicated to the proposition that nothing on earth is more important than a woman's self-fulfillment and happiness in the world.

The remarriage comedy is a genre for which Americans seem to have a unique aptitude. (Why films of this genre have virtually never been made outside the United States is an intriguing question, although certain factors are obviously pertinent. For one thing, comedies of remarriage require, as a condition, that divorce be an option for men and women; in the thirties, the heyday of the genre, precious few societies satisfied this condition.) Every national cinema, by contrast, has a tradition of films intimately related to the American melodramas – this is why "melodrama" is such a fruitful subject for a symposium like the present one. But what *is* the relationship of, say, a Chinese melodrama like *The Goddess* to its American counterparts? How do cultural differences manifest themselves in the ways the conditions of such a genre are interpreted and developed?

Before I begin to address this question, it will be helpful for me to pause to sketch the narrative of the film.

The Goddess tells the story of a woman who makes her living by walking the streets of Shanghai as a prostitute. She is struggling to bring up her young son on her own – he is an infant in the first half of the film, a boy of elementary-school age in the second.

The woman encounters a gangster type, a piglike man with a perpetual leer who is always surrounded by anonymous henchmen. He avails himself of her services for the night, then moves in, uninvited, and becomes her pimp. At a certain point, she tries to break away from him and get a job in a factory, but finds no work. When the gangster locates her once more, he makes clear that, if she tries again to escape, he will send her son away and she will never see him again. So she accepts the situation, bowing to brutal reality. In this cruel world, she needs money to support her son, and thus she, too, stands to gain from this relationship.

Years pass. The son is now a school-age boy. Neighbor women discourage their children from playing with this bastard of a prostitute, but mother and son still enjoy a pure, innocently joyful intimacy.

All these years, she has been hiding some of her earnings in a chink in the wall. The gangster is suspicious but has never succeeded in finding her secret cache. Now that the boy is old enough, she enters him in a fancy private school. She has the money, so the school accepts the boy, without really questioning the lies she tells about the boy's father.

Her son's education proceeds apace. She is happy, despite her compromises, and despite the fact that other mothers start spreading rumors, leading the other boys to pick on her son continually at school. One day, a schoolmaster observes such a scene and is concerned. (Obviously, this schoolmaster represents potential trouble. Will he find out the truth? If he does, what will become of the boy?)

Thus the stage is set for the first of the film's great emotion-charged sequences. All the parents are gathered in the school auditorium for a student talent show. Two little girls finish their spectacularly cute song-and-dance routine, and then our little hero takes the stage. He sings a poignant song about a poor newsboy and his aging parents. As he sings, the other mothers whisper knowingly in each other's ears, his own mother anxiously looks on, and, no doubt, handkerchiefs rustle and tears flow in darkened movie theaters all over Shanghai.

The rumors reach the schoolmaster in the form of an anonymous letter, and he undertakes an investigation, in the course of which he visits the boy's mother at home – the second great tear-jerking sequence in the film. In the course of his visit, he spots a telltale polkadot dress hanging on a coatrack. He also bears witness to this woman's genuine commitment to her son's education. Her love and commitment shine through most dazzlingly when she declares the truth about herself in a passionate "aria" that leaves the schoolmaster speechless with astonishment. (Cavell has pointed out that such an aria of "self-nomination," to use Peter Brook's term, is an obligatory scene in the American melodramas of the unknown woman. These scenes often feature a spectacular, virtuoso display of irony, as in Ingrid Bergman's mad scene – or mock mad scene – when she is alone with Charles Boyer at the end of *Gaslight*. In *The Goddess*, too, the woman's aria climaxes in a display of irony as she laughs derisively, bitterly, in the face of the ultimate madness of the world.)

The schoolmaster recommends to the board that the boy be allowed to remain in school. Fearing scandal, the board members vote him down, upon which he submits his resignation. (This whole sequence is intercut with the gangster discovering the hidden money.)

When she receives the letter informing her of her son's expulsion, she resolves that they will escape to some place so far away that no one will know them. This is when she discovers that the gangster has stolen her money. In a rage, she goes to his gambling den, pulls him away from his cohorts and, in an inner room, demands her money. For a moment, he seems perplexed, even a bit frightened, by her intensity. Then, dismissing his uncanny sense that this woman possesses a terrifying power, he regains his composure and tells her, with his usual leer, that he has already spent the money. In disbelief and fury, she pounds his chest with her fists. There is a brief struggle, which ends with him striking her and violently shoving her away. As he turns to leave, dismissing her, she grabs a bottle. The camera assumes his position and recedes from her, its movement matching the gangster's as he walks toward the door. With a look of grim resolution, she advances on the receding camera and strikes out violently with the bottle, attacking this brutal man and symbolically attacking the camera as well.

In prison, presumably awaiting execution for killing the gangster, she is visited by the schoolmaster, who has read about the case in the newspaper. Deeply moved, he tells her that he will raise her son as his own. Alone again in her cell, she has a vision of her son, smiling and happy – her one ray of hope, as a title puts it. The film ends.

Paul Clark speaks of Ruan Lingyu, the star of *The Goddess,* as China's Greta Garbo. I find it more helpful to think of her as a Marlene Dietrich without the theatricality, although I realize that, like all great stars, she is really unique, a world unto her self. Having viewed *The Goddess* in China a couple of years ago, I carried with me a memory of Ruan Lingyu's sad eyes. I *thought* I remembered that she played a submissive victim-figure, but this was my memory playing tricks on me. She plays a woman who is sad much of the time – she has much to be sad about – but she is strong and never meekly submits to anything. We view her in the throes of a wide range of powerful feelings, culminating in her two extraordinary explosions of emotion: She kills her gangster pimp/lover (whether or not she intends to kill him, the violence in her act is intended, and this intention is completely in character), and she tells the truth to the schoolmaster, declaring herself with astonishing passion and authority.

Throughout *The Goddess,* Wu Yonggang's camera lingers on his star as lovingly and "excessively" as von Sternberg's on Dietrich, and Ruan Lingyu emerges as fully Dietrich's equal in extravagant, breathtaking beauty. Yet there is a striking difference, as I have already indicated by saying that Ruan Lingyu is like Marlene Dietrich devoid of theatricality. When von Sternberg says "You have to understand that I am Dietrich," he is at once asserting that she is nothing without him and acknowledging that he is nothing without her. Film's creation of Dietrich is also the creation of von Sternberg, these beings are inextricably intertwined, and woman and man participate equally in their creation. By contrast, Wu Yonggang and Ruan Lingyu are *separate* beings.

Early in *The Goddess,* the woman looks at herself in the mirror and puts finishing touches to her hair and makeup before going out to walk the streets. Wu Yonggang does not cut to frame her in the mirror. If this were a von Sternberg film, we would surely be shown, and would linger over, the star's reflected image looking inscrutably yet provocatively right into the camera, at once a "fetish" and a subject mocking our guilty wish to reduce her to a fetish, an object. In contrast to Dietrich, Ruan Lingyu is not "objectified" or "fetishized." The camera does not relate to her in a guilty way, nor is *she* guilty of complicity with a guilty camera.

In the face of the camera, Ruan Lingyu is innocent in a way Marlene Dietrich is not, or claims (deceitfully?) not to be, although she, too, is no virgin. The film makes absolutely no bones about the way this "Goddess" makes her living: She sells her body. No Hollywood film even of the pre–Production Code era would be so explicit about prostitution. She does not enjoy selling her body this way, but she is not a "fallen woman" in her own eyes, or the camera's. She does not feel – and the film does not assert that she should feel – corrupted or defiled or sinful or somehow responsible for the cruelties the world threatens to inflict on her innocent son. Although *The Goddess* establishes in numerous subtle ways that Ruan Lingyu has a desirable and experienced body, in the eyes of the camera she remains pure. Except for the schoolmaster we never see a man, even the gangster, touch her with desire. (A corollary of this is that, when she kills the gangster by her own hand, no blood is drawn.)

Comparing *The Goddess* to an American melodrama like *Blonde Venus*, it is striking that "romance" in the Western sense seems virtually nonexistent in the Chinese film. This woman is not searching for fulfillment through love; what she dreams of is her son's fulfillment, which is interpreted as his education. (What constitutes an education is a central issue in the film, and we shall return to it.) *The Goddess* gives no thought to the boy's real father, as if he had none. Nor is there any sense, as there is in *Blonde Venus*, of a romance (incestuous, Freudian) between mother and son, despite the extraordinary physical intimacy that prevails between them – for example, in the wonderful sequence in which the son teaches his mother the gymnastic exercises he learned at school. Imagine if this had been Marlene Dietrich, with von Sternberg directing!

The only moments in *The Goddess* that strike this American male viewer as erotic occur in the woman's two encounters with the schoolmaster. He is drawn to her first by compassion and then by awe at her moral character, but he is also moved, repeatedly, to touch her.

When the schoolmaster pays a visit to her home as part of his investigation, there is a charged moment at which she runs her hands through her hair, then, swaying, pulls her hair tightly back, as if steadying her mind to keep from blacking out or losing control. Solicitously, he reaches out to touch her arm, but she pulls out of the frame, leaving his hand dangling for a long moment. We – and he – cannot help but be aware, at this awkward moment, that he feels a strong desire to touch her (however we may interpret this desire).

When the sequence closes with the schoolmaster patting the boy's head just after she has stroked her son's hair, we again feel the schoolmaster's desire to be touching *her.* We sense this desire even more strongly at the end of the film, when he visits her in prison. This powerfully emotional sequence climaxes in a close-up, gloriously composed and lit. Of the man's hand reaching through the bars, tenderly touching the woman's shoulder. His desire to touch her goes beyond mere kindness; there is a deep bond between them, one that I cannot fail to interpret, at least at one level, as an erotic bond.

If the schoolmaster feels passionately that there is a deep bond between them, as I cannot but believe (perhaps because I am not Chinese), he has the self-discipline to sublimate his desire – as has, for example, the heroic cadre in the face of his passionate young recruit in Xie Jin's *The Red Detachment of Women.* Without this capacity for passion, and without the self-discipline to transcend it, he would not be worthy to raise this woman's son as his own. (Then why does he not marry her? How can it be that this possibility is not even considered, as it could not fail to be if this were an American film?)

What astonishes the schoolmaster is this woman's noble, selfless dedication to her son's education. What does "education" mean to her? Is it that she wants her son to "get ahead," wants him to acquire the trappings of respectability and its attendant privileges? No. The schoolmaster, in making his case to the board (interestingly, they are dressed Chinese-style while he is impeccable in his Western suit), makes it clear that, in this corrupt society, a school's reputation has nothing to do with its ability to provide a true education. True education cannot be separated from ethical practice and moral authority. What ultimately matters is not one's place in society, for society has lost its values, but one's moral character – a fine Confucian, or Emersonian doctrine (as is the film's idea that, no matter who a boy's father is, society is responsible, we are all responsible, for his education).

In the corrupt world of *The Goddess,* the brutal gangster occupies a "low" position in the social hierarchy, yet he wields great power. Within the discourse of the film, as I understand it, he represents the link, even the equation, between male sexuality and sheer power, the rule of the fist. The film makes a further connection, perhaps equation, between the rule of the fist (hence male sexuality) and capitalist exploitation: The factories in which workers labor like slaves are framed to emphasize their conspicuously phallic smokestacks, and the Shanghai skyline itself, repeatedly invoked by the director, is a row of phallic towers.

In any case, the brutal gangster is not the cruelest villain in the world of *The Goddess.* At least he is vibrantly alive, and at least he is no hypocrite. More contemptible are the cowardly men on the school board and the hypocritical women – they would feel at home in W. C. Fields's Lompoc – who teach their children to mock a virtuous woman and her innocent son.

In identifying and condemning the brutal exploiters and the hypocrites who betray the true spirit of education, *The Goddess* is passing judgment on virtually all of Shanghai society. In this world, virtue is compelled to stand alone, joined only by the camera, only by the director, and by us.

In *The "I" of the Camera*, I have argued that, in American films following Griffith, virtue cannot declare itself, cannot be declared, except through the agency of the camera, and that the camera is always also an instrument of villainy and cannot "nominate" innocence without at the same time violating it.

In *Blonde Venus*, the camera's relationship to Dietrich is linked to that of her villainous – or at least villainy-tainted – husband. The camera's relationship to Dietrich is also linked to her son's relationship to her. At one level, this son is innocent, like the son in *The Goddess*. But *Blonde Venus* declares him also to be implicated in the world's villainy (as is the camera, as is the viewer, as is the author, as is the act of storytelling itself, as is film's art of projecting a world). At one level, the whole film springs from this "innocent" boy's guilty desire. Villainy and innocence, the camera and its subject, are, in *Blonde Venus*, two faces of one god or goddess, as inseparable as creation and destruction.

The Goddess, by contrast, implies that this woman and boy are pure, innocent, untainted, as is their intimacy with each other, as is the camera's intimacy with their intimacy. Viewing them on screen, together or apart, we experience an innocent pleasure, a joy, foreign to our experience of American movies. In a sense, the camera relates to Ruan Lingyu not as a father (as Griffith's camera relates to Lillian Gish, for example) but as a son, perhaps as *this* innocent son grown up but retaining his filial piety. The schoolmaster, like the camera, views this woman as an ideal mother – indeed, as *his* mother. As I have suggested, in *Blonde Venus*, too, at least rhetorically, the camera assumes the role of Dietrich's son. But *Blonde Venus* emphatically does not locate the mother–son relationship, or the camera's relationship to that relationship, in a region separate from the "real world" of exploitation and cruelty, as *The Goddess* does.

When we view the joyful intimacy between mother and son in *The Goddess*, the film's implication is not that what we are glimpsing is an Eden from which they must inevitably be banished for their sins.

Nor are we viewing a "phase" that must inevitably succumb to raging oedipal conflicts. The implication, rather, is that their love will never lose its innocence and joyful intimacy no matter what their fates in an unjust world, no matter what compromises the world may force them to make in the other regions of their lives. No doubt, we, too, lead compromised lives, yet *The Goddess* touches a region of purity within us when it invokes such visions of innocence, an innocence that – astonishingly, if we are familiar only with American melodramas – the camera does not threaten to violate.

In some respects *The Goddess* seems a more progressive revision of the American film melodrama. I am thinking of the features I have mentioned such as the film's unflinching acknowledgment of the woman's prostitution, the way the film shows her intimacy with her son without making it seem problematic, the fact that film does not impose a phony "love interest" on her.

Yet all these features also have a regressive aspect to them, throwing into relief the essential and profound streak of feminism of the American cinema. American melodramas are about a woman's quest for self-fulfillment when the option of marriage to Cary Grant or Spencer Tracy is ruled out – a marriage that is at once a romantic dream come true and a conversation between equals. In *The Goddess,* the woman never looks to a man for her self-fulfillment because she is not on a quest to fulfill her self. True, she is not in quest of a self because she does not doubt she already *has,* or *is,* a self. But she does not have doubts on this score because she knows her mission in life is to provide her son with an education.

But it is complicated. Although the woman's final vision is of her son, the film presents this vision in the context of its acknowledgment and affirmation of the woman herself: The woman envisions her son, but we envision *her* envisioning her son. This boy is the ideal subject of education, but it is Ruan Lingyu who is the ideal subject of Wu Yonggang's camera. This woman, mediated by film, is at the heart of *The Goddess,* as Dietrich, mediated by film, is at the heart of *Blonde Venus.* Taken literally, *The Goddess* affirms a woman's self-denial, but *as a film,* it affirms that woman's self, just as the great Hollywood melodramas affirm the selfhood of the women who are their central subjects. Within the world of *The Goddess,* Ruan Lingyu may appear to deny herself, yet her self-denial also *gives* her a self on film. *The Goddess* declares this woman to be every bit as innocent as her little boy, yet to possess an adult intelligence, knowledge, capacity for compassion, and strength – in short, the film affirms her as an exemplary human being.

The Goddess does not endorse "the patriarchy" any more than does *Blonde Venus* or any of the other American "unknown woman" melodramas. Quite the contrary, *The Goddess* decisively attacks it, although it does so in the name of an ideal father, the schoolmaster, and the values he endorses. These happen to be the values he finds perfectly incarnated – and *articulated* – by an ideal mother. For the sake of acknowledging the values this woman represents, this man is willing to renounce his social position (although, admittedly, he never takes off his tie), his privileged place in a degraded, corrupt social hierarchy. What does this woman value? Astonishingly, the film incorporates into its remarkable closing sequence a vision of what she holds most dear, as she envisions it in her final state of imprisonment.

The schoolmaster visits her in prison and swears he will look after her son as if he were the boy's real father. Then he leaves, and she is alone in her cell. Framed in medium long shot, her head is bowed. Then she looks up with a hopeless expression. Her arms dejectedly at her side, she turns and makes her way to a bare table, the camera reframing with her. There she sits, stroking her arm with her hand, her slumped position perfectly conveying her inconsolable dejection.

There is a cut to a medium close-up of her, looking down and screen left. She strokes her hair and turns her face as if to look at something offscreen to the right. Then the expressionlessness that is the perfect expression of her inner desolation miraculously gives way to a look of ecstasy. There is a title that says, in effect, that she has left only one ray of hope. Then we see her in medium shot at the far left of the frame, looking toward the blank dark background. Suddenly, as if projected onto a screen, her little boy appears in the right background of this frame. He meets her gaze – and the camera's – with a heartbreaking smile of innocence and hope, a vision real enough and unreal enough to move us, as it moves his mother, to tears.

Then the vision fades out, and the woman turns almost to face the camera, closes her eyes, sighs, slightly lowers her head, raises her head again but without opening her eyes, sighs once more, and still keeps her eyes closed as our vision of her, too, fades out and the final title appears.

So this film about education is also engaged in education, identifying and affirming what it holds to be of value in a way open only to the medium of film. Indeed, the ending of *The Goddess* – like the ending of *Stella Dallas* – is also an invocation of our condition as viewers, a declaration of the medium of film. It interprets our condition as one of hopeless imprisonment: Film is our bridge to a world of hope, a world that, *The Goddess* reminds us, is not, or is not yet, real (can it ever be?). The film does not offer a practical way of changing society so as to make this vision real. All it does – perhaps all we can ask a film to do – is to keep alive, or to breathe life into, such a vision, such a hope, of a better world.

The ending of *The Goddess* does not feel like a "happy ending" like the ending of *Blonde Venus* or *Stella Dallas.* The vision the film leaves us with is, in the end, that of a virtuous woman cast off by an unjust world. Yet, because all this woman has lived for is her son's education, this *is* a vision of happiness. This woman *is* happy, but only as long as she keeps her vision alive by closing her eyes, by shutting out the world.

Our vision of her, too, in the end fades out. The film ends, as all films must end, and we are left alone, imprisoned in a cruel, unjust world. We can keep alive our vision of this woman only if we, too, "shut our eyes." This is, at one level, what *The Goddess* calls upon us to acknowledge.

The Goddess contains several sure-fire tear-jerking passages, yet there is a reticence characteristic of this film quite different from the hyperbolic expressions of emotion we associate with melodrama. Partly, this has to do with the fact that no *violent* threat is established. After all, except for the moment the gangster grabs the woman's arm so forcefully that he leaves an imprint of his hand on her skin, he never even threatens her with physical harm. The gangster's threat is that he will harm her son, not her, and he threatens to harm the boy not by inflicting physical violence but by depriving him of an education.

Yet when the film employs parallel editing to create suspense (e.g., when it cuts back and forth between the board meeting and the gangster's search for the hidden money), or when the camera self-consciously calls attention to itself (when it frames a view of the woman through the gangster's legs, or when it composes images of factories that emphasize their phallic smokestacks, or when it assumes the gangster's place, making the woman's attack on him a symbolic attack on the camera as well), Wu Yonggang's camera *does* declare that it possess a capacity for violence, for villainy, as surely as does von Sternberg's. But in *The Goddess,* the camera's capacity for villainy somehow does not keep it from invoking visions of innocence that it does not even threaten to violate, visions that touch us, too, whatever compromises we have made with the world.

It is as if *The Goddess* divides the role of the camera (the role of the author, the role of the viewer) between two regions, one guilty and one innocent, one compromised and one pure, one public and one private. A happy marriage between public and private is a central aspiration of American films. At one level, bridging the gap between these two regions is what *The Goddess,* too, is centrally about: It is what distinguishes the heroic schoolmaster from the hypocrites on the school board. At another level, though, the film does not even contemplate bridging this gap: Keeping these regions separate is what allows the camera to invoke virtue without threatening to violate it.

In a sense, then, *The Goddess* is implicated in the hypocrisy it attacks, the duplicity of isolating one's public from one's private self. Perhaps such a compromise is inevitable in Chiang Kai-shek's, or Mao's, or Deng Xiaoping's China. (And what about George Bush's America?) But if it is inevitable, how will China ever change?

Is *The Goddess* a call for a social revolution? It is and it is not, I take it. Insofar as it is not, the film affirms the value of keeping one's eyes closed so that one's imagination can be free. Insofar as it is, it is not Mao's revolution that *The Goddess* calls for, but one akin to the new American revolution envisioned by the remarriage comedies and melodramas of the unknown women of the American cinema — a revolution that affirms the values represented by the schoolmaster and his goddess. Call these the values of education. Whatever the film's compromises, in China's current struggle between a hypocritical party and a generation of young people in quest of an education, we cannot be in doubt as to where *The Goddess* stands.

CHAPTER V

Melodrama as historical understanding: The making and the unmaking of communist history

Yuejin Wang

History and naming: The jungle in search of a beast

Peter Burke, a Renaissance historian, has suggested the deliberate employment of cinematic techniques, such as flashbacks and crosscutting, for historical narrative.[1] There is more to it than intellectual novelty. Look at the history of 1989:

First sequence: Beijing. The untimely death of Hu Yaobang, the one-time party chairman, was mourned by the Beijing students. The mourning ignited a chain of world-shocking events that began with pathos, erupted into an euphoric celebration of the temporal triumph of democracy, and ended in bloodbath in Tiananmen Square.

Second sequence: Budapest. On the screen was the exonerating memorial of Hungary's former premier Imre Nagy, who was illegally executed for his leading role in the 1956 uprising. Masses of Hungarians belatedly mourned his death.

Third sequence: Teheran. We see Iranians' frenzied farewell for Ayatollah Ruhollah Khomeini, an enormous spectacle of emotional outpouring.

Funerals, elegiac mournings, historical memorials – these events took place almost simultaneously. Furthermore, the motif of huge crowds gathered in squares was reiterated insistently on the screen. Crowds are surging everywhere in the world: in Poland, Czechoslovakia, East Germany, Hungary, the Baltic States, China. History presents itself as cinema; world events lend themselves to the now-lost grand Eisensteinian crosscutting and parallel editing; heterogeneous ideas are yoked together by violence; homogeneous scenes from heterogeneous contexts link themselves in a Kuleshovian montage with a self-assertive editing reminiscent of Dusan Makavejev's eagerness for juxtaposition.

It has already become a threadbare piece of wisdom that history is textualized. Here even before any mediating agents obtrusively intervene at heavy-handed textualization, history has already become a con-

73

struct, an artifice/artifact, and a narrative – well made yet unmeditated and (seemingly) unmediated. It organizes itself by a rhetorical intricacy that any film narrative dreams of: many-layered narrative strands, foreshortened chronology, and reiteration with subtle variance.

History now cries out for an understanding in a cinematic mode, for the unraveling of the narrative takes the form of flashbacks. We cut back to Chinese students demonstrating in 1987, demanding more freedom and bolder strokes of democratic reform. Unfortunately that led to the downfall of Hu, the party chairman, champion of political reform, who was pushed out of office by Deng Xiaoping for countenancing students' yearning towards the "bourgeois liberalization."

In view of Deng's predominant screen presence, the sequence implicitly calls for a flashback within the flashback: In 1976, Beijing students and civilians gathered in Tiananmen Square to mourn the death of the late premier Zhou Enlai and openly declared their grievance at the ruling regime. In the Chinese mind, Zhou is almost undisputedly an embodiment of virtue, although history has suppressed its memory – a secret of darkness – and never makes public Zhou's possible endorsement of the decision to send the Soviet-led tanks to trample the 1956 Hungary uprising. Again the regime found a villain who was considered the mastermind behind the massive antigovernment sentiment. The denouement of that flashback sequence ends with the removal of Deng Xiaoping from his premiership. The official denouncement capturing the headlines of *People's Daily* and vibrating on the air was that Deng was "China's Imre Nagy"! The analogy seems ingeniously appropriate: Both were premiers in a socialist country; both were believed to have obliquely ignited the rebellious fire in the public mind against the socialist orthodox.

To return to the first-removed flashback, the sequence of events in 1987, it was "China's Nagy" who removed Hu, a mastermind leader, copying Deng's own role a decade ago. To return to the present-tense narrative, it is again "China's Nagy" who removed Zhao Ziyang, yet another impersonator of the archetypal Nagy figure.

Set against these recuperated flashback sequences, the present-tense narrative presented to us on the screen is a bittersweet irony. We see the redemptive reburial of the real Nagy who died three decades ago. It is as if a mysterious and invisible director from his omnipotent point of view had intervened to edit the two shots together: the shot of Hungarians mourning the death of Nagy and the shot of "China's Nagy" purging an impersonator of that prototypical Nagy figure. Is it, according to Nietzsche, the dead burying the living,[2] or vice versa?

How does then the sequence of Ayatollah fit into the scenario? The link at the surface level is still the spectacle of massive mourning for a dead leader. The dramatic effect is the shocking discrepancy between the two different political implications of the *similar* acts/scenes of mourning. Ayatollah's body lay in state inside a refrigerated glass box and surrounded by huge crowds of mourners crying their hearts out – almost a reiteration of a shot of China in 1976, still alive in one's mind's eye. Mao was placed in a refrigerated glass coffin circled by an endless file of Chinese mourners who cried their eyes out; moreover, a documentary of the mourning scene was immediately released nation-wide so that ten billion spectators cried before the screen. The scene harks back to the Soviets' mourning for Lenin, whose body was also contained within a glass coffin placed in the Red Square as Mao's glass box is placed in Tiananmen Square, the Chinese political arena for the past century. The mourning in 1989 Beijing for the death of Hu, the embodiment of the hope for liberalization, however, completely re-verses the meaning of the spectacular mourning of 1976 for the death of Mao. In this light, to the Chinese eye, the Iranian sequence could be experienced as a return of the memory. The spatial juxtaposition be-tween the two spectacles of mourning dramatizes the temporal unfold-ing of history with its transformations, reversals, negations, antitheses, parodies, and ironies.

One sits up in rapt surprise at the intricate design of these superim-positions and dissolves of events. It is as if historical events conspire to externalize an inner or deep structure hitherto hidden from us, as if history strives to fulfill a formal construct or a cinematic apparatus, as if there is an essential structural condition to which history aspires. But what is it?

History, we are told, is repetition – prophesied by Vico as recurring cycles; telescoped by Hegel as the twice-told tale with an a priori end; fantasized by Nietzsche as the eternal return; edited by Marx as a suc-cession of tragedy and farce; and abridged by Toynbee, through his "original binocular view of history" or rather, his multiocular perspec-tive, as repeated patterns; and envisioned by Barthes as the postponed equations. But why does Kierkegaard makes a point of saying that "neither tragedy nor comedy can please him, precisely because of their perfection, he turns to the farce" – by which he means melodrama?[3]

What other terms can better capture this unfolding of history than the generic mode of melodrama? The foreshortened chronology, "the misprision and recognition of virtue,"[4] "the public recognition of, and spectacular homage to virtue,"[5] the "fundamental bipolar contrast and clash," the irreducible moral Manichaeism, the emotional excess and situational extremis, and the trajectory of peripeteia punctuated with "moments of astonishments."[6] Features of melodrama become apt vocabulary capturing our historical narrative, or perhaps any historical narrative.

History, like melodrama, defines prototype roles (of Nagy) and its later impersonators; it allows public figures to oscillate easily between the roles of hero and villain, between political leader and "public enemy"; it contains the internal shift in, or reversal of, meaning in externalized display of similar public spectacles. We experience the structural or narrative/historical a priorism: a spatialized temporality of back to future; a rapid alternation between different moments of moods (from bitterness of mourning to euphoria of temporary triumph, to absolute terror and pathos of massacre).

The funeral sequences strive after an essential melodramatic typology in its thematic structuring: tonal and rhythmic modulations, "musical patterning in a metaphorical sense."[7] As is put by Peter Brooks:

Like the oratory of the Revolution, melodrama from its inception takes as its concern and raison d'être the location, expression, and imposition of basic ethical and psychic truths. It says them over and over in clear language, it rehearses their conflicts and combats, it reenacts the menace of evil and the eventual triumph of morality made operative and evident.[8]

Our *histoire* – how aptly the French captures the history/tale coexistence! – enacts Brooks' scenario: It is *shot* through with recurrences (of funerals, or purges), reversals (from Deng as hero to Deng as villain; from Nagy as villain to Nagy as hero), rehabilitations (of the innocent wronged, i.e., Nagy, and final virtue rewarded), and a priori, the rehearsals (of future scenarios of reburial of Hu and redemption of Zhao as Nagy-figures; of massive mourning of the untimely death of some future Iranian antitotalitarian leader who in Khomeini's day would be condemned as heretic).

In this moral universe, the demarcation between virtue and evil is nonnegotiable; poetic justice is (to be) meted out. The immediate motivation – in terms of narrative logic – of Beijing students' demonstration is the urge to precipitate the acting out, by *histoire's* invisible iron hand, of poetic justice. Hu Yaobang, the hero, died an untimely death. His removal by Deng two years ago was already an outrage to the public sense of justice. The dethroned prince, as constrained by the moral imperative of melodramatic *histoire*, awaits sullenly in oblivion his restoration and redemption toward what Kent in *King Lear* would call "the promised end,"[9] expecting the descending of melodrama's deus ex machina constrained by a moral law. And we were all waiting for that ending, the day of redemption, of public recognition of the suffering virtue, as we are awaiting now anxiously the denouement of the redemption of Zhao, the Nagy figure. The *histoire*, however, went berserk or awry: Hu died ahead of Deng, who is ten years senior to Hu. A melodramatic narrative comes to a halt before it runs its normal course. Hence the public outrage, the furor, at the failure of nature/culture's smooth working out of the expected *histoire.* "Those who should have survived, dead; those who should have died, alive." A bitter proclamation posted on the campus walls of Beijing University and upheld during the demonstration articulates this frustration succinctly.[10] The imperative "should" betrays a stubborn faith in the consistency of the moral law of poetic justice indispensable to history as melodrama. The bitterness is the unwillingness to absorb any aberrations from the moral trajectory. The public staging of demonstration is therefore a compensatory act of demanding that history take its "normal" (read "melodramatic") moral course.

Melodrama's law of poetic justice generated fantasy: Villains were imagined dead. Specific time and date were offered about Deng's death after his disappearance from the screen; a vivid scenario was constructed about the assassination of Li Peng the premier. The Chinese-language press around the world perpetuated a high tale: As Li was walking across the great hall, a vengeful policeman whose sister had been killed in the massacre suddenly shot from his hip (with the dashing swing one finds in American Westerns) and severely wounded Li. The hero was in turn shot to death by Li's body guards. A modern revenge play is spun out. To the public's disappointment, Li appeared after what seems a deliberate lapse of invisibility from the camera, thus dispelling this scenario to be a mere sequence of fantasy. Even this mockery of public expectation based on melodramatic logic is still operating within the mode of melodrama, which is capable of constant astonishments – that is, Li's sudden disappearance/appearance.

Was the scenario drawn from the clues of the real screen events of Reagan and Sadat? Or was it an "intertextual" borrowing from the cinematic narrative of the aborted assassination of de Gaulle in *The Day of the Jackal,* or the failed attempt to kill Lenin in Romm's *Lenin in 1918?* The mode of melodrama becomes a mode of consciousness more deeply ingrained than we realize. The mechanism of camera obscura, used by Marx to figure our ideological refracture,[11] is now coded or built-in with the melodramatic lens. If man makes the world and shapes history after his own image, then history as it is made by man naturally takes the melodramatic turn.

Society and the perception of society move past drama into melodrama. Movies begin as Victorian theater. Nietzsche's calling for an attainment beyond good and evil is prophecy against this melodrama of progress. If Machiavelli first described the theatricalization of politics – the Prince and the paupers, the General and the general, the man and the woman, the black and the white, the young and the old, depending for their position, their very social existence, upon their externalized (Empson calls it pastoral) views of one another – then Marx first planned the recovery from this mortal slapstick.[12]

Or should we say Marx also planned the rediscovery of this "mortal slapstick"? As is also suggested by Stanley Cavell, "the ideas of "class conflict" and "classlessness," while not necessarily theatrical, are inherently liable, or phenomenologically vulnerable, to theatrical employment."[13] It is consequently not surprising to reflect that the whole communist history is especially consistent with the melodramatic logic: the oversimplification, the eternal purges, the class struggle, the designation of private property as the evil, and the chiliastic vision.

But then, so what? History as melodrama – the rhetoric brevity could after all turn out to be a thoughtless cliché that forecloses further inquiry. It is also vulnerable to the suspicion of an underlying blind faith in the telos of rationality with which history is imprisoned. "History has no telos," so enjoinders Daniel Bell, "but is only instrumental."[14] To pursue a sustained analogy of history as melodrama, the questions worth reckoning with are rather: Is there an imperative that yokes history and melodrama together? What compels us to choose melodrama as the prism to view history?

We commonly perceive history simultaneously at two levels of meaning: the factual surface, and the conceptual modeling of the events through some generic story type.[15] It follows that distortion is inevitable. Yet, as is pointed out by Hayden White, distortion could be both negative in its too willful exclusion of what should not be excluded (but then who gives the mandate?) and positive in its arrangement of events to "an integrated pattern of meaning." "The meaningless structure of mere seriality" is, accordingly, rendered comprehensible. We may say melodramatic structure offers what Fredric Jameson would call "the syntax of history":

The problem arises, however, from the apparent necessity of the mind to grasp diachrony in what are essentially "synchronic," or static and systematic, terms. Thus, it would seem that to "understand" history involves a translation of flux or change into some relatively fixed relationship between two states or moments – the "before" and the "after" of the historical transformation.[16]

The crucial point here is that "it is only more comprehensible by reference to the conceptual model which sanctioned its distortion *in this way* and *not* another."[17] "As soon as this active life-process is described," Marx urges "history ceases to be a collection of dead facts as it is with the empiricists."[18]

The economy between history and melodrama is, I would argue, not a superficial analogy; neither is the cliché quite dead. Many times with an unthinking apathy we send many things/names to their early graves by sealing them off with the murderous tag "clichés," while the cliché has not even been chewed and digested. The analogy allows a deeply embedded tension in its scheme. On the one hand, it presupposes the lordliness of the generic story type – that is, melodrama as a conceptual model – over the welter of historical facts. This presupposes an implied confidence that the chronicle of facts is placed under our teleological control through the employment – Hayden White would call it the "emplotment" – of the generic pattern called melodrama. Chaotic experience is tamed and ordered through the conceptual prism/prison. On the other hand, however, the very choice of melodrama itself has its other turbulent side: History is not imprisoned in the iron cage of the plotted melodrama, because having imprisoned this beast in the jungle or closet, we still do not know what this imprisoned beast is. This unknowability of history is well accommodated for by the knowability of the generic capacity of melodrama, which by its nature is full of surprises and astonishments – which is to say that the only thing we know about melodrama is that we do not know exactly at what moment it will surprise us, at what moment it will release the beast. But we know it will. Such is history as melodrama that takes us by surprise. In hindsight, having just watched the astonishing denouement, we realize how consistently it has fulfilled its own logic; that it comes within the range – or the web – of our telos. Yet nevertheless we were surprised. The telos is only hindsight or second thought.

Who would imagine the Berlin wall would collapse all of a sudden? And what can we say at such a historical moment? Melodramatic! By this same token, we are both affirming and denying our teleological control over the elusive trajectory of history, with its implicit promise of our ability to trace the origin and predict the future. By assigning history to the realm of melodrama, we happily legitimize and rationalize our surprise and domesticate our perplexity at what is beyond our telos, beyond our construction and design while still living under the illusion of control. With no other way of capturing or comprehending the sudden swerves and peripeteia of history, we emasculate it in the seemingly controllable cage of melodrama, thus theorizing it in an untheoretical way, retreating into a spectator's darkness to watch the darkness of history placed under the spotlight of melodramatic stage/screen. History is shortchanged, displaced, and replaced with the knowability of a melodramatic mode, which is a controlling metaphor and a malleable mode of historical understanding.

Thus, we dispel the myth of interiority by opting for another, a structure beside history instead of in history. That leads us to the questions of history and gaze.

History and the melodramatic gaze

The historical Hu-Nagy-Khomeini scenario also raises questions: Why is it that it is through the occasions of death that otherwise unrelated events, cultures, and personalities come into a close interplay, effecting some kind of mirror structure? Why does history always choose to make deaths and funerals its staples, and fetishize the dead body, so that deaths become the very landmarks and turning points of historical trajectory? These, according to Daniel Bell, are "the existential questions which confront all human beings *in the consciousness of history*."[19] Accepting the assumption that our consciousness of history is increasingly more melodramatic in structure, do we not see the connections? Is it a mere coincidence that melodrama emphatically indulges in and fetishizes the moments of death – the pathos and emotional rhetoric of excess, what Dylan Thomas calls "the feast of tear-stuffed time"?[20]

"History's dead never understand why they have lived," wrote Roland Barthes:

Caesar under Brutus's knife, Becket under that of Reginald Fitzurse, the Duke of Orleans under those of the Burgundians, the Duke de Guise under that of Henri III – each of these has been himself, achieved his true stature, only once he was dead, lying at his assassin's feet like a new man, mysterious, unaccustomed, different from the old one by all the distance of a revelation, that revelation produced by the ultimate coherence of a destiny....If these prone and still-warm dead men are saved from nothingness, it is because Michelet was already gazing upon them, the historian was already taking them over, already explaining their lives to them. He was drawing from them a raw, blind, chaotic, incomplete, absurd life, and restoring to them a clear life, a full life, embellished by an ultimate historical signification, linked to the great living (i.e., genetic) surface of History.

Thus, the historian is the man who has reversed Time,...he is the demiurge who links what was scattered, discontinuous, incomprehensible: he weaves together the threads of all lives, he knits up the great fraternity of the dead, whose formidable displacement, through Time, forms that extension of History which the historian leads while walking backwards, gathers within his gaze which decides and discloses.[21]

While obliterating meaning and difference, death also recreates meaning. Above all, paradoxically, death in melodrama/history is not going silently into the dark night; it *externalizes* all that is in the dark in life-time. This form of externality releases not only emotional excess but also the interior meaning otherwise eclipsed, marginalized, and postponed. The spectacle (the funeral, for instance), the formal gesticulation, stylistic furnishings, and the persistent reiteration of similar motives constitute a "silence made eloquent."[22] And the eloquence emanates from spectacle, mise-en-scéne, and visuality; it is addressed to our gaze.

Merging with melodrama on the occasion of death, history is imbued with the quality of, to borrow Laura Mulvey's phraseology, "to-be-looked-at-ness."[23] It is consequently revealing to note why Barthes emphasizes the historian's "gaze" vis-à-vis "the great living (i.e., genetic) surface of History." The textured history has a fascination with corpses and coffins that constitute a body of history; it foregrounds the exteriority, appearances, and surfaces that cry out – especially on occasions of funerals and memorials – for our gaze. It draws our gaze to the dramatic contours of a historical event, the peripeteia of its trajectory and its formal patterning. The signifieds of guillotines and coffins are foregrounded to become, and equate, their signifiers. The hidden signifieds are externalized. It is consequently not surprising to find that great thinkers define our position vis-à-vis history in terms of a spectator in front of a screen presence. Max Weber speaks of the "world image" and "a stand in the face of the world."[24] Marx encourages us to "visualize,"[25] and "we must look at the whole spectacle from a standpoint beyond the frontiers of Germany."[26] Marx also describes how a historical figure like Bonaparte endeavored to "keep the public gaze upon himself."[27] Buonarroti likewise in his *History* points out to whom in history "the wise man should rivet his gaze."[28]

The proliferation or omnipresence of television screens in this century has realized the metaphorical watching and gazing. History finds its incarnation on screens; it becomes a window from which one glimpses apocalypse. To the distant observer watching the melodramatic Chinese history unfolding on the screen, there is sufficient cause for bewilderment and riddle solving involved in this spectatorial experience. The spatial alignment of the screen characters in the Chinese political spotlight – who is beside whom, who is missing from the picture – are signs that reveal the intricate intrigues in the Forbidden City. Any fissure or rupture of the visual texture tells about a new maneuver behind the curtain. The weeks of invisibility and screen absence of Deng, the last emperor, in May, for instance, gave rise to the most titillating suspense in the history of melodramatic narrative and narrative history: Is Deng dead? On the life and death of one old man hinges the hope of exonerating the wronged virtues.

So the way to textualize history becomes, in the communist praxis at least, a matter of altering and reediting photographic presences to delude our gaze. Thus observed Milan Kundera:

In February 1948, Communist leader Klement Gottwald stepped out on the balcony of a Baroque palace in Prague to address the hundreds of thousands of his fellow citizens packed into Old Town Square. It was a crucial moment in Czech history – a fateful moment of the kind that occurs once or twice in a millennium.

Gottwald was flanked by his comrades, with Clementis standing next to him.

There were snow flurries, it was cold, and Gottwald was bareheaded. The solicitous Clementis took off his own fur cap and set it on Gottwald's head.

The Party propaganda section put out hundreds of thousands of copies of a photograph of that balcony with Gottwald, a fur cap on his head and comrades at his side, speaking to the nation. On that balcony the history of Communist Czechoslovakia was born. Every child knew the photograph from posters, schoolbooks, and museums.

Four years later Clementis was charged with treason and hanged. The propaganda section immediately airbrushed him out of history and, obviously, out of all the photographs as well. Ever since, Gottwald stood on that balcony alone. Where Clementis once stood, there is only bare palace wall. All that remains of Clementis is the cap on Gottwald's head.[29]

"The balcony of a Baroque palace" as a backdrop already signifies the theatricality of history's display, the object to be consumed by our gaze. The clumsy straining after a morally purified universe, while explaining why history cannot escape the heavy-handed editing like any fictional film melodrama, also suggests a constraint conditioned by history's need to foreground the smoothness of its surface like melodrama. Consequently, there seems to be no attempt at hiding the traces of the artifice of photographic reediting of history, though the intent is toward concealment and suppression of historical facts. Here is another spectacular example:

The day after Mao's funeral, all Chinese newspapers carried photos of the top leadership standing in a long line in front of the crowd at the memorial ceremony. When it was the monthlies' turn to carry the same photos, the "Gang of Four" had meanwhile been purged. The photos, already known to the Chinese public, were issued again, but this time the disgraced leaders had all disappeared from the pictures, leaving awkward gaps, like missing front teeth in an open mouth – the general effect being underlined rather than alleviated by the censor's heavy handling of the airbrush, and by his clumsy retouching of the background. To crown the cynicism of such blatant manipulation, a little later, New China News Agency issued a report denouncing Madame Mao for the way in which, in her time, she had allegedly falsified various official photographs for political purposes![30]

This praxis is predicated not only on trading reality with visuality, but also on a totalitarian will to command the mode of gaze at history. It demands that the spectator accept as unquestionable and "logical" the peripeteia of political melodrama, the *formal* necessity and *generic* imperative of the alternating rhythm of appearance and disappearance, presence and absence. There should be no surprise on our part to find some day in the future that Zhao Ziyang, the wronged Virtue, resumes his screen presence in his second coming. Our knowledge/acknowledgment – call it acceptance or complicity – with the generic imperative of history-as-melodrama has already prepared us for that ending.

So the crucial issue at stake is not so much with the artificiality of history-as-melodrama as with the coding of our gaze at History. Marx's stress on ideological perception figured as "camera obscura"[31] unwittingly becomes, in the communist praxis working under his shadow, more than a metaphor; it is now an imperative inscribed in the spectatorial experience: a willing suspension of disbelief, taking the simulacrum of history as history.

This coding of gaze finds its most explicit exemplar in *The East Is Red* (1965), a revolutionary Chinese "epic" film, which, for all its melodramatic mold, becomes an undisputed classical interpretation, or symbolic/ritualistic reenactment, of the Chinese communist history.

The film is actually what Soviet director Semyon Aranovich would call "documentary mythology."[32] The history of Chinese revolution is capsuled into a spectacular stage musical, a pageant with Zhou En-lai, the premier, as the director in chief.

Structured in a typical melodramatic mode, *The East Is Red* moves according to the archetypal communist historical scenario: from oppression to liberation, from suffering oblivion to recognition. The chronology externalizes the hidden pattern of move from spring to winter with the ambiguous summer and autumn omitted. There is no psychology of characters, as is true of melodrama; characters appear only as signs signifying their class identities.

Emphatically, the film employs rhetorical devices to constrain our mode of watching, demanding that we unconditionally accept the musical and moral Manichaeism in its way only – and no other way. The film, accordingly, inscribes not only the stage but also the spectator-in-the-text: Intermittently the camera turns around to the spectators, so that we are assimilated into that uniform spectatorial space. Moreover, the camera frequently reverts to a little boy. We are therefore invited to inhabit and merge with his point of view.

As if it were not enough, on several occasions, the child is seen covering his eyes with candy wrappers of different colors (red and green), so that he – and we – could see the chromatically transfigured stage through the transparent candy wrapper, a vision filter. The effect on us is that the screen world attains an artificial alternation of a dominate one-color world like the night party sequence in Godard's *Pierre le Fou*.

Postulating the child as a typical spectator may well be seen as an attempt to strive after some version of the Rankean conception of the historian's "innocent eye."[33] The employment of the monochromatic filters adds a further gesture toward the purification of vision, the clear-cut moral universe on the stage. The artifice invites us to follow, through this high-handed device, the orthodox public gaze. The intent may well be the insistence on conforming, on seeing as "we" (the collective) see, with the childish purity and faith, uncontaminated, unseasoned. What we experience then is a double melodrama: the staged melodrama on the one hand, with a melodramatic figure or device, and the rhetorical mediation, through the child's eye and his candy-wrapper, on the other hand. Thus when the stage shows the scenes of class oppression and rebellion, the child would – as if all by accident – use a dark blue wrapper, and when revolutionary climax is reached, the moment would call for a red wrapper.

This very melodramatic artifice itself, however, in hindsight, effectively undermines, at the same time as it underlines, the seemingly untroubled state of innocence. The high-handed intervention undoes the illusion about the "objectivity" of history. "It only required a bayonet thrust for the bubble to burst and the monster to spring forth to our eyes,"[34] to release and set free the beast in the jungle or closet. Shouldn't we have reason to imagine that the chromatically filtered screen – like the interposed flash-outs of Goddard's film, which are a Bretchian gesture of self-reflexivity – has the potential of reminding us of the concocted and mediated textuality of history?

The filmmaker in those euphoric years, inebriated with utopian visions, would not be able to comprehend the implications of those manipulative apparatuses and devices, taking them probably as no more than innocent paraphernalia to enliven the rhythm and to serve as stylistic furnishings. In retrospect, for us, however, these moments become excruciatingly apocalyptical. The washed-out redness that momentarily dominates the screen – like the flash-forth sequences of Kubrick's *Shining* (in which a child forebodes a future bloodbath) – not only anticipates the massive madness of the "all Red" (*yi pian hong*) plague in the Cultural Revolution (1966–76) but also has more apocalypse to tell. The climax of *The East Is Red* is a carnival in Tiananmen Square. The scene is momentarily covered by the child/spectator's red-colored candy wrapper to send up or highlight the euphoria of the occasion. It is shuddering to realize what a murderous omen that melodramatic stylistic gesture forebodes: The June 4 bloodbath is foretold!

The history-as-melodrama approach, therefore, does not necessarily entail oversimplification. It could reveal difference while it portends and pretends to erase it. The excessive mode of melodrama calls for our awareness of its artificiality; it points to another, which it eclipses. With that in mind, we can code our melodramatic gaze at history in a double consciousness – both inside and outside it. The more pronounced its dramatic overturns and stylistic paraphernalia, the more acutely the sense of its pointing to an otherness that could never be present.

Melodrama: Representing history or itself?

History manifests itself in, or strives after, melodrama. When film melodrama attempts to represent that grand melodrama called history, however, there is often a dramatic loss and a loss of drama: We feel the lessening of dramatic energy, momentum and meaning. Yet we still call it, or dismiss it as, melodrama. Is it a problem of naming? Do we have two different melodramas, or two different modes of melodrama, or the same drama that exists in different realms or at different levels, each having its own constraints? Why do they still share the same name, one that evokes fear and trembling, the other calling for tears and laughter? To history as melodrama, we feel the ineffable; we have different thoughts too deep for the same tears. To melodrama as history we all respond with the same amusement.[35] We cringe before the former and demur at the latter. How to explain the difference?

The history of the Chinese Cultural Revolution, for instance, is perhaps one of the most melodramatic phenomena in human experience. It created a moral universe that allowed only angels and devils. An emotional spectrum was simplified into two polar opposites: either intense love (purified into the love of Mao) or intense hate (reduced to the hate toward the class enemy). The marital bed could turn into a battlefield of class struggle. Familial intimacy – cherished for a thousand years in the shadow of the Confucian ethics – easily turned to estrangement between ideological "classes." History took on a dizzying whirlwind tempo. One day's hero was the next day's villain. Fanatics "cleave the general ear with horrid speech / Make mad the guilty and appal the free, / Confound the ignorant, and amaze indeed / The very faculties of eyes and ears."[36]

In the post–Cultural Revolution era, Chinese films have incessantly been made to "reflect" and "represent" the melodrama of this phase of history. The copying has never been quite successful; most of the efforts are bungled. Usually we attribute the failure to the employment of melodramatic mode with the unquestioned banal assumptions that melodrama as history is too exaggerated, antihistorical, or ahistorical; that history is much more complex than the oversimplified moral chiaroscuro; that history is more "serious" than theatrical send-up; that history is not susceptible to the Procrustes bed of formal/generic constraint; and that historical contours and digressions are too unpredictable to be rammed into the conceit of the two-hour traffic of melodrama. In the final analysis, melodramatic representation *overdoes* history.

Does it? Take a melodramatic conceit for instance. A familiar melodramatic figure is the correspondence between macrocosm and microcosm, and between macrocosm and body politic:[37]

> But when the planets
> In evil mixture to disorder wander,
> What plagues and what portents, what mutiny,
> What raging of the sea, shaking of earth,
> Commotion in the winds, frights changes horrors,
> Divert and crack, rend and deracinate
> The unity and married calm of states
> Quite from their fixture.[38]

This melodramatic figure *was* curiously enacted in reality fully in 1976 China. The year saw the Beijing youths' rebellious demonstration; the removal of Deng Xiaoping from office; the deaths of Mao, Zhou, and Zhu, the three most charismatic contemporary Chinese political leaders; and a historical coup d'etat by Hua, late Mao's protegee, resulting in the arrest of the Gang of Four headed by Madam Mao. This turbulent disorder in the body politic found its correspondence in macrocosm: That same year before any real political unrest erupted, China experienced one of her most catastrophic earthquakes in history, causing the disappearance of a whole city near Beijing; and it was echoed by serious calamities, including draught and famine, elsewhere in the country. What had been a rhetorical trope of melodrama was relentlessly acted out. The consequence was too profound for tears.

No melodramatic film in China afterward has been able to capture that grand melodramatic history either in scale or in depth. There is no lack of this melodramatic conceit in Chinese films: A political and moral struggle, when reaching its climax in an interior scene, would be accompanied by an outside flashing thunderbolts and thrashing torrents of rains. Instead of being awe-inspiring as it actually was in 1976, an overuse of it only causes revulsion. *When the Blue Light Flashes*, a feature film attempting to melodramatize the horrors and catastrophe of the 1976 Tangshan earthquake, for instance, as if doomed for such a project, turns out to be a bungling embarrassment. The whole film looks like a jostling rehearsal of the real event, which is endlessly postponed and finally never staged *at all*.

What – and why – is the difference between history's materialization of a melodramatic conceit and the theatrical/cinematic attempt at representation? The problem seems not so much with exaggeration or *over*dramatization as with the *under*dramatization. Preoccupied with an apocalyptical vision, we may expect the current Tiananmen *histoire* to end in a melodramatic way – the wronged virtue finally triumphant – in the near future. When it actually does, our anxiety will then be a distrust of any future film project to capture fully this enacted melodramatic history.

The problem of representation thus has its ramifications. We speak of representations, but representations of what? We have already acknowledged that history takes, or is understood to take, melodramatic turns. For melodrama to represent this history-as-melodrama is then to represent itself. Is this a tautology?

To avoid the tautology, it is tempting to evoke the Saussurian scheme: Melodrama is the *langue* of history, and film/theatrical representations – even if they are poorly done – are only specific *parole* of that essential *langue;* or the Hegelian scheme: History aspires toward the Melodramatic, as if it seeks to fulfill an Idea of the Melodrama – Hegel would call it the Spirit. The frequently bungled theatrical/cinematic attempts in practice toward the representation of history are therefore moves toward the Melodramatic, which is eternally postponed and inexhaustible. "And the medium," Stanley Cavell wrote, "is profounder than any of its instances."[39]

Thus, any melodramatic narrative attempting to capture history is actually a search for itself. Melodramatic representation of history is essentially self-representation. And understanding history is essentially to understand the generic pattern of melodrama, to understand why we spin out this artifact/artifice on which is fixed both our rapt gaze and our anguished and perplexed look, that is, our melodramatic mode of historical understanding. Are we here playing a "fort/da" game[40] with our historical consciousness: first casting it out and projecting it onto the senseless past and then desperately longing to retrieve it back through our melodramatic "representation" of that already transfigured history? Not knowing whether it is the shadow of our projection that we are recovering or that realm toward which we cast our shadow, we are never satisfied with this "representation," for the loss is never fully recovered.

Innocence unprotected: Gazing out of melodrama

No other film makes a better point about the melodramatic structure of communist history than *Innocence Unprotected* (1968), a metamelodrama made by Dusan Makavejev, the playful Yugoslavian film director. On being interviewed for *W. R.: Mysteries of Organism,* by Jonas Mekas, Dusan Makavejev makes the following confession:

MAKAVEJEV: But, coming back to my humorous version, I just wanted to have a shameless melodramatic situation, because I am personally fond of melodrama, I am not ashamed of melodrama.

JONAS: What is melodrama, to you?

MAKAVEJEV: When you are not ashamed of the soft feelings...not ashamed to cry or be happy on a very private level, without any excuse....a shameless melodrama...

JONAS:...the Mediterranean character, and the openness of emotion...

MAKAVEJEV:...theatre of life.

Makavejev did more than what he said. *Innocence Unprotected* appropriates and celebrates melodrama, while keeping it at bay and making fun of it.

Makavejev's *Innocence Unprotected* is about the first Yugoslavian film with the same title directed by Dragoljub Aleksic, a stunt man, about himself. The resulting Makavejev film is a collage combining footage from the original film, the Nazi newsreel of the occupation period, and the interviews of the old team that made the film.

The original footage in black-and-white immediately declares its melodramatic turn. The sequence in the living room where the stepmother and the Nada's (her stepdaughter) suitor make their deal and plot the marriage is shot in a typical early talkie style. Most of the shots of the sequence repeat a frontal long shot of the living room with a background door visible for characters' exits. The insistent frontality of the shots coheres to a theatrical spectatorial experience. It implies an absent spectator whose field is never undermined by a reverse shot. The camera occasionally pans and cuts to close-ups. Whenever a new character is introduced, the camera would pan to the door to show the intruder into this theatrical world; the camera would then pan from right to left as the newly arrived character walks toward the screen left.

To accentuate the melodramatic performance of the characters, close-ups show the exaggerated facial expressions: the ogling eyes (the butler ogling the exposed leg of the lying stepmother), the raised eyebrows (orphan's surprise), and the wide-open eyes.

There are marked entries and exits in the manner of stage actions. The stepmother would make an announcement of her intention to leave the matter to the suitor and her unwilling stepdaughter. And her exit, either through the door in the background or simply walking out of the frame, is a curiously prominent stage action.

The succession of actions is timed to a singular linearism. Petrovic, left alone to examine the picture handed to him by the stepmother, angrily mumbled: "Him!" He rises up. At that moment, the camera pans right. Another door is open, Nada, the daughter, comes in. When the two could not continue an animated conversation, props open the background door and the stepmother's head pokes in to survey the situation with vigilance.

These are of course taken from the footage of Aleksic's *Innocence Unprotected*. The innocence is defined in the original talkie as the innocent virtue, Nada the orphan, who has simple, pure dreams and love for Aleksic the hero. As is befitting melodrama, the virtue is harassed, beset, and threatened by the scheming villain, Petrovic. The Aleksic footage is also an immediate derivative of the archetypal Cinderella story. An unsympathetic stepmother, a suffering stepdaughter (Nada), and the prince (Aleksic) whose final kiss redeems Nada from wretchedness and delivers her from suffering. Melodrama is, after all, not about gaining illumination and revelation from suffering as it is in tragedy, but the process of delivering the suffering virtue from hell, from trying situations. The redemptive power and agent are always the pure and unwavering love and faith, and the hidden law of poetic justice by which virtue is finally to be rewarded and the villain finally to be punished. The Aleksic narrative fulfills that imperative with a dramatic reversal: Police come to the rescue of Petrovic, after he is beaten by Aleksic, only to take Petrovic himself to task.

Given the melodramatic nature of the Aleksic footage, how does it make an entry into Makavejev's film? To return to the first cited sequence. Petrovic and Nada are left alone in the living room. Petrovic breaks the ice: "I hope my company will not prove unpleasant." At these words, Nada rises and walks toward the screen left background and disappears from the frame, leaving Petrovic at the table at a loss. What follows is a sudden cut to a surprisingly beautiful medium close-up: Nada is frontally framed, looking at the camera behind a lace curtain. The lace is beautifully patterned with distinctive embroidery; it covers the whole screen with a flatness that virtually renders the film frame into a frame of classical portrait.[41] Up to this point, the film has never offered us a frontal close-up of Nada's face. She has hitherto appeared no more than a prototype role on the screen playing a character in the melodrama narrative. With this close-up, she suddenly comes alive. Her face is burdened with genuine sadness and her eyes shot with melancholy, looking into the camera with an unfathomable profundity.

This shot suddenly attains its own autonomous mood. The graphic framing dislodges her from the world of melodrama, from the Aleksic footage. Her melancholy is so profound that it transcends the superficial melodramatic world of theatricality in which she finds herself – or, rather, loses herself.

In fact, the shot is still part of the Aleksic narrative. The profundity of her gaze is our reading into Nada's essentially passive and blank look. The point is: Makavejev recognizes the potentiality in that blank look. As a filmmaker, he knows how to "rewrite" or "resketch" the face, the icon, by editing.[42] It could be imbued with renewed meaning, altered overtones, and added dimensions by grafting to new footage, linked with shots that follow it and in turn inform it. Our uncertainty about the face is transformed into a certainty. In hindsight Nada's look attains its profundity and deeper melancholy only after the gaze is redeemed by the ensuing shots.

Makavejev recognizes the moment. Nada's gazing through the window represents a longing to escape the plot (both in the sense of stepmother/Petrovic's scheming and the melodramatic plot) of the interior. The moment of escape becomes a pretext for Makavejev to liberate Nada's gaze, to extend the gaze, and to stretch the gaze into realms it would otherwise have been unable to reach. Nada's gaze has a cinematic-logical impulse calling for a reverse shot. Taking the cue, Makavejev fulfills that formal logic by providing a point-of-view shot (actually a separate footage from the contemporary newsreel), a long shot of the Belgrade street in ruins. A building emits fire and smoke. A sad melody is heard on the sound track.[43]

Cut to another long shot of a street (a closer look), which has no spatial continuity with the preceding shot. A man unloads something from a truck parked in front of a building. The camera pans with the man's right-to-left movement. A woman runs into the frame from the right matching the direction of the moving camera. The panning camera reveals more spots of fire and smoke in the distance. What follows is a succession of shots: smoke, ruined streets, collapsed buildings, rubble, dead bodies, coffins, men pulling a cart loaded with a coffin.

Commenting on this intercutting, John R. Taylor writes:

There is one point where Makavejev pulls his familiar trick of faking a reaction by intercutting two different things in such a way that one seems to comment on the other – as the suffering orphan gazes out the window in histrionic despair at her idiot plight, Makavejev cuts in news reel material of burning buildings and all the horrors of war as though this is what she is looking out at, which puts the sentimental-naive drama of Aleksic's original *Innocence Unprotected* in a different context, one justified, after all, by its historical situation, and moreover, suggests a sort of broad allegorical extension of the action as an exemplar of the eternal battle between good and evil, a notion further developed when the wicked Petrovic's molestation of Nada is paralleled by animated maps of the Nazi invasion of Russia.[44]

Or, should we say that the historical narrative generated by the newsreel is an extension of the original melodrama? The historical situation certainly "justifies," as is seen by Taylor, the sentimental naiveté of the interior melodrama, which embodies and allegorizes, in a nutshell fashion, the historical melodrama on a grander scale. Yet if we put it the other way round, the intercutting allegorizes the mode of our vision of historical reality, our limited position, our entrapped circumstances in the present. For the newsreel sequence about the historical reality is initiated by Nada's gaze from a standpoint within a melodramatic interior, as Nada is trapped, if not "imprisoned," in the melodramatic world where she looks out. Her gaze is thus coded both with a melodramatic overtone and a longing to get away from the melodramatic interiority.

The long shot of the ruined streets in wartime Belgrade has the structural coherence to qualify as her point-of-view shot. However, that is only one shot from the newsreel footage that could be sutured to her gaze, implying her ownership of the view. The whole sequence following that long shot is disembodied from any point-of-view looking out of an interior standpoint. We have cuts from one shot to another without narrative/spatial suture. Disowned by her, the succession of newsreel shots disowns her gaze as the rallying point. It is the documentary's absent spectator's gaze that motivates the cutting of the montage and the camera's panning and tilting. The wandering camera is disengaged, disembodied, and unburdened. It assumes a spatial freedom denied to Nada who is confined to the interior world. The bifurcation between the interior and the exterior tells the difference between two different generic spaces: the interior melodrama of family strife, the confined world of theatricality on the one hand, and the documented world of the historical real, the space of cosmic struggle. So the shot of Nada standing in front of the window behind the lace curtain looking out posits a moment on a threshold bridging the melodramatic world and the historical world.

Instead of situating the seeing and desiring subject in the historical real/realm to *look into* the artifice of melodrama, Makavejev reverses the paradigm.[45] The gazing subject is anchored within the film-within-film, within the world of melodrama, *looking out*. The scheme at once allegorizes and comments on our gaze toward history, the condition of our seeing the world, and the circumstantial confinement that affects our mode of seeing.

This is an epistemological allegory, or allegory of epistemology. To see and know the historical reality in its real image, the activity/mode of seeing has to be disembodied, dispersed, free-floating, and constrained by no single view point, freed from any circumstantial contingency. The montage of the war-torn Belgrade breaks away from Nada's gaze; it tells of the impossibility of Nada knowing the *whole* picture of history because of her entrapment and, above all, the entrapment of the melodramatic interior. She could only have *glimpses.*

This glimpsed possibility of a liberated field of vision and the perennial condition of limited, and generically constrained (by melodrama), gaze is the dialectical vision Makavejev has about the situation of our historical understanding.

There is no escape from melodrama. Following a long shot of a group of people pulling a cart loaded with a coffin, the film cuts back to the interior melodrama with a slight closer frontal shot of the living room. The stepmother walks in from the screen right and declares: "I'll return in an hour." Cut to the frontal close-up of Nada behind the lace curtain looking into the camera while the offscreen stepmother's voice-over is heard: "Enjoy yourself." The self-assertive declaration by the stepmother who embodies melodrama and the rhetoric of return, in addition to their diegetic relevance, has thus a symbolic overtone: The return is the eternal return of the melodrama to the lifeworld. The cutting back to the melodrama footage itself is a gesture confirming the return.

History, as the parallel editing oscillating between the interior melodramatic footage and the exterior sequences suggests, is also melodrama. The action of the interior melodrama is at one moment the villain about to pounce upon the vulnerable woman while saying: "What makes you so unhappy?" It is followed by an abrupt cut to an animated map of the Nazis closing in on Russian cities. Cut back to the interior melodrama in which the villain sets upon the woman and the two wrestle. The message is clear: Historical events unfold in a similar melodramatic fashion. The microcosm of the interior melodrama corresponds to the macrocosm of world history.

Nada not only bridges the interior and exterior shots in a spatial continuum, she is also the focal point on which is pivoted the otherwise broken chain of temporality, bridging the past, present, and future (from her standpoint). She at some point picks up, gazes at, and addresses the photograph of Aleksic. This becomes a pretext for Makavejev to order the temporal sequence of his film. Again, Makavejev reverses and subverts the normal scheme. Photographs and portraits are familiar devices to inscribe memories and bring back the past into an interplay with the present. For someone gazing at a photograph, the person figured in the photograph is usually either the deceased or the absent (to the extent of unreachable). Usually it is a device of the remembrance of the things past.

Nada gazes at the photograph and narrates stories/events centered around Aleksic, the object of her desire. Grafted onto Nada's narrating and gazing are shots of Aleksic in Nada's present and future (the old Aleksic seen in our present). Curiously, Nada narrates these scenarios in the mode of remembering, recalling, and recounting, albeit with looks of longing, dreaming, and envisioning. Makavejev thus edits a montage about the act of *remembering the future.*

Shouldn't we take this to be Makavejev's representation of the mode of historical narration and utterance in an allegorical way? Nada is so engrossed in her narration – she is telling Petrovic about Aleksic – that her narration becomes a monologue, a recital, and even an aria. The framing is again frontal, excluding Petrovic, the listener and her only audience, completely. Her facial expression and gestures are operatic. The lines become verse, as she accounts Aleksic's stunt in a sky show: "In chain, in a cage, in facing dynamite, between heaven and earth."

Up to this point, she has been addressing the offscreen Petrovic. Now she turns to face the camera and directly addresses the camera. "The fuse burns! The dynamite will blow up the cage." In narrating the apprehended explosion, it is her speech that turns explosive with a dynamic staccato. In accounting a melodramatic spectacle, she first enacts the melodrama by becoming a spectacle herself with raised eyebrows, pursed lips, and bulging eyeballs. An already melodramatic event is thus doubly melodramatic through this melodramatic narration. She depicts a frightful scenario by frightening herself in the first place; in other words, she is frightened by herself, by the melodramatic narration of which she herself is the author. "With giant's strength, he breaks the chains – saving himself and his partner from Captain Death!"

The close-up of Nada in her monologue is succeeded by a cutback into the world of the vulgar melodrama. We have a two-shot. As if standing in lieu of us, Petrovic, the only audience in the film, dismisses Nada's recital with an interruption: "An empty, silly tale!" "It's not!" Nada vehemently protests, "Look" she shows him the photograph. Cut to a shot of the photograph: two high-hung cages; fuses are burning, a man is flying to the rescue of another caged man. Reframe to a long shot of the actual spectacle. On the sound track is a chorus singing "Internationale."

Arise, ye prisoners of starvation!
Arise, ye wretched of the earth
[Close-up of Aleksic's hands breaking the binding chains]
For justice thunders condemnation,
A better world is in birth
No more tradition's chain shall bind us.
Arise, ye slaves: no more in thrall!
The earth shall rise on new foundations,
We have been naught and we shall be all.
T'is the final conflict. [Shots of the fuse, and the hands]

Let each stand in his place. [Long shot of each man in his *cage*
The international party shall be the human race.
[Explosion]

Cut back to the two-shot of Petrovic and Nada:

PETROVIC: I don't believe it.

NADA: And if you were to see him on the Pillar of Death?

Cut to the photograph of the sky show. Cut back to the medium close-
up of Nada in agony, clasping the photograph to her bosom in a typical melodramatic gesture, looking panic-stricken at the envisioned
spectacle of her own narration. The film then again cuts to the actual
spectacle.

The act of remembering the future thus has a poignant irony about
it in view of the sky-show spectacle politicized by the melos of the
"Internationale." The action of the show is the breaking of the chain
in a melodramatic fashion, because melodrama is, among other things,
about the last-minute rescue of the suffering virtue (in this respect, the
show structurally heralds or prefigures Aleksic's rescue of the molested
Nada, the damsel in distress). The breaking of the chain as a spectacle
is annotated by the song of "Internationale." The communist praxis
with Marx as its prophetic scenarist ("The proletarians have nothing
to lose but their chains. They have a world to win."[46]) is symbolically
enacted as a comical gymnastic. The pathos derives from the fact that
Aleksic is pursuing this enactment with dogged sincerity and innocence.
The motif of chain breaking recurs several times in the film, a miracle
that Aleksic relishes. Somehow, Aleksic's persistent indulgence in the
actions of chain breaking betrays a condition in which he is trapped:
the imprisonment of unthinking innocence. If he liberates the body
from its chains, he fetters the heart with chains.[47] This peripeteia of
narrative trajectory is itself melodramatic: The liberated is imprisoned
in the very process of liberation. "Each man in his place," as the melos
of "Internationale" goes, for the final struggle of the breaking of chains
and cages implies also – in retrospect – each man in his cage (as the
spectacle in the film shows) and the later Stalinist/Titoist/Maoist mandate that he remain where he is. Thus the reiterated shots throughout
the film of Aleksic posing and flaunting his muscularity, even when he
is past the proper age, and the sequence of him wrapping himself up
with iron bands become symbolically charged motifs consistent with
the above speculation.

In a way, Makavejev, through his collage, offers a cinematic scenario about the teleology of history. The telos is the domestication of
the unforeseeable future by a theoretical construct. Hegel and Marx

have each of them a teleological vision of the end of history (with Hegel, the Prussian state; with Marx, the demolition of private property and classes). Given the temporal scheme of the film, there is an added melodramatic irony. The spectacle of chain breaking is narrated by Nada as both a remembrance of some past spectacle she may have actually experienced and an envisioning of the possible scenario in which she is absent. The chain breaking *after* the moment of her narration – that is, Aleksic's action in Makavejev's footage – is what she cannot see. Nevertheless, Makavejev imposes his auteuristic will so that Nada does "see" what happens in the future – from her world of melodrama – or rather, Makavejev edits the different materials in such a way that she *seems* to see, or *as if* she sees him. The irony in the film is that technically, the montage presents us with intercutting of the shots of Nada looking adoringly offscreen into space (the 1940s footage) and the *old* Aleksic (in the 1960s footage) performing and posing as he did in his youthful years. The woman sees the youth; we see the old man. We see her gazing at what she thinks she is seeing. Yet we *know* what she is *not* seeing in the edited collage of footage from different years – the knowledge denied her as she is trapped in that 1942 melodramatic footage, the world she is doomed to inhabit. The irony is immediately about the teleological vision. Given Makavejev's immediate circumstantial world, and frequent allusions to the communist praxis, it is not too far-fetched to imagine that Nada is easily the site or figure of replacement. Substitute her with Marx, or with any teleological visionaries of history who foresee the future, the essential (melo) dramatic irony remains the same. Entrapped in the melodramatic years of the nineteenth century when class struggle was the dominant phenomenon, it is understandable for Marx to look beyond his times – as Nada does – toward the millennium. They are like Tiresias, a man who "perceived the scene, and foretold the rest,"[48] yet he is blind. In retrospect, we can envision Marx gazing into space with the same excitement Nada has, envisioning his utopia and narrating his melodramatic tale about class struggle, the triumph of the liberated proletariate, and the overthrow of the oppressing bourgeois while we see what he sees turns out to be the totalitarian imprisonment in the name of liberation of masses.

A moral law underlying a melodramatic narrative is the final reward of the virtue and the punishment of the villain. The virtue has to die – either physically or symbolically – in order to live. The trials and suffering the virtue goes through lead to the final public redemption and recognition of the wronged virtue, dead or alive. The Aleksic film transcribes this formula faithfully. Makavejev, for his confessed love for melodrama, also plays with this moral law of melodrama.

Melodrama is fascinated with death. Film melodrama necessarily fetishizes dead bodies, coffins, tombs, funerals, heavy sighs, and tears shed over the deceased who should not have died, for melodrama is emotional excess, a public display of private sentiment – what Makavejev calls the "soft feelings." The cutaway from Nada's melodramatic world to wander in the historical world of war and death is Makavejev's warm and sympathetic gesture of insisting on the genuine melodramatic energy. The montage sequence of the bombed Belgrade contains panning shots, and it is when the camera encounters the dead bodies that the camera freezes with an intense and insistent gaze upon, in one shot for instance, the dead bodies of a man and woman lying beside each other, in another shot, a dying body wriggling among the rubble. This extension and disengagement from the phony interior melodrama into the historical world to "recognize" the anonymous suffering and death can be seen as Makavejev's insistence on the genuine melodrama, his "shameless" display of "soft feelings." The use of emotional musical scores has been sparing in this film. Even when he feels tempted to put his signature on the resurrected footage, he would hand-paint the black-and-white film with color dots rather than adding real melodramatic sound tracks – "corny" music, for instance. It is when he searches and confirms the real melodrama of history that he lavishes the melancholy melos on the newsreel footage, redeeming the anonymous, quietly passing virtues with an insistent camera gaze and musical excess. It is, so to speak, Makavejev's declaration of emotion that has otherwise been so artfully concealed behind an air of intellectual playfulness and visual iconoclasm. To be melodramatic is, after all, to recognize and confirm things and values in explicit and unambiguous terms.

The emotional excess in mourning the loss of one's beloved is a leitmotif of melodrama narrative. Makavejev's mourning of the death of his country folk, the anonymous who occupy no place in the diegetic space, assigns them a *cinematic* space. When it comes to the mourning of characters who do have a place in the narrative, Makavejev, as is characteristic of him, surprises us with a violent twist.

One of the relevant reiterations of the mourning motif is the funeral of Colonel Masalovic, chef de cabinet of the Serbian prime minister, who, as the narrative voice-over tells us, "was treacherously killed.... The deceased was made a general. The sad cortege started from the cathedral. Minister Ljotic spoke of the merits of the deceased who had devotedly served the Serbian people."

This public ritual of mourning is thus also a melodramatic ritual according the deceased public recognition. The sequence of funeral as a public gathering in the film is structurally and visually a counterpoint to the sequence of masses rushing to see Aleksic's daredevil stunt show, a correspondence interlinked by similar extreme high-angle shots. The deceased, who is said to serve the "Serbian people," actually has a role neither in the narrative space nor in history.[49] Visually echoing shots of masses and public spectacle attending the stunt performance by Aleksic, who also "serves the Serbian people" with commitment and ardor, the sequence of Colonel Masalovic becomes a mirror image of that of Aleksic. His stunt is a play with the (im)possibility of death, a macabre play that caters for the Serbian masses' public gaze. Either the stunt man is alive (both Aleksic and the politician are stunt men), or he is dead. The public recognition is the same: the thronging in streets, the public eagerness to *watch* as if both activities, the sky show and the political event, share the same "to-be-looked-at-ness." In the final analysis, they are all gymnastics of nimbleness, strength, histrion- icism at the possible expense of death.

Makavejev's play with melodramatic moral law goes further. Follow- ing a scuffling sequence of the Aleksic footage of the interior melo- drama, the film cuts to a medium long-shot showing two old women holding flowers in a cemetery, joined by an old man. We then cut to a shot in the Aleksic film of Petrovic grinding his teeth. Cut back to the cemetery. We learn that these are the actors and actresses who once played roles in Aleksic's film and they come to the tomb of the actor who played Petrovic, the villain!

OLD WOMAN: I haven't seen you for twenty-six years.

OLD MAN: Just don't cry . . .

OLD WOMAN: I'm sorry.

ANOTHER WOMAN: He went early . . .

OLD MAN: Right . . .

And they are shown eating over the tomb, followed by a cut to a se- quence of people eating during wartime.

Melodrama mourns the death of the virtue. Why is it that Makavejev makes a point of shooting a "mourning" of the death of the actor who is iconographically and diegetically registered on the screen as the vil- lain? The irony pokes fun at the pathetic melodrama of communistic history: One day's hero is the next day's villain. By the same token, Aleksic, the "innocent" hero himself, had to subject himself to indict- ment and only narrowly escaped. The cemetery sequence therefore again suggests Makavejev's reflection on the pervasiveness and pervers- ity of melodramatic structure in historical reality. Now should we say the film is about melodrama or about history?

Notes

1. Peter Burke, "Historical Narrative: Revival or Regeneration," lecture given at Cornell Society for the Humanities, 4 Feb. 1988. Cited from Michael Ann Holly, "Past Looking," *Critical Inquiry* 16 (Winter 1990): 371–72.

2. Friedrich Wilhelm Nietzsche, "The Use and Abuse of History," in *The Philosophy of Nietzsche,* ed. Geoffrey Clive (New York: New American Library, 1984), p. 229.

3. Søren Kierkegaard, "Repetition: An Essay in Experimental Psychology," in *A Kierkegaard Reader,* ed. Robert Bretall (Princeton: Princeton University Press, 1946), p. 141.

4. Peter Brooks, *The Melodramatic Imagination: Balzac, Henry James, Melodrama, and the Mode of Excess* (New York: Columbia University Press, 1985), p. 36.

5. Ibid., p. 25.

6. Ibid., p. 26.

7. Ibid., p. 14.

8. Ibid., p. 15.

9. William Shakespeare, *King Lear* V. iii, ed. G. K. Hunter (Harmondsworth: Penguin, 1972), p. 180.

10. This bitterness shared by many Chinese subconsciously echoes some prototypical sentiment: "(At the thought of) crusade not yet reaching its day of triumph, thou are gone, / It makes hero's armored coats dripping with tears." Du Fu (712–70 A.D), "Shu Xiang" (The Minister of Shu), in *Quan Tang Shi (Complete Tang Poetry).* (Zhonghua Shuju, 1985), 7:2431

11. Karl Marx and Frederick Engels, *The German Ideology,* ed. C. J. Arthur (New York: International Publishers, 1988), p. 47.

12. Stanley Cavell, *The World Viewed: Reflections on the Ontology of Film* (Cambridge, Mass.: Harvard University Press, 1979), p. 93.

13. Ibid., p. 92.

14. Daniel Bell, *The Cultural Contradictions of Capitalism* (New York: Basic Books, 1978), p. 166.

15. Hayden White, *Tropics of Discourse: Essays in Cultural Criticism* (Baltimore: Johns Hopkins University Press, 1978), p. 110.

16. Fredric Jameson, *The Ideologies of Theory: Essays 1971–1986,* vol. 2, *The Syntax of History* (Minneapolis: University of Minnesota Press, 1988), p. 17.

17. White, *Tropics of Discourse,* pp. 111–12. The emphasis is mine.

18. Marx, *The German Ideology,* p. 48.

19. Bell, *Contradictions,* p. 166. The emphasis is mine.

20. Dylan Thomas, "After the Funeral," in *The Norton Anthology of Poetry,* ed. A. W. Allison et al. (New York: Norton, 1975), p. 1163.

21. Roland Barthes, *Michelet,* trans. Richard Howard (New York: Hill and Wang, 1987), pp. 82–3.

22. Thomas Elsaesser, "Tales of Sound and Fury: Observations on the Family Melodrama," in *Movies and Methods: An Anthology,* vol. 2, ed. Bill Nichols (Berkeley: University of California Press, 1985), p. 186.

23. Laura Mulvey, "Visual Pleasure and Narrative Cinema," in *Movies and Methods: An Anthology,* vol. 2, ed. Bill Nichols (Berkeley: University of California Press, 1985), p. 309.

24. Max Weber, *From Max Weber: Essays in Sociology,* ed. and trans. Gerth and Mills (New York: Oxford University Press, 1958), pp. 280–1.
25. *The Marx-Engels Reader,* ed. Robert Tucker (New York: Norton, 1978), p. 617.
26. Marx, *The German Ideology,* p. 40.
27. *The Marx-Engels Reader,* p. 617.
28. Cited from James H. Billington, *Fire in the Minds of Men: Origins of the Revolutionary Faith* (New York: Basic Books, 1980), p. 174.
29. Milan Kundera, *The Book of Laughter and Forgetting* trans. Michael Henry Heim (Harmondsworth: Penguin, 1981), p. 1.
30. Simon Leys, "Human Rights in China," in *The Burning Forest: Essays on Chinese Culture and Politics* (New York: Henry Holt, 1985), pp. 118–19.
31. Marx: "If in all ideology men and their circumstances appear upside-down as in a *camera obscura,* this phenomenon arises just as much from their historical life-process as the inversion of objects on the retina does from their physical life-process." *The German Ideology,* p. 47.
32. Semyon Aranovich gives *I Served in Stalin's Guard* (USSR, 1988), his most recently made film with a new generic category, a subtitle: *An Experiment in Documentary Mythology.*
33. White, *Tropics of Discourse,* p. 53.
34. Karl Marx, "The Eighteenth Brumaire of Louis Bonaparte," in *The Marx-Engels Reader,* p. 604.
35. I am here reversing Groucho Marx's formulation – quoted by Bell, *Contradictions,* p. 166 – that "all men cry at the same things, but laugh at different ones."
36. Shakespeare, *Hamlet* II. ii.
37. See E. M. W. Tillyard, *The Elizabethan World Picture* (New York: Vintage Books, 1941), pp. 87–100.
38. Ulysses' description in *Troilus and Cressida* constitutes a figure that is reiterated by Caesar's wife portending the heavenly disorder synchronized with Caesar's death and by Gloucester and actually tropicalized in the storm scene in *King Lear.* As an effective melodramatic trope, it is much used by Charles Dickens. In film, it is not surprising to note that it rains and thunders more often in Japanese and Korean films than it actually does climatically. *Thunderstorm* (*Lei Yu*), a film adaption based on a classical modern Chinese play, is parasitic on this conceit.
39. Cavell, *The World Viewed,* p. 103.
40. Sigmund Freud, *Beyond the Pleasure Principle,* trans. James Strachey (New York: Liveright, 1950), p. 13.
41. The implication of portrait is relevant here. A picture of a portrait is an inscription of memory of the past; it is addressed to the later-born. The addressee and the addressed thus could have a dialogue.
42. The premise could be predicated on Kuleshov's experiment with a blank face intercut with neighboring shots, which in turn inform our reading of the blank face. Though the idea of montage as collusion is critiqued by Eisenstein as too passive a reliance on external forces and replaced with Eisensteinian montage of collision, Kuleshov's aesthetics still holds true in particular cases.

Our psychological experience of Makavejev's intercutting of Nada's blank look with newsreel footage confirms that.

43. The music here becomes a signifying gesture. Up till this moment, there has been no music in the Aleksic footage of interior melodrama. The intercutting to the exterior scenes of war-torn streets added with a melancholy music becomes a trace of Makavejev's auteuristic signature. By doing so, Makavejev also adds a level of irony: The explicit melodrama of the Aleksic footage by its nature should be bound with music – melos – while it replaces music with the bickering human noise. The escape from the melodramatic sequence into the historical narrative – that is, the documentary shots of the bombed Belgrade – motivates, and is motivated, by music, the melos. Shouldn't we take this to be a subtle statement about Makavejev's attitude toward melodrama? He dismisses the superficial melodrama only to replace it with a profounder melodrama; in other words, he points to the inevitable condition of the melodramatic that underlies our mode of existence. Recalling Makavejev's confession about his preoccupation with melodrama, his love of the "soft feelings," one is tempted to read the musically attended sequence as a way of "writing" Makavejev's "shameless melodrama."

44. John Russell Taylor, *Directors and Directions: Cinema for the Seventies* (New York: Hill and Wang, 1975), pp. 247–8.

45. The typical normal paradigm would be someone in a visual narrative (a film, a photograph, or a painting) looking at an artifice – that is, a film-within-film, a photo-within-photo, or a portrait-within-portrait. This contrived scheme would create an illusion about our secured position in the real world looking at the constructed world, to use the artifice to reflect or symbolize or interact with the "real" world events. Such is the play-within-play in *Hamlet* to set a mousetrap. What if we imagine Hecuba in the play-within-play looking at Hamlet?

46. Marx and Engels, "Manifesto of the Communist Party," in *The Marx-Engels Reader,* p. 500.

47. Marx's critique of Luther ironically boomerangs: "Luther, without question, overcame servitude through devotion but only by substituting servitude through *conviction.* He shattered the faith in authority by restoring the authority of faith. He transformed the priests into laymen by turning laymen into priests. He liberated man from external religiosity by making religiosity the innermost essence of man. He liberated the body from its chains because he fettered the heart with chains." Karl Marx, "Contribution to the Critique of Hegel's *Philosophy of Right:* Introduction," in *The Marx-Engels Reader,* p. 60.

48. T. S. Eliot, "The Waste Land," line 229.

49. I owe this point to Aleksa Dilas, a Yugoslavian historian invited by Professor Vlada Petric to speak on the historical background of the film at the Carpenter Center for the Visual Arts, Harvard.

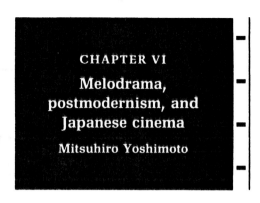

Melodrama has been one of the film genres that have been extensively studied and analyzed in the past two decades. Because of the enormous popularity of this generic form in the classical period of the American film industry, the examination of melodramatic film seems to contribute to a general study of the Hollywood cinema as an institution of industrial capitalism. Because women have been the major focus of melodramatic film both as the audience and as characters, a study of melodrama also constitutes an important part of feminist film theory.[1] And some critics have chosen to study melodrama in order to reexamine the relation between the masses and mass culture. They try to demystify the popular belief that melodrama is nothing more than a vehicle of escapism for the masses; they have uncovered in melodrama's stylistic hyperbole and exaggeration not the logic of escapism but a critique of ideology that melodramatic film is said to be propagating. In his classic essay on melodrama, Thomas Elsaesser demonstrates how a critique of American middle-class ideology of the 1950s is made in the films of Douglas Sirk through the process of condensation and displacement found in the hyperbolic use of objects and colors.[2] He goes beyond a mere formal analysis of Sirk's films by placing them in a specific sociopolitical background of the 1950s' America. What Elsaesser's essay teaches us is that the examination of melodrama as a generic form becomes meaningful only if particular texts of melodrama and their subtexts are analyzed simultaneously.

This sociocritical approach becomes particularly important when we examine the postwar Japanese cinema and melodrama. An examination of melodrama in the postwar Japanese cinema merely from a formal perspective does not lead to any significant conclusion; instead, we must place melodrama in a particular sociopolitical background of postwar Japan. Although various studies of what the melodramatic form of the Hollywood cinema signified in the 1950s' America are extremely significant, they cannot be a direct model for a study of the melodramatic form found in the postwar Japanese cinema.

Not only is the melodramatic form of the postwar Japanese cinema different from that of the 1950s' Hollywood cinema but also the sociopolitical situations of the 1950s' America and postwar Japan, though interconnected, are definitely not identical to each other. When World War II ended, the United States initially attempted to demilitarize and democratize Japan. In 1947, this experiment in the construction of a neutral, democratic country in Asia by the young officers of SCAP [the Supreme Commander of the Allied Powers] was suddenly terminated because of the policy change in Washington. In the U.S. government's pursuit of the Cold War program, Japan was strategically too important to be left alone. The reverse course was taken by the Occupation authority, and Japan was inextricably implicated as an "ally" in the U.S. hegemonic structure in East Asia. While the United States exercised power in order to maintain its hegemonic position in the world by creating the bipolar world system divided between the U.S. and Soviet blocs, Japan was in a subordinate position of a semiautonomous country, playing the surrogate role of the U.S. satellite in East Asia.

The examination of melodrama in the postwar Japanese cinema must take into account this fundamental difference between the position of the United States as the world hegemonic power and that of Japan as a semiperipheral country within the U.S. hegemonic sphere. The postwar Japanese cinema's melodramatic form becomes intelligible only if it is correlated with this difference. Our first task, then, is to find an appropriate framework or critical language that mediates melodramatic form and the specific sociopolitical subtext of postwar Japan.

One way of setting up this framework is to focus on the issue of modernity in a Japanese context. One could argue that modernity came to Japan during the 1920s when the mechanically reproducible images and artifacts analyzed by Walter Benjamin[3] flooded Japan following the great Kanto earthquake. The 1920s, which marked the emergence of an international culture of modernity, was a crucial period for the subsequent development of mass culture. For the first time, a time lag between the artistic and intellectual movements in Europe and their transplantation in other parts of the world almost disappeared. But what is more important is a rise of mass media and mass culture in the 1920s. As the American film became dominant in the world market after World War I, the Japanese cinema also lost some of its native characteristics. A new breed of directors, including those who had worked in Hollywood as actors and technicians and had just come back to Japan, introduced to the Japanese cinema the Hollywood mode of representation and technical refinement. New life-styles represented in the 1920s' films by Hollywood and by native studios played a major role in shaping the Taisho culture of modernism and Americanism.

Film as a newsreel was also important as a new kind of
An event filmed in the morning could be shown at mov
the afternoon of the same day. Radio broadcasting was s
ropolitan areas in the mid–1920s, and the number of list
grew.[4] In the publishing world, a new sales method based on sub-
scription boosted the sales of inexpensive books called *enpon*. *Enpon*
were usually sold in the form of selected works of either Japanese literature, world literature, or world thought, and millions of copies of
these books were sold. In the *enpon* boom, knowledge became a com-
modity and was mass produced.[5] What was significant about these
mass media was that they astonishingly speeded up the cycle of distribution and consumption, and it was precisely because of the ac-
celeration of the movement of materials and information that the
simultaneity and internationalism of modernity became possible. This
interdependency between modernism and mass media suggests that,
as some postmodern critics have argued, the relation between high
modernism and mass culture is not neatly characterized by a binary
opposition but is already problematic at their very origins.[6]

Thus, we could say that the 1920s was the period in which modernism and the masses appeared for the first time in Japan. However, it
was not the time when Japan was dragged into a geopolitical space of
modernity. When modernity comes to the non-West, it always takes the
form of colonial subjugation. For the non-West, modernity cannot but
signify the experience of domination by Western imperial powers.
Therefore, the non-West always resists modernity, but the outcome of
this battle is always predetermined. But to the extent that it brings advanced technology to technologically underdeveloped countries, modernity also provides the non-West with the necessary means of
fighting against the Western colonial enterprise. In the case of Japan,
the decisive encounter with modernity occurred in the mid-nineteenth
century when Commodore Perry came to Japan with gunboats and
forced Japan to end its three-hundred-year-old closed-door policy. The
fundamental aporia of modernity underlay almost every policy of the
Restoration government, and this aporia has never been resolved.
Since the mid-1970s, Japan has succeeded in transforming itself into a
hyperindustrialized "postmodern" country, and might seem to have finally escaped from the world geopolitical configuration set up by the
West. Yet, as I shall show in the last section of the paper, postmodern
Japan is still constructed on that same aporia of modernity, colonialism, and nativism.

The question is how melodrama mediates this fundamental aporia
of Japanese modernity manifested in various fields and levels of discursive practices and reality. To proceed with our inquiry, we need a
new theoretical language that can not only articulate the relation be-

tween the aporia of modernity and the melodramatic in the postwar
Japanese cinema but also negotiate between the different manifestations of the paradox of modernity in social, political, economic, and
cultural spheres. Particular attention must be paid to various generative levels of the production of narrative, including representation,
wish fulfillment, ideology, phantasm, and class allegory.[7] But before
explicating the register of these concepts, we need to clear up the
problematic of melodrama as a generic mode.

Steve Neale opens his essay on melodrama with a passage from Diderot's text, a comment on "a new theatrical genre, somewhere midway
between tragedy and comedy."[8] Although he quickly moves on to a formal analysis of melodrama and does not come back to explain the exact relation between the "origin" of melodrama in the eighteenth
century and the Hollywood melodrama in the twentieth century, Neale
still needs this historical anecdote in order to establish a genre called
melodrama as that which moves the audience to tears. Diderot's text is
not evidence for Neale's argument on the emergence of melodrama as
a tearjerker; rather, it legitimates his particular way of constructing a
melodrama genre as something distinctively different from other generic modes. Here, I do not pick up Neale's essay to criticize his "un-
scientific" use of generic category. My point, instead, is to foreground
the fact that any generic category is a construct, not a natural object
waiting to be found by cultural critics.

Does this mean that a melodramatic genre is merely a phantom created by critics so that it loses all the usefulness and significance it is
believed to have? Does the lack of preciseness in a generic category of
melodrama automatically lead either to the abandonment of that category or to a total relativization that completely nullifies the category's
operative value? Russel Merritt would say yes to all these questions.
According to Merritt, "melodrama as a coherent dramatic category
never existed, [and] it never amounted to either a total or coherent aesthetic, or even a finite repository of theatrical devices. Its chief function has been to impose critical order over a vast miscellany of
narrative texts found in six different countries spanning nearly two
centuries."[9] Merritt contends that melodrama can be defined only negatively in relation to realism; that is, what is called melodrama is
something that does not fit into the standards of realism in a particular historical moment. What is lacking in Merritt's total relativization
of the concept of melodrama is a sociohistorical awareness with regard to genre. Generic categories in general are useful because they
are critical constructs instead of natural objects; that is, genre is important for cultural studies because it is a social institution where
form and content of text are intersected and articulated with sociohistorical contradictions and ideologies. By putting a text in the context

of generic formation, the text can be rewritten, in Fredric Jameson's words, "as a synchronic unity of structurally contradictory or heterogeneous elements, generic patterns and discourses (what we may call, following Ernst Bloch, the *Ungleichzeitigkeit* or synchronic 'uneven development') within a single textual structure."[10] Even if it is a rather fuzzy category, the notion of melodrama can help us to analyze the different layers of ideological sedimentations constituting a text. The fundamental difference between Merritt and us is the difference between genre classification and genre criticism. The ultimate purpose of genre criticism is not to examine either how a particular text can be generically classified or how a particular genre is structurally constructed. What should be called a phantom is not the melodramatic genre but the "ontological status" of melodrama that Merritt is asking for.[11] If there is any meaning in carrying on genre criticism, it lies only in the dismantling and deconstruction of generic identity through a radical process of historicizing the institution of genre. As Ernesto Laclau argues,

the possibility of deconstructing all identity is the condition of asserting its historicity. Deconstructing an identity means showing the "constitutive outside" that inhabits it – that is, an "outside" that constitutes that identity, and, at the same time, questions it. But this is nothing other than asserting its contingency – that is, its radical historicity.[12]

The remaining question is how we can historicize the notion of melodrama or how this generic category can be rewritten in terms of ideological subcomponents. To deconstruct genre, we need to introduce what Fredric Jameson calls ideologeme, which is the "smallest intelligible unit of the essentially antagonistic collective discourses of social classes."[13] Through various stages of transformation, ideologeme can become either a set of abstract philosophical propositions or a value system on the one hand, or a diachronic process of transformation in the form of a protonarrative.[14] As we shall see in a moment, the ideologeme constituting melodrama takes both forms in postwar Japan.

Geoffrey Nowell-Smith argues that melodrama is a generic mode whose existence is derived from the transformation of tragedy in a new social context of the eighteenth century when the bourgeois class came into existence. In melodrama, Nowell-Smith argues, the addresser, the addressee, and the social class represented in the content are all the same: the bourgeoisie. Melodrama as a story of an oedipal family narrated from the standpoint of bourgeois subject positions is said to be a tragedy in the domestic sphere because in the equalized world of melodrama, the locus of power is not in the hands of the ruler clearly demarcated from the ruled, but it is displaced and confined within a patriarchal family.[15] Yet according to Fredric Jameson, in spite of melodrama's apparent resemblance to tragedy, it is more accurate to say that melodrama is a "degraded form of romance." For in contrast to tragedy, which unfolds the triumph of fate beyond individuals' control, at the core of melodrama can be found the ethical binary opposition between good and evil, which, situated on the level of the individual, is manifested in the form of antagonism between heroes and villains.[16] For our purpose – except for the negative connotation implied in his phrase, melodrama as a "degraded form of romance," which would be more appropriately restated as an isotope of romance – Jameson's conceptualization of melodrama as a derivative of romance is much more productive than Nowell-Smith's narrow essentialization of melodrama as an oedipal drama in a bourgeois family. The problem with a psychoanalytic theorization of melodrama as an enactment of oedipal conflict and a failure to resolve the social contradictions confined within a bourgeois family is that the possibility of psychoanalysis is dependent on the ideological model of a linear historical development with a bourgeois family as its culminating result. If we accept a definition of melodrama theorized from a psychoanalytic model, we have only two options. One is to rewrite melodrama in Japan and other non-Western countries as a Western melodrama. The other option is to conclude that because what is called melodrama in the non-West does not quite fit into a modal structure of melodrama in the West, there is after all no melodrama in the non-West. To avoid this pitfall of fixing and essentializing a melodramatic genre, we need to go back to the facts that any generic category is neither more nor less than a theoretical construct, and that the ultimate purpose of generic criticism is to deconstruct the illusion of the completeness of a genre and to analyze the layers of sedimented ideologemes constructed into a seemingly distinct genre.

Because we understand melodrama is developed as a result of generative transformation of romance, it is necessary to pay attention to how romance emerges as a genre. Jameson argues that the formation of a romance genre can be found in a transitional period of social upheaval in which two different modes of production and social institutions coexist.[17] Melodrama articulates the conflict between the old and new social structures and modes of production. In Europe, the emergence of melodrama was inseparable from the rise of the bourgeoisie and the beginning of a new class conflict. In Japan, melodrama articulated a disparity between modernity and modernization, whose "synchronic uneven development" has been the sociocultural strain on the Japanese for more than a century.[18] While modernization can be achieved by acquiring advanced technology and by fostering the development of industry, Japan has been fundamentally excluded from modernity because the possibility of the latter is dependent on the success of colonialism dividing the world into the West and non-West. But this inescapable contradiction of the modern for the non-West did not prevent Japan from modernizing itself. In order to catch up with the West, the Japanese had to believe that technology could somehow be separated from culture. Yet once the technological advancement got to the stage where Japan could compete with the Western powers, the success of technological modernization was mistakenly equated with the success of implanting modernity in Japan. As we shall see later, the contradiction of the modern articulated in the dialectic of technology and culture still forms a basis of postmodern Japan.[19]

A dominant ideologeme that appeared in prewar Japan was *risshin shusse shugi* (to rise up and get ahead in the world), which was present throughout the history of the prewar Japanese melodrama.[20] In the film circles of postwar Japan, melodrama was associated with the lack of individualism and the denial of the self. A melodramatic mentality that permitted the people to acquiesce in the creation of a fascist system was believed to have appeared because the assertion of the self had been repressed continuously. For instance, with regard to his *No Regrets for Our Youth,* made in 1946, Kurosawa once said: "At that time, I believed that the only way for Japan to make a new start was to begin by respecting the 'self' – and I still believe that. I wanted to show a woman who did just that."[21] This emphasis on the assertion of the self as a solution to the problems created by the social transformation since the Meiji Restoration had two important ramifications. On the one hand, it displaced sociohistorical contradictions produced by the difference between modernity and modernization onto the individual level. Instead of producing a genuine analysis of where Japan went wrong and how it can avoid repeating the same mistake again, this psychologizing process was another repetition of that compulsive desire to conform to the authority. The only difference was that this time the authority was not the fascist government but the G.H.Q. headed by Douglas MacArthur. On the other, if the call for the assertion of the self is restated as the question of how the subject can be constituted, it could have a significant implication for the construction of a new democratic Japan. And this was exactly what happened during the immediate postwar period, in which subjectivity was perhaps the most contested notion. In the so-called debates on subjectivity (*shutaisei ronso*), what was at stake was the question of agency and responsibility. Yet these potentially productive debates did not succeed in producing a workable concept of subjectivity. For the false equation between the construction of a subject position and the emulation of the Western subject was again established.[22]

What is significant is the emergence of the melodramatic, which does not simply designate a literary or cinematic genre but an ideologeme supporting the social formation of postwar Japan. One of the parameters of this ideologeme to be considered is Japan's relation with the West.[23] Because the Japanese believe that in the West the self is asserted and the subject as agency is firmly established, the parallel is established between two binaries, melodramatic–nonmelodramatic and Japan–the West. The word "melodramatic" in turn signifies for the Japanese their inferiority complex toward the West. To the extent that it feeds on their awareness of the lack of a Western style subjectivity in Japan, the melodramatic constantly reminds the Japanese that Japan is trapped in the geopolitical space of the Western hegemony. It is partly to facilitate the escape from this position of the "slave" that melodrama clears the space for the subject who does not act but only is acted upon; that is, the Japanese have negatively constructed a subject position from which they can fall into a delusion of being innocent victims of evil doings by others. This victim consciousness of the Japanese is a specific type of the so-called *ressentiment* articulating the colonial mentality of the Japanese, which has never been overcome for almost a century and a half.[24]

Before analyzing how the victim consciousness as a *ressentiment* generated a melodramatic film, we need to point out that, as Jameson argues, another significant characteristic of romance is its nostalgic (and sometimes utopian) happy ending. According to Jameson, this harmonious narrative closure of romance is due to the lack of unequivocal class antagonism, which, not yet clearly articulated, takes the form of an uneasy coexistence between two distinct social groups and institutions.[25] This precarious harmony organizes, for instance, the narrative of Kinoshita Keisuke's *Yabure Daiko* (*Broken Drum*) made in 1949. Kinoshita Keisuke is a leading figure of the postwar Japanese directors whose works are explicitly based on a melodramatic formula. Kinoshita's films, including such films as *A Japanese Tragedy* (1953) and *The Ballad of the Narayama* (1958), typically consist of parents sacrificing themselves for their children and children who do not understand what their parents went through in order to support a family. In *Broken Drum*, a despotic father who runs a construction company tyrannizes his wife, children, and housekeepers, who all endure his authoritarian behavior. When his construction company falls into financial difficulties, the father tries to arrange a marriage between the eldest daughter and a man whose father's money is the only means to save the failing construction company. But she meets and falls in love with a painter who has a completely different family background from her own. His parents are both artists who fell in love with each other while studying in Paris and still keep the freshness of their love even in their middle ages. Dissatisfied with his position in his father's company; the eldest son tries to become independent and to start a toy manufacturing business with his aunt. The authoritarian father does not permit his children to act of their own free will, and his wife finally runs out of patience with him and leaves the house.

The father of the eldest daughter's boyfriend is a violinist, and one of the sons, who plays the piano, composes a song in which the father is likened to a broken Japanese drum. The semantic matrix of the film detected in this careful assignment of semic elements is organized around two kinds of oppositions: between art and nonart, and between the West and Japan. In both oppositions, the first terms, art and the West, are shamelessly idealized, and the here and now – that is, the daily struggle to survive (nonart) in ruins (Japan) – is devalorized. *Broken Drum* attempts to construct a utopian space with no trace of history: It is very difficult to understand by watching this film that, defeated in the war just a few years ago, Japan is now under the U.S. occupation. Except the artist couple's sweet memory of Paris as a capital of art, the past is carefully excluded in the film. Thus, the obliteration of the dreadful past and class antagonism of the present carried out in the double transformation of life into art and Japan into the West constitutes the wish fulfillment of the film. Yet this wish fulfillment cannot be satisfied easily because it consists of two contradictory elements. On the one hand, the establishment of clear-cut binary oppositions, which is necessary for eliminating history, calls for a melodramatic opposition between villains and heroes. On the other hand, this binary opposition of melodrama cannot but introduce class antagonism into the text. In order to satisfy this contradictory demand of wish fulfillment, Kinoshita constructs *Broken Drum* based on a melodramatic formula, but the film does not have any ultimate villain who can be blamed for the characters' grievances. Although melodramatic situations abound in the film, no one seems to be responsible for those sufferings and unhappiness experienced by the melodramatic characters. At first, the father seems to be the only candidate for this villainous role, and the heroes of the democratic camp seem to triumph when the construction company goes bankrupt, and the eldest son invites the father to become a manager of the small toy company he and his aunt have just started. However, the father in the end does not occupy the position of villain. Toward the end of the film, there is the only flashback sequence of the film in which the father's remembrance of how he clawed his way up from extreme poverty to become the successful manager of his own construction business is shown in a rapid montage. When we see his extreme suffering as a penniless manual laborer and understand what a plate of curry and rice (*kare raisu*) meant to him in that miserable condition, our sympathy is not with his bourgeois children but with this despotic father. Thus, this short flashback sequence seems to fulfill the wish fulfillment that all of us are victims of unfortunate historical circumstances, so that nobody should be blamed for grievances suffered by us. However, this wish fulfillment is satisfied only by paying the heavy price: History and class consciousness, which have been carefully excluded from the manifest text of the film, inadvertently creep into this flashback sequence. Having the feeling of documentary footage recording a real historical event, the flashback is quite incongruous with the rest of the film, which is clearly coded as a fantasy. For the first time in the film, class antagonism is presented without being transformed into a wish-fulfilling opposition between art and nonart. Perhaps the audience is affected by the flashback sequence but does not remember what is shown there. Regardless, by using a melodramatic mode whose essential element is temporality, nobody can erase history. History always comes back to haunt any attempt of that sort.

2

The erosion of melodramatic film started to happen in the mid–1950s, which were not only the crucial years for the construction of postwar Japan but also a turning point for the postwar Japanese cinema. In the political sphere, the unification of forces was realized both in the conservative and progressive camps, and led to the establishment of the so-called 1955 System in which the Liberal Democratic Party firmly entrenched itself as the ruling party. Its dominance has never been challenged by the second largest party, the Japan Socialist Party, until recently. In 1956, the Japanese government declared in the *Economic White Paper* that because the gross national product had surpassed the prewar level, the postwar was finally over. In the same year, the literary critic Nakano Yoshio published an essay called "Mohaya 'sengo' de wa nai" ("It Is No Longer Postwar").[26] In this essay, Nakano's declaration was not based on the economic recovery after the war's devastation. Instead, Nakano argued for the end of the postwar because the notion of the postwar had been used as an easy way out of the complex problems with which the Japanese had been faced during the 1945–55 period. Nakano contended that in the name of the postwar, any serious tasks, including a difficult negotiation with the Soviet Union to conclude a peace treaty, were not rationally carried out but simply evaded. The "postwar" had been the key to the solution of every problem because it relieved people of facing reality and enabled them to take action based on mere emotion. Nakano was particularly weary of Japan's incorporation into the cold war structure as an American ally and of Japan's ambition to become again a great imperial power under the military umbrella of the United States. Instead of clinging to the illusion of rising to a great power, according to Nakano, Japan should ally itself with the minor powers of the Third World.

As the film critic Sato Tadao argues, most of the important films produced between 1945 and the mid–1950s were based on the assumption that people were good, but society was evil.[27] In this simplistic scheme, the social evil and oppression were so powerful that characters in films could do nothing but passively remain in the position of the oppressed, and the total helplessness of characters trapped in a melodramatic situation induced the sentimental reaction of the audience. This melodramatic sentimentality of the Japanese cinema has some parallels with the "postwar" mentality criticized by Nakano. For both are a product of the so-called victim consciousness: We are merely powerless, innocent people, so that whatever problem we are faced with is not the result of our own action but that of the overwhelming social evil and constraint of which we are only victims. But as Japan regained its sovereignty as the San Francisco Treaty came into effect in 1952, and also became a supporting/supported player of the world system that had the United States at its center, the notions of the "postwar" and the melodramatic were no longer adequate to answer a crucial question of subjectivity. What was at stake in Japan in the 1950s was how the Japanese could transform themselves from the passive recipients of the results of the actions taken by others into active subjects taking responsibility for their own actions.

It is in this context that directors like Masumura Yasuzo and Nakahira Ko launched a critique of the Japanese cinema both in practice and in criticism. Masumura was particularly vocal about his dislike of the melodramatic structure of the Japanese cinema, in which no character with a strong sense of self and individual freedom was said to be found. He believed that the Japanese cinema could not have appealing characters without individuality, subjectivity, freedom, and responsibility in Japanese society. The challenge Masumura had to meet was whether it was possible to make a nonmelodramatic film when reality itself was melodramatic – when the existing social situation contained so many remnants of "feudalism," which did not foster the ideals of bourgeois individualism. Masumura's solution was to create strong characters who would not conform to the prevailing social customs best characterized as melodramatic even if nobody could find individuals like those characters in real society. Masumura hoped that someday reality would catch up with the ideal he created on screen.[28]

Whether Masumura's strategy came to fruition is very questionable. For his argument was based on the doubtful assumptions that history develops from the premodern to the modern in a linear fashion; that the West had reached the highest stage of social development achieved by democratic, liberated individuals; and that the West, which had accomplished the great task of liberating individuals from the yoke of premodern social constraint, was the ideal to be caught up with by all other societies. Masumura was labeled *kindai shugisha* (modernist) by Oshima Nagisa precisely because of this wishful thinking that the mechanical grafting of modernity onto postwar Japan of the 1950s would somehow miraculously solve social contradictions and transform Japan into a replica of the West. For Oshima, no matter how hopeless Japanese society appears, one must confront and start with that miserable reality. From his perspective, melodrama is not a genre of film in which there is no trace of bourgeois notions of individualism and freedom; instead, any film is called melodramatic so long as it does not directly face up to a real social situation and its contradictions. In other words, the problematic of the melodramatic cannot be confined within the question of genre, but it has more to do with to what extent one would genuinely deal with ugly reality saturated with premodern elements of conservatism.[29]

What was at stake in the debate on melodrama was the possibility of constituting new types of subjectivities. *Kindai shugisha* and new wave directors both agreed that the capitalistic mode of production had not changed the "premodern" mode of social formation; on the contrary, the development of capitalism in Japan had been supported and facilitated by premodern institutions and communal ideologies. Moreover, despite his criticism of Masumura as a *kindai shugisha.* Oshima shared with Masumura the same assumption, according to which the premodern was paired with the melodramatic and the modern with the nonmelodramatic. Oshima disagreed with Masumura over how to construct a nonmelodramatic subject, but to the extent that he did not fundamentally question the West-centered model of a linear historical development, Oshima did not completely escape from the paradigm presented by *kindai shugisha.* This ideological limitation of new wave directors and *kindai shugisha* prompts us to take a second look at a history of the postwar Japanese cinema constructed by this new generation of university-educated directors and by both Japanese and Western film critics who either shared or accepted that particular construction of Japanese film history. As a way of undertaking this task, I shall reexamine a filmmaker they reproached for the aloofness from social reality and for formal rigidity: Ozu Yasujiro.

Throughout his career, Ozu worked at the Shochiku Company, which was known, on the one hand, for its production of "women's films labeled as 'Ofuna flavor' – warm, sentimental, subscribing to myths of basic human goodness, romantic love and maternal righteousness,"[30] and on the other, for its marketing of Oshima, Yoshida, Shinoda, and others as *Shochiku nuberu bagu* (Shochiku new wave). These two different aspects of Shochiku studios did not coexist harmoniously because, regardless of the studio executives' marketing strategies, new wave directors started their careers specifically as a rebellion against those directors making films in the tradition of Shochiku Ofuna flavor. Imamura Shohei worked for Ozu as an assistant director, but his dissatisfaction with what he thought of as Ozu's formal rigidity and repetition made him leave his position and even Shochiku itself. The fight between Ozu and the new wave director Yoshida Yoshishige is also very well known. New wave directors saw in Ozu's films only a skillful formal exercise with total indifference toward contemporary social reality. Meanwhile, Japanese critics saw in Ozu's films what they thought were unique characteristics of traditional Japanese culture. A convenient label was created, and Ozu was said to be the most Japanese of all the Japanese directors.

This characterization was also accepted by the American critics Paul Schrader and Donald Richie. For both of them, Ozu was a Zen master who made films based on transcendental aesthetics.[31] According to David Desser's classification, Ozu is a representative film director of the classical paradigm whose narrative is chronological, episodic, cyclical, mythic, and transcendental.[32] Because Desser's position on Ozu is based on the combination of Schrader, Richie, and Bordwell, it is worth examining his argument in order to position ourselves in relation to the existing critical literature on Ozu's films.

Desser classifies the Japanese cinema into three distinct paradigms: the classical, the modern, and the modernist. Desser argues that the narrative mode of Ozu's films is classical and best understood as an equivalent to the narrative mode of the Japanese novel, "especially as practiced by authors like Shiga Naoya, Natsume Soseki, Tanizaki Junichiro, and most particularly, Kawabata Yasunari, Japan's Nobel Laureate and arguably its greatest novelist."[33] This passage strikes us as so strange that it makes us wonder what he really means by the classical paradigm of Japanese cinema. For the Japanese novel (*shosetsu*) has diverse modes of narration, and the writers he mentions cannot be lumped together as the representative Japanese authors writing in the same narrative mode. Because I cannot go into the issue of narrative modes in Japanese literature here, I would like to simply point out that nobody can think of any other writers representing such different schools of modern Japanese prose fiction than those four whom Desser chooses to support his argument on what he calls the classical paradigm of Japanese cinema. For instance, Tanizaki and Kawabata are contemporaries, but the types of texts they wrote are diametrically opposite. Whereas Kawabata devised a narrational mode that aestheticized and dehistoricized reality, Tanizaki constructed textual strategies that confronted the ugly side of reality and challenged not only Kawabata's tactics of aestheticization but also a tradition of the so-called

I-novel (*shishosetsu*), of which Shiga Naoya was a representative writer.[34]

But the most serious problem with Desser's argument lies in his classification of the Japanese cinema into three different types based on such notions as classical, modern, and modernist. We must continuously question the historical model underlying these terms, which are nonoperative as critical concepts. These three terms correspond to a linear historical development mimicking the master narrative of the Western imperial powers. For instance, Desser explains the transition from the classical to the modern paradigm as follows:

In the shift from the classical to the modern paradigm, we find a shift in the attitude toward the status quo. From acceptance of life's problems, we find the emergence of the individual who fights against his circumstances; we find, in short, the emergence of bourgeois individualism. This individualism is expressed in a narrative mode which emphasizes chronological, causal, linear, and historical thinking. The paradigm here called modern is in all important respects modeled on the classical Hollywood style.[35]

Is being either traditional or classical the same as being subservient to the status quo? Does Desser mean to say that until bourgeois individualism was introduced to Japan, the Japanese had simply accepted and never revolted against authority? Is he arguing that the Japanese had to be taught by Westerners even to change their own history? Desser may well say that he is not talking about traditional Japan but only films made by such "classical masters" as Ozu, Mizoguchi, and Naruse. But this kind of objection would not hold because these directors are called "classical masters" precisely because they are said to utilize a classical tradition of Japanese culture in the first place. The question is of course which tradition Desser is talking about. For tradition is not something we find out there, but is continuously constructed and deconstructed in a particular sociohistorical context.[36] The fact that a "traditional Japan" repeatedly appears not just in Desser's but also in many other critics' writings (including Noel Burch's) is an ideological construct necessary to reaffirm the Western hegemonic structure in which Japan is acknowledged as the Other.

Among the Western film critics, it is David Bordwell who has succeeded in demystifing the myth of Ozu's Japaneseness.[37] Bordwell tries to show how much Japanese society was penetrated by the Hollywood cinema and Western mass culture in general; how Ozu himself was attracted by the Hollywood cinema and a new life-style of modernity; and how Ozu displaced, in spite of his fascination with the Hollywood cinema, narrative from the center of his films. Following Noel Burch, David Bordwell calls the narrative mode of Ozu's films "parametric," and Ozu is said to be a modernist filmmaker in the same rank with Bresson, Dryer, and Godard.[38] The assumption underlying Bordwell's demystification of Ozu as an embodiment of Japanese tradition is the existence of the "international style" of the Hollywood cinema, and it enables him to measure all other types of cinema against this normative mode of film production. Bordwell has succeeded in freeing Ozu from the image of the quintessential Japanese director only by retrapping him in the discursive field of international modernism. The question is to what extent Bordwell's modernist position is different from the position of those American and Japanese critics who see Ozu as an embodiment of the essence of Japanese culture. But this question is misleading to the extent that it creates a false dichotomy between modernist and nonmodernist positions. For the only major difference between the two positions is that while Desser, Richie, Schrader, and others appropriate difference as the other, Bordwell erases difference as the same. The two seemingly opposite positions on Ozu are merely two aspects of modernization theory, and Ozu as a traditionalist and Ozu as a modernist are only mirror images of each other.[39]

Since the end of World War II, Ozu had been the major figure at Shochiku's Ofuna studios, yet his films, which dealt with highly melodramatic situations, did not quite fit into stereotypes of "Ofuna flavor" films. In the guise of the "most Japanese of all Japanese directors," Ozu in fact deconstructed the most Japanese of all Japanese genres, family melodrama. This deconstruction was achieved by his will to construction (*kochiku*) and his refusal to give in to *jinen* (nature).[40] In Ozu's films, everything seems "unnatural." Characters behave in a peculiarly subdued way, and as we can see in the acting of Ryu Chishu, the quintessential Ozu actor, diction and elocution are also far from natural. The inconspicuous titles and similar plots blur the boundaries between films, and sometimes make us wonder where one film ends and where another one starts. A minute attention paid to pictorial aspects, including colors and the geometric construction of each shot and a sequence of shots, defies the law of realism to such an extent that the visual surface stands out from the narrative.

What these various manifestations of "unnaturalness" in Ozu's films signify becomes clearer when we compare them to the unrealistic character behavior in Masumura Yasuzo's films. The unnaturalness of Masumura's films are derived from his faith in the transplantation of Western individualism and humanism to postwar Japan. The extreme exaggeration of characters' behavior and a quick tempo are introduced in Masumura's films in order not only to escape from sentimental emotionalism of melodrama prevalent in the Japanese cinema but also to emulate the ideal of a liberated individual supposedly found in Europe. In Ozu's films, however, the melodramatic is not simply replaced by bourgeois individualism of the West. Instead, we find the melodramatic is deconstructed on every level of the textuality of his films. While the melodramatic as an ideologeme provides an imaginary solution to the contradiction of the Japanese modern, Ozu instead makes us confront that contradiction by refusing to let go the will to construction (*kochiku*).[41]

3

Starting from the late 1950s, and definitely by the end of the 1960s, the melodramatic ceased to be a working ideologeme of Japanese social formation. For more than ten years, the melodramatic gave an imaginary solution to the contradiction of modern Japan, the disparity between modernity and modernization. The decline of melodrama happened when the melodramatic started to be replaced by a very different social reality. In the 1960s, after the failure of the public protest against the renewal of the United States–Japan mutual security treaty (*Anpo*), mass movements of protest and dissension against the system gradually disappeared.[42] What emerged, instead, in this vacuum was the LDP's plan of doubling the national income (*kokumin shotoku baizo keikaku*) and the final transformation of Japan from an agrarian to industrial society. When this income-doubling policy actually turned out to be successful, the ideologeme of the melodramatic became obsolete. The Japanese who had been haunted by the fundamental aporia of modernity since the mid-nineteenth century finally seemed to be liberated from colonial structure by a high-growth economy propelled by technological innovation. The question is whether the melodramatic did really disappear or whether it has merely become unconscious.

To the extent that the disappearance of the melodramatic from the surface of social reality was a result of the seeming sublimation of the Japanese modernity's contradiction, it can be said that the simultaneous decline of the Japanese cinema and melodrama was a harbinger of the coming of the so-called postmodern age. Here we are stepping into a murky territory. Postmodernism, which is supposedly a cultural phenomenon of economically advanced Western countries, does not seem at first to have any direct connection to the Japanese melodramatic. If there is any meaning whatsoever in talking about the relation between the melodramatic as a type of ideologeme and the postmodern as a new mode of social formation, no matter how messy its outcome is, we cannot avoid the task of rethinking the highly contested notion of postmodernism.

The fact that a number of books and articles on postmodernism have been published recently might make us believe we no longer have to start a discussion on postmodernism with that seemingly perennial question: What is postmodernism? Although I shall not review here important literature and debates on postmodernism, on the definition of which there is no clear consensus, I believe most of us would agree that a newly emerging sociocultural situation in the postindustrial West has certain common features that would be best characterized as postmodern. I would like to emphasize that I mean by postmodernism a newly emerging social formation and its cultural manifestation of postindustrial capitalism; that is, I do not make such a distinction between a "utopian postmodernism" of critical theory and art or a "postmodernism of resistance" and a "commercial postmodernism" of popular culture or a "postmodernism of reaction"[43] because this type of thinking simply replays a symptom of what characterizes a modern paradigm without providing an adequate critical language putting a distinct social system of the postmodern in an appropriate historical context. From Fredric Jameson's notions of schizophrenia and pastiche to Baudrillard's simulation and fatal strategies, postmodernism, understood simultaneously as a radical break from and as a reflection on the modern, is inseparable from the expansion of multinational capital and global information network.

From the perspective just described, Japan would be one of the most apt examples of postmodern society. How extensively Japanese capital has penetrated into every corner of the world requires no demonstration. In the cultural sphere, Japan has transformed itself into a new type of audiovisual information society: Constantly dismantled and reconstructed buildings and shops, sophisticated television commercials, millions of copies of comics read by all age groups, fashion created by designers acclaimed in Paris, theater and musical performances of all kinds, and new "high-tech" gadgets introduced on a daily basis are part of what constitutes the imaginary landscape of the postmodern city of Tokyo. The significance of this imaginary landscape becomes clearer when we realize how important the image of the postmodern Japanese city has been for cyberpunk fiction and recent American science fiction film.[44] Furthermore, this connection between American and Japanese postmodern culture cannot be isolated from the transformation of the world economic system by multinational capital. For instance, the conflation of the expansion of Japanese capital on a multinational scale and the development of postindustrial capitalism in the form of the audiovisualization of society has surfaced in the recent takeover by Sony of CBS Records and Columbia Pictures.

However, the status of Japan as a postmodern society becomes uncertain when the question of the postmodern is resituated in the context of Japan as a non-Western country. For it is questionable whether the non-West has ever had even the modern, to say nothing of the postmodern. As I have already indicated, for the non-West, the coming of modernity and that of colonial subjugation have always been inseparable. In most cases, the non-West's incorporation into the geopolitical space of modernity has taken the form of colonization by the technologically advanced West. On rare occasions, some non-Western countries have succeeded in learning advanced technology and modernizing themselves. Yet the success of modernization has not necessarily been accompanied by modernity. The non-West is from the very beginning deprived of attaining its own centered subjectivity in the world fundamentally transformed by the master narrative of the Enlightenment imposed on itself. The non-West can achieve the goal of modernizing itself by the advancement of technology, yet modernity remains always unattainable to the non-West because what constitutes modernity is precisely the exclusion of the non-West from the modern, "universal" West. The paradox of modernity for the non-West is if the non-West somehow succeeds in obtaining modernity, that would also be the end of modernity or, in Hegelian words, the "end of History"; that is, the non-West can achieve modernity only by destroying it.

According to the Hegelian philosopher Alexandre Kojeve, this "end of History" does not belong to the unforeseeable future but has already been realized. Kojeve argues that it is Japan that has already reached the state of posthistorical society characterized by the end of Man and by the supreme reign of snobbery.

[In Japan] I was able to observe a Society that is one of a kind, because it alone has for almost three centuries experienced life at the "end of History" — that is, in the absence of all civil or external war (following the liquidation of feudalism by the roturier Hideyoshi and the artificial isolation of the country conceived and realized by his noble successor Yieasu). Now, the existence of the Japanese nobles, who ceased to risk their lives (even in duel) and yet did not for that begin to work, was anything but animal.

"Post-historical" Japanese civilization undertook ways diametrically opposed to the "American way." No doubt, there were no longer in Japan any Religion, Morals, or Politics in the "European" or "historical" sense of these words. But *Snobbery* in its pure form created disciplines negating the "natural" or "animal" given which in effectiveness far surpassed those that arose, in Japan or elsewhere, from "historical" Action — that is, from warlike and revolutionary Fights or from forced Work. To be sure, the peaks (equalled nowhere else) of specifically Japanese snobbery — the Noh Theater, the ceremony of tea, and the art of bouquets of flowers — were still to remain the exclusive prerogative of the nobles and the rich. But in spite of persistent economic and political inequalities, all Japanese without exception are currently in a position to live according to totally *formalized* values — that is, values completely empty of all "human" content in the "historical" sense. Thus, in the extreme, every Japanese is in principle capable of committing, from pure snobbery, a perfectly "gratuitous" *suicide* (the classical epee of the samurai can be replaced by an airplane or torpedo), which has nothing to do with the *risk* of life in a Fight waged for the sake of "historical" values that have social or political content. This seems to allow one to believe that the recently begun interaction between Japan and the Western World will finally lead not to a rebarbarization of the Japanese but to a "Japanization" of the Westerners (including the Russians).[45]

Yet a Japan Kojeve is talking about is a Japan incorporated into a Hegelian world system, so that the "Japanization" of the West does not at all mean a triumph of Japan, the non-West, but that of Hegelian philosophy and therefore that of Western civilization, which invented this world view. What Kojeve attempts to accomplish is a final containment of the non-West within the horizon of the Enlightenment project. In other words, instead of bringing modernity to its end, the "end of History" signifies none other than the final triumph of modernity.[46]

The complex and murky nature of our discussion comes from the fact that Japan constitutes a place for the intersection of these two different but interrelated discursive fields of postmodernism. On the one hand, the development of postindustrial capitalism has brought about in Japan the emergence of hyperconsumer culture, and it is very difficult not to use the concept of postmodernism to describe and analyze this cultural condition. On the other, the pernicious ideology of modernity still dominates and sustains the geopolitical configuration of the world divided into the West and the non-West, and "postmodern" Japan is still part of this world system. At the moment, we do not have a precise critical language that lets us weave in and out between two divergent notions of postmodernism. We have to think through this problematic of the postmodern instead of yielding to the temptation to argue that Japan has already overcome the modern. But this is exactly what has been claimed by the conservative intellectuals recently. Japan's high-growth economy and the development of postindustrial capitalism have created the illusion that the fundamental disparity between modernity and modernization experienced by non-Western countries is finally sublated. According to the conservatives, Japan has successfully overcome the modern, so that the West is no longer a model to be caught up with. On the contrary, they say, it is Japan that would be a model to be followed by both the West and the non-West.

What we are witnessing right now is a return of the overcoming the modern syndrome in Japan and the collaboration between the resurgent Japanese right wing and some Western intellectuals. This collaboration is not necessarily carried out consciously, and sometimes, even the good intentions on the part of Western intellectuals inadvertently contribute to a collaborative process. For instance, Noel Burch's *To the Distant Observer* is a first-rate example of film scholarship on the Japanese cinema, and nobody who wants to study this subject can possibly ignore Burch's achievement. Nevertheless, throughout the book, there is an unsettling undertone whose implication should get more attention. In the conclusion to a study of Kurosawa as a "late avatar of a tradition," Burch states that

in a sense, this entire book has been intended as an indictment of Western (capitalist) cultural imperialism. Japan, of course, is now an imperialist nation in her own right; and it is not surprising that in order to accede to this status, traditional values have ultimately had to be distorted or repressed — traditional values which, in themselves, as I have tried to point out, are not necessarily 'bad' – it all depends on the use to which they are put. Needless to say, Japanese capitalism has preserved, in forms chosen by it, those which suit its requirements. However, in my view it is important for the future of Japanese society that there be kept alive concepts and attitudes which may be bound up with such features as the neo-feudal paternalism of the modern firm or the veritable apartheid inflicted on Japanese women, but which at the same time have truly progressive potentialities, assuming the transformation of production relationships.[47]

What is disturbing in Burch's argument is his static view of tradition. Contrary to what Burch says, there is no such thing as pure, uncontaminated, tradition. For the purpose of pursuing its imperialist enterprise, Japan did not "distort" traditional values but simply created them. But let us suppose, for the argument's sake, there are undistorted, true traditional values as Burch assumes. According to Burch, when the "transformation of production relationships" is accomplished, those traditional values can "have progressive potentialities." But of course when production relations and a mode of production change, "traditional values" are also transformed. How can the mode of production be changed without affecting "traditional values" at the same time? Burch's argument is based on the sociological compartmentalization of different aspects of social formation and particularly on the reification of tradition. Burch states exactly what the Japanese right wing wants to hear, and by reifying tradition, he inadvertently contributes to the neonationalists' attempt to conflate "Japanese tradition" with postmodernism.[48]

Neonationalists argue that Japan had already had postmodern culture even before modernity came to Japan with a threat of colonization. This argument seemingly solves the contradiction of the Japanese modern. For on the one hand, it valorizes "tradition" uncontaminated by the influence of modernity; on the other, it makes Japan superior to the West to the extent that Japan was already in the state of the postmodern well before the West had reached to that stage. Obviously, this neonationalist argument is only a parody of what Kojeve calls the "end of History" and the "Japanization of the West." But we cannot dismiss this argument as nonsense because it is becoming more and more prevalent. "Postmodern Japan" is constructed on the process of dehistoricization and a parodic mimicry of the critique of modernity in the name of tradition with "progressive potentialities." As the distinction between the old and the new has been annulled by the smooth opposition-free space of hyperconsumer culture, melodrama has also disappeared. For no matter how elusive it is, a certain historical consciousness can always be found at the core of melodrama. The fall of the melodramatic since the early 1970s is inseparable from the process of spatialization, dehistoricization, and depoliticization plaguing "postmodern Japan." Melodrama as a genre has, practically speaking, disappeared; however, because the fundamental contradiction between modernity and modernization not only remains but is increasingly aggravating, the melodramatic has not died but has merely become unconscious. We have to wait and see if the melodramatic unconscious someday becomes conscious again and contributes to a revitalization of historical consciousness in the near future.

Notes

1. See Thomas Elsaesser, "Desire Denied, Deferred or Squared?" *Screen* 29, 3 (Summer 1988): 106–15.
2. Thomas Elsaesser, "Tales of Sound and Fury: Observations on the Family Melodrama," in *Movies and Methods,* vol. 2, ed. Bill Nichols (Berkeley: University of California Press, 1985), pp. 165–89.
3. Walter Benjamin, "The Work of Art in the Age of Mechanical Reproduction," in *Illuminations: Essays and Reflections* (New York: Schocken Books, 1969), pp. 217–51.
4. For more detailed information on Taisho culture, see Minami Hiroshi and Shakai shinri kenkusho, *Taisho bunka: 1905–1927* (Tokyo: Keiso shobo, 1965).
5. Watanabe Kazutami, *Hayashi Tatsuo to sono jidai* (Tokyo: Iwanami shoten, 1988), pp. 27–33.
6. For instance, see Andreas Huyssen, *After the Great Divide: Modernism, Mass Culture, Postmodernism* (Bloomington: Indiana University Press, 1986).
7. These are the critical concepts used by Fredric Jameson. See his *The Political Unconscious: Narrative as a Socially Symbolic Act* (Ithaca, N.Y.: Cornell University Press, 1981).
8. Steve Neale, "Melodrama and Tears," *Screen* 27, 6 (Nov.–Dec. 1986): 6.
9. Russell Merritt, "Melodrama: Postmortem for a Phantom Genre," *Wide Angle* 5, 3 (1983):28.
10. Jameson, *Political Unconscious,* p. 141.
11. Merritt, "Melodrama," p. 25.
12. Ernesto Laclau, "Building a New Left: An Interview with Ernesto Laclau," *Strategies* 1 (Fall 1989):24.
13. Jameson, *Political Unconscious,* p. 76.

14. Ibid., p. 115.

15. Geoffrey Nowell-Smith, "Minnelli and Melodrama," in *Movies and Methods*, vol. 2, ed., Bill Nichols (Berkeley: University of California Press, 1985), pp. 190–4.

16. Jameson, *Political Unconscious,* p. 116.

17. Ibid., p. 148.

18. The following anecdote provided by Tsurumi Shunsuke aptly illustrates this "synchronic uneven development" in modern Japan: "A Mexican anthropologist, Ricardo d'Amare, tells of a Swedish engineer whose faith in Europe was shattered by what he saw on his trip to Japan. He had been raised in the belief that European civilization was like a magnificent tapestry, science and art embedded in love and a religious upbringing. In Japan he found odd techniques and beliefs of obviously European lineage combined piecemeal and functioning efficiently at a low cost. The people did not seem versed in the humanistic culture of Europe, but they none the less accomplished time-saving jobs in a way that was expedient enough. This Swedish engineer succumbed to a nervous breakdown. Perhaps he was an unusually susceptible character, but even so his story exemplifies a way of looking at Japanese culture which is humiliating to Europeans, and in being humiliating it teaches them something." Shunsuke Tsurumi, *A Cultural History of Postwar Japan: 1945–1980* (London: KPI, 1987), p. 126.

19. See Tetsuo Najita, "On Culture and Technology in Postmodern Japan," *South Atlantic Quarterly* 87, 3 (Summer 1988): 401–18.

20. Sato Tadao, "Toki jidai," in *Koza nihon eiga 3 toki no jidai*, ed., Imamura Shohei, Sato Tadao, Shindo Kaneto, Tsurumi Shunsuke, and Yamada Yoji (Tokyo: Iwanami shoten, 1986), p. 27.

21. Donald Richie, *The Films of Akira Kurosawa*, rev. ed. (Berkeley: University of California Press, 1984), p. 37.

22. See Masao Miyoshi, "Dare ga kettei shi dare ga katatte iru no ka: sengo nihon ni okeru shutaisei to seiyo," in *Sengo nihon no seishinshi: sono saikento* ed., Tetsuo Najita, Maeda Ai, and Kamishima Jiro (Tokyo: Iwanami shoten, 1988), pp. 277–309.

23. Another important parameter of the melodramatic as an ideologeme is the intellectuals' relation with the masses.

24. On *ressentiment,* see Jameson, *Political Unconscious*, pp. 185–205, and Gilles Deleuze, *Nietzsche and Philosophy*, trans. Hugh Tomlinson (New York: Columbia University Press, 1983), pp. 111–46.

25. Jameson *Political Unconscious*, p. 148.

26. Nakano Yoshio, "Mohaya 'sengo' de wa nai," in *Nakano Yoshio shu*, vol. 2 (Tokyo: Chikuma shobo, 1987), pp. 148–65.

27. Sato Tadao, *Oshima Nagisa no sekai* (Tokyo: Asahi bunko, 1986), pp. 45–8.

28. Masumuro Yasuzo, "Masumura Yasuzo no eiga ron," *Imeji foramu 79* (March 1987): 34–7. See also Oshima Nagisa, " 'Kindai shugi' tojo no koro," *Imeji foramu 79* (March 1987): 28–9.

29. Sato, *Oshima Nagisa no sekai*, pp. 50–3.

30. Audie Bock, *Japanese Film Directors* (Tokyo: Kodansha International, 1978), p. 199.

31. Paul Schrader, *Transcendental Style in Film: Ozu, Bresson, Dreyer* (Berkeley: University of California Press, 1972); Donald Richie, *Ozu* (Berkeley: University of California Press, 1974).

32. David Desser, *Eros Plus Massacre: An Introduction to the Japanese New Wave Cinema* (Bloomington: Indiana University Press, 1988).

33. Desser, *Eros Plus Massacre*, p. 17.

34. On *shisosetsu*, see Edward Fowler, *The Rhetoric of Confession: Shishosetsu in Early Twentieth-Century Japanese Fiction* (Berkeley: University of California Press, 1988).

35. Desser, *Eros Plus Massacre*, p. 20.

36. On the "invention of tradition," see Eric Hobsbawm and Terence Ranger, eds., *The Invention of Tradition* (Cambridge: Cambridge University Press, 1983).

37. A Japanese critic who set out to accomplish a similar goal is Hasumi Shigehiko. See his *Kantoku Ozu Yasujiro* (Tokyo: Chikuma shobo, 1983). For how influential Hasumi is in the scene of contemporary Japanese film criticism, see Shinko Suga, "Japanese Films in the 80s: Interview with Tadao Sato," *Framework* 36 (1989): 90.

38. David Bordwell, *Ozu and the Poetics of Cinema* (Princeton: Princeton University Press, 1988).

39. How can we escape from this trap of modernist perspectives? If there is any positive aspect of postmodernism, it is its focus not on a generality of international style but specificities of regional styles grounded on particular sociohistorical situations at particular locations. But the studies of Ozu's films from the perspective of a postmodernism understood in this sense are yet to come out either here or in Japan.

40. For a relation among *jinen, kochiku,* the modern, and the postmodern, see Karatani Kojin, *Hihyo to posuto modan* (Tokyo: Fukutake shoten, 1985), pp. 9–49.

41. It is interesting to see that Imamura Shohei, once a vehement critic of Ozu, has recently come back to the world of Ozu in his *Kuroi Ame (Black Rain)*. Imamura's repectful remark on Ozu might indicate that Ozu and Imamura, two directors who seem to have nothing in common, share similar concerns, particularly skepticism toward modern Japan. See an interview with Imamura published in *Imeji foramu* 111 (July 1989): 74–5.

42. Of course, public protests did not disappear immediately. For instance, there was a very powerful anti–Vietnam War movement lead by a committed writer Oda Makoto. Yet these remaining protest movements did not involve a great number of liberal college professors, intellectuals, and workers as the mass protest did in 1960.

43. E. Ann Kaplan, "Introduction," in *Postmodernism and Its Discontents: Theories, Practices*, ed. E. Ann Kaplan (London: Verso, 1988), pp. 4–5; Hal Foster, "Postmodernism: A Preface," in *The Anti-Aesthetic: Essays on Postmodern Culture*, ed. Hal Foster (Port Townsend: Bay Press, 1983), pp. xi–xii; Huyssen, *After the Great Divide*, pp. 220–1.

44. See, for instance, my "The Postmodern and Mass Images in Japan," *Public Culture* 1, 2 (Spring 1989): 8–25.

45. Alexandre Kojeve, *Introduction to the Reading of Hegel*, trans. James H. Nichols, Jr. (Ithaca, N.Y.: Cornell University Press, 1980), pp. 161–2.

46. The Enlightenment and colonialism have transformed the world into the world of modernity, which constitutes an absolute horizon of containment for the non-West. To the extent that the non-West strives to break away from this horizon of containment, the "postmodern" is a much more meaningful notion for the non-West than for the West. In Japan, for instance, the first significant "postmodern" debate took place during World War II in the form of overcoming the modern syndrome. In 1942, the round-table discussion on "overcoming the modern" (*kindai no chokoku*) was organized by the literary magazine *Bungakukai*, to which the leading intellectuals of that period were invited. The significance of this and other related discussions seemed to be forgotten, but since the early 1980s, as the postmodern becomes a topic of heated debates, the "overcoming the modern" has resurfaced and been rediscussed in the Japanese intellectual scene. On the symposium on "overcoming the modern" and its implications, see H. D. Harootunian, "Visible Discourses/Invisible Ideologies," *South Atlantic Quarterly* 87, 3 (Summer 1988): 445–74; Naoki Sakai, "Modernity and Its Critique: The Problem of Universalism and Particularism," *South Atlantic Quarterly* 87, 3 (Summer 1988): 475–504; Kosaka Masaaki, Nishitani Keiji, Koyama Iwao, and Suzuki Shigetaka, *Sekaishi teki tachiba to Nihon* (Tokyo: Chuo koronsha, 1943); Matsumoto Ken'ichi, ed., *Kindai no chokoku* (Tokyo: Fusanbo, 1979); Hiromatsu Wataru, *'Kindai no chokoku' ron: showa shisoshi e no ichi dansho* (Tokyo: Asahi shinbunsha, 1980); Takeuchi Yoshimi, "Kindai no chokoku," in Matsumoto, *Kindai no chokoku*, pp. 273–341; Kuno Osamu and Yoshimoto Takaaki, "Senso, shiso, teiko," in Yoshimoto Takaaki, *Yoshimoto Takaaki zen chosaku shu*, vol. 14 (Tokyo: Keiso shobo, 1972), pp. 385–97; and Hiromatsu Wataru, Asada Akira, Ichikawa Hiroshi, and Karatani Kojin, " 'Kindai no chokoku' to Nishida tetsugaku: kankei no naimenteki jokyo kara fujo suru 'nihon' to yu mukonkyona jishin," *Kikan Shicho* 4 (1989): 6–38;

47. Noel Burch, *To the Distant Observer: Form and Meaning in the Japanese Cinema* (Berkeley: University of California Press, 1979), p. 323.

48. The French sociologist Michel Maffesoli argues that Japan "most exemplarily represents the postmodern" because it has successfully achieved modernization and acquired highly developed technology while conserving traditional elements at the same time. Needless to say, this kind of definition of postmodernism – the combination of the modern technology and the premodern archaic – has nothing to do with our discussion of the ambiguity of the postmodern. See Michel Maffesoli, Nakamura Yujiro, Mizubayashi Akira, and Ichikawa Hiroshi, "Shakaigakuteki ninshiki to posuto modan: Dionusosu teki chi ni yoru shakai no zentaiteki nin'shiki o mezashite," *Kikan Shicho* 4 (1989): 170–1.

References

Benjamin, Walter (1969). "The Work of Art in the Age of Mechanical Reproduction." In *Illuminations: Essays and Reflections*, 217–51. New York: Schocken Books.

Bock, Audie (1978). *Japanese Film Directors*. Tokyo: Kodansha International.

Bordwell, David (1988). *Ozu and the Poetics of Cinema*. Princeton: Princeton University Press.

Burch, Noel (1979). *To the Distant Observer: Form and Meaning in the Japanese Cinema*. Berkeley: University of California Press.

Deleuze, Gilles (1983). *Nietzsche and Philosophy*. Trans. Hugh Tomlinson. New York: Columbia University Press.

Desser, David (1988). *Eros Plus Massacre: An Introduction to the Japanese New Wave Cinema*. Bloomington: Indiana University Press.

Elsaesser, Thomas (1985). "Tales of Sound and Fury: Observations on the Family Melodrama." In *Movies and Methods: An Anthology*. Vol. 2, ed. Bill Nichols, 165–89. Berkeley: University of California Press.

—(1988). "Desire Denied, Dererred or Squared?" *Screen* 29, 3 (Summer):106–15.

Foster, Hal (1983). "Postmodernism: A Preface." In *The Anti-Aesthetic: Essays on Postmodern Culture,* edited by Hal Foster, ix–xvi. Port Townsend: Bay Press.

Fowler, Edward (1988). *The Rhetoric of Confession: Shishosetsu in Early Twentieth-Century Japanese Fiction*. Berkeley: University of California Press.

Harootunian, H. D. (1988). "Visible Discourses/Invisible Ideologies." *South Atlantic Quarterly* 87, 3 (Summer):445–74.

Hasumi Shigehiko (1983). *Kantoku Ozu Yasujiro*. Tokyo: Chikuma shobo.

Hiromatsu Wataru (1980). *'Kindai no chokoku' ron: showa shisoshi e no ichi dansho*. Tokyo: Asahi shinbunsha.

Hiromatsu Wataru, Asada Akira, Ichikawa Hiroshi, and Karatani Kojin (1989). " 'Kindai no chokoku' to Nishida tetsugaku: kankei no naimenteki jokyo kara fujo suru 'nihon' to yu mukonkyona jishin." *Kikan Shicho* 4:6–38.

Hobsbawm, Eric, and Terence Ranger, eds. (1983). *The Invention of Tradition*. Cambridge: Cambridge University Press.

Huyssen, Andreas (1986). *After the Great Divide: Modernism, Mass Culture, Postmodernism*. Bloomington: Indiana University Press.

Imamura Shohei (1989). An interview. *Imeji foramu* 111 (July):64–82.

Jameson, Fredric (1981). *The Political Unconscious: Narrative as a Socially Symbolic Act*. Ithaca, N.Y.: Cornell University Press.

Kaplan, E. Ann (1988). "Introduction." In *Postmodernism and Its Discontents: Theories, Practices,* ed. E. Ann Kaplan. London: Verso.

Karatani Kojin (1985). *Hihyo to posuto modan*. Tokyo: Fukutake shoten.

Kojeve, Alexandre (1980). *Introduction to the Reading of Hegel*. Trans. James H. Nichols, Jr. Ithaca, N.Y.: Cornell University Press.

Kosaka Masaaki, Nishitani Keiji, Koyama Iwao, and Suzuki Shigetaka (1943). *Sekaishi teki tachiba to Nihon*. Tokyo: Chuo koronsha.

Kuno Osamu and Yoshimoto Takaaki (1972). "Senso, shiso, teiko." In *Yoshimoto Takaaki zen chosaku shu,* vol. 14, ed. Yoshimoto Takaaki, 385–97. Tokyo: Keiso shobo.

Laclau, Ernesto (1989). "Building a New Left: An Interview with Ernesto Laclau." *Strategies* 1 (Fall):10–28.

Maffesoli, Michel, Nakamura Yujiro, Mizubayashi Akira, and Ichikawa Hiroshi (1989). "Shakaigakuteki ninshiki to posuto modan: Dionusosu teki chi ni yoru shakai no zentaiteki nin'shiki o mezashite." *Kikan Shicho* 4:158–77.

Masao, Miyoshi (1988). "Dare ga kettei shi dare ga katatte iru no ka: sengo nihon ni okeru shutaisei to seiyo." In *Sengo nihon no seishinshi: sono saikento,* ed. Tetsuo Najita, Maeda Ai, and Kamishima Jiro, 277–309. Tokyo: Iwanami shoten.

Masumura Yasuzo (1987). "Masumura Yasuzo no eiga ron." *Imeji foramu 79* (March):34–7.

Matsumoto Ken'ichi, ed. (1979). *Kindai no chokoku.* Tokyo: Fusanbo.

Merritt, Russell (1983). "Melodrama: Postmortem for a Phantom Genre." *Wide Angle* 5, 3:24–31.

Minami Hiroshi, and Shakai shinri kenkusho (1965). *Taisho bunka: 1905– 1927.* Tokyo: Keiso shobo.

Najita, Tetsuo (1988). "On Culture and Technology in Postmodern Japan." *South Atlantic Quarterly* 87, 3 (Summer):401–18.

Nakano Yoshio (1984). "Mohaya 'sengo' de wa nai." In *Nakano Yoshio shu,* 2:148–65. Tokyo: Chikuma shobo.

Neale, Steve. (1986). "Melodrama and Tears." *Screen* 27, 6 (Nov.–Dec.):6–22.

Nowell-Smith, Geoffrey (1985). "Minnelli and Melodrama." In *Movies and Methods: An Anthology,* vol. 2., ed. Bill Nichols, 190–4. Berkeley: University of California Press.

Oshima Nagisa (1987). " 'Kindai shugi' tojo no koro." *Imeji foramu 79* (March):28–9.

Richie, Donald (1974). *Ozu.* Berkeley: University of California Press.

—(1984). *The Films of Akira Kurosawa.* Rev. ed. Berkeley: University of California Press.

Sakai, Naoki (1988). "Modernity and Its Critique: The Problem of Universalism and Particularism." *South Atlantic Quarterly* 87, 3 (Summer):475–504.

Sato Tadao (1986). "Toki jidai." In *Koza nihon eiga 3: toki no jidai,* ed. Imamura Shohei, Sato Tadao, Shindo Kaneto, Tsurumi Shunsuke, and Yamada Yoji. Tokyo: Iwanami shoten.

—(1987). *Oshima Nagisa no sekai.* Tokyo: Asahi bunko.

Schrader, Paul (1972). *Transcendental Style in Film: Ozu, Bresson, Dreyer.* Berkeley: University of California Press.

Suga, Shinko (1989). "Japanese Films in the 80s: Interview with Tadao Sato." *Framework* 36:87–91.

Takeuchi Yoshimi (1979). "Kindai no chokoku." In *Kindai no chokoku,* ed. Matsamoto Ken'ichi, 273–341. Tokyo: Fusanbo.

Tsurumi Shunsuke (1987). *A Cultural History of Postwar Japan: 1945–1980.* London: KPI.

Watanabe Kazutami (1988). *Hayashi Tatsuo to sono jidai.* Tokyo: Iwanami shoten.

Yoshimoto, Mitsuhiro (1989). "The Postmodern and Mass Images in Japan." *Public Culture* 1, 2 (Spring):8–25.

CHAPTER VII

Inscribing the subject: The
melodramatization of
gender in *An Actor's
Revenge*

Scott Nygren

In *The Revenge of Yukinojo* [Ichikawa]
triumphed over his material so completely
that the result is something of a masterpiece – though just what kind is difficult to
say.

Donald Richie

Ichikawa's film *An Actor's Revenge* (*Yukinojo Henge*, 1963) has long
been acknowledged as an eccentric "masterpiece."[1] In this chapter, I
would like to consider the film as the site of contestatory discourses of
power and gender identification, through a play of apparently contradictory theatrical and cinematic styles. Specifically, the film foregrounds melodrama as a style that uneasily pivots between traditional
Kabuki theater and Western cinematic realism. As such, it invites a reconsideration of the role of Shimpa, the Japanese melodramatic theater popular between 1890 and 1920, in its relation to cinema and
Japanese culture.

Shimpa derived from a form of political theater designed to promote
liberal political thought prior to the 1890 establishment of the first
Japanese constitution and embodied emerging middle-class values
parallel to the role melodrama played in France after the Revolution.[2]
All but forgotten after the triumph of Shingeki, or Western-style realist
theater, and Shingeki-influenced cinema, Shimpa marks a boundary
between what later would become clearly delineated Western and Japanese traditions in both political organization and narrative representation. These different traditions came to be known as "feudalism" and
"humanism," yet both terms are sweeping generalizations that erase
the complexity and contradictions within each tradition. As such, they
mythologize cultural difference as a polarization of unitary transhistorical forms.

This chapter argues that *An Actor's Revenge* sets Kabuki and Western melodrama against one another, as two forms of excess, in order to
destabilize the assumptions inherent in each. "Feudal" and "human-

127

ist" distributions of power are both undermined through an ironic intertextual bracketing of modes of representation associated with each. These modes can be seen to regulate the distribution of power and the relative positioning of women within discursive formations.

At the same time, gender destabilization in the film provides a means of discussing the difficult question of psychoanalysis in a Japanese context. Gender identification is undermined by the deliberate casting of Kazuo Hasegawa (Yukinojo) as an *onnagatta*, the type of male Kabuki actor who specializes in playing female roles, and the actress Ayako Wakao in romantic love scenes. This juxtaposition recalls the historical moment in Japanese film when women first replaced *onnagatta* in female roles during the 1920s and undermines any simple sense of what constitutes gender identification.

Textual features

According to Donald Richie, Ichikawa was assigned to remake *An Actor's Revenge* as punishment, "almost a calculated insult," by the Daiei studio after their dissatisfaction with his productions of *Conflagration* (*Enjo*, 1958), *Bonchi* (*Bonchi*, 1960), and *The Outcast* (*Hakai*, 1962). This "old tearjerker," or "tired melodrama," was seen by the director and his wife Natto Wada (who adapted the scenario) as "so bad as to be good."[3] In short, the scenario is conceived as a melodrama at the historic moment when negative attitudes toward the form begin to reverse into a positive appreciation. Appropriated shortly after its release into the Western concepts of "camp" and pop art, Ichikawa's reinscription of melodrama can perhaps now be reexamined on its own terms.

The story centers on Yukinojo, a celebrated Kabuki actor during the Tokugawa period who, as an *onnagatta* or *oyama*, specializes in female roles. During a performance at the Ichimura Theater in Edo (Tokyo), he recognizes Lord Dobe and the merchant Kawaguchiya, who were responsible for the ruin and suicide of his parents. He seeks vengeance through subterfuge, most significantly through the manipulation of Lord Dobe's daughter Namiji who has fallen in love with him. Economic depression has produced a rash of burglars, who by turns interfere with or assist Yukinojo's schemes. Eventually, Yukinojo traps his enemies by a charade in which he pretends to be the ghost of his dead father, and overcome by exposure and guilt, they kill themselves.

The story is filled with instances of social corruption and class power. Lord Dobe and Kawaguchiya exemplify the alliance of samurai and merchant classes that dominates Tokugawa Japan. Kawaguchiya's speculation in the rice market is characterized as greed responsible for the famine and uprising that devastates the city. Lord Dobe claims that the Shogun is in his power because of Namiji, linking his corruption directly to the nominal ruler. When the story of Yukinojo's father Matsuuraya is told at the end of the film, Lord Dobe is revealed as the former magistrate of Nagasaki, the sole Japanese city where even limited trade with the West was permitted during the rigid isolation of the country enforced by the Tokugawa Shogunate. Lord Dobe had been bribed by Hiroyama, whose "rare clock" had been smuggled from abroad, and then conspired with Hiroyama and Matsuuraya's clerk Kawaguchiya to blame Yukinojo's father for the crime. Matsuuraya, driven mad by the false accusations, committed suicide.

At the same time, numerous roles are mirrored by parallel relationships or names. Ohatsu, a woman boss of a band of burglars, is infatuated with Yukinojo, mirroring across class lines Yukinojo's aristocratic affair with Namiji. Yukinojo's "real" name in the film is Yukitaro (Yukinojo is his stage name, which partially explains why his enemies don't recognize him), a name mirrored in Yukitaro's rival Yamitaro, a burglar and Ohatsu's principal cohort. In a tour-de-force performance not untypical of Kabuki, the same actor plays the roles of both Yukitaro and Yamitaro. This doubling is then noted within the film when Yamitaro claims he feels as if Yukitaro were his brother, and again when Ohatsu remarks that their profiles are similar. Yamitaro is in turn rivaled by another burglar Hirutaro (*Yami* means dark and *Hiru* means light), Yukitaro is rivaled by yet another burglar Heima Kadokura (a former fellow student of the sword instructor Issoshai at the Tenshin School, where the school "secrets" are recorded on a piece of paper that turns out to be blank), and so on.

Part of the doubling cuts across the difference between stage performance in Kabuki and offstage "life," that is, the film's representation of the characters' social context. Ichikawa's film has been often noted as an antirealist experiment with all the artificial and theatrical devices available to a filmmaker at the Daiei studio in Kyoto. Yukinojo maintains his *onnagatta* costume and performance both onstage and off, creating several layers of sexual ambiguity during love scenes, especially with Namiji. The wide screen becomes an arena for graphic display: A horizontal fan fills the screen against a red background, a fight is filmed as slashing swords isolated by light against total darkness, a rope stretches completely across the screen (again isolated against darkness) with the characters pulling the rope offscreen. In addition, any sense of historical realism seems willfully and even frivolously violated. Authentic Kabuki music alternates with a muted jazz trumpet or violins and vibrophone, and outdoor scenes can seem conspicuously painted as if to recall Western landscapes. Traditional Kabuki and Western-style cinema reflect each other as equally artificial constructs.

The effect of all these proliferating plot turns, conspiratorial revelations, character doublings, and formal devices is to create a narrative maze in which rational comprehension of all detail becomes difficult or perhaps impossible on first viewing. Narrative clarity tends to dissolve into an illusion of infinite recession, as in a hall of mirrors. In this, the story is not unlike the Byzantine workings of many Kabuki plays (or eighteenth-century opera in the West), but the film does not stop there.

Plural intertextuality

If *An Actor's Revenge* seems like a labyrinthine text in itself, another part of its fascination comes from a layering of intertextual references so complex that the effect of infinitely receding mirrors extends well into the social fabric of Japanese film history and cross-cultural influences between Japan and the West. First, Ichikawa's film is a remake of Teinosuke Kinugasa's *The Revenge of Yukinojo* (*Yukinojo Henge*, 1935), a film made during the militarist period of closure against the West as strict as that of the Tokugawa regime in which the story is set. As in the Ichikawa film, the Yukinojo character in the original film also maintained his *onnagatta* role both on- and offstage, and the same actor again performed the roles of both Yukinojo and the burglar (and in the first film, of Yukinojo's mother as well). Further, as is well known, Ichikawa specifically chose the same actor who had starred in the 1935 film to recreate his role in the 1963 version, and Ichikawa's scenarist Natto Wada adapted the original scenario by Daisuke Ito and Kinugasa, which had been based on a novel by Otokichi Mikami.

Interestingly, the actor involved had changed his name between films, reversing the film character's adoption of a stage name after he left Nagasaki. When the actor had moved from Shochiku to Toho, he had been forced to leave his stage name of Chojiro Hayashi behind and revert to his birth name of Kazuo Hasegawa. In a famous incident, a Korean gangster hired in part by the Shochiku labor-gang boss slashed Hasegawa in the face with a razor; only afterward did the public sympathize with the change and accept his new name.[4] Hayashi/Hasegawa's face was then reconstructed through extensive plastic surgery, making his "real" face as much an artificial construction as that of his *onnagatta*'s role's makeup. Shortly after Ichikawa's film, Kobo Abe's novel *The Face of Another* would make the trope of plastic surgery and new identity a metaphor for the Japanese experience of cultural change; by 1966, Hiroshi Teshigahara had made Abe's novel into a film.

In 1963, Ichikawa's choice of Hasegawa for the role of Yukinojo already suggested the violence of identity change between the militarist period and the post-Occupation cinema of "modern" Japan. This disjunction specifically resonates with the difference between Kabuki tradition and Western realism: The enforced mythologies of militarism that attributed divine origin to the emperor had been displaced by the humanist realism of the American Occupation as vehicle of an equally imposed ideology. For those Japanese who had lived through the militant enforcement of such contradictory ideologies, a cynical distance tended to undermine absolute belief in any single system of meaning, as can be seen in the films of the Japanese New Wave contemporaneous with Ichikawa's film.

But many more ironies surround the names of personnel associated with *An Actor's Revenge*. Kinugasa, the director and coscenarist of the first version, is best known in the West both for his experimental films of the 1920s, *A Crazy Page (Kurutta Ippeiji*, 1926) and *Crossways (Jujiro*, 1928), and for his later *Gate of Hell (Jigokuman*, 1953). However, Kinugasa was himself originally an *onnagatta* at the Nikkatsu film studio and played the heroine in such films as Eizo Tanaka's *The Living Corpse (Ikeru Shikabane*, 1917). Kinugasa led the 1922 *onnagatta's* strike against Nikkatsu to protest the introduction of women to play female roles in films, before making a career change and becoming a director. Although Kinugasa had between these two periods reversed himself to lead the fight to modernize Japanese filmmaking, his 1935 production of a film narrative centering on an *onnagatta's* revenge unavoidably recalls the conflict between traditional Kabuki stylization and Western cinematic realism earlier in Japanese film history.

Unfortunately, few complete films from this period survive, even at the Film Center of the National Museum of Modern Art in Tokyo or in the Matsuda collection, and *The Living Corpse* is so far extant only through written descriptions.[5] This was the period when *onnagatta* and *benshi* dominated Japanese film production, together with the exaggerated Shimpa techniques for which Tanaka was primarily known. Tanaka however idolized Ibsen and attempted to introduce "new-style" films beginning with *The Living Corpse*, substituting such devices of Western realism as location shooting for the theatricality of Shimpa. According to Anderson and Richie, Kinugasa's female appearance in the film was contradicted only by the heavy workmen's boots that he wore due to the heavy mud encountered during November shooting. However, no one objected because "the audience had not yet been trained to expect the illusion of complete reality."[6]

The Living Corpse, then, apparently participated in a remarkably mixed style of film in some ways unique to Japan, but also characteristic of the intersection of traditional non-Western aesthetics with cinematic representation. The omniscient style of camera narration characteristic of Western realism is framed by the *benshi* as interpretive narrator, location realism combines with contradictory costume elements, and photographic realism combines with *onnagatta*. This mixed text is conceived as a move against the theatricality of Shimpa, and marks what is perhaps Kinugasa's most important role as an actor in early cinema. Although Kinugasa's relationship to Western modernism has been debated, concerning his avant-garde films like *A Crazy Page,*[7] the effect that his disjunctive stylistic background had on his interest in antirealist filmmaking has yet to be discussed. Ichikawa, in remaking *An Actor's Revenge,* is in some ways more faithful to Kinugasa's film experience than Kinugasa's original version could be. Through his deliberate undermining of cinematic realism by studio theatricality, Ichikawa reconsiders precisely those early conditions of production that helped shape Kinugasa's wildly diverse career and incorporates those into his remake as a critique of the text.

Daisuke Ito, who cowrote the original *Actor's Revenge* scenario with Kinugasa, was himself a major director of silent films. Ito originated the *chambara* or sword-fight film, which recreated the fight scenes of previously filmed Kabuki and Shimpa plays with greater cinematic realism. Curiously, *chambara* films are linked with ideas of left-wing social activism, which circulated in Japan during the 1920s, and often feature an outlaw hero fighting against a corrupt and oppressive social order. The most famous actor portraying such outlaw heroes was Tsumasaburo Bando, but Hayashi/Hasegawa was almost as popular.

Although again few films survive, it is possible to draw some guarded conclusions from Ito's only extant silent film, *Jirokichi the Ratkid (Oatsuræ Jirokichi goshi,* 1931), together with Buntaro Futagawa's *The Outlaw (Orochi,* 1925) and Tsuruhiko Tanaka's *The Red Bat (Beni Komori,* 1931).[8] All these films can be considered as part of the Ito school, through their increased physicality of performance combined with dynamic camerawork and editing during combat sequences. Most interestingly, a comparison of *The Outlaw* and *Jirokichi* suggests the kind of innovations Ito introduced. *The Outlaw,* in contemporary terms, is a far more experimental film. The climatic fight scene at the end of the film is represented through a series of stylized combat tableaux directly transposed from Kabuki: The central character is tied in by police ropes drawn across the screen like a spider's web, and a close-up presents his face in cross-eyed anguish as if in a Sharaku *ukiyo-e* (Edo-era woodblock print) portrait of a Kabuki actor. Intercut with this, the film rapidly jumps across static compositions of the surrounding police in a machine-gun rhythm of stacatto Soviet-style montage. Accordingly, *The Outlaw* follows a paradoxical pattern of inversions where Western modernism and Japanese traditional aesthetics seem to coincide, as I have discussed elsewhere.[9] In contrast, Ito's own film *Jirokichi* radically eliminates both such theatrical effects and disjunctive montage, substituting a dynamic style of physical performance and cutting on action to center attention on character within narrative continuity. Yet even in *Jirokichi,* as Burch has noted of Ito's style as perpetuated in *The Red Bat,* visual stylization exceeds Western continuity norms. Rapid swish pans (e.g., between two men at a tense moment) interrupt Western conventions of narrative action but in Ito seem designed to intensify viewer involvement with screen action.

It is perhaps impossible to reconstruct with any historical certainty how the *benshi* (or *katsuben,* as *benshi* for cinema were called) interacted with specific films. However, if Shunsui Matsuda's *benshi* performances on the soundtracks that now accompany both *The Outlaw* and *Jirokichi* are any evidence, then *benshi* performance may also have been modified in relation to shifts of visual style. In Matsuda's *The Outlaw,* the *benshi's* voice frequently interrupts the action, as for example to introduce each new character who appears on screen. This produces an unintentional Brechtian effect of distancing the viewer from total identification with the action. In contrast, in Matsuda's *Jirokichi,* the *benshi* narration conforms far more precisely to the outlines of the action visualized on screen, again inviting a more direct identification with the central character within narrative continuity. If this is not simply coincidence, the difference is highly suggestive of possible innovations within the mixed textual construction of *katsuben* performance.

Accordingly, such tropes as national xenophobic isolation, a name change masking violence, the transposition of the *onnagatta* role within cinematic realism, and sword fights against social oppression all extend past Ichikawa's film text into its social and historical context. Ichikawa's easy mixture of realist and antirealist devices recalls and transforms the discordant styles within a text that characterized early Japanese cinema. Of course, one could object that any Japanese film could be traced to its origins in early cinema, but such an objection would miss the point. Ichikawa's *An Actor's Revenge,* through its concatenation of specific and highly charged intertextual citations, invites consideration of the cultural and cross-cultural contexts in which narratives are produced. These contexts are situated at the intersection of Japanese traditional theater and Western cinematic realism, and are addressed in *An Actor's Revenge* by a rereading of melodrama.

Melodrama as avant-garde

In the histories of Japanese cinema available in English, melodrama is usually treated briefly. The predominant view is that melodrama can be equated with Shimpa, or "New School Theater," the form of Japanese theater characteristic of the Meiji era. Shimpa originated in the 1890s and maintained a dominant popularity from about 1900 to the mid–1920s, and was the primary source both of cinematic style and of film actors and directors during the early period. Shingeki, or "Modern Theater," thereafter displaced Shimpa as a primary cultural influence, beginning with experiments in theater in 1909 and becoming dominant in cinema by the 1930s.

Opinion has then often diverged in ways that leave Shimpa equally marginalized. Most often, Shimpa has been dismissed by both Japanese and American writers as a transitional, "half-modern" movement, not yet sufficiently realist to sustain audience attention as a fully adequate representation of the modern age. Tadao Sato, for example, argues that its character types were drawn from Kabuki and dismisses its "antiquated forms" once Shingeki appears.[10] Donald Richie refers to Shimpa as "almost instantly fossilized" and again contrasts it to a Shingeki-influenced cinema that seems obviously superior because "Shingeki at least concerned itself with a kind of reality."[11] Faubion Bowers, in his classic postwar text on Japanese theater, dismissed early Shimpa as silly and insignificant melodrama and again reserves praise for the "serious" theater with realism that followed.[12] Alternatively, Burch praises Shimpa, but as a form of resistance to Western models of narrative form that preserved elements of traditional Japanese theater. Burch argues that the originators and practitioners of Shimpa knew little or nothing about the Western models they were supposedly emulating and, as a result, unavoidably recapitulated the traditions they sought to abandon.[13] The difficulty with either of these positions is that neither examines Shimpa on its own terms. Both instead immediately slide past Shimpa to another form privileged as "serious" in its influence on cinema, regardless of whether realism or an antirealist reading of Kabuki is so privileged.

Yet Shimpa, even when it is described by its detractors, is clearly an energized intersection of conflicting forms, an unstable and multiple movement that functioned as a pivot between traditional Japan and the modernized West. Shimpa directly derives from the "Political Dramas" (*soshi geki*) originated by the Liberal Group in 1888 to promote the polic ʾs and platforms at stake once the Meiji constitution would be put into effect in 1890. Yet Shimpa is also clearly related to efforts made to reform Kabuki, to imports of Western plays, and to contradictions between Western and Kabuki norms of representation. In Kabuki, Danjuro IX's nationalistic "Plays of Living History" (beginning in 1878) and Kikugoro V's "Cropped Hair Plays" (beginning in 1879) both radically broke with the prescriptive stylization of Kabuki that characterized the late Tokugawa period. Danjuro sought to eliminate the inconsistencies of traditional Kabuki texts and rewrite them as unified nationalistic propaganda based on historical research. Kikugoro first adapted a Western play into Japanese and staged performances in contemporary dress; cropped hair indicated the recent abolition of feudal social distinctions and the hairstyles that had signified them. Both Danjuro and Kikugoro adapted Western models of narrative construction (history, theater) to promote the social and political agendas of modernization, yet pursued these representational goals within the framework of Kabuki.[14] As a consequence, both produced performances that mixed styles as freely as Shimpa.

Shimpa as a term first refers to the work of Kawakami Otojiro, beginning in 1891 with his elimination of overt political material from the "Political Dramas" he had been writing. Enough legends surround this "sensational charlatan," who is acknowledged as the "father of modern drama in Japan," that he seems like a Meiji version of O-Kuni, the woman whose dance in the bed of the Kamo River supposedly created Kabuki. One narrative claims that an audience member once murdered one of Otojiro's fictional villains, because he was supposedly unable to distinguish art and life even in the initial stages of realist aesthetics.[15] (Godard restages a similar story in *Les Carabiniers* about the confusion of art and life for viewers of early cinema.) Another narrative claims that Otojiro, after touring Europe and America with Shimpa, returned to Japan in 1902 to stage a version of *Hamlet* in which the central character entered on a bicycle.[16] This particular story (also appreciated by Burch) joins Shakespeare with a signifier of the European avant-garde, because the bicycle was in the late nineteenth century the principal emblem of the modern among Bohemians.[17] European tradition appears avant-garde in Japan, in a mirror reversal of the paradoxical link of Japanese tradition and Western modernism noted in *The Outlaw*.[18] In his work on the *Origins of Modern Japanese Literature*, Kojin Karatani also notes that the onset of the modern period in Japan is characterized by a series of such inversions.[19]

Shimpa after 1895 was capable of mixing forms of representation in a way that can perhaps only be appreciated in the West after the postmodernist reevaluation of pastiche and contradictory styles within the same work. Both men and women appeared on stage at the same time in female roles,[20] a circumstance often criticized as partially regressive or progressive but not appreciated as a meaningful contradiction in itself that usefully problematizes representation. Shimpa also first combined film with live performance in "chain-drama" (*rensa-geki*), as early as 1904 and as late as 1922, with significant popularity beginning in 1908.[21] In this mode of representation, exterior scenes were shot on film and alternated on stage with live performances for interiors. In its capacity for such innovative mixed forms, what is called melodrama or Shimpa in Japan ironically seems to share certain features with what in Europe is called avant-garde: a passion for the politics of representation, a distancing from total identification with any single system of meaning, and a disruption of the ontology and epistemology of the image.

Shimpa, it could be argued, was a volatile generator of tropes that first marked the collision of Japan and the West. As such, this marginalized form functioned to help produce the determining tropes that served to orient Japan's entry into the modern period, and which are later repressed in dominant forms of representation from the 1930s on. Ichikawa's *An Actor's Revenge* redirects our attention to what is called Japanese melodrama, through a text informed by a complex intertextual understanding of melodrama's multiple determinants. The determining tropes of Shimpa then begin to self-destruct through representational contradictions made apparent by their recontextualization in an era of dominant cinematic realism. The film reinstates the representational indeterminacy of the period when Shimpa was dominant, and signification had not yet become comfortably polarized into the mythologized terms of tradition and realism.

In *An Actor's Revenge,* melodrama appears as a boundary site between Kabuki and cinematic realism. Through an inversion, by which melodrama is reprioritized long after it had been conceived as superceded by realism, the style is made to comment on the logocentric assumption that realism is central. In part, the film recalls the historical origins of realism for Japan in a mode of excess, undermining realism's pretensions to an origin in an objective, mute nature. *An Actor's Revenge* retells a melodramatic story of love and vengeance by freely mixing realist and antirealist devices and, by so doing, suggests that a totalized illusion of realism depends on a denial of sexual difference and of class violence. Through a strategy of excess, realism is seen as grounded in a desire for power over the other, both ideologically and sexually.

On the other hand, Ichikawa's reinscription of melodrama also relocates Kabuki as a necessarily complementary mode of excess. By 1912, Nikkatsu had divided its production into Shimpa ("New School"), which signified the production of dramas in contemporary settings at its Tokyo studio, in contrast to Kyuha ("Old School"), the period dramas produced at Kyoto.[22] From the historical break that marked the emergence of Japanese melodrama, Shimpa and Kabuki reinvented one another, each in a way that mixed traditional–modern and Japanese –Western values. As a result, neither Kabuki nor Shimpa is the Tokugawa theater or European melodrama it may at first appear to be. At Nikkatsu, Shimpa worked to redefine the parameters of period drama, not as a tableau transposition of Kabuki, but as a domain in which a middle-class Meiji personality-type confronted tradition. At the same time, Shimpa preserved the character stereotypes of Kabuki, producing a specifically Japanese version of melodrama. As described by Sato, these types are the *tateyaku* ("standing role"), the *nimaeme* ("second"), and the *onnagatta*. The *tateyaku* is the male lead of the Kabuki troupe, who represents the idealized *bushido* samurai and never places romantic love or family interests above his loyalty to the feudal lord. The *nimaeme*, in contrast, were weak men who fell in love with geisha or prostitutes and preferred to commit suicide with them rather than subordinate emotional intimacy to *bushido*. The *onnagatta* played all female roles, but especially the idealized woman whose virtue is demonstrated by the degree of sacrifice she endures. Sato argues that these values contrast sharply with feudal ideology in the West, in which warrior virtue is identified with romantic idealism. In Shimpa excess functions to reinforce polarized values of good and evil, as in Western melodrama, but the ideological terms so valorized are quite different.

Kabuki was itself often a form of social protest against a corrupt Tokugawa regime. Sato relates the Kabuki male-character split to the difference between samurai tradition and the emerging merchant class during the Tokugawa period, with their respectively different attitudes about the role of women. Ito's active translation of such protest elements into left-wing *chambara* films reinscribed Shimpa melodrama as a critique of emerging Japanese capitalism, constructing a parallel style from different sources to the Western melodrama that had emerged in the West during the capitalist development of industrialization. In Ito's reweaving of the multiple determinants that characterize a specifically Japanese mode of melodrama, the *tateyaku* becomes the vehicle for an Old Left trope of heroic socialism. The ironies of this formation become especially obvious once feminism emerges as a component of social critique.

Kinugasa's mid-1930s *chambara* is more ambiguous: Although his narrative's representation of a corrupt elite might suggest an extension of Ito's critique to the militarists by then in power, Yukinojo's dedication to his vengeance also suggests an ethical purity valorized by Japanese fascism. Given the intensifying repression of dissent during the 1930s, Kinugasa's text hides behind a double reading: The corrupt elite could just as easily be read as the dominant Westernized class that revolutionary fascism considered itself to be fighting against. Ichikawa's satirical quotation of the trope of a corrupt dominant class after the Occupation recalls both Ito's and Kinugasa's prior usages. Early *chambara's* anticapitalist protest is recalled in the context of renewed post-Occupation capitalist development, but so are the ambiguous consequences of such protest during the militarist period and the Occupation.

By satirical displacement, Ichikawa does not so much negate the social critique of *chambara* as turn our attention elsewhere. The film problematizes an identification of social activism with an unconsidered conjuncture of *tateyaku* and a realist aesthetic. As such, a principal target of the film's critique becomes the samurai humanism of postwar period films by Kurosawa and others, including such "masterpieces" celebrated in the West as *Seven Samurai* (*Shichinin no Samurai*, 1954). Although Richie has argued that Mifune is "definitely a post-war type," Sato argues that Kurosawa's casting of Toshiro Mifune is a classic example of the *tateyaku* role.[23] Yet, Mifune's role in *Seven Samurai*, as has often been noted, is to defend the peasants rather than exploit them. Kurosawa's samurai tend to revive early *chambara's* reinscription of *tateyaku* as socialist protest, but shift the politics by developing the character of individual samurai. The *tateyaku* role is reinscribed once again to suggest humanist individualism, but still within the value system of Japanese melodrama, the traces of which remain in Japanese cinema long after the surface style of exaggerated action has disappeared. In *Seven Samurai*, the enemy has also been recast from an oppressive dominant class to the chaos of uncontrolled criminals, a shift that ironically returns the samurai to a position of legitimate, if temporary, authority over the peasants who mistrust them. Ichikawa's Yukinojo in part satirizes this recuperation of democratic activism (whether socialist or humanist) by the unavoidably rigid hierarchies of feudal heroics condensed within the figure of the *tateyaku*. Equally important, his film undermines the embedding of this contradictory figure within the naturalizing form of a totalized realism.

In Ichikawa's *An Actor's Revenge*, the "truth" of both social oppression (Yukinojo's reenactment of his father's ghost to confront his enemies) and of sexual difference (Yukinojo's theatrical construction of sexual identity juxtaposed with Namiji as voyeuristic object) is represented as a confrontation of the theatrical against a dominant realism. The most significant danger is the violence of representations embedded in ideological rigidity, and the effective response is not vengeance but *jouissance*, a play of forms. If the characteristic activity of *chambara* from Ito through Mifune is to valorize a negational rage against social oppression, then the figure of Yukinojo works to undermine the categorical absolutism enforced by negation. Through its parody of the Hasegawa type of social protest, *tateyaku*, Ichikawa's melodrama works to reverse the tendency toward representational identification with totalitarian control that has characterized both the left under Stalinism and the humanism of corporate hierarchization. In contrast to the similar concerns of Oshima's *Night and Fog in Japan* (*Nihon no Yoru to Kiri*, 1960), Ichikawa further plays with the problem of how to reinscribe violence into a positive project of textual pleasure that unlocks the anxious isolation of the subject.

Gender indeterminacy

The parody of Yukinojo functions as a playful critique of what Lacan would call the paranoid construction of the cogito, and its dependence on a categorically objectified other to defend itself against anxiety. Nowhere is this parody more fully developed in *An Actor's Revenge* than in the treatment of gender. The juxtaposition of *onnagatta* and actress in a love scene generates contradictory tensions that cannot be resolved within any expectation of a unified text. This juxtaposition recalls the same mix of performers of female roles in Shimpa, at the "origins" of "modern cinema," but here recedes into an indeterminacy that cannot be contained by an imaginary progress toward one representation or the other.

This destabilization rests on the simple device of sustaining the images of both *onnagatta* and actress within the conventions of a love scene characteristic of realist continuity, inviting the same emotional transference and identification with character that classic cinema constructs. As a result, the viewing subject is placed in an untenable position. It is not just that identification is undermined by transgressive sexual implications, but that those implications become undecidable. If the images of what appear to be two women together suggest a lesbian relationship, then an eroticized image of an *onnagatta* as a male offstage also shifts the appearance of female costume toward transvestism. Is the woman a voyeuristic object of male desire mirrored back by the man's cross-dressing? Or the man an image of the woman's narcissistic desire for a weak *namaeme*, literalized in the form of emasculation? The effect of receding mirrors earlier observed both textually and intertextually is here reinscribed at the position of emotional identification to trouble the formation of the subject.

One might object that such tensions are a mirage created by seeing the film out of context, that *onnagatta* are completely conventional in Japanese tradition, and that only Westerners would imagine sexual complexity by misreading an *onnagatta* as if he were a transvestite. Yet this objection overlooks the 1958 passage of the antiprostitution law in Japan, a law designed to bring Japanese sexual practices into conformity with the appearances demanded by the West. It also overlooks Ichikawa's many previous films such as *Conflagration, Odd Obsession* (*Kagi*, 1959), *Bonchi*, and *The Outcast*, which specifically represent a neurotic or perverse psychology in a Japanese context, some adapted from novels by Tanizaki and Mishima, which themselves are psychoanalytically informed. Since the Meiji period, numerous translations of Western texts (both books and films) have circulated in Japan, often the same texts through which Westerners develop their own unconscious assumptions or reading formations through which they interpret the world. Unavoidably, many Japanese have become well aware of how Westerners are likely to view certain things and have often incorporated Western discursive formations into their own work. Tanizaki and Mishima are but two examples. Wim Wenders's nostalgia in *Tokyo-ga* for an imaginary Ozu-style Japan to the contrary, no pure Japan has ever existed. This fantasy is of recent invention and is inextricably linked in Japan with a xenophobic and authoritarian right wing seeking justification for an imaginary cultural superiority over Japan's Asian neighbors and the West. In the United States, a fantasy of an innate Japanese difference is linked with a similar narcissism, one that imagines that only ignorance of Western formations of knowledge and power would explain any limit to American cultural totalization.

Cultural difference remains but not through ignorance of the West. Multiple determinants always affect the complex intertextual formations we call culture, never any single source. Accordingly, as *An Actor's Revenge* seems to demonstrate so well, texts that invite multiple and even contradictory readings can be constructed. The process of cross-cultural translation is unavoidable, and the film functioned from the outset in both Japanese and Western readings, a doubling that contributes to its effect of receding mirrors.

For Lacan, of course, mirror identifications are a mark of the mirror stage and its unavoidable component of undifferentiated aggressivity.[24] Lacan argues that during the period when a child first identifies the image in the mirror as a signifier of the self, that image is still relatively undifferentiated and remains transferrable among other children. This phenomenon, which he terms a transitive relationship, means that children at this stage are unable to conceptually distinguish between others and themselves. Transitivism leads to both the spontaneous identification of children with one another and, simultaneously, to intense unresolvable disputes whenever desires come into conflict, because the child has no conceptual apparatus to distinguish intersubjective difference clearly. For Lacan, this apparatus requires the locating of the self in language, a project accomplished through gender differentiation. Accordingly, Lacan warns against appeals to emotional identification, often produced in the name of "humanism," as a means of resolving conflict.

In these terms, the undecidability of gender relationship in the *on-*

nagatta–actress love scenes becomes a mark of its cinematic "language," and its displacement of fetishized love object toward a representation of jouissance. Located at the site of narrative and visual mirroring, *onnagatta* and actress become interchangeable or transitive. The classic realist camera image that constitutes woman as the object of the gaze is equated with the theatrical construction of the idealized female object by the male. In other words, the realist image that embeds woman in a naturalized objectification is itself seen as a mask, and the "truth" of the realist image is recast as a mask of power.

The formation of the body in representation becomes a contested terrain through the sexually ambiguous figure of Yukinojo, so that mastery of the other by reduction to a unitary object becomes impossible. Reciprocally, the plural representation of gender raises the questions of authorship and authority in textual construction. Ichikawa has never been identified with the single set of concerns classically used to identify the body of work belonging to an auteur. Instead, his work has been remarkably diverse and open to a play of contradictory forms, similarly impossible to master by reduction to a unitary object.

In Yukinojo, the body becomes a scene of teaching, in the sense in which Gregory Ulmer refers to Lacan's seminars as a combination of the psychoanalytic scene and pedagogy. However, here the disciplinary boundaries that frame the possibility of the subject are themselves called into question.

Notes

1. Donald Richie, *Japanese Cinema* (Garden City, N.Y.: Doubleday, 1971), p. 191.
2. See Peter Brooks, *The Melodramatic Imagination: Balzac, Henry James, Melodrama, and the Mode of Excess* (New Haven: Yale University Press, 1976).
3. Richie, *Japanese Cinema*, pp. 190–1.
4. Joseph L. Anderson and Donald Richie, *The Japanese Film: Art and Industry* (Princeton: Princeton University Press, 1982), pp. 86–7.
5. Regarding the scarcity of surviving materials from this era, see Noel Burch, *To the Distant Observer: Form and Meaning in the Japanese Cinema* (Berkeley: University of California Press, 1979), p. 111.
6. Anderson and Richie, *Japanese Film*, p. 39.
7. See James Peterson, "A War of Utter Rebellion: Kinugasa's *Page of Madness* and the Japanese Avant-Garde of the 1920's," *Cinema Journal* (forthcoming), and Burch, *Distant Observer*, pp. 123–39. Peterson argues that Kinugasa was a modernist, while Burch sees him as a traditionalist.
8. See also Burch, *Distant Observer*, pp. 110–16. In his discussion of Ito, Burch provides a formalist critique of *The Red Bat*, the only film from this school he had been able to see. He does not, however, discuss the influence of

socialism on *chambara,* and instead sees the form as an expression of a dominant class. I am indebted to Larry Greenberg of Matsuda Films and Kyoko Hirano of the Japan Society for their assistance in permitting me to see *Orochi* and *Jirokichi,* and to Akira Shimizu of the Japan Film Library Council and the Film Center of the National Museum of Modern Art in Tokyo for enabling me to see *The Red Bat.*

9. Scott Nygren, "Reconsidering Modernism: Japanese Film and the Postmodern Context," *Wide Angle* 11, 3 (July 1989).

10. Tadao Sato, *Currents in Japanese Cinema,* trans. Gregory Barrett (Tokyo: Kodansha International, 1982), p. 20.

11. Richie, *Japanese Cinema,* pp. 7–8.

12. Faubion Bowers, *Japanese Theater* (Rutland, Vt.: Charles E. Tuttle, 1952; 4th ed., 1982), pp. 208–12.

13. Burch, *Distant Observer,* pp. 59–60.

14. Bowers, *Japanese Theatre,* pp. 201–8.

15. Ibid., pp. 208–11.

16. Ibid., p. 210. See also Burch, *Distant Observer,* pp. 59–60.

17. Roger Shattuck, *The Banquet Years* (London: Cape, 1969).

18. Nygren, "Reconsidering Modernism."

19. See Brett DeBary, "Karatani Kojin's *Origins of Modern Japanese Literature,*" and Kojin Karatani, "One Spirit, Two Nineteenth Centuries," *South Atlantic Quarterly* 87, 3 (Summer 1988): 591–628.

20. Bowers, *Japanese Theater,* p. 212.

21. Anderson and Richie, *Japanese Film,* pp. 27–8.

22. Ibid., p. 31.

23. Ibid., p. 403; Sato, *Japanese Cinema,* p. 19.

24. Jacques Lacan, "Aggressivity in Psychoanalysis," in *Écrits,* trans. Alan Sheridan (New York: Norton, 1977), pp. 8–29; selected from *Écrits* (Paris: Éditions du Seuil, 1966).

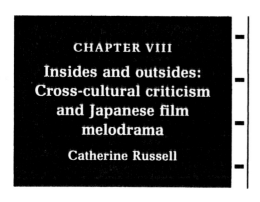

CHAPTER VIII

**Insides and outsides:
Cross-cultural criticism
and Japanese film
melodrama**

Catherine Russell

Japanese cinema presents a number of difficulties to a discipline of theory and criticism that has been developed in the West. While it is important not to apply inappropriate concepts to Japanese culture, it is equally dangerous to essentialize this national cinema as if it were immune to Western influence. Once we get beyond the exoticism of Orientalist critical discourse and anchor Japanese film in sociohistorical terms, we are in the domain of ethnography.[1] What I would like to suggest here, by way of the melodramas of Ozu and Mizoguchi, is that Japanese ethnography has a specific ideological cast, and that national identity in Japan has a particularly melodramatic structure.

Much has been written about the mistakes made by a number of Western critics in construing Japanese formalism as radical modernism.[2] Melodrama, unlike modernism, has deep roots in Japanese cultural history and might even be said to dominate Japanese cinema as a kind of metagenre to the same extent that it informs North American narrative film.[3] In fact, emotional intensity is a key attribute of the so-called Japanese "character." If a Western critic such as Ian Buruma can say that "every Japanese is equipped with a non-verbal emotional transmitter which functions only with other Japanese,"[4] then an examination of the discourse of melodrama in Japan should shed some light on the representation of Japaneseness in the cinema.

Let me suggest, first of all, the degree to which theories of American melodrama "fit" the Japanese form, and the point at which they diverge. The dominant theorization of *Hollywood* melodrama is based on a Freudian model of desire and repression.[5] The "too much" of everything that characterizes the melodramatic form is a "victory over repression," not through narrative but form,[6] and melodrama is redeemed from the trash bin of sentimentality by virtue of its modernist traits of anti-illusionism. The social forces responsible for the plight of melodramatic protagonists are contaminated by way of a challenge to realist representation; the intensity of suffering exceeds the codes of realism as well as the limits of the visible and the knowable.

143

Peter Brooks claims that Western melodrama dates from the French Revolution and is closely tied to the rise of the bourgeois class. With the legislation of the law of virtue, the Manichaean polarities of good and evil were secularized and given the social form of antiaristocratic rebellion,[7] which was eventually reified in the form of nineteenth-century opera.[8] This theory of melodrama does not claim that all melodrama realizes its radical potential but tends to imply a theory of writerly texts and radical readership. The symptoms of Hollywood melodrama are the symptoms of social contradictions and the genre becomes, effectively, a psychoanalysis of the culture in which it is produced.[9] Western melodrama is an expression of latency and interiority, an eruption that takes place on the surface of discourse which points in its very excessiveness to something that escapes representation.

Japanese melodrama seems also to emerge with the rise of the bourgeoisie in the Tokugawa period. The *bunraku* puppet plays and Kabuki plays of Chikamatsu Monzaemon (1653–1725) are not usually described as melodrama, probably because of the discredit the label tends to bear, and yet these are narratives of great emotional intensity, heightened by music, gesture and mise-en-scène.[10] In fact two central melodramatic strategies that Peter Brooks dwells on, the "aesthetics of astonishment" and "the text of muteness," are exemplified in Kabuki and *bunraku*, respectively.

It is Roland Barthes who first alerts us to the difficulties in transposing a Western conception of melodrama to the Japanese context. In his discussion of *bunraku*, he claims that "excess is given only within the very code of excess...the signifier cunningly does nothing but turn itself inside out, like a glove."[11] If in fact there is "no depth" as Barthes suggests in *Empire of Signs*, "nothing to grasp" behind Japanese signifiers; if all Japanese texts are as empty as he claims, then perhaps all Western readings of Japan are misreadings. Maybe we cannot forget our metaphysics and read Japanese culture in its own terms. Does this mean we should give up and go home and resume our stance of "we are the world"?

On the other hand, perhaps Japan is a culture of *experience* rather than reading, and perhaps the void against which its signifiers are produced has dimensions that are unknown beyond that experience of being Japanese. This indeed, seems to me to be the central dynamic of Japanese melodrama; the unspeakable realm of desire is an emotionally charged expression of national identity that escapes realist modes of representation and is displaced into a discourse of excess. And it is precisely the failure of the outsider, the non-Japanese, to understand Japan that maintains these dynamics. Barthes concludes his analysis of *bunraku* with the observation that Westerners cannot understand it because for us "to attack meaning is to hide or invert it but never to 'absent' it. . . . What is expelled from the [Japanese] stage is hysteria." In the presence of the puppet manipulators on stage "work is substituted for inwardness . . . the *inside* no longer commands the *outside*."[12]

To some extent this is in keeping with Brooks's theory of melodrama, which does aspire to an aesthetics of form and textuality, but it is crucial that Western melodrama postulates "a signified in excess of the possibilities of the signifier."[13] Claims on meaning from the psychological interior of Western melodrama are unsubstantial but "large," whereas Barthes's version of Japanese melodrama negates the very possibility of a signified; the only claim on meaning is meaninglessness. By restricting his analysis of Japanese representational praxis to "traditional" forms, Barthes evades the problem of their transformation in the twentieth century. How "meaning" can be exempted from cinematic representation, which "signifies" on so many (indexical, symbolic, and iconic) levels, and how Japanese cinema might retain its Japaneseness despite this, are questions that lie beyond the limits of Barthes's "Japan."

Barthes's interpretation of the Japanese signifier informs Noel Burch's account of Japanese cinema. It is the essential Japaneseness of directors Ozu and Mizoguchi that make them so different from Hollywood, and from the perspective of Brechtian modernism, therefore antibourgeois and politically "progressive."[14] Burch's appreciation of the discursive qualities of Japanese formalism, its systematic departure from Western codes of realism, leads him to the rather contradictory conclusion that the high point of this radical Japanese cinema was precisely in the wartime production of imperialist propaganda. Both Ozu and Mizoguchi contributed to this militarist program, and few would deny that the war years did see a refinement of the traditionalist elements and their characteristic styles.

Although both Ozu and Mizoguchi have been recognized as melodramatists, this aspect of their work has tended to be sublimated by modernist aesthetics.[15] D. William Davis has described Mizoguchi's and Ozu's wartime films, among others in the 1930s and 1940s, as actually subverting the militarist ideology that commissioned a revival of traditional Japanese style, insofar as the style "takes on a life of its own." His analysis of these films concentrates precisely on the *excess* of spectacle: "violent hysteria" and sweeping scenic long takes in the case of Mizoguchi and Ozu's "excessive" rigor and emphasis on patriarchy.[16] These melodramatic strategies are symptomatic of a politics of representation in which emotional expression pushes the limits of discourse beyond the representable. Analysis of the melodramatic dimension of Mizoguchi's and Ozu's characteristic narrative styles suggests that it is precisely essential Japaneseness that struggles within the realist representation of narrative cinema. The "unspeakable," or

more precisely, "unseeable" interiority of classical Japanese film melodrama may best be characterized as an ethnographic realm of desire.

Mizoguchi's melodrama, first of all, raises a key question about the
Japanese *feminisuto* tradition. Sato Tadao sums up the attitude that
informs Mizoguchi's depiction of women's oppression:

The image of a woman suffering uncomplainingly can imbue us with admiration for a virtuous existence almost beyond our reach, rich in endurance and
courage. One can idealize her rather than merely pity her, and this can lead to
what I call the worship of womanhood, a special Japanese brand of feminism.[17]

Images such as Miyagi in *Ugetsu Monogatari,* the Kinuyo Tanaka
characters in *My Love Burns* and *Sansho the Bailiff,* Osan in *The Crucified Lovers,* and Oharu and Princess Yang Kwei Fei in the films
named after them, are powerful enough, according to Sato, to stand as
an indictment against oppression by the whole male sex.[18] Joan Mellen
endorses this view in her discussion of Mizoguchi, whose heroines she
sees as rebelling against their prescribed social roles and challenging
the norms of feudal patriarchy. The fact that they usually end up sacrificing themselves on the altar of this just cause is simply "the price to
pay for spiritual transcendence. It has awaited all revolutionaries."[19]

Mizoguchi's heroines die for making a choice, a "choice" informed
by the Japanese version of a melodramatic "moral occult":[20] *giri* and
ninjo.[21] These terms embody a range of polarities, but they refer most
immediately to the contradiction between obligations to society – including one's family, village, class, trade, or business (*giri*) – and individual human feelings (*ninjo*). Interdependent, symbiotic moral
principles of exteriority and interiority,[22] *giri* and *ninjo,* sometimes interpreted as restraint and emotion, are forever at war within the Japanese melodramatic psyche, and it is only in death that the struggle
can be overcome. In Mizoguchi's narratives, as in Chikamatsu's, it is
above all a balance between these two principles that is desired and
attained. *Ninjo* for Mizoguchi, is closely tied to woman's desire, but it
is neither suppressed by nor triumphant over *giri.* As Sato suggests, it
is a desire for virtue rather than expression; and it is characterized by
endurance and lack of complaining, hardly revolutionary principles of
either political resistance or feminism.

The excesses of Mizoguchi's stylistics – in particular his use of indigenous music, sudden eruptions of violence, elaborate decor, mediating foreground objects, and tableaux of suffering females – do
point to an absent signified, but it belongs less to the character's desire than the spectator's desire for spectacle. As Osan passes a crowd
on the way to her death at the end of *The Crucified Lovers,* one peas-

ant whispers to another that she looks more beautiful and happy than ever. The perfect balance between *giri* and *ninjo* has the effect of emptying the violence of its potentiality.

Moreover, the *feminisuto* tradition is indicative of the fundamental role of the mother in Japanese culture and psychoanalysis. Despite the distinctly patriarchal shape of the emperor system, it is the mother who secures the Japaneseness of the Japanese family. In his central text on Japanese psychoanalysis, *The Anatomy of Dependence,* Doi Takeo describes the infant's preoedipal relation to the mother as the determining structure "not only of the psychological makeup of the individual Japanese but of the structure of Japanese society as a whole." It seems to be generally accepted that Japanese men appreciate maternal characteristics in women so that they can recover an infantile relationship of dependency and indulgence, an attitude called *amae,* with their wives. Furthermore, the suggestion that the Japanese psyche deemphasizes the individualizing mechanism of the oedipal complex explains the so-called Japanese group mentality. Doi explains that

the Japanese term *uchi* (inside) as used in words such as *miuchi* (family circle) or *nakamauchi* (circle of friends or colleagues) refers mainly to the group to which the individual belongs and not, as with English terms such as "private," to the individual himself. In Japan, little value is attributed to the individual's private realm as distinct from the group.[23]

Outside this inner circle, which of course can be ideologically extended to include the family of Japan, are foreigners, epitomized in classical times by the Chinese and in modern times both by "the West" and by racially inferior Asians.

While Doi's theory has obvious explanatory power that makes it especially attractive to Western scholars of Japanese culture,[24] we should be prepared to treat Doi as we now read Freud, as symptomatic of the culture he attempts to explain. If Peter Brooks can describe Freudian theory as melodramatic in structure, positing a repressed interiority that struggles, through the discourse of analysis, to emerge from the dream work and the repression imposed by the family structure,[25] the same can be said of Doi's version of Freud, with the important difference that it is Japanese identity rather than personal identity that is the privileged category. The egolessness of Doi's Japanese subject is more than compensated for by the ethnocentricity of the "Japanese character" in his theory.

Equally important is a recognition that his analysis is actually drawn from the uniqueness of the Japanese language, where he discovers the central untranslatable term *amae.* Refering in Japanese to the relationship of dependency and indulgence originally experienced with the mother and maintained in adult relationships of intimacy, the word has no English referent, which is precisely what makes it so important to Japanese psychoanalysis. Furthermore, the balancing of *giri* and *ninjo* is a representation of *amae*, but *ninjo*, the category of emotion, is for Doi the privileged literary expression of *amae*, which he justifies again by the suggestion that it is incomprehensible to the non-Japanese.[26]

Doi's theory is in fact a constitutive feature of *nihonjinron*, or the interdisciplinary Japanese study of Japanese identity, which historically runs parallel to Western modernism. H. D. Harootunian, in a book suggestively titled *Things Seen and Unseen*, historicizes *nihonjinron* as a decadent form of *kokugaku* or the discourse of Japanese nativism that began to be written in the Tokugawa period. Emerging with the rise of the bourgeoisie, it was, like Western melodrama, originally a radical narrative, challenging "the entrenched domination of Chinese culture in Japanese life," which the ruling Edo oligarchy manipulated as an instrument of power. *Kokugaku* involved the "elimination of culture itself as a category," and the terms of being Japanese were derived from experience. Harootunian sums up the nativist strategy as the following:

Nativism, in its Tokugawa incarnation, rescued daily life, custom, and "household duties" – the alterity of an official discourse that privileged mental over manual labour – and converted them into the content of discursive knowledge. ... This new form of knowledge presupposed closing all distances between subject and object.... No difference was supposed to intervene between what humans did and made and what they could possibly know; practice and hermeneutics became the same thing.[27]

The collapse of signification noted by Barthes was, according to Harootunian, the result of the nativist determination to restrict knowledge to "things seen and heard" in order to counter the cultural authority of the Tokugawa social hierarchy. "The way to reunite mental and manual labour was to return to the identity of speech and work as activities centered in the body" (p. 74). The language of work, worship, and the body (e.g., bowing) becomes a discourse with more profundity, veracity, and emotion than that of textuality or performance, modes of expression that came to be known as "deceptive." An example of this valorization of transparency might be the peasants' pot making in Mizoguchi's *Ugetsu Monogatari*, which is represented as a more "sincere" craft than the classical arts associated with the aristocratic Lady Wakasa. In 1952 Japan, *kokugaku* is for Mizoguchi a nonimperialist, pacifist mode of traditionalism through which "Japaneseness" might be resurrected after its censorship during the Occupation period.

The ideology of *kokugaku* was institutionalized as a form of nationalism with modernization. During the Meiji period cultural praxis, far from being banished, came to supersede political praxis in the formation of a hegemonic order of cultural identity. While the nativist theorists of *kokugaku* insisted on a transparency of language in which nothing would be hidden, an inside–outside discursive paradigm developed with the Meiji restoration in which *kokugaku* itself became the repressed content of representation. Barthes's identification of the "exemption of meaning" with the impenetrability of Japanese culture is consistent with *nihonjinron* ideology, which depends on a cultural "outside" for its definition of Japanese specificity. That this inside–outside paradigm has melodramatic contours is suggested by Doi Takeo, for whom "desire" in the Japanese psyche is a desire to move "inside" the divisibility of subject and object, self and others, to lose oneself in another person.

The goal of egolessness, associated with Zen aesthetics, becomes melodramatic when it is narrativized within a discourse of history. Harootunian argues that whereas the "Other" of Western ideology refers to the irrational, inferior, and Oriental, the Japanese Other is "the repressed alterity of a more authentic life that had existed prior to the imperative of Western rationality."[28] Whereas the primary category of otherness in Tokugawa nativism was "the ancients," the pre-Chinese ancestry, in *nihonjinron* it is the rural peasantry. When the identity of "the ordinary and abiding people," the folk of Japan, was fixed in the early twentieth century as the privileged subject of *kokugaku*, the zen of daily life became linked to a pastoral nationhood. In the context of a rapidly industrializing and urbanizing Japan, the rural "folk" were made invisible and the discourse became one of "incurable nostalgia."

This observation is eminently applicable to the director who has been described as "the most Japanese" of Japanese directors, Ozu Yasujiro. A number of critics have described Ozu as a zen master of the cinema, deploying traditionalism both narratively and stylistically as a spiritual transcendence of industrialized Japan.[29] The traditional Japanese aesthetic of *mono no aware* that informs Ozu's films, the "sympathetic sadness" of the transience of life, is contingent upon the emotional union of ego with nature.[30] David Bordwell, eschewing the "essentially Japanese" argument altogether and situating the films in a more sociohistorical context, explains Ozu's theme of transience as a repeated depiction of the "broken promises of Meiji." Although many younger Japanese filmmakers see Ozu's conservatism as reactionary, Bordwell sees Ozu's films as "liberal protests against the failure of the state's social responsibility."[31] These readings actually coincide if we consider Ozu's films as melodramas in which psychological interiority paradoxically refers to an egolessness of Japanese history, the privileged content of *nihonjinron.*

Especially in Ozu's postwar work, family melodramas of arranged marriages, generational differences, and dying patriarchs, a sense of loss pervades. In *Late Summer,* for example, the smoke from the crematorium chimney is the last sign of the father who operated a family business that will now be sold to a corporation. Setsuko Hara, the dead patriarch's widowed daughter-in-law, vows to remain single and deny a prospective suitor, for no other reason than *giri* to the dissolving family she has married into. The younger daughter of the family, however, decides to marry the man of her own choice. Like so many of Ozu's films, the desires of individual characters are indistinguishable from a more pervasive sense of something missing, something of which the characters have been robbed by modern Japan. In this film Chishu Ryu makes a cameo appearance in the final scene as a peasant in a field near the crematorium, personifying the *kokugaku* that is signified by Setsuko Hara's resignation to widowhood.

Stylistically, it may seem contradictory to speak of "excess" in connection with Ozu, whose quietude remains unparalleled in contemporary cinema. But could we not consider those pillow shots, empty frames, and nondiegetic images of objects and locales, along with Ozu's systematic decentered and discontinuous editing patterns that have been so exhaustively documented by formalist critics,[32] as excessive in themselves? Ozu's refusal to adopt the codes of Hollywood illusionism results in an excess of film language, of signs and signifiers. If indeed a *satori* experience is the effect of this excess, as so many other critics have suggested, perhaps it is best described as Barthes describes the haiku, as "a panic suspension of language." But rather than being *abolished* by this "vicious infinity of language" as Barthes suggests of the haiku,[33] "secondary thought" (signification) is produced as a supplement, marking the limits of cinematic language to produce "Japaneseness."

The emotional restraint of the typical Ozu performance may indeed lack the expressionism of Western melodrama. In Barthes's words, "emotion no longer floods, no longer submerges, but becomes a reading,"[34] and yet can anyone deny the intensity of the characters played by Ozu's emblematic actors Chishu Ryu and Setsuko Hara? Their mutual resignation to the mortality of the Japanese family at the end of *Tokyo Story* is voluminous and deeply inward. The discontinuities of Ozu's idiosyncratic editing (and to a large extent this applies to Naruse as well) are compensated for by a naturalistic performance style — a highly refined body language that conveys most of the film's emotional intensity.

If *nihonjinron* has ideologically fueled a suppression of the "folk's" revolutionary potential, this passivity is emblematized in Ozu's stylistics. And yet the failure to communicate takes place very specifically within the apparatus of the cinema, which insists on a separation of subject and object in the structure of spectacle. Ozu's systematic subversion of point-of-view editing has the effect of alienating individuals within the phenomenology of cinematic representation.[35] As Harootunian has suggested, essential Japaneseness, in its original nativist formulation, is rendered politically impotent as soon as it is represented because it depends on an experiential epistemology. Its aestheticization is its end. Therefore it may well be that the repressed struggle of Ozu's melodrama involves an incompatibility of *mono no aware* with the phenomenology of cinema.

An absent signified seethes beneath the surplus of Ozu's signifiers, a signified content that is perhaps neither reactionary nor progressive, but points to *nihonjinron* and beyond, to the content of *kokugaku* and the promise of the communality of the folk. Now reduced to salarymen and secretaries in an increasingly alienating environment, what struggle against the contemporary realism of Ozu's cinema are memory and experience.[36] The essential Japaneseness that lurks within Ryu and Hara and informs Ozu's refined stylistics evades representation precisely because it is inseparable from the past, the radicality of which depended precisely on an evasion of representation.

When the New Wave Japanese filmmakers of the 1960s searched for a new language of representation for a New Japan, melodramatic strategies of sex and violence were deployed in a new regime of excess. Oshima's revisions of Mizoguchi's woman-centered melodramas, *Cruel Story of Youth* and *The Sun's Burial,* are indebted to Vincente Minnelli and Nicholas Ray for their expressive use of color and wide screen.[37] Shinoda's 1969 version of Chikamatsu, *Double Suicide,* likewise upsets the balance of the Japanese "moral occult" by sexualizing the protagonists and demonizing the codes of *giri.*[38] Indeed Oshima's writing in the 1960s insists on subjectivity as an absolutely necessary means of defining freedom "from the congeniality of our all being Japanese."[39] Many other directors, including Kurosawa, Immamura, and Tatami, engage with melodrama, and it is high time both Japanese and non-Japanese critics examined their strategies of excess, irony, and formalism with respect to *nihonjinron* and desire.

The difficulties facing the foreign critic, the outsider, would seem to be intensified by the recognition that the privileged interior content of classical Japanese cinema, its emotional depth, is predicated on our exclusion. And yet once we penetrate the formal surfaces of this national cinema to the secrets latent within, it is crucial that we question our own respect for the cultural other and come to terms with *nihonjinron.* As bourgeois ideology it provides far fewer loopholes for resistance than its Western realist and individualist counterpart. What has paraded before Western critics in the guise of emptiness and spirituality is also the self-indulgence of *nihonjinron*, and it begs to be historicized and recognized as the hidden desire of a different melodrama.

Notes

1. David Bordwell proposes as much in "Our Dream Cinema: Western Historiography and the Japanese Film," *Film Reader* 4 (1979).
2. Kristin Thompson and David Bordwell, "Space and Narrative in the Films of Ozu," *Screen* 17, 2 (Summer 1976): 41–75; Noel Burch, *To the Distant Observer: Form and Meaning in the Japanese Cinema* (Berkeley: University of California Press, 1979). For criticism of this approach, see especially Peter Lehman, "The Mysterious Orient, the Crystal Clear Orient, the Non-existent Orient: Dilemmas of Western Scholars of Japanese Film," and Kirihara, "Critical Polarities and the Study of Japanese Film Style," both in *Journal of Film and Video* 39 (Winter 1987); Scott Nygren, "Reconsidering Modernism: Japanese Film and the Postmodern Context," *Wide Angle* 11, 3 (July 1989).

Bordwell himself has attempted to broaden his perspective in his recent book *Ozu and the Poetics of Cinema* (London: BFI Publishing, 1988). It is unfortunately only in the opening chapters to what is basically a neoformalist approach to Ozu that Bordwell situates Ozu's extensive oeuvre within the Japanese sociohistorical context.

3. Oshima has described melodrama as the most traditional form of cinema in Japan. Oshima Nagisa, *Écrits (1956–1978): Dissolution et jaillissement* (France: Editions Gallimard, 1980), p. 26.
4. Ian Buruma, *Behind the Mask: On Sexual Demons, Sacred Mothers, Transvestites, Gangsters, Drifters and Other Japanese Cultural Heroes* (New York: Pantheon, 1984), p. 176.
5. Thomas Elsaesser, "Tales of Sound and Fury: Observations on the Family Melodrama," in *Movies and Methods: An Anthology* vol 2, ed. Bill Nichols (Berkeley: University of California Press, 1985), pp. 165–89.
6. Peter Brooks, *The Melodramatic Imagination: Balzac, Henry James, Melodrama, and the Mode of Excess* (New York: Columbia University Press 1976), p. 41.
7. Brooks, *Melodramatic Imagination*, p. 15; Elsaesser, "Tales of Sound and Fury," p. 169.
8. The perversity of opera is partially explained by Clément in terms of the flights of soprano vocalization that express all that cannot be contained by narratives of imperialist patriarchy. It is a register of desire, a feminist imagination, which Catherine Clément is attracted to in an opera such as *Madame Butterfly, Opera, or the Undoing of Women*, trans. Betsey Wing (Minneapolis: University of Minnesota Press, 1988), p. 47.
9. Geoffrey Nowell-Smith compares Minnelli's mise-en-scène to Freudian conversion hysteria, in which "the energy attached to an idea that has been repressed returns converted into a bodily symptom. The 'return of the repressed' takes place, not in conscious discourse, but displaced onto the body of the

patient. In the melodrama, where there is always material which cannot be expressed in discourse..., a conversion can take place into the body of the text." "Minelli and Melodrama," *Home Is Where the Heart Is: Studies in Melodrama and the Woman's Film,* ed. Christine Gledhill (London: BFI Publishing, 1987), p. 73.

10. Divine forces are not responsible for the characters' downfall, but social forces, which are often personified in Manichaean terms. Familiar melodramatic traits include the setting of many of the plays in the gay quarters of Edo; the polarization of female characters as either courtesans or mothers; the dramatization of class mobility and limitations; narrative devices of eavesdropping, misunderstandings, and coincidence; and a narrative momentum of inevitability. Typical narratives concern love suicides (in *bunraku*) and the falls of great families (in Kabuki), often based on historical events. Onstage narrators and musicians, the antecedents of the *benshi* of Japanese silent film, are as responsible for increasing the affectivity of the performances as they are for supplying dialogue and commentary. Much the same is true of the *benshi.* See Donald Kirihara, "A Reconsideration of the Institution of the Benshi," *Film Reader 6* (1985).

11. Roland Barthes, *Empire of Signs,* trans. Richard Howard (New York: Hill and Wang, 1982), p. 49.

12. Ibid., p. 62.

13. Brooks, *Melodramatic Imagination,* p. 199.

14. Burch, *To the Distant Observer.*

15. Audie Bock describes many of Mizoguchi's early, lost, silent films as melodramas in her filmography, but the term drops out of her synopses of the later works (Audie Bock, *Japanese Film Directors* [New York: Kodansha International, 1985], pp. 55–61). David Bordwell concedes that Ozu occasionally worked in the genre, but suggests that it clashes with his characteristic "abstraction" (*Ozu,* p. 339). The films that he specifically designates as melodrama (meaning Western melodrama) include: *Now Are the Dreams of Youth* (1932), *Until the Day We Meet Again* (1933), *Woman of Tokyo* (1933), *Story of Floating Weeds* (1934), and *Tokyo Twilight* (1957).

16. D. William Davis, "Back to Japan: Militarism and Monumentalism in Prewar Japanese Cinema," *Wide Angle* 11, 3 (July 1989).

17. Sato Tadao, *Currents in Japanese Cinema,* trans. Gregory Barrett (Tokyo: Kodansha International, 1982), p. 78.

18. Ibid., p. 77. Sato does not name these films, but the discussion of *feminisuto* precedes his analysis of Mizoguchi, whom others have unambiguously characterized as exemplary of this ideology. (Bock, *Japanese Film Directors,* p. 40; Buruma, *Behind the Mask,* p. 33.)

19. Joan Mellen, *The Waves at Genji's Door: Japan through Its Cinema* (New York: Pantheon, 1976), p. 269.

20. The term "moral occult" is central to Brooks's theory of melodrama. It refers to the invisible realm of moral feeling that is not transcendent or handed down from above, but comes from within melodramatic personae, with equivalent authority to that of divine law.

21. The deaths of Mizoguchi's heroines should be distinguished from those of American melodramas, such as *Broken Blossoms, Letter from an Unknown*

Woman, Dark Victory, Some Came Running, and *Imitation of Life.* The women of these films accomplish nothing in their deaths, which is what makes them textual victims, cruelly excluded from a society that cannot accommodate their desires.

22. Peter N. Dale, *The Myth of Japanese Uniqueness* (London: Croom Helm, 1986), p. 105. Dale specifically links *giri* and *ninjo* to Japanese perceptions of social outsides and more personable insides, and further, to Japaneseness and non-Japaneseness.

23. Doi Takeo, *Anatomy of Dependence* (Tokyo: Kodansha International, 1971), p. 42.

24. Peter N. Dale offers a multitude of examples of how Doi's central term *amae* has entered the mainstream of Japanese studies across a spectrum of disciplines, including history, politics and sociology; *Japanese Uniqueness,* pp. 147–8.

25. Brooks, *Melodramatic Imagination,* pp. 79–80.

26. Doi, *Anatomy of Dependence,* p. 22.

27. H. D. Harootunian, *Things Seen and Unseen: Discourse and Ideology in Tokugawa Nativism* (Chicago: University of Chicago Press, 1988), p. 410.

28. Ibid., p. 413.

29. Paul Schrader, *Transcendental Style in Film: Ozu, Bresson, Dryer* (Berkeley: University of California Press, 1972), pp. 15–55.

30. Donald Richie, *Ozu* (Berkeley: University of California Press, 1974).

31. Bordwell, *Ozu,* p. 42.

32. Kristin Thompson and David Bordwell, "Space and Narrative in the Films of Ozu," *Screen* 17, 2 (Summer 1976): 41–75; Burch, *To the Distant Observer.*

33. Barthes, *Empire of Signs,* p. 75.

34. Ibid., p. 54.

35. Sato attributes the typical frontality of Ozu's medium close-ups and the lack of "correct" eyeline matching to the Japanese avoidance of confrontation. It is more the shared vision of scenery between two characters than the meeting of glances that constitutes empathy. Sato, *Japanese Cinema,* p. 196.

36. It is significant in this respect that Ozu's films contain few if any flashbacks. Not even photographs provide access to the past through memory. See Bordwell, *Ozu,* pp. 53–4.

37. Specific references include the red, white, and blue lights of *Cruel Story,* which recall the mise-en-scène of *Some Came Running;* and the red jacket and steep precipices of *Sun's Burial,* which recall *Rebel without a Cause.* See Maureen Turim, "Oshima's Cruel Tales of Youth and Politics," *Journal of Film and Video* 39 (Winter 1987).

38. David Desser, *Eros Plus Massacre: An Introduction to the Japanese New Wave Cinema* (Bloomington: Indiana University Press, 1988), p. 178.

39. Joan Mellen, *Voices from the Japanese Cinema* (New York: Liveright, 1975), p. 264. See also Oshima Nagisa, *Écrits (1956–1978).*

CHAPTER IX

Psyches, ideologies, and melodrama: The United States and Japan

Maureen Turim

A truly comparative theory of filmic melodrama needs to consider its derivation, history, and function in various countries. Are we speaking of the same phenomenon when we use the term to refer to films of heightened emotional involvement in highly personalized fictions, but produced in different countries? Theories of filmic melodrama tend either to concentrate on the British and American melodrama or to treat melodrama generally, in universal terms, without referring to a specific national history.[1] Some corrective to this can be offered by considering other national treatments of melodrama, for example, the case of France, which developed the earliest, and perhaps the most distinctive and varied, theatrical tradition of melodrama and subsequently a long and varied history of filmic melodrama.

In relation to this, we need to examine how melodrama rests on its theatrical heritage: This means figuring out both what that theatrical tradition was and how aspects of melodrama expanded to permeate nineteenth-century culture, as evidenced in the romantic novel, the history painting, and nineteenth-century opera and symphonic composition. So if we first consider how melodrama developed, it is not because we believe that a study of origins will alone explain and limit what melodrama has come to be, but rather that the history of the formation of melodrama can in fact suggestively expand how we look at melodrama today.

One can say that melodrama began and grew relatively simultaneously in several European countries, notably France, Britain, Italy, and Germany. I say relatively, for as we shall see, French melodrama and melodrama theory emerged earlier and was a more distinct form than in other European countries; still, Italian opera is so distinctly coterminous with melodrama that there is much to debate in seeking origins and lineage. It is far more intriguing to see a convergence of models of expression coalescing to form melodrama as we now know it.

In some instances, the conditions of production were strikingly similar. For example, musical pantomime was inaugurated to circumvent patent laws in both England and France; melodrama was born out of a shared impulse to compete with the official theaters linked to royal decree and the aristocracy.[2] So in both instances, melodrama represents a more popular theatrical form, the beginnings, along with the music hall, of a mass entertainment, to be consumed by the urban proletariat and the bourgeoisie, though precisely how this class-defined audience was addressed and constituted varied from country to country and decade to decade. One can also note the exchange that occurred among these European countries, including the immediate translation and performance of plays, as well as the less direct borrowings from one country to another. Further, many basic constituents of melodrama's narrative form and mise-en-scène are similar in each of the countries in which it developed. In all cases, melodrama is characterized by increased attention to the visual elements of stage production tending toward expressive excess, the repetitive casting of character types in moral dilemmas and physical dangers, the circumstantial convergence of events, and the blending and juxtaposition of conflicting tones.

Today, the subgenre of the domestic melodrama is emphasized exclusively in attempts to define the filmic genre. Historical epics, gangster films, and horror films are seen as different genres, distinct from melodrama. This is at least partially a result of the tendency I mentioned earlier of certain theorists to consider late nineteenth-century British and American melodramas as the precedent for filmic melodrama. Once the earlier history of melodrama is considered, we see the immense importance of the historical, supernatural, colonial, criminal, and mystery melodramas. They provide the antecedents for the historical epic, the gangster film, and the horror film. It certainly is necessary to consider the wide range of expression and subgenres that constitute the nineteenth-century melodrama.

National tendencies and contexts for theatrical melodrama also were quite different one from another. In France, for example, the development of melodrama differed in at least three distinct ways from the parallel histories of its neighbors. One is the way in which the classical French drama formed a particularly restrained point of departure, much more restricted by formal laws than the Shakespearean tragedy. The second major factor differentiating French melodrama is the French Revolution, which affected the theater both directly and by shifting entirely the cultural and class context. As Frank Rahill (1967, 20) notes, "The popular audience and the commercial theater came into their own simultaneously at the Revolution to complement each other." Third, there are the specifics of the boulevard du Temple, or the "boulevard du crime," as it came to be known for its architectonic disposition of the melodrama theaters, which drew a mixture of bourgeois and working-class audiences. French melodrama was subsequently largely subsumed by romanticism and naturalism; that is to say, melodramatic tropes survived but were tied to explanations of causality and context, eventually leading to what is on the surface antithetical to melodrama, realism, but what on closer examination constitutes an embarrassed toning down of the melodramatic traits that inform it.

British melodrama, on the other hand, was built from the heritage of Shakespearean tragedy, a form that has retrospectively been seen as already both populist and melodramatic by several theorists. It developed after 1843, in the midst of class turmoil generated by industrialization but in the absence of any distinct political revolution. If the formal opposition between high and popular culture, tragedy and melodrama, is not as distinct perhaps as in France, ironically, it is expressed as an antagonism against melodrama as a lower form with greater vehemence. A strong motif of the British melodrama (also present in continental melodramas) is the mixing of classes due to circumstances in which true class identities are temporarily concealed.

American melodrama, on the other hand, grew in the wake of the revolution in the virtual absence of a theatrical tradition. By the time theaters were built in the United States, the "high" culture they imported and emulated from Europe was defined by melodrama. Democratic notions of plurality and universality superseded class consciousness even when characters were drawn from distinct and opposing classes.

The necessity for a specificity to the cultural heritage of melodrama in film is all the more evident in the case of Japan, where the emergence of the form followed a different history. In general, melodrama in Japan is in part an importation of European modes, in part a realignment of Japanese modes of expression emerging in Japanese popular cultural forms such as Kabuki. The development of Kabuki has certain parallels to the development of melodrama in the West; Kabuki's role as a theater of the rising merchant class, officially forbidden to the samurai, borrowing heavily from dance, suggests that, like melodrama, its innovative form was grounded in an appeal to a new class of theatergoers. There is also some ground to a formula that posits Kabuki's relationship to Noh as similar to melodrama's to Shakespearean or French classical tragedy. The high-art theatrical traditions in each case are greatly modified, particularly as concerns the formal functions of poetic language, but are still intertextually significant in providing structures of conflict and notions of performance for the emerging forms to assimilate. Further, Kabuki plots and expressive gestures are similar to some used in European melodramas, and music and spectacle play an important role. Yet Kabuki is not simply Japan's melodrama, as by the time of the emergence of melodrama in Europe and Japan's exposure to that form, Kabuki had defined its own classical traditions as stylized theater. The emotional identifications and contemporaneous settings that inspire melodrama are mitigated in Kabuki by its remaining fixed in its late seventeenth-century form.

A significant difference in Japan's development of the melodrama is that it is perceived as a foreign importation. Further, there is never any direct heritage of the performance of fully staged classical melodrama. Melodrama is instead inherited via its influence on Western theatrical and literary form in both late romanticism and early realism. When the Japanese borrowed the tropes of melodrama this was often perceived as adopting Western realism. The works of Ibsen, for example, were read and performed in Japan at this time; though his works are far removed in some sense from the spectacular aspects of melodrama, their domestic conflicts and emotional tensions do borrow from late melodrama. The Japanese borrowings from late nineteenth-century Western theater became pronounced around 1890, occurring simultaneously with the first Japanese performances of Western tragedies such as Shakespeare's.[3] The emergence first of Shimpa, a modern Meiji theatrical form, and then of Shingeki, which stripped Shimpa of many of its remaining ties to Kabuki, paved the way for the development of filmic melodramas that concentrated on domestic conflicts in modern-day Japan.

American and Japanese melodramatic adaptations have, then, an intriguing parallel in that they both assimilated a European tradition that was somewhat foreign to immediate sociocultural circumstances, but which could be easily embraced by certain sectors because these European artifacts spoke to the changing conditions in political and industrial structures these countries were experiencing. For example, in the United States, melodramatic structures were easily absorbed by the nascent homegrown cultural form, the Western. Similarly, the historical melodrama became inflected with democratic interpolations of a mass audience of citizens in ways that both parallel the British and French traditions and exceed and transform them.

In Japan, the sword-fight narrative easily moved from its structure in Kabuki to its melodramatic autonomy as a filmic genre, the *chambara*. Similarly, the Japanese theatrical heritage provided an even more profound supernatural symbolism than the European tradition. The supernatural that in Noh was based on religious beliefs and in Kabuki was absorbed as symbolic, if not necessarily religious form, blended with Western melodrama's supernatural to create a hybrid form of the supernatural melodrama that ironically has looked specifically Japanese to contemporary Western audiences ignorant of the supernatural in their own melodrama tradition.

Japanese and American assimilation of the melodramatic, then, each in its own way, lent itself to the interspersal of cultural forms. That Japanese filmic expression has itself been influenced most heavily by American film makes the assimilation and development of melodramatic form a most complicated matter of intertextuality. An example of this interspersal of textualities and traditions can be seen in the popularity of Errol Flynn in Japan as an influence on the silent *chambara* film. Griffith's adaptation of *Orphans of the Storm,* fascinating as an example of an American rendering of a traditional French theatrical melodrama, was exported to Japan upon its release in 1921. Along with other similar films, it familiarized a mass Japanese audience with European melodrama via the circuitous route of a specifically American treatment.

Japan and the United States are fascinating sites on which to examine the reinterpretation and revitalization of the melodrama. Comparative analysis of films of the 1920s and 1930s in each country would show how each national cinema explored the tropes of melodrama, often under the guise of a quest for greater filmic realism. Without pursuing the details of such a comparison of these periods here, I hope I have indicated how melodrama could become the most complex of intertexts for the silent film, as it in fact stimulated numerous genres and developing national traditions. Only in certain cases were the spectacular elements and absolute oppositions of melodrama retained; with the blending of melodrama and realism came the contemporary, limited sense of the filmic melodrama – what in the United States came to be known as the "woman's film." This restricted notion of melodrama as filmic genre confined the melodramatic to the domestic or family melodrama with increasing concern for psychological depth of characters. By the sound period, the melodrama as film genre was firmly established in each country along parallel lines of structuration, characterization, and audience appeal. It is to these sound melodramas that I now wish to turn my attention.

I wish to look at parallel melodramas in Japan and the United States; the four I have chosen as my focus are *Tender Comrade* (1943) and *Possessed* (1947) from the United States and *No Regrets for Our Youth* (1946) and *Floating Clouds* (1955) from Japan. All are late melodramatic forms. Except for *Possessed,* which is a psychological melodrama that largely divorces itself from the direct historical representations, the others all blend the domestic melodrama with the historical melodrama; all inscribe their characters with the psychological density we associate with the particular generic permutation known as the psychological melodrama. I have chosen these particular films due to the overlaps in structures they represent; they are all concerned with obsessive love, with a woman who has lost her lover. They all use flashbacks to explore the power and signification of memory. With the exception of *Floating Clouds*, they are all films I include in my book, *Flashbacks in Film: Memory and History* (1989). Here I want to build on the analyses offered in the book by reframing the questions I ask of them as I address the issue of the specificity of national cinemas' use of melodrama. Although the films date from relatively similar periods (sound film in its classic formulation), the U.S. examples date from the war and immediate postwar period, whereas the Japanese films are both from the postwar period, with *Floating Clouds* coming a long time after the others. *Floating Clouds* begins its fictional narration in 1946 and flashes back to depict the war years, so that its setting as fiction does coincide temporarily with the others. The discrepant production dates, however, are significant and have historical determinations that I shall address in my analysis. First, I am interested in looking at similarities and differences among these films as versions of the same narrative structure, a process that Gérard Genette has termed the "palimpseste," combining structuralist theory of myth with poststructuralist theories of intertextuality (Genette 1982).

Anyone familiar with *Possessed* and *Floating Clouds* may have been struck by how the two films call out for comparison and will understand my reasons for doing so. Both treat heroines who are obsessed with men who were once their lovers, but who have jilted them. They can both be taken as fictional studies of female obsession and masochism in psychoanalytical terms. The "myth" here is psychoanalytical – the story of a woman's obsessive love. Yet in approaching either film psychoanalytically, methodological caution must be taken to locate that psychoanalytic analysis outside of or beyond the film's own presentation of character psychology. *Possessed* can be seen as deforming psychoanalysis in order to perpetuate mythic characterizations of the female, whereas *Floating Clouds* assiduously avoids its mention.

I will begin by pursuing this comparison between these two films alone. *Floating Clouds*, however, has a historical, directly political dimension that *Possessed* attains only through an extratextual reading. If we left the comparison with just these two films, it would certainly skew the analysis. In fact, the historical, referential dimension of *Floating Clouds* is not only found in other Japanese melodramas such as *No Regrets for Our Youth*, it is similar to such U.S. melodramas as *Tender Comrade*. So a second phase of the comparison will treat historical reference and its ideological function. These, then, are the connections that define the four-film corpus; the questions I wish to explore are: How do such concepts as psychology, nostalgia, political circumstance, group identity, and individuality define the female self within these melodramas? Are we able to determine distinctly Japanese or American aspects to the treatment of these concepts?

The contrast between *Possessed* and *Floating Clouds* is instructive, first because *Possessed*, directed by Curtis Bernhardt for Warner's in 1947, is among the psychological melodramas that take as their heroine a woman who is from the outset considered mentally disturbed if not psychotic. This set of melodramas aims to represent the memory processes of the disturbed psyches of the heroines. The film's structure as a series of flashback memories is crucial since it allows for the segmentation of the narration into three "sessions" and the positioning of the audience as "listening" with a psychoanalytic regard, like the patient's doctors represented in the fiction.

However, once the dissolve takes us inside the flashbacks, the concern with memory is abandoned as a mimetic goal in favor of a reexperiencing of the descent into madness. This reliving of the past is in turn compromised by the conventional imperatives of Hollywood film narration. Even so, the subjective experience of the woman reacting to her distorted vision of the surrounding world is given a mimetic rendering through the inclusion of both auditory and visual hallucinations. Contained in this complex narrational compromise is a view of female madness that is warped, bent out of shape both by ideological premises and the effects of the compromise strategy itself.

The idea of a heroine pronounced from the outset to be clinically insane is not unique to the American melodrama. However, American melodrama does attempt to psychologize its characters more completely than do European forms; the German *Secrets of the Soul* (Pabst, 1926) certainly preceded this genre of films in the United States, but remains exceptional for its internal mobilization of psychoanalysis to cure its character. If characters in German expressionist or French impressionist melodramas are insane or neurotic, only occasionally is this treated clinically. Still this representation of insanity is not only not foreign to European film, it can be found in Japanese film; *Page of Madness* (Kinugasa, 1926) centers its examination of an insane asylum on two women patients, one in particular who is given past experiences, the drowning of her child, that depict at least partially the genesis of her insanity.

Still, we can generalize that in European and American fiction and film character psychology is coded differently from that in Japanese traditions. The overarching tendency in Japanese film is to assign characters traits and even show their dynamic transformation without belaboring and dissecting, through coded revelations and commentary, the internal psychological frame and ambivalences that "cause" such configurations. The development of character psychology tends to be more understated and the mode of presenting it more external. I am not saying here that Japanese characters in melodramas are flat characters as opposed to round American representations; both national traditions grant their character's psyche, and in both instances psychology motivates action. I am saying rather that the representation of a character's psyche is often more indirect and ambiguous in Japanese films. In contrast, the U.S. melodrama throughout its history, but especially since the 1930s, has sought above all else to establish and reiterate character psychology; it has become obsessed with assigning motivations for all actions (though sometimes these are layered so thickly that they become multiple and contradictory). It often seeks and labels causes in early childhood experiences or in present social milieu or in innate or inherited deviance.

To look at how *Possessed* and *Floating Clouds* exemplify this difference, let's examine the coding of character psychology in each. *Possessed* has received much critical attention from psychoanalytical feminism for the manner in which it treats a woman, Louise Howell (Joan Crawford), lost, "possessed" by desire.

In the opening scene, she is absent from the present in which she circulates, roaming the streets in a distracted state, until she is inducted into a hospital ward where she will be treated. The terms of this treatment "Psycho" turn out to not merely be an element of hospital jargon; it is reiterated by a wall plaque indicating this ward. It serves as a sign for the bizarre vision of psychoanalysis that the film conveys. While the psychoanalytic treatment itself is the motivational source of the flashbacks, it is implausibly represented as a drug-induced magic that can extract an explanatory story. Three sessions produce three episodes within a linear narration of the past, a coherent retelling by the patient of the past years of her life. "Narcosynthesis" is the term given to the injection that will make the patient, diagnosed as in a catatonic stupor and suffering from complete "mutism," talk.

Louise Howell's enunciation is markedly incoherent. The phrases are fragmented, concealing as much as they reveal. Like the language of psychotics, words are generated that conceal other words that must remain unsaid. And the film form soon invites the spectator into further participation in Louise's mental state by presenting her auditory fantasy as the reality of the sound track. We hear the sound of a Schumann sonata that she is supposedly imagining, while her plea to "make them play it softer" results in the volume being lowered. This rendering of an auditory phantasm in conjunction with the disjunct and relatively opaque verbal narration contrasts with the filmic rendering of Louise's verbalization of her memories. Continuity supplants the awkward phrases of a jarred psyche; the film images fill in, creating a misleading nondisjunction. Yet in a sense, another film emerges from within the contradictions and from the subtle graphic signs of the dissolves and the patterns of repetition within the flashback narrative structure. In this "other" film, one "hears" more of Louise's subjective experience, more of the functioning of the unconscious, more of the social circumstances that limit a woman's options to deviant behaviors. Implicitly, *Possessed* exposes some of what might possess a female psyche to strike out with violence, for in the end Louise Howell murders her former lover. However, it simultaneously covers that knowledge with structural and discursive encasements whose function it is to regulate and thus obfuscate this view of the female unconscious. This contradiction is ideologically determined, a cultural trace of a society that cannot ignore a problem, nor face it honestly.

In contrast, the heroine, Yukiko, in *Floating Clouds* never attains the state of disorder assigned Louise Howell in *Possessed*. Her obsession never precipitates a psychotic break and a murder; we might say that it remains neurotic, but the film text itself never indicates any such term. Like *Letter from an Unknown Woman* and *Camille*, it provides the material for a psychoanalytic reading as a study of obsessional neurosis only indirectly and symbolically.

We are introduced to Yukiko through documentary footage depicting the repatriation of Japanese from Indochina following the surrender in 1946. After two shots of the actual returnees, Yukiko is presented in the foreground in a fairly convincing process shot. Yet the discrepancy between documentary footage and the superimposed fictional presence accents Yukiko as alone in this crowd, her gaze fixed off to her right to indicate her self-absorption. She will soon be actually alone, briefly appearing to wander the streets of Tokyo, not unlike the first images of *Possessed* that show Louise Howell wandering the streets alone. Yet when Yukiko arrives at her destination, her former lover's house, we retrospectively realize that she knew where to find him.

There is, then, an interesting contrast to the way the lover and the past love are represented in the two films. In *Floating Clouds* the reunion of lovers in Tokyo following the war is an awkward coda to an affair that is now foreclosed. The past of that affair is indicated by two flashbacks, each from Yukiko's focalization. The first occurs when her lover leaves her waiting on the street outside his house, while he returns to dress so that they can rendezvous at a hotel, the second in the midst of a conversation between them following this brief encounter. They are by far the most subjective and revelatory moments of the film, the only indications we are given for Yukiko's obsession with this man, the only moments of "direct" psychological explanation. We shall come back to a fuller analysis of these images of the past later on, but for now what is significant is that they portray Yukiko's past involvement with this man as a romantic and fulfilling seduction. This past of love and relative luxury contrasts with the squalor of surroundings and the denial of love in the present. We do know that Yukiko had always known her lover was married, but she is depicted as unable to construct any other meaningful life for herself upon learning that her wartime lover has no intention of divorcing his wife to marry her, as being obsessed only with him, as unable to accept his loss. She continues to seek his love, to accept the degradation he causes her, and lives only for his intermittent attention to her. This obsession is ultimately given explanation by the contrast between the ideal images of the past and the abject conditions of the present.

Loss in *Possessed* takes the form of the first symbolic narrative event told in the flashback; Louise Howell loses David Sutton as a lover. In a scene in David's lakeside house, Louise is shown dressing after their afternoon swim, a discreet double entendre that the film uses to suggest their sexual activities. David announces the end of their relationship, as his response to her bold declaration of love and possessive desire, "I want a monopoly on you." A boat ride across the lake is the means by which David returns Louise to her employer's house, depositing her on the dock. It is to this same dock that David returns in a later sequence after having gone to Canada on a business venture financed by Louise's boss, Dean Graham. The intervening sequences establish Louise's position as private nurse to Graham's invalid wife, who suffers from jealous fantasies of her husband's infidelity with Louise. David's return evokes Louise's humiliating supplication for his attention, alternating with vicious threats and accusations. Her manner of speaking becomes increasingly agitated, manic, until the sequence ends with an image of turbulence on the water as David once again "leaves." This dissolves to Louise in the present, once again calling "David."

The loss of David is thus repeated with the first flashback, presented both times in conjunction with the dock and water imagery. This repetition is characteristic of dream structure; the film, like a dream, is doubling its representation, compulsively marking the loss of the man as a symbolic cause of Louise's psychosis. The return to the present shows Louise once again rambling, voicing paranoid delusions. The doctors begin their diagnosis on the basis of the narrative we have just "heard." They call it the "beginning of a persecution complex" and a "schizoid detachment" that will grow, nourished by her "obsessions." The diagnosis presents a paradox, since nothing within the flashback supports this conclusion. However, Louise's verbal narration in the present is a disjointed discourse that might suggest possible paranoia or schizophrenia.

We can note then a difference in psychological coding and attitude between *Possessed* and *Floating Clouds*. The first thing this difference suggests is that by 1946 in the United States, female obsessive love had the potential to be seen as negative, a destructive threat to the self, medicalized within a fictional discourse and given a male frame through which we are not so much to understand it, as to cure it through the magic of contemporary science. This was not always the case, nor is it always the case in melodramas made contemporaneously.

Melodramas can treat obsessive love in at least three distinct ways, each indicating a difference in attitude both on the surface and symbolically. The first type depicts the woman as the heroine whose obsessive love is a measure of her worth. For example, in Griffith's *True-Heart Susie* (1917), obsessive love is an indication of female loyalty and strength of character. The woman temporarily suffers from male neglect and lack of reciprocity, but the love itself reaches and redeems the neglectful man, and the ending confirms the romantic couple. In a second type, typified by two films that are adaptations from literature maintaining their period setting, *Camille* (George Cukor, 1936, from the Dumas novel)[4] and *Letter from an Unknown Woman* (Max Ophuls, 1948, from the Stefan Zweig novel), the woman is depicted as victim of her obsessive love. Obsessive love, if no longer a plus, is still a sign of a good, if unfortunate, character. The woman who loves obsessively is above all a victim. She is pure in her love, but mistreated through no fault of her own. The male is charged with inadequacy as he fails to love and appreciate her. Such love symbolically causes the woman's death (though her illness is circumstantial, consumption, tuberculosis, she is ill, ultimately, from loving too much). This is, of course, the pattern in *Floating Clouds.* In contrast, the medicalized and juridical versions of obsessive love see it as a symptom whose results are disastrous for all involved. It is often combined with other desires, such as class ascendancy, and thus, far from being pure, is tainted with ulterior motives. The male may be just as callous as in the previous case of woman as victim of obsessive love, but his treachery is less centralized or even excused due to extenuating circumstances.

The move from one treatment of obsessive love to another is correlated with changes in the construction of female identities that involve some ironic inversions. The most "sympathetic" view of obsessive love seems to assume that women are subservient and receive their identities through the men who court them. Men are then made responsible for the women who love them. In contrast, the most "critical view" of obsessive love assumes that women *can* attain far more autonomy and independence; if they have chosen to remain obsessed with those men who abandon them, it is a failure to achieve an independence to which they should have access. The view in which the woman is still considered a victim within obsessional love, then, can be seen as a historically transitional phase, one that occurs when women are granted a certain autonomy without being expected to have abandoned their dependency on men and to have achieved self-determination. That in the American melodrama this transitional state can be associated with the past and with Europe (Paris, Vienna) is intriguing; once obsessional love is no longer sanctioned by narrative as the force of female goodness, such unsanctified yet sympathetically rendered passion is presented as foreign.

All of these narratives of obsessional love toy with the structure of desire that Freudian psychoanalysis terms "obsessional neurosis." Freud's most famous case history of obsessional neurosis is his treatment of the "Rat man" in which obsessive ideas, fears, and images are traced to sexual repression and childhood anxieties (Freud 1963). Guilt is a strong component in the etiology of the obsessive neurosis. Obsessional love may or may not be a symptom of obsessional neurosis; often the obsessions that a neurotic suffers are so strong as to foreclose romantic attachments. However, love itself can be seen as containing elements of the obsessive in it: a loss of self to the other, a fixation on the other as object, and the inability to let go of the love object or substitute another. For women, culturally, this danger in love of enclosing at its core the structure of an obsessional neurosis is great, for the constitution of the self has been culturally circumscribed and rendered secondary to subservience to the other if not to love itself.

While all of these films treat obsessive love, and while *Possessed* links this to a psychotic break, the configuration of obsessional neurosis receives only indirect representation in all of them. The structure of obsessional neurosis is symbolically mapped onto other aspects of these narratives. It is usually not recovered in the oedipal configurations of childhood, but instead projected onto the incestuous interactions of the future. Thus we find other strong similarities in their narrative structure, ironic incestuous liaisons that will continue to cross and knot. Both heroines find themselves linked with another man, or men who are to serve as substitutes for the lost lover, but who cannot affect her to discharge the obsessional hold the lost lover maintains. In *Possessed* that man is an older, father figure, whose wife, before her suicide, manifested paranoid delusions about just such a relationship. In *Floating Clouds* the substitutions are serial, including an American GI. In both films the "lost" male lovers are in turn linked to younger women whom they substitute successfully for the heroine. In *Possessed* the younger woman is the stepdaughter, whereas in *Floating Clouds,* she is a woman the "lost" lover meets while Yukiko and he attempt to reconstruct their affair at a spa. In addition, Yukiko herself treats her lover's wife with disdain, claiming to have mistaken her upon their first meeting as his mother; she is in turn treated in the same way when she confronts the younger replacement for herself.

All of these substitutions and incestuous configurations indicate a slippage in the representation between obsessional love and incestuous desire. This is not so much an examination or a reflection of the etiology of obsession as it is an ironic displacement of such an examination. The psyche and therefore the subject in these fictions is always given indirect and displaced representation, despite the formulation of psychological characters. If the psyche receives symbolic configuration in such narrative structurations, historical context can either be posited as a determining construct or absented from direct figuration in the melodrama. Of course, even when it is absent, it may be displaced and symbolically figured through other means.

Possessed avoids direct historical contextualization. Like many melodramas, in representing the personal and the domestic, the inside, it situates itself outside the specificities of history. We might be tempted to read it, and especially the earlier story from which it was adapted, as a home-front melodrama, or conversely, read it as a postwar trauma melodrama, but it situates the lover's absence and returns in private business and not the military. *Floating Clouds,* in contrast, contextualizes its obsessional love as first evoked when the heroine was overseas, in Indochina during the Pacific War. As such, it belongs to the group of melodramas that interlace the personal and the historical, the psyche with political contexts.

It is the flashbacks that establish the war as memory and as context for obsessional love. The situation that would place Japanese foresters in Indochina is not directly and overtly stated in the film. The historical collaboration between the French Vichy regime controlling Indochina and the Japanese war effort is, however, evoked in the imagery. This French imperialist context is indicated in the elaborate French mansion setting, the Cointreau served after dinner, and the presence of Vietnamese servants, including a very attractive woman whose repeated close-up glances at the suggestion of a romantic or sexual liaison with him. These flashbacks then, in choosing Indochina, rather than an occupation site in which Japanese culture alone ruled, represent what it is for the Japanese to acquire the taste of European culture, to substitute themselves for the French.

Within the flashback, this is highlighted by the shots of Yukiko in Western dress, particularly one in which a dissolve ending the previous scene takes us into a shot of her running toward the camera in a white frock. These images indicate a narcissistic component to her memory of her love affair; her memory images represent a longing for herself as free, as European, as sophisticated. All we need do is contrast this image with the shots of the traditional wife to see this as a fantasy depiction of a liberating aspect of Western culture for Japanese women. The flashbacks to Indochina link romance with a release from Japanese tradition and conventional roles. Further, they link romance with Japanese economic power. A return to romance in Indochina is for this Japanese couple the best of all possible worlds.

Moreover, the occupation is then depicted as responsible for Yukiko's inability to give up the obsession. A woman without English skills is presented as unemployable during the occupation, and she is depicted as needing to return repeatedly to her former lover for economic reasons. The economic and political scene is charged with determining the psyche and its fixations. Both Yukiko and her lovers are economically and emotionally devastated by the loss of the war and the occupation itself. The war and the occupation then also "excuse" male inaction, duplicity, and bad faith. Only travel to remote rural Japan allows the couple to reunite, and then only briefly before Yukiko dies.

All of this is evocative of the complexity of the representation of history within the melodrama. Whereas the ideological writing of history by the historical melodrama's grandiose rendering of historical events at least foregrounds ideological purpose, the same sort of positioning in domestic or family melodramas set in specific historical contexts may not be so evident. Personalized versions such as *Orphans of the Storm* in one sense use the historical as backdrop for domestic melodrama and are not often treated as serious historical representations. This formulation is misleading, though, because the domestic melodrama here becomes fused with historical, and the consequence is an interweave of ideological treatments of personal and political motivations and casualties. Rare is the historical melodrama in which personal, psychological, and essentially domestic concerns are not part of the vision of history conveyed. Equally, most domestic melodramas manipulate referential coding of the historical in defining personal relations.

It is in this context that I will compare *Floating Clouds* and *Possessed* to another pair of melodramas, *Tender Comrade* and *No Regrets for Our Youth*. For as we shall see, what is at stake here in the use of melodrama for political ends is the wrenching of obsessive love out of its more critical treatment by this time in the history of the melodrama and reinvesting it with virtues that it no longer has in *Possessed*, nor does it so simply have in *Floating Clouds*.

Kurosawa's *No Regrets for Our Youth* (*Waga seishun ni kui nashi*, 1946; the title actually translates as "no regrets in my life"), like many of the American melodramas of the war and postwar period, uses the flashback to symbolize the weight of history. The manner in which it does so is quite different from Naruse's melodrama and, in fact, quite singular in Japanese film up to this point. This film, based on the real events surrounding the political censorship of a professor and his student in the 1930s, adds a love story to the tale of political opposition to provide a personalized chronicle of Japanese leftists during the rise to power of the military and the right wing. It uses its flashbacks as part of a discourse on the ideology of memory, tradition, and nostalgia, a discourse it works out in terms of fictional symbolic representations.

What I wish to highlight here is the focus on the woman whose relationship to politics is one of obsessional love. The film begins in 1933 at Kyoto University when the professor's daughter, Yuki (Setsuko Hara), is picnicking at Mt. Yoshida with a group of her father's students, including two rivals for her affection, Noge, the leader of a radical faction, and Itakawa, a more sedate personality who eventually drops out of the struggle to become an official within the military government. The romantic rivalry is played out with a series of matched traveling shots on a chase by the two men of Yuki through the woods characteristic of Kurosawa's graphically rich style of filming action sequences. This hike and picnic surrounded by wildflowers, an idyll at springtime so dear to Japanese notions of pleasure, provides one image of youth to which the film will return later on. This pleasant scene is interrupted by gunshots and the discovery of a soldier wounded during war-game exercises.

From this introduction of contrasts, the film turns to the Zengakuren (student group) struggle for academic freedom when Yuki's father is fired by the Ministry of Education. The student rebellion is crushed by political repression, with Professor Yagihara telling his former students, "Your struggle was not wasted. When spring comes flowers will bloom again," establishing with these words a reference to the first springtime picnic scene. The radical Noge continues the struggle and is imprisoned. Yuki's bourgeois tastes and loyalty to her father separate her from Noge in spirit. In a ration line in 1938, Yuki meets Itakawa, who has become a government employee in Tokyo, where she has become a secretary. Itakawa tells her of Noge's whereabouts and also that he thinks Noge has changed as a result of his five-year imprisonment. However, Itakawa's perception is superficial; Noge seems different only because his activities are more clandestine. Yuki watches Noge from a distance through several seasons depicted in a montage sequence. Finally they meet, rekindle the romance, and marry; however, Noge's political activities are not directly discussed. Yuki is still a somewhat passive and traditional Japanese wife, whose sphere is their apartment.

It is at this point that the flashbacks and the complex commentary on nostalgia for the past and the relationship of the past to the present and future of Japan begins. A first flashback to the picnic occurs when Yuki evokes their youth. For Yuki, like her father, the springtime idyll represented a lost and idealized past for which she longs when confronted with the threat to their security posed by her husband's antiwar activities. Noge's memories are verbal rather than visual. He simply recalls the struggle to "defend freedom in school."

This contrasting retrospection introduces two sequences that depict a difference in attitude and political maturity between Yuki and Noge. The first is a scene of them in the audience of a movie theater. Noge laughs heartily along with the film, while she cries at his side, apparently lost in her thoughts of fear about the future. Following this scene, they return home, where they discuss the role of the past, present, and future in providing the meaning of their lives. Noge explains to Yuki his philosophy of personal and political history. His philosophy not only establishes his character but sets the precedent for Yuki's later conversion to Noge's credo. First he says he knows the truth will be known ten years from now and people will thank the resistance. Then he tells of a moment of "weakness" when he left home ten years ago to his father's scolding and his mother's tears. This moment of doubt has since been resolved, and his comment on it now is the assertion that there are "no regrets in my life." This rejection of filial subservience in favor of other ideals, in this case a commitment to political struggle characteristic of the Communists, is an especially strong departure within a Japanese context that prizes self-sacrifice to the family unit and to authorities. Underlying the difference between Noge's and Yuki's visions of the past is the ideological conflict between the tenets of political activism and Japanese tradition. However, as the film resolves this conflict, it is not simply Noge's view that triumphs, but rather a complex synthesis in which Noge's parents will return later in the film as part of Yuki's means of formulating her own version of her husband's credo.

When Noge is arrested as a spy, Yuki is also held for questioning; in jail, as she looks out the cell window, there is a second flashback to the picnic. This time to the scene of the chase through the woods. Yuki is again shown contrasting her present situation with a moment of happiness in the past. Her memory is still primarily nostalgic, unlike Noge's view of life that sees the past as the foundation of the present struggle and the future as its vindication. However, after Noge is tortured to death in prison, Yuki undergoes a transformation. She comes to subscribe to Noge's perspective on life and political struggle, but adds to his lesson a reconciliation with his past that he never made. This is made clear when Yuki decides to move to Noge's natal village to live with his peasant father and mother, to earn their respect for herself and her dead husband despite the villagers' persecution of them for being a family of spies. Working in the rice paddy, she has an auditory flashback to Noge's words in the earlier scene of philosophical explanation. His voice-over echoes from the past with such lines as "I have no regrets for my life" and "ten years from now people will know."

The final flashback in the film indicates how Yuki's values have changed; during her visit to her parents' house in Kyoto following the war, the image dissolves from her hands at the piano keyboard to an image of her hands in the water of the rice paddy as she worked. This memory image from her recent past is interpreted by Yuki as also an indication of what her future now should be, as she once again decides to leave her middle-class home to return to her husband's family. This resolution is an odd mixture of traditional Japanese behavior (a widow traditionally was expected to remain with her deceased husband's family) and a Maoist position on solidarity with peasants as an expression of commitment to leftist politics. In a sense, Yuki's final position is much more a return to nostalgia than it is the assimilation of her husband's credo. The difference is only in the object of her nostalgic longing. Rather than a sequence of youthful play and seduction, her nostalgia is now aimed at her husband's past. When Noge stated that he had "no regrets for my youth," it was a statement of a decisive break with tradition that was not at all nostalgic, whereas Yuki's means of incorporating this credo is to substitute her husband's past for her own bourgeois heritage and to construct a life that combines elements of this past and of tradition as her means of approaching the present and the future.

In doing so, Yuki becomes yet another version of the obsessive love heroine of melodrama. She is a highly politically motivated version, a version recuperated to serve impressive ideological ends. Yet this very act of recuperation of the obsessive heroine has other ideological consequences as well. Though the film might appear to be one of the few flashback films to date to represent the nostalgia inherent in flashbacks critically, finally it backs away from the radicality of this position to one that reconciles, symbolically, nostalgia with a new set of principles and objects of that nostalgic longing.

Further, the displacement of the nostalgic object has as its ultimate consequence the dismissal of a bourgeois and urban life in favor of solidarity with peasant farmers. This can be interpreted as a political allegory, especially given the influence of the Japanese Communist Party on the scenario through the pressure exerted by the labor union of film technicians at Shochiko studios, cited in several sources.[5] In fact, the historical figure after whom Noge is modeled was a Communist Party member, though this is not mentioned in the film, probably due to the censorship authority of the U.S. occupation forces. That antibourgeois and antiliberal message is easily explained in this context, a position quite different from the kind of humanism one finds in other Kurosawa films. Beyond this, it is fascinating that at the level of political allegory the film suggests a Maoist solution rather than one more characteristic of Soviet communism, though to some extent this constitutes a prefiguration within a Japanese context of the Maoist philosophy that gained such currency after the Chinese revolution of 1949. Explaining the narrative in these terms, we find that the wife of a former student radical who died as a war resistor, specifically one writing against Japanese imperial penetration of East Asia, finds her means of continuing his goals by working in the fields alongside peasants, working to modify their right-wing nationalist sentiments. As a Maoist parable, this film suggests the significance of the peasants as a force of resistance, though the film modifies this by reference to the traditional aspect of Yuki's act of returning to her husband's family. The final flashback that substitutes the image of hands working the fields for hands playing the piano is the quintessence of Maoism. One finds then in *No Regrets for Our Youth* a complicated use of flashbacks for historical/political commentary.

Similarly to Yuki in *No Regrets for Our Youth,* the heroine of *Tender Comrade* (Edward Dymytryk, 1943, from a script by Dalton Trumbo) is a politically recuperated version of the heroine of obsessive love. The film structures its tale of its female, home-front heroine as a coming-of-age story, where the past represents immaturity and the war teaches lessons. The flashback structure provides a complexly ironic alternation of tone, contrasting the serious moments of war with the frivolities of peacetime romance. This alternation of tone might seem either odd or innovative in the context of 1940s filmic melodrama, where a greater consistency of tone is the norm, but it is in fact a trait of the theatrical melodrama tradition. Alternating tonalities were still common in early silent melodramas, but less so by the time this film was made. The ideological strands woven through these contrasted moments are quite ambiguous.

The film opens on the morning of Chris Jones's (Robert Ryan) departure for overseas as his wife, Jo (Ginger Rogers), hurries him off to Union Station. A teasing banter reminiscent of sibling squabbles sets a light comedic tone for this initial scene, which is dispelled in the actual departure scene, whose camera angles emphasize the characters' subjective views of being torn apart from each other.

After this opening of contrasting moods, the film chronicles Jo's home-front occupation, showing her operating a forklift at Douglass Aircraft and later urging her friends to form a collective living situation to sustain each other economically and emotionally through the war. "War Widows Local 37," as Jo jokingly terms their project in running their household as a "democracy" where resources are pooled, becomes the main concern of the present-tense narrative, providing an illustration of home-front issues such as fidelity and loneliness, rationing versus hoarding, and treatment of a German immigrant who joins their household as a cook. The narrative implicitly explores the possibility of wage-earning women cooperating in an experimental form of socialism, a leftist concern that is never directly thematized, for obvious reasons.

The flashbacks contrast in tone. The first two occur at night, after the household members retire to their separate bedrooms, leaving Jo alone with her photograph of Chris on her nightstand and her thoughts of the past, while the last flashback occurs when she is alone in the hospital after giving birth to her and Chris's child. Sentimentality is suggested by the introduction and conclusion of each flashback with an image of a couple meeting in a soft-focus landscape dominated by sky and clouds, yet the tone of each flashback recalls the comic treatment of the film's opening, and each narrates a fight between the young couple, each presenting an ironic view of the remembered past. A series of comically related disputes whose themes are Jo's feeling she's not receiving enough attention and the difficulty of caring for a neighbor's child are what the flashbacks recall. Considering that Jo performs a leadership role in the women's collectively run household, the disputes between Jo and Chris point out the sharp contrast between the headstrong bride and the mature, autonomous person she becomes by the film's end.

The flashbacks are not just comic, they are ironic, as each theme quickly is counterpointed in a manner that refers to the present action of the narrative. Even though frivolous and personal, the flashbacks involve serious references to the war; Chris ignores Jo because he is preoccupied with increasingly frightening international news, and during the difficulties of handling their neighbor's baby their own fears of parenthood are overshadowed by the newspaper headline that announces the drafting of married men. The irony of this flashback is doubled by its maternity-hospital frame. The flashbacks also convey Jo's dissatisfaction with her role as a housewife, though her complaints are undercut by the comic treatment and the contrast to Chris's concern with the impending war. Whatever resonance there is to the complaint of this future defense-plant worker that she is merely a "cheap housekeeper" as she piles unironed shirts at her inattentive husband's feet is subsumed in the aura of guilt that the flashbacks acquire as her complaints are remembered in Chris's absence, while he is fighting overseas. It is as if the reminiscences are wrought with regret: "If only Chris were here now I wouldn't complain about a thing." This edge of guilt surfaces as Jo tells her friend after she returns home with the baby, "Most of the fights I had with Chris were over nothing at all." The war is marked as a maturation process, one that turns children into parents and selfish individuals into collectively minded persons whose fulfillment comes as a direct outgrowth of their participation in a social process. However, guilt is linked, as we have said, to obsessional neurosis; here obsessional love is indirectly depicted as feeding on the guilt of the wartime home front. The ironic tone of the flashbacks and their insertion in the present as moments of reminiscence spurred by loneliness and longing for the absent male generate ambiguous and sometimes contradictory messages. Much of the feminist potential in the focus on Jo and the women's collective is actually mitigated by the flashbacks and their framing.

The final sequence suggests a way that the audience might have absorbed these contradictions into an interpretation that does not have such an unsettling multiplicity of messages and such a disturbing recognition that the prewar experience of American women was perhaps not ideal. Upon receiving a telegram announcing Chris's death in action, Jo wakes up her baby. As she holds the child, there is an auditory flashback to Chris's serious words of farewell at Union Station, where he stated his plans for after the war. Then Jo addresses her infant son, telling him of the meaning of his father's sacrifice. This final presentation of dead father to infant son represents the incorporation of the past into the future and of the flashbacks into the present drama. Jo's monologue suggests the importance of memory images in the formation of human values, so that this closing scene serves as a metacommentary on the flashback strategy of Hollywood's wartime films; even when the past is presented as comic, ironic, or insufficient, it bears within it promise for the future different from that which the present of war seems to allow.

Memories, even those of individual foibles and marital differences, are here endowed with the power to establish identity and serve identification with a heritage and a cause. In the case of other films that do not use flashbacks, the narrative as a whole can become this sort of fictional "memory" that can be taken as a representation of our social memory. Flashback films, on the other hand, imbed the process by which memory forms the individual and the social group within the narrative. They narrate what it means to remember. They indicate what the power of memory can be for a fictional character while becoming a similar extension of that memory formation for their audience. Through their structuring of memory sequences as subjective recall of historical and personal experience, these films structurally underscore the process by which memories are granted the power to define the individual and the social group that identifies with the remembered experience of another's story.

Given these general statements of the ideological functioning of fictive memory depiction, certain differences between melodramas like *Possessed* and *Floating Clouds*, on one hand, and *No Regrets* and *Tender Comrade*, on the other, are all the more striking. In *No Regrets* and *Tender Comrade*, where the female psyche is positioned within a very specifically wrought political frame, obsessional love can be colored with an extremely positive connotation. The narrative invests in circumstances surrounding obsessional love, resanctifying and reinvesting in the sacrifice "I," the good girl who loves beyond her self, loves selflessly, the hero worthy of her love. It is as if the heroine of *True-Heart Susie* can be resurrected by a rather astonishing leap backward into the history of melodrama. An earlier heroine can be made to serve not Victorian morality, but antifascist resistance and Maoist realignments in *No Regrets* or left-wing affiliation with patriotic militarism in *Tender Comrade*. Yet when the psyche is so positioned ideologically, the warp endemic to melodrama is exposed from another angle. If melodrama in its symbolic narratives proposes many psychoanalytical formations, we cannot simply take melodrama to illustrate the truth of the psyche, even symbolically. It deforms those formations as context necessitates.

No Regrets and *Tender Comrade* urge us to forget the cost of female sacrifice to obsessional love by so ennobling it; while the heroines of these films are depicted as incapable of redefining their lives after loss except as extravagant rededication to the act of mourning, this memorial function of the heroine is, if not actually hidden, at least disguised. In contrast, by thematizing that sacrifice, *Floating Clouds*, like *Camille* and *Letter from an Unknown Woman*, foregrounds the cost the other films can't afford to admit. Still this sacrifice is aestheticized and romanticized. *Possessed* extravagantly theatricalizes the cost of obsessional love and is least accommodating to it. Yet it in turn is least sympathetic toward its heroine, judging her harshly. The paradox is that while these melodramas treat obsessive love differently, each feeds off the motivating energy of the obsession. Each enacts the obsession, replays it. Melodrama is obsessive.

Here we come to a far more fundamental questioning of melodrama as form. For all it can do in symbolization of the psyche and in raising questions of the subject in history, as these designed symbolizations overlap and cross, there seems always in this symbolizing embodiment in melodramatic form more of the symptom than of the analysis. Melodrama has determined limits. If melodrama derives its force from symbolizing the psyche or dramatizing the historical moment, we must also remember that its character psychology is constructed to serve the force of this narrative mode or its ideological preoccupations. It seems that much of the valorization of melodrama as a women's genre, much of the recent spectator-study-based approval melodrama is receiving for speaking to women's psychoanalytical dilemmas, fails to take into account precisely these paradoxes.

In conclusion, let me return to a question with which I opened this chapter, the problem of comparative study of melodrama across cultural traditions and histories, across national boundaries. One thing I have shown is that neither national typing nor chronological and contextual periodization is as obvious or even as possible as is often assumed. Here we have looked at four films made in two different countries during relatively the same period. We have found striking similarities between two pairs of films formed across those national boundaries, coupled with striking differences between the films coming from the same country. Historical readings, genre studies, and studies of national cinemas by methodological proclivity have favored the typologies that seem so hard to produce here, once comparative methodologies and deconstructive principles are brought into play.

Admittedly, my comparisons also show a greater restraint and understatement in the Japanese films, even as they mobilize rather flamboyant melodramatic tropes, in contrast with a greater figurative reiteration, symbolic saturation, and metacommentary in the American examples. It is my hypothesis that this difference in degree can be to some extent traced to the residual force of the different histories, the different patterns in which the theatrical melodrama was assimilated in each case. Yet this difference should not be taken as more than it is, a difference in degree. For I have found more that is similar at the level of underlying structures than I had at first expected. This is not because the melodramas represent the truth in its universal or even its psychoanalytical or literary aspects; it is because they represent similar myths that similar cultures are simultaneously and quite emotionally calling into being. Our "real" is fundamentally melodramatic.

Notes

1. See, for example, Elsaesser (1972), which discusses only the British tradition of melodrama as a model for analyzing American film. This has been continued in the feminist readings of melodrama by Linda Williams (1984), Christine Gledhill (1987), and E. Ann Kaplan (1987).
2. According to Frank Rahill (1967), the British patent system began with a grant in 1660 by Charles II to Drury Lane and Covent Garden with "the exclusive acting rights to the spoken drama." These were extended to Haymarket in

1705 (p. 135). The privileges of the patent houses were revoked in 1843 with the passage of the Theatrical Regulation Act (p. 119). In France the patents were originally granted to the Opéra in 1669 and 1672, forbidding singing in other theaters, and to the Comédie Française in 1680, forbidding other theaters to use dialogue (Goimard 1980, 19). These patents were revoked in 1791 by a law that stipulated that any citizen could "build a public theater and there put on plays of all genres" (Thomasseau 1984, 5; my translation). This section of the chapter concerning French melodrama is drawn from an earlier article of mine (Turim 1987).
3. Faubion Bowers (1974, 208–12) uses the term "melodrama" pejoratively in reference to political dramas and Shimpa. See also Sato (1982).
4. *Camille* was also adapted in Hollywood silent films of 1915, 1917, and 1921.
5. Anderson and Richie (1982, 163–5). Joan Mellen (1976, 44) discusses a scene that is not in the American print of the film: "Kurosawa shows her, as a child, painting airplanes and locomotives and involved with 'other mechanical things,' unlike other girls – suggesting, quite prophetically, that a non-sexist educational experience will produce a new kind of woman, one equal to men in every way." From Mellen's description it is possible that this scene is a flashback deleted from some prints and intriguing for its feminist implications. However, Mellen's interpretation of the film seems to force it into a far more radically feminist statement than is necessarily evident in the film text.

References

Anderson, Joseph L., and Donald Richie (1982). *The Japanese Film: Art and Industry.* Princeton: Princeton University Press.
Bowers, Faubion (1974). *Japanese Theater.* Rutland, Vt.: Charles E. Tuttle.
Elsaesser, Thomas (1972). "Tales of Sound and Fury: Observations on the Family Melodrama." *Monogram* 4:2–15.
Freud, Sigmund (1963). *Three Case Histories.* New York: Collier.
Genette, Gérard (1982). *Palimpsestes.* Paris: Editions du Seuil.
Gledhill, Christine, ed. (1987). *Home Is Where the Heart Is: Studies in Melodrama and the Woman's Film.* London: BFI Publishing.
Goimard, Jacques (1980). "Le Mélodrame: Le mot et la chose." *Les Cahiers de la cinémathèque* 28.
Kaplan, E. Ann (1987). "Mothering, Feminism and Representation: The Maternal in Melodrama and the Women's Film 1910–1940." in *Home Is Where the Heart Is: Studies in Melodrama and the Woman's Film,* ed. Christine Gledhill. London: BFI Publishing.
Mellen, Joan (1976). *The Waves at Genji's Door: Japan through Its Cinema.* New York: Pantheon.
Rahill, Frank (1967). *The World of Melodrama.* Philadelphia: University of Pennsylvania Press.
Sato Tadao (1982). *Currents in Japanese Cinema.* Trans. Gregory Barrett. Tokyo: Kodansha International.

Thomasseau, Jean-Marie (1984). *Le mélodrame.* Paris: Presse Universitaire de France.

Turim, Maureen (1987). "French Melodrama: Theory of a Specific History." *Theatre Journal* 39, 3:307–27.

—— (1989). *Flashbacks in Film: Memory and History.* New York: Routledge.

Williams, Linda (1984). " 'Something Else Besides a Mother': *Stella Dallas* and the Maternal Melodrama." *Cinema Journal* 24, 1:2–27.

CHAPTER X

Negotiating the transition
to capitalism:
The case of *Andaz*

Paul Willemen

The critical recovery of Douglas Sirk's work in the early 1970s sparked a renewal of interest in melodrama in film studies and in popular culture theories. Subsequently, under the impetus of a certain genre of feminist cultural politics, allied with an emphasis on the complexities of consumption (not to say consumerism) and a desire to reevaluate areas of cultural production of which women were said to be the dominant consumers, this interest in cinematic melodrama was extended to the discussion – and in my view the positive valuation – of soap operas and of written romances. Unfortunately, all this work has concerned itself exclusively (except in some Latin American countries – and that work has not been translated and widely circulated because of it) with the products of the Anglo-Saxon media monopolies in film and television as well as in publishing. And these discussions have systematically neglected to see those cultural products and practices as part and parcel of "advanced industrial" media monopolies and their efforts to dominate a global market.

The relations between texts and viewers or consumers have also been discussed exclusively within that framework, without taking any notice of its place and function within strategies for world market domination. The Latin American work on telenovelas (e.g., the work of Michelle Mattelart [1986]) is not taken into account in any of the major books on melodrama, and neither is the work by Chinese critics on Hong Kong melodrama. Egyptian and Asian melodramas are hardly even referred to. This is a classic instance of a projective, universalizing appropriation: The study of the British and of the North American melodramatic production has been presented as constitutive of the genre, as the prototype of the universal genre of melodrama. Other types of melodrama or melodramas from other cultural spheres can then only be discussed in relation to or as a deviation from the Anglo-American norm. Therefore, from this ethnocentric point of view, the relations between viewers/consumers and melodramatic texts that can be discerned by studying the melodramatic productions generated by the dominant, monopolizing institutions of the Anglo-American media industries would hold good for all melodramatic production anywhere in the world, regardless of the historical conditions for which or within which that production arose. The clear implication of these melodrama studies is that the Hollywood norm of narration in film as well as in television was elevated into an ideal type against which the products of other cultures are to be measured.

At the same time, those studies increasingly evinced a parrotlike identification with preconstituted social groups. In this case: the fantasy construct of a female mass audience. The argument ran something like this (I am parodying, but only very slightly): Since all these ordinary women delight in melodramatic productions, and since we must identify with the oppressed, it must follow that melodramatic productions are to be valued positively, since to value the genre negatively is tantamount to despising its consumers. The possibility that the capitalist organization of the mass production of media texts could also have severely damaging and disabling effects both on the products and on the consumers was not to be countenanced. Moreover, melodrama studies degenerated into the study of consumer preferences that could only benefit the monopoly producers (and advertising agencies selling particular consumer groups to television) instead of trying to establish critical criteria or modes of analysis that would allow us to make distinctions between different aspects of particular melodramatic productions. In order to avoid confronting the complexities of the way capitalist production affects people via, among other things, texts, many film and television studies practitioners elaborated an exceedingly simplistic and misleading discourse on pleasure while accusing critics of puritan elitism (usually by accusing them of clinging to the high–low culture dichotomy).

In addition, the possibility that what we in the West call melodramas might operate differently in other social formations and in other historical periods was not addressed either – and still isn't. In other words, a genre that had been feminized (see Andreas Huyssen [1986] on the feminization of industrially produced popular culture) by Western "high" culture has been claimed by women media commentators as, indeed, a women's cultural form with special affinity with women's concerns and desires. Which is how a category called into being and defined by the patriarchal bourgeoisie of the industrializing nineteenth century came to be promoted as the repository of women's popular culture. The only difference was that these commentators attached a positive instead of negative value to it. Except, of course, as an economic practice: As a source of profits, it was valued very positively indeed. And it still is: See, for instance, the passionate defense of North American soap operas by representatives of Rupert Murdoch's Sky Tele-

vision and by Saatchi & Saatchi in the British "deregulation of
television" debates on the grounds that television should give the people, the consumers, what they want and that advertisers are ready and
waiting to assist with this fundamentally democratic reorganization of
the media (killing off public service broadcasting in the process and
outlawing as "elitist" any attempt to invoke notions of critical quality
in the democracy argument).

Consequently, melodrama studies did not ask questions that might
have emerged from comparative studies. The study of melodrama in
Western film and television studies has remained imprisoned in this
arbitrarily (but ever so conveniently, from the point of view of the Anglo-American advertising giants) defined universalizing and populist
problematic, which has so dramatically handicapped the work.

More recent studies (for instance, the recent work of Charlotte
Brundson [1990]) are beginning to rectify this state of affairs, although
mostly outside of film and television studies, which still lag lamenta-
bly behind in this respect.

All I want to do here is to point to some aspects of the way Mehboob Khan's melodrama *Andaz* can be used to suggest some questions
not asked in any of the existing film-melodrama books I am familiar
with. This Indian melodrama asks me, a Western critic, questions
about the framework within which Western notions of melodrama have
been elaborated. I do not pretend to be able to extrapolate from this
one film any conclusions about Indian melodrama as such nor about
the Indian cinema in the years just after Indian independence. I want
to constitute it as an interlocutor able to bring into focus questions
about deficiencies within my own, Western cultural framework.

First, a few words about the director by way of an introduction.
Mehboob Khan, the son of a policeman, was born in 1909 in a village
in Gujarat. In 1925, he ran away from home to Bombay, where he
eventually entered the film industry. He became an actor in 1934, and
in 1935 he directed his first feature. In 1942 he founded his own production company, and he moved into his own studios in 1952. He
made the all-time Indian blockbuster *Mother India* in 1957. It was a
glossy remake of a film he had made in 1940 called *Aurat*. He made
Andaz in 1949, barely two years after India threw off British rule. His
next film, *Aan*, made in 1952, was one of the first Indian films in tech-
nicolor. Its narrative opposed the corrupt world of the maharajas to
the purity of the peasants, but he had also taken the opportunity to
castigate peasant rebellion at the same time. It is of some interest
to know that, although he was not a communist, he adopted the ham-
mer and sickle as the emblem for his productions. He died in Bombay
in 1963.

Western critics, especially Henri Micciollo, attribute a kind of popular-populist progressivism to Khan, a progressivism apparently hampered by his recourse to melodramatic conventions. Micciollo even goes so far as to compare *Mother India* to *Mother Courage,* no doubt seduced by the echoes in the titles and a Catholic love of heroically suffering mothers. Critics also often refer to Khan's humble origins as an explanation for his alleged progressivism. In fact, in India, being a policeman in the pay of the British was not all that humble, but let us accept that Khan stemmed from the bottom ranks of the petite bourgeoisie.

According to the Indian critic Kishore Valicha (1988), *Andaz* was a particularly important film: "Following independence there was a trend towards urban sophistication. This was epitomised in *Andaz.*... [It] did several things at once: it immortalised the love triangle and focussed attention on youth. Indeed, *Andaz* became a norm for a long time."

We do not have to accept any of the reasons given by Kishore Valicha to believe that the film was indeed regarded as a norm for some time after. Its musical director, Naushad, was regarded as a most distinctive composer; it was the second film in which the notorious couple of Raj Kapoor and Nargis acted together; and it was Dilip Kumar's breakthrough film.

It would be easy to criticize the film for its technical inadequacies (e.g., some notable continuity hiccups, as in the first scene between Nargis and the father in bed) and for other slips, such as the scene where Dilip Kumar plays the piano and a whole orchestra can be heard striking up on the soundtrack, but no piano. However, I want to focus on the film in its capacity as a modernization melodrama in the context of a particular Indian nationalist ideology. I think it is worth reminding ourselves that, like all nationalisms and especially nationalisms forged in the context of national independence struggles, Indian nationalism was a complex amalgam of many different and even politically opposed currents and positions.

In a remarkable book on the subject, Bipan Chandra's *Nationalism and Colonialism in Modern India* (1979), the author commented that the capitalist strategy of nursing and opposing the formerly (in 1936) socialist Nehru, but above all of supporting the right wing in the congress, had succeeded by 1947 in making Nehru into an acceptable prime minister of independent India, and the dominant sectors of capitalism were ready to cooperate with him in the task of building up its economy along the capitalist path.

In that context, the social configuration presented by *Andaz* is of considerable interest. The central family nexus of father and daughter is presented in an absolutist, precapitalist manner. The matrix of the familial relations is rigorously paternalistic, and its values are presented as symbolizing tradition. The father's discourse is referred to in the film as incarnating Indian tradition and customs. Moreover, that father–daughter nexus is the dramatic pivot of the drama: Pressures for change (presented primarily by her wearing Western clothing and adopting Western gestural patterns along with them) will be shown as impacting on the father–daughter relationship and will be judged acceptable or not depending on whether they allow the father's value-world to be transmitted to and internalized by the daughter. The family is obviously presented as extremely well off, but the sources of its wealth, the dead labor hoarded by the family, are not examined. Nevertheless, they appear directly related to Westernization, as is demonstrated by the life-style and clothes at the beginning of the film. However, by not making the generation of the familial wealth an issue at the beginning of the film, the impression is created, largely by omission, that this wealth is rooted in some "traditional" organization of Indian society. However, the reproduction of that wealth, of the life-style and the values that go with it, is now dependent on capitalist enterprise.

It is significant that the family's relation with capitalism, with the actual site of production, is mediated through a hired company president and that interactions with capitalism take place in the domestic home and in the boardroom exclusively. In other words, the family presents all the hallmarks of a landowning aristocracy negotiating its profitable relationship with newly flourishing capitalism and its attendant institutions, but the film conflates the two and thus allows the actual position of the family to remain conveniently vague, partaking of the colonially induced capitalism while simultaneously incarnating a continuation of feudal relations.

There are various references to the fact that "foreign melodies cannot be played on Indian strings" and that "alien flowers do not grow in Indian soil." While such lines are obviously part of the political nationalism that energized the independence struggle, capitalism and industrial enterprise are not to be seen as either an alien flower or a foreign melody. Capitalism is presented, through the family's business interests, as organically and traditionally Indian. And insofar as the symbols of Indian Tradition are at stake in capitalist enterprise, capitalism is itself absorbed into Indian Tradition and is therefore not a source of conflict. Or it should not be, at any rate.

But it is, and that is the subterranean point of the film. The father, who is revealed to have an impaired heart and who soon dies, is echoed by the wheelchair-ridden mother of the son-in-law. She too incarnates traditional values and is a damaged person, forming a strange parental couple with the father. Interestingly, neither the heroine's mother nor the husband's father plays a role, leaving the parental terrain, the world of traditional Indian values, to the damaged parental couple represented in the narrative. It is worth noting that this parental world in charge of traditional India represents the preindependence period, colonial India. To present colonial India as the site of Tradition gives a peculiarly ironic twist to that parental couple, although Mehboob Khan presumably meant to suggest that the Indian bourgeoisie, although damaged by colonial rule, nevertheless remained the embodiment of the True India, of Eternal India, indeed, of Mother India. This move then equates Indian nationalism with the capitalist right wing of Congress, allowing the new bourgeoisie to masquerade as the guardians of Indian authenticity. Bipan Chandra's thesis about Nehru and Congress at the time of independence is thus incarnated in this film by the two parental figures, leaving us with the equation of independent India with Widowed India, a no doubt unintended and paradoxical implication for a strongly patriarchal social order. And an implication the effects of which also spill over into the portrayal of the capitalist who cannot get the girl as well as in the depiction at the beginning of the film of the girl whose man is radically absent (present only in her thoughts). Everything in the film suggests that the elimination of the British has acquired the overtones of parricide.

The dramatic tension of the narrative is then played out in relation to a literal act of reproduction: the daughter's marriage and the child she bears. The family fortune may be treated as aristocratic wealth, but the daughter's dilemma is that she should reconcile the modifications brought by capitalism – and the need to reproduce wealth through capitalist enterprise – with the need to reproduce a precapitalist conception of Indian Tradition, a tradition constructed as predating colonial rule and damaged by colonial rule but nevertheless a tradition that, although precapitalist, is embodied in and by capitalists as well as by an aristocratic playboy.

The contradiction is played out in relation to Nargis's two suitors: One is an infantile spoiled brat who incarnates precapitalist social and familial relations; the other is a diligent manager of the family's involvement with capitalist social relations. What is of interest here is that the precapitalist figure is presented as infantile and feeble though invested with all the authority of traditional absolutist patriarchy, while it is illegitimate for the New Man to reproduce himself, to reproduce anything but the capitalism he is put in charge of. The Pater Familias even warns his daughter not to be "friendly in the new way" with his hired company director. The New Man of capitalism is very much an orphan: He has no parents at all. He is decreed to be the inheritor, or rather the guardian, of the father's traditional legacy, but he fails because he misreads tradition itself. He misreads it because it is embodied in the daughter in the form of a subtext, an implied code rather than an overt one. The daughter is the pivot in this network, since it is in her that an overt text and a hidden one continually combine: an overt text first misread by one suitor, then by her husband, and a hidden text first misread by the suitor, then a different hidden one misread by the husband, until she emphatically acknowledges the impossibility of inhabiting two codes and makes the implicit one explicit in her final words, spoken from behind prison bars and addressed to her husband and child: "I should have listened to my father ...all my misfortunes are my own fault because I should have accepted the subordinate role assigned to women in feudal India."

The film's problem, then, has little to do with women's desires as such: These are only of interest to the narrative in so far as they allow for the presentation of conflicts between more abstract historical and socioeconomic forces. The daughter is not constructed as a character in the Western sense of being an individual subject to the rules of some psychological verisimilitude. She is a figure, a function, a carrier of specific and in this case conflicting social forces. She is not a character. She is an agent.

The problem addressed by the film is a political conundrum: Capitalist enterprise should not affect or interfere with precapitalist relations and the associated traditional moral codes regulating social reproduction. In the new India, precapitalist social relations should fuse with capitalism, leaving the culture and the traditional hierarchical arrangements undisturbed, repairing what was damaged by colonialism. An indigenous and independent capitalism should simply allow an updated form of Old India to come into existence. That capitalism only came in with colonial rule and that the Indian bourgeoisie was therefore a colonial creation are tactfully overlooked – except, arguably, in the damaged status of the parental generation and in the sterility of the New Man and in the very ambiguity of the family's class position. The fact that capitalist social relations must necessarily destroy the precapitalist values and family forms is also simply swept under the carpet, although that is in fact the source of the drama.

Other aspects of Mehboob Khan's notion of Old India, of Mother India, have to be kept in mind here: His notion of a pure (and docile) peasantry is documented in *Aan* and in *Mother India*. To this pure peasantry corresponds an equally pure because equally traditional aristocratic sector which, according to *Andaz*, is now unfortunately being weakened by the need to incorporate a Protestant work ethic into the constellation of autocratic indolence and innate moral superiority. This is also an element that Khan later revised when he represented autocratically indolent figures as the baddies in *Mother India* at a time when he could blame the negative aspects of capitalist exploitation, in a displaced manner, on the backward remnants of a landed aristocracy. The result was that he presented villians that combined cupidity and aristocratic autocracy, with the consequent shift of purity and Indian Tradition toward the peasantry (rather than toward an urban proletariat, which must have been far too urgently present to urban audiences for such a strategy to be acceptable). Nevertheless, active resistance to the ruling structures was still presented as totally unacceptable and as the source of even greater misery. In contrast, the work of Satyajit Ray in the late 1950s, while deploying a very similar ruralist myth of preindustrial innocence, refrained from representing peasant rebellion as an unmitigated evil.

In *Andaz,* the desired fusion of capitalism and Old India is presented as impossible: The father dies and the functions he combined in his person are split across two male characters, the two suitors of his daughter. The film opts in the end for a reassertion of precapitalist social relations, or at least for a mode of social organization that emerged under colonial rule and that is now presented as India's traditional values. Nargis is given a life sentence of containment (she is literally removed from the social fabric) and tearfully admits that she should have listened to her dad and spurned all these alien, modern customs, thus finally legitimating the conservation of tradition over the need for capitalist change. This makes *Andaz* a film advocating the perpetuation of the colonial Indian elite. The only difference – although it is a substantial one – is that now, with independence, this elite has to take charge of its own wealth creation, a responsibility previously rigorously controlled and directed by the British colonizers. With the disappearance of the British, control functions become more complex and have to be split into the perpetuation of social status and the creation of wealth. Khan subordinates wealth creation to the perpetuation of status – class difference – but registers, in *Andaz,* the tragic impossibility of that arch-conservative choice, which in the end means the assertion of an unquestionable legitimacy of a brutally enforced patriarchal rule.

It is, of course, also possible to read many more tensions in the narrative and its mise-en-scène: For instance, the light-colored hair of the child may be construed as signifying the contradiction between tradition and capitalism as well, especially perhaps evoking in a subterranean manner the fact that capitalism in India is irrevocably colored by Western colonization. But the essential point I want to make here remains: *Andaz* is a melodrama that presents the tensions and contradictions involved in the adaptation of precapitalist social relations to a capitalist environment, while forgetting that the Indian bourgeoisie is itself a colonial legacy.

This raises for me the following question: To what extent is this same set of tensions a dynamic and a constructive force in Western melodrama? Michael Denning's (1987) study of North American dime novels between 1880 and 1920 would suggest that the melodramatic plots used in those stories rehearse the same types of conflicts but propose different solutions. The worker hero marries the boss's daughter and becomes foreman or manager in his turn. Aristocratic privilege and prejudice are depicted negatively, and the negative sides of capitalism are seen as stemming from an undue residue of precapitalist values surviving into the world of capitalism. Perhaps it should go without saying that those narratives expend a great deal of energy in ruling out possible resolutions in a socialist direction: The real villains beyond redemption – and often killed in the course of the narrative – are the socialist troublemakers, depicted as agitators and terrorists.

If we should consider melodrama in the West as a way of negotiating the transition from absolutism to capitalism, from the feudal aristocracy to the industrial bourgeoisie as the ruling class, or at least as presenting the problems of capitalist modernization, then the presentation of the family in such narratives would be determined precisely by the need to reconcile the drama of lineage and reproduction with the drama of social-structural change. This in turn would provide the frame within which the female protagonists are elaborated as the privileged sites or agents for the enacting of the tensions and contradictions involved in the process of social reproduction. And although it is possible to project Western character conventions with their notions of individuality into such a frame, it would be a mistake to analyze the role of women in melodrama outside of the framework which structures and locates them as signifying figures, as agencies. In other words, female protagonists may well be constructed as people who insist on their needs and desires in the face of a hostile patriarchal culture and social necessity, but they are permitted to do so only within the framework and the problematic of the melodramatic genre's social function and inscription: which is to accommodate the survival of precapitalist relations within capitalism in order to legitimate and maintain capitalist social relations, that is, capitalism with an allegedly human face.

A particular melodrama will then have fulfilled its function if it evokes the possibility of emancipatory pleasures inherent in a process of social change (these are mostly presented as the pleasures of consumption) and then succeeds in organizing those pleasures in such a way that the dominant gratifications dispensed by the film or by the text become associated with conservative values. In Western melodrama, such conservative values would then be the affirmation of "traditional" values in the context of capitalist modernization. Melodrama is the drama of capitalist modernization, framed in such a way as to exclude the very possibility of change in a socialist direction.

References

Brundson, Charlotte (1990). "Problems of Quality." *Screen* 31, I.

Chandra, Bipan (1979). *Nationalism and Colonialism in Modern India.* New Delhi: Orient Longman.

Denning, Michael (1987). *Mechanic Accents: Dime Novels and Working-Class Culture in America.* London: Verso.

Huyssen, Andreas (1986). "Mass Culture as Woman: Modernism's Other." In *After the Great Divide.* Bloomington: Indiana University Press.

Mattelart, Michelle (1986). *Women, Media and Crisis: Femininity and Disorder.* London: Comedia.

Valicha, Kishore (1988). *The Moving Image: A Study of Indian Cinema.* London: Sangam Books.

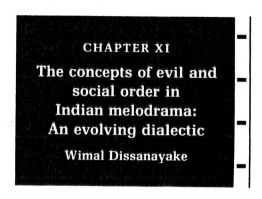

CHAPTER XI

The concepts of evil and social order in Indian melodrama: An evolving dialectic

Wimal Dissanayake

The objective of this chapter is to examine three of the most popular films made in India in relation to the concepts of evil and social order, and to analyze how these concepts as discursive practices have been undergoing a transformation as a consequence of diverse social and cultural factors.

Indologists, by and large, have subscribed to the notion that there is no problem of evil in Indian culture, and philosophers and religionists have sought to explicate it in relation to philosophical works. However, as Wendy Doniger O'Flaherty has ably pointed out, it is to mythology that we should turn if we are to obtain a clearer and more representative picture of the nature and significance of evil in Indian culture and imagination. As she says, "The theodicy that is developed in Hindu mythology demonstrates a more popular, general, and spontaneous attitude toward evil than may be found in the more complex arguments of the Hindu theologians" (O'Flaherty 1976, 8).

In the generality of Indian myths, evil is perceived as an outcome of greed and lust. According to the celebrated Indian epic *The Mahabharata,*

Formerly, Prajapati brought forth pure creatures, who were truthful and virtuous. These creatures joined the gods in the sky whenever they wished, and they lived and died by their own wish. In another time, those who dwelt on earth were overcome by desire and anger, and they were abandoned by the gods. Then by their foul deeds, these evil ones were trapped in the chain of rebirth, and they became atheists. (O'Flaherty 1976, 23)

According to a statement in the *Skanda Purana.*

In the Golden Age, people were happy and equal. There was no distinction between high and low, no law of separate classes. Then some time, people became greedy, and the wishing-trees disappeared and passions arose. (O'Flaherty 1976, 23)

Traditional Indian culture takes a very realistic attitude to the concept of evil, treating it as an entity that is both inescapable and important to social order. According to many cycles of myths, God created evil as a positive element in the universe with the intention of allowing goodness to define itself in opposition to evil. In a much venerated classical text on ethics, it is said that

In order to distinguish actions, the creator separated *dharma* and *adharma,* and made the pairs of opposites such as happiness and unhappiness. And whatever he assigned to each at the first creation, truth and falsehood, that quality clung spontaneously to it. (O'Flaherty 1976, 47)

In this regard, the following comment by O'Flaherty is very apposite:

In Hinduism, evil must be rightly ordered and kept in its place, away from the gods, distributed among men or demons or both. Only in this way would there be a true balance, a true plenitude; were evil to weaken altogether, weaken the gods, or to disappear altogether – were all men to become virtuous, or all demons godly – there would be no universe at all, for their would be no "contrasting pairs." In this view, God is powerful and good; he chooses to place evil and suffering in the universe, not because he is forced to do so by Karma, nor because he is so evil that he enjoys seeing others suffer, but because if he wishes to create a universe at all, it is by definition necessary for that universe to contain evil as well as good. (O'Flaherty 1976, 49)

In traditional Indian culture, as in most other cultures, evil was perceived as an unwholesome force. In the case of India, however, the relationship between self and social order was not a simple one where evil was seen as a negative and goodness a positive. As has been pointed out, the gods are responsible for the creation of evil for a variety of reasons: in traditional Hinduism, because *dharma* is only possible and valuable and *adharma* exists to act as a foil to it; in mythology dealing with asceticism, because the gods are afraid that human beings will acquire too much power and overcome them; and in devotional mythology, because God wishes to come down to the level of evil and to participate in it with the intention of liberating humankind. So in Indian culture, while the negativity of evil was recognized, it was also valued as a force necessary for the maintenance of the social order.

It is against this background of thinking that we need to discuss the three Indian melodramas that constitute the subject of this paper: *Fate (Kismet), Vagabond (Awaara),* and *Flames (Sholay).* There are some interesting points of affinity that need to be pointed out at the outset. *Kismet, Awaara,* and *Sholay* are three of the most popular films made in India. All three can be categorized as melodramas and have as their leading actors some of the most well known stars in the Indian screen. All three films were produced in Hindi and deal with stories related to robbery and outlaws. The heroes of all three films are unconventional in that they operate from the wrong side of the law. Moreover, in terms of good and villainy, *Kismet, Awaara,* and *Sholay* differ appreciably from the general run of Hindi film melodramas.

According to traditional Indian aestheticians, a hero in a play had to be handsome, courageous, virtuous, of noble birth, and so on, as opposed to the villain, who presented the exact opposite set of attributes. For example, in *The Dasharupa,* a classical treatise on Indian dramaturgy, it is said that the hero of a play should be

well-bred, charming, liberal, clever, affable, popular, upright, eloquent, of exalted lineage, resolute, young, endowed with intelligence, energy, memory, wisdom, skill in the arts, pride, heroic, mighty, vigorous, familiar with the codes, and a just observer of laws. (Haas 1962)

In contrast, his opponent is "avaricious, stubborn, criminal and vicious." This distinction, with minor modifications, is found not only in classical theater but in folk theater as well. In the domain of cinema, too, one may discern a general conformity to this stipulated opposition. What is interesting about the heroes of the three films under consideration in this chapter, *Kismet, Awaara,* and *Sholay,* is that they represent a commingling of the attributes of the hero and his antagonist, as enunciated in the classical treatises and given expression in traditional works, popular and folk as well as classical.

Kismet

Kismet is one of the longest running Indian films of all times. It ran for three years to full houses in the same theater in Calcutta, breaking all previous records. *Kismet* tells the story of Shekhar, who as a child runs away from home and grows up to become an expert thief. He falls in love with Rani, who is an ex-dancer and now almost an invalid, and their relationship propels the story of this film forward.

Shekhar, a good-looking young thief, one day happens to observe a man stealing a watch from an old man. He quickly picks the thief's pocket and decides to pursue him. The thief goes into a jewelry shop, where stolen goods are bought. There the owner of the shop introduces Shekhar to Banke, whose pocket Shekhar had just picked. Banke, realizing that he has been outfoxed by Shekhar, seeks to enter into an alliance with him. But much to his dismay, Shekhar sees the old man, whose watch was just stolen, coming into the jewelry shop with the intention of hawking his watch, so that he can attend a theater perfor-

mance. Shekhar, overcome by remorse, decides to take him to the theater performance. There, to his great surprise, he comes to know that
the old man with him now used to be the owner of that very theater,
and that the lead singer is actually his daughter.

It so happens that Rani, the old man's daughter, was once a tal-
ented dancer. One day, under the influence of liquor, the old man had
ordered her to dance nonstop until she collapsed out of sheer exhaus-
tion. Rani never danced again, and now walked on crutches. To make
matters even stranger, the present owner of the theater, Indrajitbabu,
had once worked for the old man and was now someone from whom
the old man borrowed money.

The performance is over, and the old man disappears. As Rani is
searching for her father, she is very nearly run over by a car but for the
timely intervention of Shekhar, who quickly pulls her aside. Rani had
seen him with his father and takes him to be one of his father's
friends. Indrajitbabu and his wife appear on the scene, and Shekhar,
who had observed the gold necklace she was wearing, deftly steals it.
As the police are in the vicinity, he decides to conceal it in Rani's carriage. Before he is able to recover it, however, the carriage disappears.
Shekhar finds his way to Rani's house and takes back the necklace.
Rani wakes up and sees him. She is under the impression that he has
come with his father and asks him to stay the night over with them in
their house. The following day Indrajitbabu's manager demands that
her father pay back a loan that he had obtained from his client. Shekhar, rising to the occasion, suggests that he will rent a room in their
house so as to facilitate the paying back of the loan.

The police inspector who arrives at Indrajitbabu's house to investi-
gate the theft of the necklace learns about the sad story of the man's
eldest son, Madan. Madan had grown up to be a mischievous child,
and one day as punishment, his father had ejected him from the
house. He had never returned. Mohan is Indrajitbabu's younger son,
and he is in love with Lila, Rani's sister. In the meantime, Shekhar is
paying back the old man's loan by stealing from Indrajitbabu's manager. Rani anxiously hopes that one day she will be able to walk without the crutches, and a doctor tells Shekhar that it can be done if he is
prepared to spend a substantial sum of money. Shekhar also comes to
know that the necklace he had stolen from Indrajitbabu's wife had
originally been a gift Rani had been given by his father, and which
later they had been forced to sell. Shekhar gives Rani the necklace,
and each expresses true feelings for the other. Despite Shekhar's ad-
vice to the contrary, Rani wears the necklace to the theater, and Indrajitbabu's wife detects it and calls the police. The police arrive on the
scene and demand that she tell them where she had gotten the necklace, but Rani does not answer. At that point Shekhar rushes in and

confesses that he stole it. Rani is overwhelmed by shame and does not want to have anything to do with him.

Mohan, in the meantime, goes away to continue his higher education, unaware of the fact that his girlfriend is pregnant, and Indrajit-babu rudely dismisses the liaison between his son and Lila. Meanwhile, Rani is operated on and is cured. However, she finds out, much to her chagrin, that the money for the operation had come from Shekhar. At this point, as fate would have it, the police inspector, who has been following the entire case very carefully, comes to the realization that Shekhar is in point of fact Indrajitbabu's long lost son, Madan. All charges against him are dropped, and all are happily reunited, as Indrajitbabu finally accepts Rani and Lila as his daughters-in-law.

The story of *Kismet* conforms to the characteristic pattern of Indian melodrama, not only in the way that the digesis is constructed, but also in the way song and dance counterpoint the digesis. *Kismet* contains eight songs that became extremely popular with the Indian moviegoing public. It creates a symbolic world that is all too familiar to the audiences.

Although this film follows broadly the contours of Indian melodrama, it also departs significantly from the accepted model. For example, the hero of the film, Shekhar, does not conform to the conventions of Indian melodrama: He is a thief who operates from the other side of the law, and this goes against the usual image of a hero. On the other hand, although a thief, he is an affable and good-hearted one, and his appearance, demeanor, and behavior strengthen this impression. This also contradicts the accepted semiotics of villainy. As in most Indian melodramas, romance takes center stage, but is here grafted onto a character who, according to standard practice, would hardly qualify to be the romantic hero.

Although *Kismet* deals with the life of an outlaw and with social distinctions, at the end of the film we realize that the thief Shekhar is none other than the elder son of Indrajitbabu, and family union metonymically legitimizes the existing social order. If questions of class and exploitation are temporarily raised, they are quickly submerged in the happy family reunion and the romantic fulfillments. The film attributes everything to the power of fate, and accepts it as a given. Hence, the concept of evil that is contained in the film in no way serves to question the existing social order or extend its discursive boundaries.

Awaara

Awaara by Raj Kapoor combines romance, social commentary, music, and melodrama in a way that appealed enormously to the moviegoing public. Indeed, its popularity was not confined to India, and as a result of this film, Raj Kapoor became a well-known name in the Arab world, China, Southeast Asia, and the Soviet Union.

The story centers around the life of Raj, a boy growing up in the slums of Bombay. Judge Raghunath, a conservative man, is firmly convinced that only children of gentlemen can climb up the social ladder and enjoy the kind of social recognition that he does. By the same token, he subscribes to the notion that the children of criminals are bound to be eternally condemned to a life of depravity and darkness. As a consequence of a series of events depicted in the film, this conviction is seriously challenged.

Bharati, Judge Raghunath's wife, is abducted by the notorious criminal Jagga, who resolved to become a criminal in the first place, when Judge Raghunath erroneously convicted him of a crime he had not committed. Because Jagga's father was a feared criminal, Judge Raghunath, in keeping with his philosophy, arrived at the conclusion that Jagga had committed the crime. Jagga later returns the wife, but the news of her abduction as well as her pregnancy quickly spreads in the community, much to the anger and worry of Raghunath. Clearly upset by the circulating gossip, he decides to discard his wife. Bharati gives birth to a son in the slums, and he is named Raj. Jagga is obviously happy with the turn of events. Bharati takes Raj to Bombay with the intention of bringing him up in a way that would be in accord with the reputation and social standing of his father. Raj is admitted to a school where he meets Rita and takes an intense liking to her. But as Raj is unable to pay his school fees, he is thrown out of school and enters the dark and dangerous world of crime. It so happens that his friend Rita is the daughter of a friend of Raghunath. Many years later, the paths of Raj and Rita cross again. Now Rita is a young attorney and Raj a criminal, and their earlier friendship during school days blossoms into love. Raghunath, of course, has no inkling of who Raj is, but is somehow suspicious of him. Rita invites Raj to her house for her twenty-first birthday, and Raj accepts the invitation, but is now confronted with the problem of buying her a good gift. When he sees Judge Raghunath on the street carrying a box of jewelry for Rita, he knocks him down and steals an expensive necklace from it. At the party, the Judge recognizes Raj as the one who had stolen the necklace. He is horrified and livid with anger. To make matters worse, he realizes that Raj has given Rita the necklace, but Raj leaves the birthday party before he is caught. This sequence of events prompts Rita to look into Raj's life and background. As a consequence, she arrives at the conclusion that Raj is none other than Raghunath's son. (As in *Kismet*, here, too, we begin to see how the topoi of necklaces and mistaken identities play a crucial role in the propulsion of the story.)

As a criminal, Raj has increasingly come under the influence of Jagga and is aware of it. He wishes to free himself from his dominion and, in sheer desperation, kills Jagga. As Raj's lawyer, Rita accuses Raghunath in court of having succumbed to unfounded suspicions about his wife's infidelity and blames him for his son becoming a felon. Had he not behaved irrationally, Raj would not be leading the kind of life to which he was not condemned. But Raghunath refuses to face the fact that the criminal who is being tried is his son. For his part, Raj, who has by now been made aware that he is in point of fact Judge Raghunath's son, is deeply hurt by all this. He makes a speech, siding with all those children who have, like him, grown up in a sordid environment and ended up on the wrong side of the law. He stresses the fact that criminality is not a product of heredity but of social environment. Raj's speech makes a deep impression on Raghunath, who finally comes to accept that Raj is his son. He visits him in prison and admits his guilt. Raj is given a three-year prison term, and he assures Rita that after his release he will lead a good life.

Awaara is a characteristic Indian melodrama, with song and dance contributing to the enhancement of the whole spectacle. In *Awaara,* the melodrama combines narrative and spectacle in a more integrated fashion than in *Kismet.* Consider the famous dream sequence in the film, which has been executed with much dexterity and takes place at a significant juncture in the filmic digesis. It exemplifies graphically the problems facing Raj and points at the vast social gap that separates him from Rita. The dream sequence serves to fulfill two important functions. On the one hand, it forces Raj to face the reality of his situation and make up his mind. On the other, it serves to externalize, in terms of readily graspable visual icons and culturally embedded signifiers, the conflict encountered by the hero.

The dream sequence consists of three parts, each with distinctive themes, visual and musical. The first transports us to the idyllic world of Raj and Rita. We see a flight of steps leading to a spiral tower amidst vast, fluffy clouds. Beautiful damsels dressed in white dance on and around the steps. We see Rita at the bottom of the flight of steps, beckoning Raj, giving expression to her desire. In stark contrast, the second part depicts the interior of the hell to which Raj is condemned. Here, instead of the icons of romance and desire, we see grotesque skulls with bulging eyes; instead of the beautiful damsels, we observe sinister-looking figures wearing horns. Raj desperately cries out for help, as the flames are on the verge of consuming him, and he is unable to free himself from the threatening demons.

No sooner does he cry out than he is transported back to the romantic scene with the fluffy clouds and the flight of steps, and Rita at the center. As she walks up the steps, she begins to sing joyfully. This sequence, while spectacular and inventive, underlines the disparity between the two worlds that Raj lives in, and the iconography of the dream sequence serves to enforce this point. We are, at first, shown the flight of stairs from bottom up, emblematizing the social gap between Raj and Rita, and as the song ends, we are shown Rita leading Raj up the flight of steps. In the eyes of Raj, as well as the audience, uniting with Rita means moving up in the world socially. Furthermore, because all this is depicted through a dream sequence, it serves to establish the point that, although Raj is a poor criminal from the underworld, he is also the son of Justice Raghunath, and the social gap between Raj and Rita is illusory.

As in *Kismet,* in *Awaara* the idea of social evil is at the heart of the film. However, whereas in *Kismet* it was explicated, rationalized, and evaluated in terms of the inevitability of fate, in *Awaara,* it is a product of the social order. Raghunath's conviction that criminals are born and not made is severely challenged by the film, and he himself comes to accept its baselessness. The statements made by Rita and Raj also serve to underline this belief. In *Awaara,* therefore, we see a greater emphasis on the social dimension of evil than in *Kismet.* However, this mode of thinking is not allowed to result in an extension of the discursive boundaries related to social order, because the emphasis is placed on the romance and the genealogy of the family. As I have pointed out elsewhere, Raj Kapoor's is a cinema of security (1988). He achieves this sense of security by harmonizing various discourses like tradition and modernity, and social protest and maintenance of the status quo, and this is clearly in evidence in *Awaara.*

Sholay

Sholay is reputed to be the most popular Indian film ever made. (The dialogues contained in *Sholay* have been released on long-playing records and sold to the public, creating a new market in the process. These dialogues are often played on loudspeakers at fairs, weddings, commemorations of all kinds, and religious ceremonies, much to the amusement of the attending audiences. In addition, a whole slew of *Sholay*-brand commodities such as jeans, belts, and jackets have entered the market as well.) *Sholay* can best be described as an Indianized Western. It deals with the lives and the conflicts experienced by a group of characters who forcefully dramatize the pervasiveness of evil in society.

Thakur Saheb is a retired police officer and a rural landlord. He hires two trigger-happy jailbirds to hunt down a gang of bandits led by Gabbar Singh, who are terrorizing villagers, including those in his own village. Some time in the past, the Thakur, then a young police officer, arrested Gabbar Singh. However, the thug succeeded in escaping from prison and avenged himself by brutally killing the Thakur's family, and cutting off his arms. How the hired gunmen fight Gabbar Singh and the violence that ensues form the bulk of the story. The film ends with Thakur Saheb seeking his vengeance by trampling Gabbar Singh to near death, and the police arriving on the scene. *Sholay* brought to the Indian screen some of the most brutal and repulsive scenes of human violence and depravity. And what is interesting is that these were executed without any qualms or feelings of guilt. There was a matter-of-factness to the acts of violence that was new to Indian cinema.

The opening sequences of *Sholay* demonstrate the kind sensibility and rhetorical strategies this film brought to Indian cinema. A train enters Chandan Pur station. Ram Lal, Thakur's servant, is awaiting the arrival of the jailer. The jailer gets off the train, and he and Ram Kaka mount two horses. The whistling of the train is heard on the soundtrack. The theme song comes on as the camera follows the two horsemen across terrain where the action is to take place, then tracks them as they go past rocks and boulders, trees, bushes, and pools and on to the village of Ram Garh, where they arrive at the Thakur's house. The house fills the entire frame of the screen, exuding a sense of tranquillity, as goats are seen grazing around it. The guitar music in the theme song intimates the mixture of Western and Eastern sensibility that the film represents. *Sholay,* which has been dismissed as a "curry Western," no doubt gains in discursive force as a consequence of that intertextual memory. The hills, boulders, open sky, and vast empty spaces captured in long shots bring to mind the natural ambience of Westerns.

The Thakur, draped in a large shawl, observes their arrival in silence and walks up to them. The jailer has come in response to his letter. The Thakur shows the jailer a photograph, and he recognizes the men in it as Veeru and Jaidev, two highly professional crooks. The Thakur then says that he is aware of the crooks' backgrounds, and that along with their despicable attributes, they also possess some good qualities. He recalls an incident after their capture in Jabalpur, when he was taking the two men to the police station on a freight train. Through a flashback, we see the young police officer Thukur with the two felons, Veeru and Jaidev, with their hands bound. Of the two, Veeru is shown as the more talkative and personable. He comes across as a simple man who enjoys life and accepts whatever it might bring him. Jaidev, on the other hand, is quiet, confident, and self-possessed. Not given to sentimentality or reflection, he has a certain sense of practicality. The train suddenly stops with a jolt, and we see a blockage of the railway tracks. The foreman is shot, the driver wounded, and the train starts moving backward. "You want to test our courage?" asks Jai. "There is still time to think it over," adds Veeru. They extend their handcuffed wrists to the Thakur, and their hands frame his face. The Thakur fires at their handcuffs and frees them, warning them not to try to escape. The next 640 shots are action shots executed with a great deal of competence and technical skill. Every now and then slow motion is used to heighten the dramatic effects. There is virtually no dialogue, and the editing is quick and forceful. The camera very fluidly registers the actions and reactions of the combatants as they engage in a drama of violence.

We are spontaneously drawn into the conflict, as the bandits on their horses chase the moving train. Our eyes follow the bullets as the camera charges toward the bandits. After emerging from a tunnel, the train crashes through a pile of wood blocking the tracks, and there appears to be a moment of silence. However, the battle is not yet over and the bandits are now on the train. The ropes tied around the petrol drums in one of the wagons snaps as the fight continues, and the petrol spills out. Veeru takes out the burning coal from the engine with a shovel. It is shown in close-up as the conductor watches the coal being hurled. A low angle shot in slow motion captures it. The live coal descends on the bandits as rain and is followed by the explosion of the petrol wagon and the flames engulfing it. The Thakur is shot and is pulled back into the train as the last of the bandits is thrown out of the train. The two friends turn to each other, and one says, "Let's get the hell out of here." The Thakur then stumbles in, warning them not to try to escape, but falls down unconscious. Veeru and Jai pause to discuss their next move. If they choose to leave, the Thakur will almost surely die, and if they stay, they will have to go behind bars. Veeru asks Jai to toss a coin saying "heads, we take him to the hospital, and tails, we escape." Jai opens his hand and heads win.

At this point, the film comes out of the flashback as the Thakur says, "If they had so desired, they could have left me and escaped. They are scoundrels, but brave. They are considered dangerous, but know how to fight. They are bad, but human. I need those two. Please find them for me." This sequence very clearly establishes the courage, fiber, and moral values of Veeru and Jai. Their decision to stay with the Thakur serves to win over the sympathy of the audience, and in point of fact, the hero of the film gets split into three in an interesting twist. The Thakur, armless and powerless against his enemies, acquires the strength of the two jailbirds whom he hires, and who become, not only instruments of his revenge, but also an extension of his personality.

The unapologetic violence and its visual correlates – the nature and the disposition of the two hired jailbirds, the sense of evil that permeates the entire film – are well caught in these initial sequences, and indicate a significant departure from the two earlier films discussed, Kismet and Awaara. To be sure, both in terms of content and style, Sholay is heavily indebted to American Westerns. However, the director has endeavored to assimilate the imported elements into the fabric of Indian melodrama. It is indeed apparent that the textual energies of the film have been expended in widening the discursive boundaries of popular Indian cinema, reconstituting the dialect of evil and social order at a different ontological and epistemological plane.

In Kismet, the presence of evil is explained in terms of a transcendental fate, whereas in Awaara, it is correlated with the social environment in which human beings happen to grow up. However, in both films, the family wealth and privilege, coupled with the heavy romantic overlay, prevent any serious engagement with social issues. In Sholay, on the other hand, evil is gratuitous, pervasive, inescapable, and is attached to a psychology of cynicism. In Kismet and Awaara, the selfhood of the protagonists is ultimately defined in terms of family genealogy, whereas in Sholay, the selfhood of Veeru and Jai are defined in terms of the violence that surrounds them. Moreover, in both Kismet and Awaara, the heroes are rooted in the specific social ambience in which the narrative takes place, whereas in Sholay, they are rootless, as the Hindi film audience was increasingly becoming. Sholay ushered in a new sensibility to the Indian screen, a new stage in the evolving dialectic between violence and social order.

Another significant feature of Sholay, and one that relates to its reception by audiences, has to do with the character of Gabbar Singh. He is portrayed as an archvillain who destroyed the Thakur's family in cold blood, cut off his arms, and terrorized villages, thereby transgressing all known social norms. Hence, one would expect him to be disliked by audiences. However, in a detailed study of the reaction to the film by the Indian audience, it was found that the preponderance of the moviegoing public liked Gabbar Singh. Viewers were enamoured of his dialogues and his delivery. It is not that the audience lacks a concept of evil or a moral imagination. Rather, the audiences applaud Gabbar Singh as played by Amjad Khan even as they realize that he is morally depraved and a despicable character. The element of spectacle has been privileged over the narrative in a way that was not seen in earlier Indian melodramas.

Another point merits close attention. In most Indian melodramas, the female body, as the object of fetishized male desire and the inscription of male dominance and power, is centrally situated in the filmic discourse. In both *Kismet* and *Awaara,* with the high premium placed on the eroticization of the human body and the primacy of the somatic genealogy, the body is crucial to the reading of the films. In *Sholay,* too, the body is of pivotal significance, but, there is an appreciable difference. In the case of *Sholay,* the male body takes precedence as it becomes the battleground both literally and figuratively – Thakur Saheb's arms are cut off by Gabbar Singh, and his hegemonic power and the countermoves to it are dramatized by the body, which becomes the central arena for the contestation of ideological meaning in a way that is not perceived in earlier Indian melodramas. The human body becomes the terrain on which good and evil vie for supremacy, and a realizing force of social order.

Although *Kismet* and *Awaara,* by selecting thieves and felons as the protagonists, initiated a new and interesting discussion of evil and social order, they still rigorously circumscribed the traditional cultural codings and, hence, their orthodox resolutions of the conflicts engendered by the narrative. In *Sholay* too, at the end, the villainous Gabbar Singh is brought to justice. But the way it is done – the positive coding of violence, the inflections of human evil – opens up a new discursive space within the dialectic between evil and social order. All three films deal with social deviants, but in the case of *Sholay,* the humanly constructed nature and shape of deviance, conflicts of interest, power differentials, competing values, and the structure of legal arrangements that underpin social order are brought to the fore of the filmic discourse and thematized in a provocative new way.

The visualization of violence in *Sholay* has the effect of glamorizing it, a phenomenon new to Indian melodrama. The low-angle shots investing the actors with an added aura, the slow motions, and freezes serve to secure this effect. There is also a certain uninhibitedness in the depiction of violence. Two of the most gruesome scenes in the film are the decimation of the Thakur's family and the amputation of his arms by Gabbar Singh. We hear the sounds of gunshots, and four members of the Thakur's family are killed. We do not see the killer, only a freeze, and then, one by one, each of the family members falls to the ground. Then an extremely long shot captures a tiny moving figure. We then cut to a mid-shot of Gabbar Singh with an ambiguous smile spread across his face. His grandson comes out running, as Gabbar Singh walks toward him with a fierce air. The self-contented look of Gabbar Singh is contrasted with the terror in the child's eyes. He quite matter-of-factly takes out his gun: The soundtrack registers the gun shot. A cut to the engine of a train follows, and subsequently, we are shown how the Thakur is placed under the gallows, and how Gabbar places two swords on his shoulders and lifts them. A cut to a long shot of his shawl and to the sleeves of his shirt dangling in the air conveys a kind of visual representation of violence in new Indian cinema.

Apart from the behavior of Gabbar Singh, the actions and attitudes of Veeru and Jai, too, bear on the question of violence. They adopt a casual attitude that reflects a cynical spirit. They are hired to do a job, and that is all that matters. Amitabh Bachchan, who plays the role of Jai in *Sholay*, attained great popular recognition for his role as an angry young man in *Chain (Zanzeer)*, a role he has played over and over to the delight of the audiences. Veeru and Jai have the courage to defy convention. Death is of no concern to them: It is what they accomplish before death that matters. They seek to prove to themselves that they are a power to be reckoned with in society. Their actions focus on evil and social order in a way not seen in earlier Indian films. Amitabh Bachchan plays the role of a man of few words, who rarely displays his emotion, is never given to self-reflection, and tries to define himself in terms of physical action. He becomes a kind of symbol that concretizes the destructive powers of evil that pervade society, as well as its inevitability.

Fredric Jameson believes that all third world cultural texts should be read as national allegories. This is, no doubt, a controversial statement, one that does not seem to pay adequate attention to the rich cultural traditions of third world countries that have evolved over a long period of time, nor to the diversity of the cultural texts. However, in the case of *Sholay*, it can justifiably be said that the film works at the level of national allegory. The lack of comforting narratives that offer the security of stable logics, the phenomenon of the social order being constantly undercut by ambiguities of meaning, and the absence of human feeling and the concomitant devaluation of human life dramatized in the film all have significance within the film's allegory about the Indian nation. The film, in its own melodramatic way, brings out a social thematics that has a deep relevance to Indian society as a whole.

By portraying violence as a ubiquitous force of a society in which rational voices are hard to find, and by dramatizing how evil produced by society itself constantly explodes into human destruction, *Sholay* jolts the Indian audience into a new awareness of the relationship between violence and social order. In earlier Indian film melodramas, when human violence and the consequences that follow were depicted, they were made endurable and comprehensible in terms of a larger framework of moral evaluation. In *Sholay*, no such moral framework exists; the film throws into bold relief the power of evil and the inability of society, which produced it in the first place, to contain it within an accepted scheme of moral adjudication and retribution.

As has been rightly pointed out, the foundations of the popular

Hindi cinema were laid in the 1940s. This foundation includes the financial institutions associated with the industry as well as the content, form, and style of the films, which, in turn, were shaped by the circumambient social forces. Produced in 1943, *Kismet*, in its content, form, and narrative conventions, represents the assimilation of these forces.

The 1940s witnessed India seeking to come to terms with the forces of modernity at a mass level, and this necessitated a rethinking of traditional values and the morphology of the cultural heritage. Produced in 1943, *Kismet*, in its own way, reflects the preoccupation with the issue. The social world that is depicted in the film is being rapidly modernized as it yields to newer civilizational forces. At the same time, there is an attempt to cling to tradition and comforting cultural memory as a way of countenancing the newer disruptive social forces. For example, as Iqbal Masud points out, the love relationship in *Kismet* can best be understood in relation to the traditional love stories of Laila-Majnu and Radha-Krishna. The overall valorization of fate in the affairs of humankind also testifies to the hankering after tradition and well-traversed paths of human meaning. Therefore, what we find in this film is a narrativization of the commingling of traditional and modern discourses that one finds in the wider society. The film seems to be saying that evil is undoubtedly a product of social order, but that there is a traditionally ordained higher scheme of things in terms of which evil can be explained and domesticated.

Awaara was produced in 1951. Hindi cinema of the 1950s constituted an outgrowth of the city culture that was beginning to spread out in postindependence India and, hence, the city became the locus of action and the *topos* of narrativity in many of the films produced in this period. The city with its attractions and resources, as well as its dehumanizing counterforces, came to serve as an emblem of the modernity into which India was stepping. The rich upper classes enjoying the benefits of the newly found opulence, while the poorer classes were struggling to eke out a living in dark slums against severe odds, presented a socially generated binarity and character types that scriptwriters and film directors were quick to transform into filmic images. *Awaara* shows this proclivity very clearly. However, working within an accepted tradition of melodrama and subscribing to a residual optimism, *Awaara* resolves the social conflict, as symbolized by the main characters, by resorting to a traditionally accepted strategy of family reconciliation. The questioning of social order in the film, such as it is, does not result in challenging its basic tenets or a widening of the horizon of discourse, and this is in keeping with the mood of the time.

Sholay was produced in 1975. By then, the social scene in India and the sensibilities of the people had changed appreciably, leading to a sense of disenchantment, at times bordering on cynicism. As Masud has remarked,

India in the seventies became a good place to escape from. War in 1971; social unrest; emergency; a weak coalition government, the restoration of the mainstream party; the steadily increasing inflation eroding the power base of the old middle class; the rise of the new rich – brash robber barons; the proliferation of the urban poor in the sprawling slums; their steadily growing links with the mafia – smugglers, drug traffickers and plain criminals who connected at the other end to the *nouveau riche.* (1987)

In addition, we began to witness India getting increasingly caught up in the world system, and how the forces of late capitalism, as symbolized by the two hired jailbirds, were beginning to enter the rural culture. The entire film constitutes a spectacle of evil – evil that is socially grounded, self-generated, and irrevocable. *Sholay* underlines the need to reexamine the parameters of social order as a way of understanding pervasive and mindless violence, and eventually eliminating it. Hence, here we find a new dialectic between evil and social order (evil testing the social order), which urges a rethinking of the nature of society as it comes to grips with late capitalism.

Veeru and Jai exist outside the accepted social values. The concept of the family, which almost always provides narrative closure to Indian melodramas, is conspicuously absent in *Sholay*. The Thakur's family is decimated earlier in the film, and what we find is a group of people, who have no anchorage in the institution of the family, confronting their destiny through the instrumentalities of evil. In this film the violence seems to invest the brutal, the vicious, and the hideous with an aesthetic value. Violence becomes the lynchpin of the signification system of the outsiders and the inarticulate. The sanguine faith in the existing social order is seriously questioned. Through evil they are reaching out to a new social order. Is *Sholay* saying that, as in the traditional Hindu myths referred to at the beginning of this paper, the present age of violence and the extinction of traditional certitudes should lead to a more tranquil and prosperous age? That the flames suggested by the title of the film are burning up the existing social order so that a better one may take its place? If so, the film is reaffirming the positive function of evil insisted on by traditional Hindu mythology.

Bibliography

Berger, Peter, and Thomas Luckman (1967). *The Social Construction of Reality.* New York: Anchor Books.

Brooks, Peter (1976). *The Melodramatic Imagination: Balzac, Henry James and the Mode of Excess.* New Haven: Yale University Press.

Dissanayake, Wimal, and Malti Sahai (1988). *Raj Kapoor's Films: Harmony of Discourses.* New Delhi: Vikas Publishers.

Geertz, Clifford (1980). *Negara.* Princeton: Princeton University Press.

Haas, George C. O. (1962). *The Dasarupa.* Delhi: Motilal Banarsidas.

MacIver, R. M. (1937). *Sociology.* New York: Farrar and Rinehart.

O'Flaherty, Wendy Doniger (1976). *The Origins of Evil in Hindu Mythology.* Berkeley: University of California Press.

Parkin, David (1985). *The Anthropology of Evil.* Oxford: Basil Blackwell.

Ricoeur, Paul (1967). *The Symbolism of Evil.* New York: Harper and Row.

Siwek, Paul (1951). *The Philosophy of Evil.* New York: Ronald Press.

Voegelin, Eric (1952). *The New Science of Politics.* Chicago: Chicago University Press.

Williams, Raymond (1966). *Modern Tragedy.* London: Chatto and Windus.

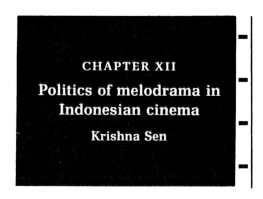

CHAPTER XII
Politics of melodrama in Indonesian cinema

Krishna Sen

Some years ago I was on a panel discussing Asian cinemas at the Melbourne Film Festival with Tuti Indra Malaon, arguably one of Indonesia's greatest melodramatic actresses, and Teguh Karya, probably Indonesia's most famous living director.[1] The festival had, the previous night, shown their film *Ibunda (Mother)* (Teguh Karya, 1985), starring Tuti in the title role as the mother. One Australian woman, for whom this was the first encounter with Indonesian cinema, speaking from the floor thanked Tuti and Teguh profusely for making this film, which she said had "entered her dreams last night." She was grateful because of the way in which the awful conflicts were all magically resolved in the last crucial minutes of the film. In her effusive endorsement of *Ibunda,* she had opened up the vexed question of the source of the melodramatic pleasure: Does it lie in the expressive excess of conflict (and its attendant sorrow, loss, and pain) or in the reassuring escapism of happy endings? Is it a genre of acquiescence or of resistance, of expressing difference or securing indifference?

This chapter, as a tentative first effort (in the English language, at any rate) to look at melodrama as a genre in Indonesian cinema, will not presume to answer these wider theoretical questions. But rather the questions are there to mark the common grounds on which inquiries about melodrama in different societies can be based and how the insights emerging out of Western theories may inform, and be informed by, work on other cinemas. (Living and working in the cultural West of the geographical south, I cringe a little at the language-politics of the East–West divide. But it still seems to be the best available shorthand.) At the same time, of course, one needs to be cautious in using "Western" critical categories when talking about (for want of a better term) "non-Western" cinemas. As Christine Gledhill points out, "how far the melodramatic aesthetics extends to non-Western cultures...is a matter of debate." And indeed in relation to the cinemas of Asia, we cannot be certain "that the term 'melodrama' constitutes legitimate categorisation rather than superficial resemblance" (1987, 2).

As a word, "melodrama" has currency in most film cultures of Asia, including Indonesia. But its discursive constitution need not be the same across intercultural boundaries. The works of Brooks in literature and Elsaesser in cinema show the historical and national transformations that the genre has undergone in the Euro-American contexts. This chapter explores, speculatively rather than conclusively, the dual problem of defining and historicizing Indonesian melodrama films. I should say, however, that my "historicizing" venture is not to discover the date of the first Indonesian melodrama, but to explore the historical circumstances in which melodrama becomes the dominant aesthetic form in Indonesian cinema.

That last comment asserts the importance of melodrama in Indonesian cinema. That *Ibunda*, which the Indonesian discourses categorized as a melodrama, swept up all the major Indonesian film awards in 1986 is symptomatic of this importance. An overwhelming majority of the annual film awards in Indonesia through the past two decades have gone to melodrama films.[2] These awards are decided not by the popular appeal of the film, but by a small group of prominent artists and intellectuals appointed as "annual film festival jury" by the minister of information (Sen 1987, 107–9). Awards thus mean not only popular success of the genre (such as melodrama has had in the Western context) but an aesthetic recognition rather different from the pejorative way in which the genre has been traditionally cast in the West (and indeed continues to be conceived except by a handful of film and literary theorists).[3]

New order invention of melodrama[4]

At the administrative level, the generic divisions of contemporary Indonesian cinema are easy to get at. The Censorship Board categorizes every film under a dozen or so standardized headings. These divisions are, on the whole, reproduced by the reviews in the press and by the annual film festivals. One of these categories is "drama/melodrama." The English term is used (drama is synonymous with melodrama), and there is no Indonesian translation in common circulation. No doubt, working backward with a theory of melodrama (worked out in the Western context), we would be able to fit a large part of older/traditional Indonesian literature and performing arts into the category of melodrama. But the currency of the term as applied to a body of indigenous cultural products, by indigenous readers, audiences and critics, seems to go back only to about the 1950s.[5] The latest edition (1988) of the standard Indonesian dictionary, *Kamus Besar Bahasa Indonesia*, describes melodrama as plays and films with "contemporary," "sentimental," and "serious" stories. On semantic grounds, then, the best entry point into Indonesian melodrama may well be melodramatic film, whether of Hollywood or Bombay, from which the Indonesian genre most directly takes its name, rather than attempting to find its indigenous antecedents.

Thematically films categorized as melodrama in Indonesia are about relationships between adult men and women who are married. They focus either on family crises or on prostitution. Not surprisingly, these themes have long been common in Indonesian cinema. Interestingly, however, it was only in the 1970s that "melodrama" became part, and indeed the principal component, of "good" cinema in Indonesia. Prior to 1962–3 (when the film industry ground to a halt, for reasons I shall come to later), films that won awards and critical acclaim in Indonesia were almost always ones categorized as historical/nationalist, films about Indonesian resistance to the Dutch (see Sen 1988). The shift in the work of Usmar Ismail, now regarded as the father of Indonesian cinema, is symptomatic of the displacement of the historical/nationalist genre by melodrama as the dominant aesthetics of Indonesian cinema.

Usmar consolidated his position as Indonesia's leading filmmaker in the 1950s. Between 1950 and 1962 he made fourteen films. With one exception (his last and least successful film of that period), all of his works were categorized as either comedy or historical. The political and economic crisis in the 1960s, which virtually destroyed the film industry, and Usmar's own involvement in right-wing politics, put a stop to his film work for almost eight years (see Sen 1985, 1–50). From about 1968, film production started to return to pre–1960 levels. In many ways, this was a new film industry in new political circumstances. A bloody civil war that started in October 1965 had ended with the elimination of all left-wing movements by the Indonesian army, and the New Order had emerged with the promise of an open economy and, for many, the reality of muzzled political and cultural expression.

In 1970, only months before his death, Usmar made *Ananda*, his second and last New Order film, a melodrama about the life and death of a young woman as a prostitute. Ananda, a form of address that best translates as "my child," is the name of the film's female protagonist. The name is thus the anchoring metaphor that plays on the childlikeness of the woman. Her innocence is emphasized in the opening minutes of the film as she is pursued by men in her village but remains entirely unaware of her appeal to men. She eventually falls in love with a university student who seduces her and then marries another woman. This experience suddenly transforms Ananda into a woman fully aware of the power of her body, which she now starts to use as a nightclub performer and prostitute to earn a living and torment men. Eventually she meets Halim, the only man ever to care about her rather than merely desire her. But he is married, thus unable to give her the protection in marriage that she begs. Ananda's association with the world of crime ultimately leads to her being murdered. The closing scene finds Halim sitting at her deathbed shedding tears of regret at his inability to save her.

Ananda is a victim. First of her parent's lack of affection, then of men's predatory sexuality, and finally of her own uncontrollable passions and the inability of the society to protect her. *Ananda* was popular and set the pattern for a large number of highly successful melodrama films all centering on women, who as victims of circumstances, become prostitutes and eventually die, regretting the way they have been forced to lead their lives but unable to change the course of events.

For the victim, of the victim

The films Usmar made prior to *Ananda* had a crucial narrative difference from his last film. In every one of his earlier films, the narrative progressed along the lines of the protagonists' efforts to change their lives and the conditions of the society around them. These were texts that, imbued with the confidence of a nation that had just won its independence from the colonial Dutch, registered the transformative possibilities of human action. These texts constructed heroes who acted in and upon history and moved it along. Textually the spectator was positioned to identify himself or herself with the hero, the historical agent of nation building.

There were victims in these films, of course. Victims of the villainous Dutch and, especially in Usmar's comedies, victims of corrupt, ambitious nationalist leaders. But these victims transformed themselves, and if they died, that death was a symbolic sacrifice to the forces of history, not a life wasted. I would argue that the pleasure of the historical films and of the comedies is a ritual, social pleasure of collective victory. By contrast, in *Ananda*, the world is seen from the point of view of the victim. The pleasure of this perspective is one of passive individual identification with the victim, in the recognition of one's own circumstantial inability to act. The protagonist here is *acted upon*, caused by others to be the way she is, rather than *acting*, to create herself and her circumstances. Nor is her would-be savior free to act; he is prevented from saving her by his social circumstances, his monogamous marriage.

Some of this parallels Elsaesser's (1972, 2–15) now classic observations on Hollywood's family melodrama. But there are differences in which one can locate the specifically New Order Indonesian transformations of the genre. Brooks and Sypher have seen the conflict of polar opposites, articulated in the "heroine–villain–hero triad" as the central paradigm of melodrama – of nineteenth-century European melodrama, at any rate. If they are correct, then Indonesian melodrama is markedly different. In *Ananda,* which marks a beginning and sets the tone of the "prostitution films" as a subgenre of melodrama, the villain is conspicuously absent. The young man who seduces and then leaves Ananda for a rich wife is seen for less than three minutes. Other men whose desires she unintentionally stirs by her beauty are faceless and largely powerless. Villainy is not then concentrated in any character or any institution but rather dispersed through everyone, including the victim herself and every social institution. So dispersed, the villain is in fact not visible except as some theoretical concept of fate or social reality. Melodrama here is thus centrally about the victim, but without any target to which to direct the blame for this victimization.

The shift in the dominant textual structure of Indonesian cinema from historical/nationalist in the 1950s to melodramatic in the 1970s can be located, at least in part, in the transformations that the nation's politics and society had undergone in the mid-1960s. Indonesian politics in the 1950s was one of mass mobilization. The nationalist leader Sukarno had headed the state since independence and consolidated his control of the government from 1957 onward. No doubt his control depended on a multiplicity of international and national political factors. But with no specific political party behind him, part of Sukarno's political strategy was based on his charismatic appeal to large sections of the Indonesian population. At the same time fierce rivalry of ideologically opposed political camps, since the late 1950s, led to demonstrations of rival mass bases of the various political parties. (For an account of the escalating political mobilization during this period, see Ricklefs 1981, 245–71.)

The overt political difference of right- and left-wing cinema notwithstanding (and there was plenty of overt politics in cinema; see Sen 1985), there was a degree of correspondence between the historically and socially located potential film audience and the textually constructed spectator. The dominant historical genre of the 1950s incorporated the politics of mass mobilization. Like Sukarno's political speeches (see Feith and Castles 1970, 98–122), the historical film was also able to ignore partisan politics and address its audience as a victorious nation on the move toward greatness, defined, in the first instance, by opposition to the colonial Dutch villains.

Civil war broke out in October 1965. The army under the leadership of Suharto suppressed a coup by its own junior ranks in the early hours of 1 October (Anderson and McVey 1971) and presented itself as the defender of the people against the Communist Party. In the following year or so, somewhere between 200,000 and 500,000 Indonesians were killed, and thousands were involved in carrying out the killings (May 1978, 91–128). The army emerged by 1967 as the country's ruler. Its power base was the institutional hierarchy, organization, and arms, not popular support. The horrors of mass politics had been demonstrated. After 1965, the greatest shared national memory was no longer the war of independence against the Dutch; it was the civil war. The nation could no longer be comfortably imagined by its collective opposition to outsiders. Whatever your politics – communist, military, or Islamic – the enemy was now within.

Civil war and the narrative of household drama

When the film industry started to recover in 1968–9, after some four years with very few productions, the public space of national and communal life, which had been the mainstay of historical films and comedy respectively, seemed out of bounds for cinema. State censorship had gagged anything that could possibly look like left-wing politics, any overt reference to class or regional conflict, and there was an unspoken ban on any reference to the recent political massacres (Sen 1987, 130–42). The trauma of recent history was too ugly and too confusing for a commercial, mainstream film industry such as Indonesia's. Film narrative thus turned its attention to the private space of the household. Pressures to ensure that a film's authors not be construed as communist sympathizers meant that on the whole films dealt with middle-class and prosperous households. But the Indonesian household is not only that of the family in the Western sense; it includes servants. Ironically then the private melodramatic space of a household in the Indonesian context cannot be "realistically" constructed without the incorporation of class difference within the household.

The 1978 melodramatic classic *Pengemis Dan Tukang Becak (The Beggar and the Trishaw Pedaler),* directed by Wim Umboh, foregrounds class conflict within the household. Wim Umboh, something of the grand old man of Indonesian melodrama, had been directing films since 1955. But he only assumed the status of a "great filmmaker" in the 1970s, reflecting the rising status of melodrama as the dominant genre. *Pengemis Dan Tukang Becak* won three out of the twelve national film awards for 1978 and immense popular success.

The film opens with Ratih, the only daughter of rich parents, adopting as her servant Sri, a child of her own age. Sri leaves the orphanage and grows up in the wealthy household of Ratih's parents. The intimacy of two young girls growing up together never offsets the mistress–servant inequality between them. Sri listens to Ratih as her confidante and overhears her young mistress making love to different young men each night. Sri knows Ratih more intimately than anyone else and silently keeps Ratih's promiscuous secrets until Ratih becomes pregnant.

Ratih's pregnancy, caused by some unidentifiable male, disturbs the comfortable construction of the family and the household so far assumed by the film. Her parents arrange to marry Ratih off to Joko, a debauched, bankrupt gambler, who himself has illegitimate children he refuses to acknowledge. Joko agrees to marry Ratih for financial gains, and Ratih refuses to consummate the marriage. She expressly states that they must each reserve the right to have relationships with other people. Ratih also refuses to care for her daughter Ajeng, so that Sri becomes the real caregiver.

The household finally breaks apart when Joko attempts to rape Sri, and Sri is evicted by Ratih's mother, the mistress of the house. Later the same night, Ajeng leaves home with Sri. The moment when Sri steals back into the house to get Ajeng, the child, for the first time in the film, addresses the servant as "Ibu" (mother). Although in Indonesia the term "Ibu" is commonly used to address older women generally, the surrogate mother–child relationship between Ajeng and Sri is overdetermined in a number of earlier images. (For instance, only Sri is ever seen as feeding the baby Ajeng or holding her.)

The rest of the film is played out in the slums and streets, rather than in the privatized space of the wall-bound home in which it had been contained so far. Sri and Ajeng enter into other surrogate family relationships as they slip from poverty into destitution. The first of these is formed with the trishaw pedaler, Parto, which in terms of real/reel time lasts as long as Sri's time with Ratih's family (although in the fiction's time frame it is much shorter). Eventually, in their attempt to escape from the police search initiated by Ajeng's natural mother and her husband, Sri, Parto, and Ajeng get to Jakarta, where Parto gets separated from Sri and Ajeng. Two other surrogate families are formed at this point. Parto is adopted into the home of an aging trishaw pedaler, who no longer has the strength to work. So Parto drives the trishaw in return for the family acknowledging him as a relative, because he legally needs to have a family in Jakarta in order to work in that city. Meanwhile, Sri and Ajeng are joined by a homeless child, Mamit.

A series of coincidences lands Sri, Ajeng, Mamit, and Parto in the same hospital. When Parto finds Sri and Ajeng, their split up "family" is reconstituted, this time with Mamit incorporated into it. At the same time the police recognize Sri in the hospital and inform Ratih and Joko, Ajeng's legal family. Ratih and Joko have by now become a real married couple and want "their" daughter to return home. Ajeng demands that Sri and Mamit must also come home with her. The parents agree. Noticeably in this scene Ajeng calls Sri "Bu Sri" returning her from the status of the mother to that of the maid. The household within which the film started is finally reintegrated, again with Mamit as part of it.

In effect, that original household is reproduced in the next generation. Joko and Ratih now take the place that Ratih's parents occupied in the unit at the start of the film, Ajeng and Mamit take the position of Ratih and Sri, and Sri takes the position of the elderly maid of the household, when Sri first arrived.

Clearly the definition of what constitutes the primary unit of the society is at stake. The people who share the space called home are not members of any biological family. Units sharing responsibility for each other are formed either by affection or social need (Ratih's social need to be married because she is pregnant, for instance). And yet the units that are formed on the streets and in the shacks are somehow not the ideal. They are units of shared pain, which cannot be overcome until the ideal unit is repositioned within the ideal home. Reproduction of family relations is at the same time the reproduction of the middle-class household. And it is the home where class contradiction is both expressed and ultimately resolved not through change but through a return to an individualized, private, harmonized hierarchy. The questioning of inequality, in a society that offers nothing but destitution to a servant who through no fault of her own has left her master's protection, a society that allows the rich to get away with criminal injustice, is never answered but is overtaken as the nostalgic dream of a restored past comes true. The bonding that takes place between Parto, Sri, Ajeng, and Mamit by the shared identity of their social experience is rendered temporary and aberrant, by the circular motion of the narrative, which begins and ends in images that reproduce the structure of happy-home snapshots. Within the narrative of household conflicts, Indonesian melodrama both metaphorically acknowledges the political unconscious of the civil war, the war within, and the class contradictions that nearly ripped the nation apart and dissolves class contradiction into a set of hierarchical but mutual dependencies within the unequally shared space of the home.

A note on silence

Mulvey, following Elsaesser (1972) and Brooks (1985), suggests that the melodramatic mode of expression "must speak through symptom, on the knife-edge between meaning and silence, demanding interpretation rather than a direct, unmediated understanding of what is said"

(1986, 92). The play on silence in *Pengemis Dan Tukang Becak* literally constitutes the powerless as speechless. The child Sri never speaks at all. She speaks for the first time in the film when she refuses Ratih's command to help abort the fetus. At the critical moment of her life, when Ratih's husband, Joko, attempts to rape her, she only screams wordlessly. The only verbal comment on the incident comes from Ratih's mother's voice accusing Sri of tempting Joko.

As Sri leaves her mistress's household, and moves for the first time among her class equals, she begins to speak her needs and feelings. Significantly though, when she relates the attempted rape to the trishaw pedaler Parto, who has come to care for her, the flashback is entirely without human voice. In the flashback Sri opens her mouth in a soundless scream. The unspeakable crimes of the upper class may be visible, but they remain unspoken and inexplicable.

The metaphor of the speechless as powerless is reinforced later in the film with the introduction of Mamit, who becomes a companion for Sri and Ajeng in the final quarter of the film, when they have been reduced to total destitution. Apart from whispering his name to Ajeng, Mamit says absolutely nothing throughout the film. Mamit, perhaps five years old, alone and hungry, first appears outside a roadside food-stall where Sri and Ajeng have spent their last money to buy food. Mamit waits silently for the stall owner to throw out the leftover food from the customers' plates. But every time the scraps of food arrive, he is pushed aside by older boys. Reading Sri's silent concern, he finally walks to her table and smiles. Sri and Ajeng share their last meal with him. When they leave the stall, Mamit follows them around until Sri and Ajeng accept him as part of this very strange family unit.

In a particularly memorable scene, following the practice of roadside car cleaners, Mamit jumps onto the front of a car and, ripping off his own torn tee shirt, proceeds to clean the windscreen. The driver, completely ignoring his efforts, turns on the windscreen wiper and water. The expressive powers and the social weakness of silence are evoked simultaneously. Mamit's silence means that he is neither seen nor heard by the people in the film, who constantly push him aside at every effort he makes to fend for himself, but at the same time it establishes his special communication with the spectator. His silence speaks contradictorily to members of the community in the text, on the one hand, and the community addressed by the text, on the other.

In the closing sequence of the film, the first reunion, that between Parto, Sri, and the two children, is entirely without verbal language. The visual and musical rhythm of this union is disrupted by the arrival of Ratih and Joko, as Ratih speaks to her child, and Ajeng responds with speech. Throughout the conversation between the mother and daughter, which would also decide the futures of Mamit and Sri, the two of them remain silent. In being reintegrated into the hierarchy of the home, Sri surrenders her authority to speak. Does the restoration of the harmonious hierarchy demand the silencing of the lower class? Does the post-1965 socially and historically constituted Indonesian audience hear in this silence an echo of its own inability to speak out?

Concluding questions

Given the preliminary nature of this inquiry, it would be inappropriate to come to definite conclusions. I have attempted to think through some notion of historical moments in Indonesian sociopolitical change as spawning the dominant aesthetics of its film industry. The mass mobilization of pre–1965 politics is framed in the historical film text whose paradigmatic narrative looks forward to a future. Melodrama on the other hand is the text of control, perhaps even of repression. The New Order bred the genre of acquiescence and despair, rather than of hope and change.

Grimstead and Vicinus have argued that "melodrama's challenge lies not in confronting how things are, but rather in asserting how they ought to be" (in Gledhill 1987, 21). The sudden inexplicable "happy endings" of *Pengemis* and other films of its ilk can perhaps be understood as the "ought-to-be" fantasies taking over the "how-things-are" lived experiences. The narrative structure of the Indonesian household melodrama is best described as circular, starting with a social harmony of the household that is disrupted as the story moves outside the house, to be restored in the last few minutes of the film. But the resolution comes from fate, coincidence, accidents, not through anyone specifically working toward the goal of the restoration.

Perhaps the harmony of the extended and unequal "family" of Indonesia, born from excluding the Dutch "outsider," has been destroyed by the events of 1965. No one really knows how to restore the whole that existed in the past. But the dream persists. Melodrama in Indonesia is about this hope of recovering the past. It is, quite literally, about containing contradictions, about expressing difference, without allowing it to rip the text and the imagined nation/audience it addresses apart. Melodrama thus becomes the dominant aesthetics of Indonesian cinema precisely at the historical moment when fundamental social contradictions, breaking the nation apart, have just been suppressed by the new military rulers of the country.

Because I have based some of this argument in the contrast between what the genres "historical" and "melodrama" mean in the context of Indonesian cinema, let me end by briefly returning to the historical genre. There was a period in the early 1970s when there was not a single film that could be categorized as historical. In the late 1970s and more in the early 1980s, there has been a revival of the historical genre. The question is, whether this is a return to or a transformation of the conventions that defined the genre of that name before 1965, or has it been marked by the containment, repression, and restoration paradigm of post-1965 political and cinematic practices.

The film that in many ways marked a return of the historical genre was Teguh Karya's *Nopember 1828*. It was made the same year as *Pengemis* and the two films shared between them nine out of the twelve Indonesian film awards for 1978. Interestingly, *Nopember 1828*, like its great melodramatic contemporary, starts in the peaceful harmony of a walled space, albeit a village not a house, and ends there with the harmony restored. The Dutch come into the village and go when they are defeated. But the villagers' victory signifies restoration of the past peace, not any change marking a future.[6]

Melodrama has in common with mythology and psychoanalysis a sense of eternalness, in contrast to the temporal and spatial specificity and change that marks history as a mode of thinking. When Indonesian films about nationalist struggles against the Dutch have revived the historical mode, rather than being simply historical inflections of the melodramatic, perhaps we shall begin to read through these a change in Indonesian politics.

Notes

1. This essay is dedicated to Tuti Indra Malaon, one of Indonesia's most loved actresses, who died on 20 September 1989. The essay concerns some of the works and people she cared about greatly. I hope I have appraised them lovingly and critically but without any pretense of "academic distance." In politics, nostalgia, and melodrama there is no place for the dispassionate!
2. The Indonesian film archives, Sinematek, produces an annual list of films, including a full list of nominations under twelve or thirteen basic categories for the annual film awards. Most years, especially since the late 1970s, there have also been special publications for the annual film festivals, with greater details on nominated films, including their generic categorization and story line. Even a cursory look through these indicates that more than half the awards each year have gone to films categorized as melodrama.
3. At another level, however, both Indonesian cinema and melodrama have been marked off as "uneducated, urban lower class, entertainment" (see Sen 1989, 1) in the "educated" literary discussions in Indonesia, much as in their Euro-American counterparts. Thus in the overall cultural discourse, cinema and melodrama are not just within the category of "low" culture, but perhaps even defining characteristics of it. From this position there is, in fact, at times an identity between cinema and melodrama – that is, all of Indonesian cinema comes to be seen as melodrama by some bureaucrats and intellectuals who administer the industry.

4. "New Order" was the name given by the supporters of Suharto to the new government (and by extension the new phase of history that was established when the military captured power in a violent coup and civil war in 1965. The same military rulers are still in power in Indonesia.

5. As far as I can establish, the term first entered the Indonesian language dictionaries in 1953 in *Kamus Umum*. And until the term entered the Indonesian language, English-to-Indonesian dictionaries unable to find a translation used long descriptions to explain melodrama. In a 1949 dictionary, *Ksatrya-Dictionary*, the English term "melodrama" is explained in Indonesian as "permainan sandiwara penuh dengan kejadian2 sedih tetapi berachir dengan gembira," that is, "a stage performance full of sad occurrences but with a happy ending."

6. For a more detailed discussion of this film, see Sen (1988, 56–8). Hanan (1988, 25–47) also discusses the film in detail, but with very different questions and conclusions.

References

Anderson, Benedict (1983). *Imagined Communities: Reflections on the Origin and Spread of Nationalism*. London: Verso.

Anderson, Benedict, and Ruth McVey (1971). *A Preliminary Analysis of the October 1, 1965, Coup in Indonesia*. Ithaca, N.Y.: Cornell University Press.

Brooks, Peter (1985). *The Melodramatic Imagination: Balzac, Henry James, Melodrama, and the Mode of Excess*. New York: Columbia University Press.

Elsaesser, Thomas (1972). "Tales of Sound and Fury: Observations on the Family Melodrama." *Monogram* no. 4:2–15.

Feith, Herbert, and Lance Castles, ed. (1970). *Indonesian Political Thinking, 1945–1965*. Ithaca, N.Y.: Cornell University Press.

Gledhill, Christine, ed. (1987). *Home Is Where the Heart Is: Studies in Melodrama and the Woman's Film*. London: BFI Publishing.

Hanan, David (1988). "Film and Cultural Difference: November 1828." In *Histories and Stories: Cinema in New Order Indonesia*, ed. Krishna Sen, 25–47. Melbourne: Monash University.

Jameson, Fredric (1981). *The Political Unconscious: Narrative as Socially Symbolic Act*. Ithaca, N.Y.: Cornell University Press.

Kamus Besar Bahasa Indonesia (1988). Balai Pustaka, Department of Education and Culture, Jakarta.

Kamus Umum (1953). Balai Pustaka, Jakarta.

Ksatrya-Dictionary: Kamus Inggris-Indonesia, Indonesia-Inggris (1949). Perpustakaan Kesatria, Medan.

May, Brian (1978). *The Indonesian Tragedy*. London: Routledge and Kegan Paul.

Mulvey, Laura (1986). "Melodrama In and Out of Home." In *High Theory/Low Culture: Analysing Popular Television and Film*, ed. Colin MacCabe, 80–100. Manchester: Manchester University Press.

Ricklefs, Merle (1981). *A History of Modern Indonesia*. London: Macmillan.

Sen, Krishna (1985). "Hidden from History: Aspects of Indonesian Cinema 1955–65." *Review of Indonesian and Malaysian Affairs* 19, 2:1–50.

—(1987). "Indonesian Films 1965–1982: Perceptions of Society and History." Ph.D. diss., Monash University. [A revised version titled *Framing of Indonesia* is forthcoming from Zed Press]

—(1988). "Filming 'History' under the New Order." In *Histories and Stories: Cinema in New Order Indonesia,* ed. Krishna Sen, 49–59. Melbourne: Monash University.

—(1989). "Power and Poverty in New Order Cinema: Conflicts on Screen." In *Creating Indonesian Cultures,* ed. Paul Alexander, 1–20, Sydney: Oceania.

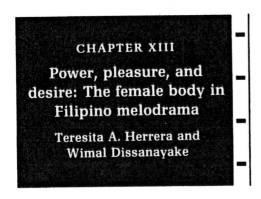

CHAPTER XIII

Power, pleasure, and desire: The female body in Filipino melodrama

Teresita A. Herrera and
Wimal Dissanayake

Significance is inherent in the human body.
Julia Kristeva

Laurey Mulvey's "Visual Pleasure and Narrative Cinema" has shaped much of the current thinking on the representation of women in cinema.[1] However, that essay does not pay adequate attention to the role of the audience and the complex ways in which meanings are negotiated with filmic texts: how viewers' backgrounds, histories, and lived experiences come into play in the production of meaning. The interplay between textual subjectivity (woman) and social subjectivity (women) cannot be ignored, and in our forays into Filipino melodrama we have realized the value of keeping this principle in mind. In this chapter, we examine three Filipino melodramas from the perspective of two Western-educated Asian viewers: one a Filipina and the other a non-Filipino male.

In most national cinemas, the construction of femininity in terms of the human body figures prominently in melodramas, and the Philippines is no exception. In Filipino melodrama in general, the symbolic constitution of womanhood in the filmic enunciation and the discourse on the female body are closely related, bringing into play questions of power, pleasure, and desire. In the present chapter, we demonstrate this by examining two typical Filipino melodramas that narrativize shifting structurations of power, pleasure, and desire within a quintessentially patriarchal social order, denying female subjectivity its ontological validity, and a third film that challenges textual systems that foreground the female body in this way as a means of negating women's autonomy. In the world of Filipino melodrama, the female is generally constructed as a symbolic product of patriarchal desire. The female becomes an object of male gaze as her subjectivity is denied, and any attempt to destabilize this widely circulated image results in her being stigmatized as treacherous, sinister, and possessed of an unassuageable sexual appetite, which could disman-

218

tle the existing social order. Being a product of the male gaze in the cinematic representation, she continues to be enchained as an object of male voyeurism. Efforts at escaping her condition only result in tragedy.

A premise of this essay is that questions of femininity, evil, villainy, domination, submissiveness, and their cinematic representations are culturally constructed and, hence, vary from country to country and tradition to tradition. However, the way in which popular cinema in the Philippines operates, the way in which it is received and appreciated by the moviegoing public, and the way it is influenced by Western discourses, both social and mass cultural, lead it to play a dominant role in the shaping of the discourse on the representation of women in mass art as opposed to folk arts. Moreover, the popular filmmakers have internalized the cultural codes, ideologies, and narrative strategies of Hollywood cinema in which, according to the influential theory first proposed by Mulvey, the camera becomes an instrument of the male gaze.

Texts are generated within discursive spaces opened up by lived practices. These practices mature and gain in depth and ideological definition over time; they are internalized by the members of a given society as the concomitant of the very fact of living in that society. Hollywood cinema as a discursive practice plays a crucial role in the lifeworld of Filipinos who frequent movie houses. E. Ann Kaplan has questioned whether the Chinese cinema arises from the same desires for replacing the lost object, for introspection, displacement, and projection, that psychoanalytic theory has attributed to cinema in the West.[2] Such a question has deep relevance to the Filipino situation as well. However, in the case of the Philippines, there seems to be a far greater overlap with the Western discourses than is the case in China. Having said this, it is also important to underline the need to challenge the transhistorical and essentialist aspect of the cinepsychological approach and bring it face to face with the forces of cultural construction by raising the question whether alternate codes of cultural representation bring with them alternate ideologies of spectatorship.

In Filipino melodrama, women are represented as either objects of patriarchal desire or as icons of social disruption that threaten the stability of the social order; often the two are interconnected. The gendered polarities in these melodramas serve to provide a discursive space wherein the males can define themselves against the objects of desire or disruption that are the females.

The past decade or so has seen a sharp increase in interest within film study in the human body as a symbolic construct, as a reality continually produced and reproduced in society. The mapping out of the modalities of construction of the human body, understandably enough, leads into discussions of politics, ethics, and questions of knowledge and power. The ground-breaking work of Foucault, Elias, and Kantorawicz and the writings of Nietzsche from whom they took their cue have largely inspired this newfound interest.

Focusing on a hermeneutic of dominance and submission, we wish to call attention to the ways in which, in Filipino film melodramas, the female body is specularized, situating women rhetorically as objects under the dominion of male gaze and desire.

Karnal (Of the Flesh), as the title suggests, is a film dealing with the female body and the symbolic construction of femininity. It is a story of passion, jealousy, and ostracism, set in a remote Philippine village in the early twentieth century when the country was still an American colony. The film textualizes the patriarchal nature of feudalistic society during those hard times.

Although the story and screenplay were written by a man, Ricardo Lee, it was inspired by a true story, "To Take a Life," written by a woman magazine writer, Teresita Anover Rodriguez. It is also directed by a woman, Marilou Diaz-Abaya, a well-respected director in Philippine cinema. Narrated by a nameless woman storyteller, played by veteran Filipino actress Charito Solis, the story gives a sense of symbiosis between the past and the present – the period of the next generation, as exemplified by the narrator. An aura of mystery surrounds the storyteller, as one feels she is somehow connected with the story, although she has only heard it from her mother, who one presumes is a native of the place and has experienced the events firsthand.

Yet, her very narration of the story shows her to be a woman in control over the situation. She is presented as a well-dressed upper-class Spanish *mestiza* Filipina matron living in the old stately but somewhat decrepit mansion, which is also the setting of the narrative and a metaphor for the inevitable tragedy.

She talks about Narsing (Phillip Salvador), a prodigal son, who returns to the village with his wife, Puring (Cecille Castillo), from Manila where he fled three years ago to escape his father's tyranny. He gets a cold welcome from his widowed father, Gusting (played by veteran actor Vic Silayan), landlord of a mango plantation and former *cabeza de barangay* (village head). His married sister, Doray (Grace Amilbangsa), who still lives in the big house with her husband, Menandro, their father's overseer, gives him a warmer welcome.

Narsing is completely dominated by his father, who makes clear his dislike of the city, and anything or anyone connected with it. This includes Narsing's wife, who reminds him of his own wife, Elena, who has died. He reiterates his role as *padre de familia* (head of the family) and tells his son he must work for his and his wife's keep as long as they are in his house. Narsing silently acquiesces and retires with his wife, whom he had earlier introduced to the villagers.

One sees in Narsing an emblem of the impotence of the Filipino people in the face of tyranny and oppression. Since his youth, he has been afraid of his father, describing his fear as "almost having to pee in my pants" when he faces him. He tells his wife about his desire to beat his father in games in his youth, and, when his father rises to his full height and gives the victory sign, Narsing wanted to pull him down and kill him. His contained violence erupted in frequent bouts of jealousy concretized in constant beatings of his wife – a pattern set by his father, whom he outwardly hated but secretly idolized. He longs to return to Manila, which he equates with his unconquerable father, and he is determined to prove himself to both.

Puring is a city girl, more liberated and rebellious than the women in the village. She personifies Hegel's "eternal irony of femininity," projecting an image of an obedient and faithful wife yet leading a double life with a lover. At first, missing the frenzy of city life, and finding town life too sleepy for her, she ventures out of the house and into the village one day, just looking for adventure. The move prompts Narsing to beat her, then make love to her. Loneliness and rebellion inspire her to have a brief affair with Gorio, the village deaf-mute (Joel Torre).

Her otherness in a male-dominated society knows no bounds. The hegemonic social view of city women as loose and easy makes her the target of sexual fantasies of village swains. She reaches the extreme of her marginality when her own father-in-law, seeing in her a resemblance to his dead wife, attempts to rape her. He is prevented from doing so only by his daughter's arrival.

Doray, Narsing's sister, is the epitome of the oppressed village Filipina, dominated by men all her life – her father, her brother, her husband whom she does not love, and her lover whom she yearns to be with. She tells Puring about their dead mother, Elena, who was the subject of their father's jealous temper. His constant beatings drove Elena to rebel and seek other men, which produced another round of beatings. Elena kills herself after Gusting parades her naked around the village, as punishment for her infidelity.

Gusting, the feudal lord, is not the benevolent father figure but a slave driver who tyrannizes his plantation workers, the village people whom he dominated when he was *cabeza de barangay*, and now tyrannizes his family whom he loves but to whom he is merciless. His power over the village dissipated after his wife's suicide, but he still keeps his family and his own workers in thrall.

History seems to repeat itself when Gusting discovers his daughter-in-law keeping a tryst with her lover and drags her to Narsing for supposed justice. Narsing turns on him when he finds out about his attempted rape of Puring. The melodrama reaches a crescendo when Narsing chops off his father's head in his rage. His solitary dragging of his father's coffin throughout the village is reminiscent of the *penitencia*, the Philippine practice of carrying the cross as penitence for one's sins, derived from Spanish Catholic rites.

Narsing is jailed, but, in spite of his defense of his wife, or maybe because it caused his father's killing and thereby his guilt, he punishes Puring by forbidding her to see him. Doray punishes Puring too, by driving her out of the house. Completely oppressed, ostracized by the villagers, and moreover, pregnant with Narsing's child, she seeks refuge in the house of Gorio, her former lover. When she is about to deliver, the village midwife refuses to tend to her, and she is left to Gorio's humble ministrations. The village abounds with rumors about her "devil baby." Finally, in desperation, she kills her malformed baby.

Narsing hears about this and his resolve to escape is strengthened. When he does, he threatens to kill Puring, but their love prevails and they reunite. The two attempt to escape the soldiers in pursuit, helped inadequately by the faithful Gorio, but Narsing is caught. Jailed again, he kills himself in prison.

Doray reconciles with Puring and bids goodbye to go to Manila, ostensibly to arrange her brother's funeral, but really to escape from her unhappy marriage. She goes to her former lover, José, and begets a daughter by him.

Puring is not as successful. She does leave the town, bidding goodbye to Gorio, but does not escape marginality in society. She never returns to the village but gossip says she has become a prostitute, selling her body to American soldiers in the city of her birth. This is possible because Philippine society marginalizes widows and separated wives, treating them like virgins who are defiled if they remarry.

The story ends with the narrator's revelation that she is Doray's only child. She talks about the contradiction of her mother's life, her futile attempt to escape the tyranny of the life she had lived, a life she does not really escape because she became as tyrannical as her father.

The storyteller takes her destiny in her own hands and never gets married. She says this is so that the strain of cruelty in her blood would not be inherited by any offspring. In truth, she wants to escape the ostracism that leaving her children would have caused in this patriarchal society.

The film is a commentary on feudal times, which can also apply to present times in some places, especially in Asia, where women dare not defy their husbands or their fathers, where workers dare not rebel against their lords and masters. It shows the dominant patriarchal structure pervasive in a society where women must know their place. Woe to the woman who strays.

In this film, the concept of the body is central. The story revolves around the body of Puring and the camera gazes at her with delight. Narsing, his father, Gorio, as well as the village gossips find her body alluring, and her whole life is narrativized in terms of the body. Having come as an alien body to the village, she is portrayed as the destroyer of many lives, leading some to gory deaths. Her desire, her yearning for fulfillment and self-definition, is always subordinate to others' pleasure of her body. What we primarily see in the textual system is a seemingly simple equation: femininity = eroticism = body. The ways in which the camera searches Puring out and dwells pleasurably on her body reflects how the inscription of femininity by the masculine gaze is crucial to the narrative technique, even though *Karnal* was directed by a woman.

This does not mean that *Karnal* contains no "resisting" elements. For example, in the closing sequences of the film, we are shown Puring moving away from the camera, her body becoming smaller and smaller as she leaves for Manila, leaving behind a feeling that the men who came into contact with her are partly responsible for her plight. A young woman stranded and lonely, going away by herself into uncharted territory, and overwhelmed by unforeseen calamities carries great emotional force for Filipino viewers, suggesting that this woman is a victim and that society bears a burden of guilt. This implication of guilt has the effect of deconstructing the putatively simple relationship between the voyeuristic male gaze and the female body that is its object. Similarly, the relationship between Puring and the deaf and dumb Gorio challenges the putative supremacy of the male gaze.

Salome, the second film that we wish to discuss in this chapter, exhausts all possible situations of female oppression. Written by Ricardo Lee, too, it is directed by actress-director Laurice Guillen, whose portrayal of Cory Aquino in the television miniseries, *Dangerous Life,* associates her with the president in the eyes of the Philippine public.

It is another film set in a rural background in the Philippines – a fishing and farming village. The plot revolves around a gypsy couple who go from town to town looking for their "place in the sun." The husband, Karyo (played by actor Johnny Delgado), a coconut farmer and gamecock hobbyist, finds that his lovely childless wife, Salome (played by Gina Alajar), is invariably not accepted in the villages they go to. It is Hegel's "eternal irony of femininity" at work here again – an outwardly passive, obedient, and faithful wife who rebels against the system by using her feminine wiles to seduce every man she meets.

The story also makes use of traditional Filipino myths, such as the myth of the mermaids from the deep who come to seek revenge against the fishermen who disturbed their quiet lives. An old man's repeated reference to the mermaids has so psyched the villagers that they believe Salome could be a reincarnation of one of these creatures. And so, when Salome reports to the police station that she killed the stranger from the city (played by Dennis Roldan) because he threatened her honor and her husband's honor, the villagers do not believe her. Salome's true character of covered-up deceit surfaces as the story unfolds, with different versions of how she killed the man.

At first, the film audience's pity is aroused for this wronged woman, threatened with rape by a stranger, whom she kills to protect her own and her husband's honor. Then, another image of an adulterous but driven woman looms as a consequence of her tale to her lawyer: an image of her being restricted to the house and a part of the seashore by a jealous husband, her being attracted to the stranger and having a liaison with him, her husband finding out, and her finally killing her lover to end it all.

The whole village, biased against her in the first place, consolidates forces to prove her guilty in court. However, there is no actual witness to her liaison with the stranger, except a boy, her only friend in town, who perjures himself to save her from the death sentence. She is pronounced not guilty by the court. But the story does not stop there. She is ostracized by the village and even mauled by a fierce woman (played by Armida Siguion-Reyna) who claims she caused the death of her son who was infatuated with her. Only her husband and her friend, the boy, stand by her side through her suffering.

Then, the audience is presented with another image of Salome – an out-and-out seductress who "eats men," as the town gossips put it. Not only that – she would kill the stranger, her lover, because he spurned her. Salome lapses into anomie and gradually loses her will to live because of her lover's death. In the end, one gets the true picture of Salome – a neglected wife whose loneliness drove her to adultery with the stranger, her only lover till then. It is her husband Karyo's jealousy and domination that drives her to kill her lover that day, and not her hurt pride. Karyo reveals this just before he ends their lives by the sea.

Salome's depiction of Hegel's "eternal irony of femininity" – her passivity and obedience that in return annuls the law that governs her – is problematic. In the end, she allows the law to dominate her when she bows to her husband's command to kill her lover. By society's norms, she was expected to kill her lover, either to protect her honor and her husband's honor, or because she was spurned, or because her husband told her to do so to avenge his shame. From a feminist vantage point, she should have taken the law in her own hands and escaped with her lover. But she was pressured by her culture to subjugate her own desire for fulfillment and happiness.

If *Karnal* deals with the human body as an object of male desire, *Salome* dramatizes how the female body becomes both the physical and symbolic terrain on which male domination is enacted and male power inscribed. Salome, with all the biblical connotations her name carries, is portrayed as a woman of questionable morals causing unhappiness to the lives of those with whom she comes in contact. Once again, we see that her suffering, her misery, is the outcome of the power of the patriarchal social order that is valorized in the film. The erotically coded scenes are consciously designed to stimulate desire even as they lead her closer and closer to tragedy. Salome's misfortune can best be read as the sufferings of a woman entrapped in a male-dominated society, her body becoming a site for the display of that male power; this naturally positions the spectator as the dominating bearer of the patriarchal gaze. However, in this film too, there are points of resistance that challenge the scopic regime of the male and the pleasure emanating from it. For example, throughout the film, there are culturally anchored references to a mermaid that contrast its mythical body with the human body of Salome, allowing the audience moments of ironic detachment that undermine the simple sadistic and masochistic identifications the film primarily calls for.

Ina, Kapatid, Anak (Mother, Sister, Daughter) is a film written and directed by males, Mel Chionglo and the nationalist Lino Brocka, respectively, but it narrativizes the conflicted experiences of women in a way that embraces a feminist perspective.

This film deals with three women, all marginalized by society, who seek to transcend their powerlessness and determine their own destinies. It is a story of Emilia, the *ina* (mother), played by veteran Filipino actress Charito Solis, a typical oppressed Filipino woman: educated, but relegated to the house because of an ailing father, a henpecked husband, and a teenage daughter. Emilia finally shows her hidden resentment of the social role she has to play when she resists her sister's domination of everything and everybody she holds dear by declaring her prior claim on all of them.

Pura, the *kapatid* (sister), portrayed by the celebrated Lolita Rodriguez, plays a woman who has transcended her marginalized role by escaping her oppressive environment and putting down new roots in a supposedly more liberal society. Having just come from the United States, Pura returns to the Philippines ostensibly to be there at her dying father's bedside, but her real intention is to prove to her family that success can be achieved by cutting ties to one's inherited cultural past.

This lesson has made an impression on her teenage niece, Erlinda, the *anak,* Emilia's daughter, played by Rio Locsin. Erlinda hero-worships her successful aunt Pura, and yearns to escape the tyranny of her mother, Emilia. She meets a young man working at the carnival and decides to elope with him to Manila, the big city of her dreams. Her efforts are foiled by her mother, who wants her to finish her studies so she can have a better chance to survive if she moves to the city in the future.

Emilia sees herself in her daughter and wants to overcome her failure to go beyond her traditional role as housewife and part-time piano teacher. She feigns passivity in her role as doting daughter to an invalid father, but she expresses her sense of rebellion by being a shrew to her husband and daughter. At the end, she is shown to be once more the queen of her house and home.

Pura's attempt to sell the ancestral house is thwarted because of her status as society's Other: She is the bastard daughter of her father's liaison with a maid. Her otherness has been thrown at her by her sister ever since she lived in that house. Her boyfriend was stolen by her sister, who married him. This was what caused her sudden departure to the United States. She is honored as a prized citizen of the town, but this is short-lived after Emilia refuses to allow the sale of the house. This failure rankles, her, but she leaves at the end after making peace with her sister, a common bond emerging out of unrequited love.

Manoling, the husband, played by Ric Rodrigo, is not the domineering Filipino "macho man." He is more a shrew's "under the *saya*" (or under the *skirt,* meaning, henpecked) husband who gives up power over his wife because of the *utang na loob* (debt of gratitude) he owes her father for placing him in his job as public servant. He rebels at his being made the Other in his father-in-law's house by inviting some of his poorer drinking companions and their families to live in the ground floor. He shows his machismo only by drinking heavily and by going to the cheap dance halls to forget his misery in the arms of a paid dancer. He is pathetic, and Pura, his former girlfriend, does not hesitate to tell him so. The contrast between Pura's iron will and Manoling's weak nature testifies to the feminist agenda at work in this film. Basically, the story boils down to the question: Does one get out of an oppressive situation by attempting to escape, as Pura did, or by holding one's own and making something out of it, as Emilia did?

The Philippine patriarchal society exercising its "hegemony of meaning," as Roland Barthes put it, dictates that a woman's place is at home, taking care of the children, the old and the sick, and doing housework, whereas the man's place is at work, after which he can go out with his friends and colleagues to drink or to be entertained. Emilia initially couldn't get out of the system or the terrorism of Barthes's "regime of meaning." So what she did was try to subvert it from within by pretending to be submissive to its "law," staying in the house but actually dominating her husband and daughter and practically "reigning" over the household. Pura got out of the system by transplanting herself into a more liberal system that recognizes merit in career women although still marginalizing women in other ways. She gains the grudging admiration of her townmates and the adoration of her niece, but she does not gain her half-sister's respect until the end, when she finally wins her grudging friendship by forging a bond of mutual understanding.

The whole film is a study of feminism as it operates in the Philippines, where the movement is still young. A significant achievement of the movement is the acceptance of a woman as president in a traditionally patriarchal political system – *working*, in contrast to being a titular nominal head.

Ina, Kapatid, Anak differs significantly in content and style from the other two Filipino melodramas we have discussed, in that this is a film whose main characters are women who seek to obtain proprietorship over their bodies and to control their destinies. The problems and frustrations, joys and sorrows, of women in Filipino society are here narrativized in a way that denies the primacy accorded to the male gaze in the other two films. In this film, Lino Brocka privileges female subjectivities over the compulsions of a patriarchal social order. In the narrative strategies adopted to present the reality of the female characters, Brocka challenges the exclusionary practices of a male-dominated culture valorized in other Filipino melodramas. In this film, instead of the male viewers voyeuristically watching the bodies of women who are the objects of their desire, we find the leading characters, all of whom are women, rearranging their lives in a way that brings out their distinct identities as cultural subjects. Brocka makes no attempt to hide the weaknesses and shortcomings of his characters, and this makes the film all the more persuasive.

Some analysts have attempted to explain the root of Filipino women's oppression in their religions. Sister Mary Mananzan, a feminist Filipino nun, backed by the findings of an ecumenical consultation of church women in Manila in 1985, affirms this statement as being valid among Filipinos.[3] The participants, coming from seven Asian countries, saw the root of women's oppression in religions. However, they also concluded an equally strong conviction that there are liberating forces in religion, but we shall confine ourselves to a discussion of Philippine religions and female oppression in society.

Mananzan says there are no traditions of women goddesses in Philippine history, unlike the Egyptian religion's goddess Isis and Hinduism's different goddesses. However, there are Filipino legends about *diwatas* (female spirits) like Maria Makiling, who supposedly inhabited a mountain and brought peace, calm, order, and well-being in the community. However, Maria's legend still showed the androgenous nature of the Filipino society that created her. Her father, the Supreme Spirit, discovered her liaison with a human being and forbade it on pain of not being able to transform herself back into a spirit from her present human form. Maria Makiling left her lover, promising to leave him a sign to remember her by. She obediently returned to her father's spirit world, but left her imprint on the mountain. Today, it is said that Mount Makiling's twin peaks are in the form of a woman's breasts – Maria's symbol of her love. Yet, this symbolism and Maria's abandonment of her lover at her father's command both bespeak of the patriarchy of Filipino society. There is a similarity between her female subjectivity and that of Salome's acquiescence to her husband's command to kill her lover to prove her love for the former. The trait is also found in Emilia's giving up her ambition toward a career in exchange for her devotion to a sick father, because duty compelled her to respond to the latter's prior need of her attention. It is likewise in Puring's silence in the face of her father-in-law's sexual abuse to spare her husband's recognition of his father's carnality.

It is interesting to know, however, that the word for God, *Bathala*, does not have a sexist connotation, according to Mananzan. She said that in primitive Tagalog script, it consisted of three consonants: *ba-tha-la*. The first consonant is the first syllable of the word *babae* (woman), which symbolizes generation; the third is the first syllable of *lalake* (man), which symbolizes potency; and the second is an aspirated *h*, which means light or spirit. So she says the word "God" in Filipino means the union of man and woman in light.[4] Yet, the Filipino's regard for God is still in a hierarchical and patriarchal light, with Mary as an intercessor for his favors. Mary is also regarded as a good female model – subservient to the Father's and the Son's wishes at all times.

Another author, Leonardo Mercado, a Filipino theologian, talked about the way a Filipino views the human body. He says: "For the Filipino, the sacred and the profane are intertwined. Thus a mother after giving birth gives a meal-offering as thanksgiving to God. The Filipino is so close to nature that he sees the divine reflected in creation. The various natural signs (rainbow, moon, birds, etc.) give a message of the divine."[5] He distinguishes between the incarnational world view, which he says the Filipino has, and the dualistic world view, which originated from the Greeks. With Plato and the Neoplatonists, proponents of the latter view stressed the dualism between matter and spirit, between natural and supernatural, between body and soul. Spirit cannot be reduced to matter or vice versa. With this dualism goes the dualism between the profane and the sacred.[6] Thus, he says that, with the existentialists, the Filipino does not say "I have a body" but "I am a body." He adds that a Filipino does not think that lust or carnal desires spring from the body for they involve the whole man.[7] So, he concludes that if God created the world, then the world is not profane for the Filipino. This may explain the ease with which many Catholic Filipinos, who are in the majority, engage in extramarital relations but stay married to their wives. They find no conflict between having a mistress on the side and still being considered a good family provider. A typical husband treats his wife and his mistress equally well, without neglecting either one. Both are expected, however, to accept the situation gracefully. To go beyond – to seek a separation or attempt to have him for herself – would be to lose him forever. Given most Filipino women's economic dependence on their men, neither could afford this. But with the advent of modernism and two-career marriages, this situation is slowly losing its grip on Filipino society.

On miracles, Mercado says that because the Other World is in contact with the present world, the Filipino naturally expects that miracles happen. *Milagro* (miracle) is used differently in Philippine languages. It can mean the unusual, as when a man who is always absent appears in town. It can also mean a great possibility, as when somebody buys a sweepstakes ticket and hopes for a "miracle" of winning the national lottery. Third, miracle is also used for the extraordinary. Thus, if a wooden statue suddenly weeps, the statue is said to perform a miracle. These three meanings of miracle are interconnected. The incarnational world view of Filipinos expects that divine interventions are a part of life, that the Other Life or Heaven is in contact with the present.[8] Thus, in the three films reviewed, the extraordinary is a miracle that comes after forbearance of something accepted as the will of God. Puring's tolerance of Narsing's jealous practice of keeping her confined in the house, Emilia's acceptance of her fate as her father's nurse, and Salome's acquiescence to her husband's relegation of her status as housewife all speak of the Filipino's fatalism. This is a belief that *Bahala na* (God will provide) somehow if they conform to society's expectations. Then, God will reward them with a "miracle" – Narsing will repudiate his father out of love for Puring (she did not really expect Narsing to kill Gusting); Erlinda will finish her studies and succeed in a career that will be Emilia's fulfillment of her dream; Salome will be proved innocent by the court and everything will be back the way it was before. Of course, reality went beyond expectation and miracles turned into nightmares as Puring and Salome discovered. Only Emilia, who took her destiny into her own hands, was able to fulfill her dream and transcend her initial female subjectivity.

Another author, Benigno Beltran, in speaking about the symbolic universe of the Filipino, says that it is that of "a people who assume that we always know more than we can understand and we always understand more than we can say."[9] He adds that the mark of intelligence among Filipinos is "knowing how to be oblique when asking questions or making a request; it might even be hiding one's own thoughts if these might disturb smooth interpersonal relations."[10] Beltran agrees with Mercado that Filipinos do not share the Platonic ideal of absolute intelligibility out of which this intellectualism of Western culture arose. He adds that there is much allusion and obliqueness in Filipino speech. Examples of this obliqueness in speech abound in these three films. One example occurs when the village people communicated his wife's adultery to Salome's husband by beer songs and "chicken" mimicry. Another is the ostracism of Puring by the village people and her sister-in-law, suggesting their belief in her guilt after Narsing's slaying of her father and his imprisonment. Or one can see it in Emilia's final gesture of friendship to her half-sister as her expression of gratitude to Pura's help in getting Erlinda to change her elopement plans.

In spite of these cultural considerations, *Karnal* and *Salome* typify the general run of melodramas, which exploit the female body to construct femininity in a way that validates patriarchal power, pleasure, and desire. *Ina, Kapatid, Anak* moves forward toward a more challenging textualization that embraces a feminist agenda, an agenda the film articulates in characteristically Filipino cultural terms.

Notes

1. Laurey Mulvey, "Visual Pleasure and Narrative Cinema." *Screen* 16, 3 (1975): 6–18.
2. E. Ann Kaplan, "Problematizing Cross-Cultural Analysis," *Wide Angle* 11, 2 (1989): 40–50.
3. Sr. Mary Mananzan, in *Religion and Society,* ed. Mary Rosario Battung et al. (Manila, Philippines: Forum for Interdisciplinary Endeavors and Studies, 1988), p. 107.
4. Ibid., p. 109.
5. Leonardo Mercado, *Elements of Filipino Theology* (Tacloban, Philippines: Divine Word University Publications, 1975), p. 25.
6. Ibid., pp. 27–28.
7. Ibid., pp. 29–30.

8. Ibid.

9. Benigno P. Beltran, *The Christology of the Inarticulate* (Manila: Divine Word University Publications, 1987), p. 206.

10. Ibid.

CHAPTER XIV

The register of nightmare: Melodrama as it (dis)appears in Australian film

Susan Dermody

There was a dilemma for me in the writing of this essay. First, I felt a certain obligation to "represent" Australian film and to speak about its relationship to the term "melodrama." And yet recent Australian film presents a relatively impoverished surface when it comes to melodrama in the full sense of the term, so the case is a rather negative one.

Second, as I began thinking about this chapter, the interesting things that arose were the more philosophical questions about the importance, or not, of the form at this moment in time. While I feel an old interest and attraction toward melodrama, and gratitude that its embrace in the recent past has reenabled proper attention to be paid to trash and low forms of popular narrative, I also feel a curious caution toward it as a form. Its dynamic is a peculiarly rich and yet *stuck* one. I am interested first in making this ambivalence a conscious one, before feeling for the influence of the form on Australian film, and speculating on why it is not a genuine staple or compelling presence in our visual culture, despite the melodramatic effects discernible in almost every film and their persistence across television varieties of soap and serial.

There seems to me to be a need to recover a nineteenth-century sense of the particular register of dramatic form that may properly be called melodramatic before its scarcity in Australian film at the far end of the twentieth century can be considered.

I

Guilty pleasures, and dreadful ones

The question of melodrama — how it works, how it holds us, what kind of meaning it permits — is proving to be one of the more enduring interests left over from the set of orthodoxies of 1970s' film theory.

Maybe this is because of the way that melodrama, and any response to it, is deeply embedded in conscious and unconscious ambivalence. There's no final end to the tease of melodrama. It is inherently unsatisfying in a way that is very satisfying when writing about melodrama. The object, at its best, is so saturated with conflicted and mixed desires, and yet, or and so, the exploration of the object almost never can reach a satiated conclusion. In some circumstances, of viewing and writing, this can feel good: You can laugh, you can cry, and you can be left with an unsatisfactorily happy ending that leaves the process open, itchy, interesting.

Then there's the pleasure of being mixed up with a bad object, and of grubbing about in the silt layers of popular culture. Here's how one traditional source defines melodrama:

A play based on a romantic plot, with little regard for convincing motivation and with an excessive appeal to the emotions of the audience. The object is to keep the audience thrilled by the awakening, no matter how, of strong feelings of pity or horror or joy. Poetic justice is superficially secured, the characters (who are either very good or very bad) being rewarded or punished according to their deeds. Though typically a melodrama has a happy ending, tragedies which use much of the same technique are sometimes referred to as melodramatic. (Holman 1972, 312–13)

The same source refers to these characteristics as "deplorable," but it's easy for us to deplore that in its turn and earn points for taking pleasure, even an educated guilty pleasure, in the excessiveness, perversity, obviousness, and sheer popularity of the form.

Another particular pleasure for women, in looking closely at melodrama, is rather like the one afforded by the vast domain of psychoanalysis; indeed, the two are curled about one another. Here is the mystery of what binds us as social, gendered beings to a set of relations, feelings, and actions, stated, indeed overstated, with wounding clarity. Here it is again, and again, the undoing of women. And the breathless sense that always accompanies this wounding moment, that all of this melodramatic display will not alter one whit the mystery or its bondage.

Melodrama merely tests so far as to guarantee the power of the forces that hold us in place, if we choose to see in melodrama's terms, as victims and villains. The villainy in the extraordinarily rich and complicated melodrama of Freudian psychoanalysis is a very subtle and inexorable one; we can point to the "fact" that women lack, that it can then never be known what it is that they want, that this want threatens the frail piece of flesh where it is not missing and ensures the more elusive phallus of its power and centerpiece in the whole composition of this system of meaning – of the flesh and bones of psyche.

Who is villain, here, who is the victim? Not anybody, but everybody, so we are all both guilty and excused.

It is on the occasions when melodrama coalesces with such a powerful romance of psyche as this that the interest can really be aroused, even though the pleasure must always be tinged (tainted?) with masochism, for a woman spectator or writer. How can they *say* that! It's horrible, it's so *true!* How can they dare to say it? Look, they're saying it out loud! And now they're covering it over again, dropping the curtain, rolling end titles. Time for the lights to come back on. Time to look sheepishly at one another again.

And so the special predilection of feminist film theory and writing for Freud and for the Oedipal drama of so much film melodrama and television soap, especially for the women's film, the domestic melodrama of the 1940s and 1950s, and its motley descendants in film and television over the three decades in between.

So, also, the interest among women writers on film[1] in some aspects of 1970s and 1980s horror film where you can make out the melodrama of the monstrous feminine taking place in particularly striking form. Like the series of profoundly abject[2] encounters with the Mother of them all in *Alien* and *Aliens*. Or the primal scene of hysterical birth in *The Brood,* of menstruation in *Carrie,* of the female outwardly possessed of her own monstrosity in *The Exorcist.*

This is just the start of the short list; there are dozens, and interestingly, the ones that attract our real fascination are the ones with enough psyche in them to be melodramas of profound *unconscious* ambivalence, sometimes masked by a display of the conscious variety. Horror films almost all display at their most prized moments the body of woman undone and sacrificed in some form; we're all quite used to that. But these I have been picking out – and the list really starts in the 1960s with *Psycho,* of course – dare directly to pose the feminine as *problem* and then sometimes position a woman as combatant, as hero, in facing the threat.

The conscious in combat with the unconscious is as common as romance form, but it is rare to have women named as the bearers of consciousness, as its defendants – or even as fully conscious human beings, free enough of the undertow of the id and its deep-sea monstrosities to be trusted with the central active role in the eternal battle of melodrama. And so *Alien/Aliens* especially seduces and betrays our fascination by sending in a heroine to do battle with the immortal enemy of the monstrous feminine. We're talking not so much guilty pleasures now, as *dreadful* ones. As nineteenth-century parlor art, entertainments, novels, and pseudoscientific sociobiology knew so well.

So what is this "melodrama" as I am using it (assuming that C. Hugh Holman's stab at a definition is blinded by judgment and far short of the mark)? And second, why haven't I so far mentioned a single Australian example to illustrate my argument?

What does it mean: To weep?

Two main sources have influenced my thinking on melodramatic form and aesthetics: Eric Bentley's *The Life of Melodrama* (1967) and Peter Brooks's *The Melodramatic Imagination* (1976). Thomas Elsaesser's "Tales of Sound and Fury" (1972) and Catherine Clement's *Opera, or the Undoing of Women* (1989) have added detail (about film and opera, respectively) to the contours of the argument.

All of these works have considerable consonance. Brooks, so frequently cited in the melodrama literature, seems to work partly in a lineage from Bentley's excellent, much earlier work of definition and persuasion toward the object; Elsaesser influenced much of the 1970s work on the recuperation of film melodrama, especially 1950s weepies, even though he spoke somewhat from the margins (and never in *Screen*); and Clement has written something that has ached to be written, it seems to me – a rich observation of how calmly and consistently the economy of desire in grand opera calls for the killing of at least one woman at its height of passion, and how unremarked this central fact goes in the discourse of "opera loving." Her rich embellishment of how the economy of textual desire deals with women in the particular melodramatic instance of opera is awfully familiar, and evocative, after years of looking at the question of how the feminine is posed in film and how the females are dealt with.

All of these writers work from a sympathy toward melodramatic form and a lush sense of its landscape, but with a certain clearheadedness about its limits of workability, about where the posture of the form gives way to imposture or swooning collapse, and where the love it excites must grow more cautious.

What are the lineaments of melodrama that emerge between these accounts? Bentley begins in a defense of the weepie. "Tears are a relatively unexplored ocean," he writes, and quotes George Bernard Shaw: "Tears in adult life are the natural expression of happiness as laughter is at all ages the natural recognition of destruction, confusion and ruin" (Bentley 1967, 197). This seems like a healthy, self-aware sense of the paradoxical good fun of a weepie, and yet of the tension, in the experience of melodrama, between the adult and the infantile.

Melodrama answers to the sense that self-pity and a good cry have their uses, and that the space in which it is possible to publicly lament is now a shrunken one, of stage and film and television miniseries. It slides in between tragedy and farce, evoking pity for the hero, but more impressively, fear of the villain; it is about the power to feel and project fear, and, of course, a sense of evil. It works (when it works) by virtue of the art of proper exaggeration, not too mechanical or awkward, but not empty of feeling, and this is a key to judging its particular registers both of performance and plot.

The intensity of feeling that creates childhood fantasy and adult dreams is what also justifies formal exaggeration – or is it lack of inhibition? – in art. "It is as children and as dreamers – one might melodramatically add 'as neurotics and savages too' – that we enjoy melodrama" (Bentley 1967, 204). And so the paranoid or persecutory logic of the plot, where even the weather and landscape conspire with the fear and villainy and strong emotion. And the long arm of coincidence, which pushes aside probability again and again, to enclose the possibilities of plot in a sense of fate, to ensure excruciating agonies, to bring things full circle, to stage amazing revelations that will drop the happy ending into place with a slightly false click. "Like farce, this genre may be said, not to tumble into absurdity by accident, but to revel in it on purpose. To question the absurd in it is to challenge not the conclusion but the premise" (Bentley 1967, 203).

And, of course, the grandiosity of melodramatic acting. To the extent that we are all ham actors in our dreams, *"melodrama is the Naturalism of the dream life"* (Bentley 1967, 207; italics in original). The elevated rhetoric, the loaded lines of melodrama at its peak moments, follows on naturally from this. "Ordinary conversation would be incongruous and anti-climactic" (Bentley 1967, 207). What we're seeing and hearing (when it is risked, and carried off, these days) is the remnants of a once far richer corporeal expression, that we've politely denied ourselves, a body writ large.

You see what we're missing when you watch ethnographic films about Trobriand Islanders[3] or New Guinea highlanders,[4] or news footage of black South African funerals, demonstrations, street theater. Faces and bodies and voices that are all drawn into the articulation of this strong feeling, then this one. And you understand *that* we are missing it when you see the worry about the (in)security of the body's borders, spilling over and flooding the screen in so much film horror and pornography.

(But how far can melodramatic gesture and performance be risked, now? As I will explore in the second part of this chapter, I'm tempted to think that it needs very particular arenas, in which to be permitted, "indulged," so far are we historically removed from the original moment of melodrama and culturally – and carefully – distanced from its antecedent life in the body, the body writ large.)

The high Victorian rhetoric of melodrama as we still faintly hear it was already the lag-end – the rags and tatters ... of something that had once been splendid ... Hugo ... German *Sturm und Drang* Drama.... In England the postmedieval drama begins with the establishment of a melodramatic rhetoric in Marlowe's *Tamburlaine,* and melodramatic rhetoric subserved tragedy, or declined into bombast and banality, or merely served its natural purpose as the proper style of melodrama, until about 1850. (Bentley 1967, 207)

It can still be heard in Australia as late as the sound films of Charles Chauvel (whose barely submerged enterprise of speaking, in high melodrama terms, the "family melodrama" of relations between Australia and the mother country, England, has been brilliantly explored by Stuart Cunningham [1990]), and in much 1930s and 1940s newsreel and government documentary narration. But it makes us laugh now. It has been replaced by laconic understatement of feeling, and rich, compensatory idiomatic expressions (often very bodily in their metaphor), to signify strong, inviting Australianness. That our politicians spoke mainly in "high melodrama" until as recently as wartime Labor Prime Minister Curtin still comes as a shock to the ears.

To return to the question of where this exaggeration or lack of inhibition comes from, and what it carries with it – Bentley has a position on this that for me powerfully organizes the whole question of melodrama. He argues that there is a genteel tradition in the maintenance of everyday twentieth-century life (remember he was writing in the mid-1960s, when the postindustrial, postmodern inflection of that life was beginning but hardly understood), one that steadily maintains attention to the cultivation of the ordinary, in the face of the extraordinary discoveries of theoretical physics and the mass atrocities of "modern behavior."

If this is true, then there is a constant hunger to glimpse the wild and gigantic, behind the "arras" of a world seen in monochrome and miniature (or swept from sight as any kind of original reference, in a wash of signs and simulacra). There is a need to awaken the imagination, and to the extent that melodrama aligns with childhood feelings, melodrama is a possible strategy for delivering such an awakening, or at least arousing the right hunger. Melodrama belongs to the magical phase of childhood (and theater) when thoughts seem omnipotent, when *I want* and *I can* have not been distinguished, when "the larger reality has not been given any diplomatic recognition" (Bentley 1967, 217). Our own innocence is axiomatic; in melodrama proper, any interloper is a threat and a monster; and the ending will be happy because that is what we feel it *has* to be (Bentley 1967, 217).[5]

So there is a ceiling to the expectations that can be had of melodrama, just as there is to the expectations of what a child can do. For the sake of the children, the household, world peace, or whatever needs to be maintained, we agree on ideals of nonmagnified feeling, as standards. But "what we all have are the magnified feelings of the child, the neurotic, the savage.... Though the melodramatic vision is not the worst, it is also not the best. It is 'good up to a point,' and the point is childhood, neuroticism, primitivity" (Bentley 1967, 217).

And then there is the constant hazard of melodrama, that the lurid and the gigantic fall quickly into stereotype, and stereotype is awfully easy to summon up but very hard to handle.

The missing middle ground

Brooks's work is far more currently known in the melodrama literature and needs only gestures to show how it differs from and relates to the way that Bentley constellates melodrama. Brooks's emphasis is on melodrama as the anxiously forceful and spectacular enactment of *moral* imperatives, the struggle between strictly polarized forces of good and evil, conscious and unconscious, in a postsacred world. His sense of the form is very conditioned by the historical and political moment of melodrama as *the* form of our time, the form that was called forth by the conditions of postrevolutionary France and Europe. The epistemological moment it illustrates and contributes to is the one in which the shattering of the myth of Christendom (the Enlightenment) was acted out as the end of its cohesive society (the French Revolution) and its forms, tragedy and comedy.

"It comes into being in a world where the traditional imperatives of truth and ethics have been violently thrown into question, yet where the promulgation of truth and ethics, their instauration as a way of life, is of immediate daily political concern" (Brooks 1976, 15). The revolution *is* one of the great Manichaeistic melodramas, dependent for its meaning on the excision of any middle ground, and staged on postsacred ground, from which the authority of God as the last instance of all meaning has been withdrawn. "The Revolution attempts to sacralize law itself, the Republic as the institution of morality. Yet it necessarily produces melodrama instead, incessant struggle against enemies, without and within...who must be confronted and expunged, over and over, to assure the triumph of virtue" (Brooks 1976, 15).

And so, his premise: "We may legitimately claim that melodrama becomes the principal mode for uncovering, demonstrating and making operative the essential moral universe in a post-sacred era" (Brooks 1976, 15).

Especially so because of that other post-Enlightenment phenomenon, romanticism, which may be partly understood as a reaction to the loss of the sacred and its unifying effect. Romanticism may also be seen as offering as substitute the new sacred of the individual, the personal, giving rise to the melodrama of endless individual acts of self-understanding and moral imperative, with no point of "terminal reconciliation" (Brooks 1976, 16). It becomes impossible to conceive sacralization other than in personal terms. Personality makes its claim to sacred status. And the ego demands to be the measure of all things. This is the air that melodrama breathes.

For Brooks, what brings on the contortionist struggle of melodrama to speak the unspeakable is the *impossibility* of the desire for the sacred; the form is about this impossibility, is its embodiment. And so there is an occult edge to the melodrama's sense of morality. If the most important things for melodrama – which I take to be the ethical drama in a person's life, the ethical implications of their psychic drama – cannot be easily *seen*, then they must be wrested forth from behind the facade of life, of things, of appearances. "Precisely to the extent that (melodramatists) feel themselves dealing in concepts and issues that have no certain status or justification, they have recourse to the demonstrative, heightened representations of melodrama" (Brooks 1976, 21).[6]

And so, in the perpetual absence of a middle ground, we have the aesthetics of astonishment, of the total enjoyment of excruciating situations in their unadulterated state, the experience of nightmare.

"Melodrama regularly simulates the experience of nightmare, where virtue, representative of the ego, lies supine, helpless, while menace plays out its occult designs. The end of the nightmare is an awakening brought about by the expulsion of the villain, the person in whom all evil is seen to be concentrated, and a reaffirmation of the society of 'decent people' " (Brooks 1976, 203). God may be in doubt, in the post-Enlightenment melodrama world, but the Devil is not; he never stops incarnating, or even appearing as himself. Perhaps the archetypal story of melodrama is paradise lost, but now with paradise never to be regained.

Characters in this world don't have psychology but are psychology, the pure psychic signs of its melodrama – Father, Daughter, Persecutor, Judge, Duty, Obedience, Justice. The space created by their interplay is like the Freudian dream text, a web of pure, exteriorized signs (Brooks 1976, 36). Characters speak directly their moral/emotional perceptions of the world (think of daytime soap opera), a vocabulary of moral and psychological abstractions, presented as revelation.[7]

"Nothing is understood, all is overstated. Such moments provide us with the joy of a full emotional indulgence" (Brooks 1976, 41).

Brooks's work meets Bentley's most closely on the terrain of dream, as I have indicated, and from here he moves toward the question of psychoanalysis. He sees all of Western thought and culture as dominated by systems of conflict that are "systems of expressionistic clarification," organized under the episteme of melodrama, most obviously those of Hegel, Marx, and Freud. "Psychoanalysis can be read as a systematic realisation of the melodramatic aesthetic, applied to the structures and dynamics of the mind" (Brooks 1976, 201). The eternal conflictual universe of Eros versus Thanatos, and notions like excess, repression, enactment, return – again, we are breathing the distinct air of melodrama.

And finally, I cannot resist including his insight on the melodrama of politics in our era, our arms race era, where virtue and evil are fully personalized again.

Rarely can there be the suggestion of illumination or reconciliation in terms of a higher order of synthesis.... The modern political leader is forced to posit a continuous battle with an enemy. If it is not another suborning political power or leader, it may be a natural scourge on which "war" is declared, poverty, hunger, inflation.... (Brooks 1976, 203)

Think of the rhetoric of the early Reagan era, when "limited thermonuclear war" was being considered possible in "the European theater" (of war), in the eternal *Star Wars*–style battle with "the evil empire." More particularly, as the 1990s begin, think of any right-wing religious fundamentalist rhetoric in its political aspect. The bells that this insight starts ringing for me are alarm bells.

Analysis interminable

The melodramatic imagination is still a tuning fork that resonates to the tone of much experience, of "current times," even these officially flattened, postmodern times, lost in hyperreal space. It can still provoke the imagination, even while the flow of placeless, processed imagery threatens to pacify and overwhelm that faculty. It can still contact a sense of the marvelous, even if its power is waning as melodrama disappears in its pure form, or its original register, from cultural life in electronically mediated reality. Certainly, it still persists in that strong remnant of nineteenth-century, romantic art in our time, the horror film.

And yet I wonder whether it is still so strategically appropriate to privilege the form in theory, and whether we should be tuning in to the lateral message it emits, by way of the meaning of its form, a little more carefully.

Christine Gledhill has recently analyzed the history of the theoretical emergence of melodrama through the past two decades of film writing and shown how restricted the term has grown, to the point where it has virtually been collapsed into one particular variant, the domestic melodrama/woman's weepie/television soap opera, as a kind of loose but insistent cluster (Gledhill 1988, 5–39). She traces how this restricted usage came about through a succession of theoretical projects in the 1970s and 1980s, each focused slightly differently on realism as the antivalue.[8] Her general rethinking of the ambiguous relationship between melodrama and realism (and the question of the representation of women in either) is timely and useful.

American 1950s family melodrama appealed to the Marxist and Lacanian projects of film theory in the 1970s because the films embodied dire contradiction, both formally and thematically, and broke open under the strain. Cracks at the seams. Realism's presumed desire for seamlessness defeated from within, caught in the act. "Formal contradiction became a new source of critical value because it allowed apparently ideologically complicit films to be read 'against the grain' for their covert critique of the represented status quo" (Gledhill 1988, 6).

And what a status quo it was! Eisenhower America, the whole, great conservative, consumerist feast, riddled with oedipal and family romance. Douglas Sirk's films, especially, seemed to provide a series of wonderfully hysterical texts. But "whether a Sirkian capability could be legitimately attributed to melodramas as a whole, or whether Sirk constituted a special case in relation to other 50s melodramas" (Gledhill 1988, 9) – or, indeed, whether reading against the grain was any kind of likelihood for audiences then, especially those still dreaming of entering the feast – were questions rarely asked.

Melodrama fetishizes contradiction (the extreme polarity of its field of meaning, the clenched embrace of opposites locked in eternal combat) in a way that endeared it to Marxist criticism, which could see such texts as laying bare the (melo)drama of dialectical struggle. But the slight hitch is that melodrama never steps outside of its own terms for a moment, and those terms are predicated on the perpetually missing middle ground. It is a form designed never to be able to imagine a profound form of resolution, an intellectual or emotional embrace of opposites – never, in a sense, to be able to complete the third step of a Hegelian dialectic.

And melodrama tends to assign its characters primary psychic roles – father, mother, child – and to exteriorize psychic conflict and structures – in its perpetual "melodrama of psychology" (Brooks 1976, 35–36, cited in Gledhill 1988, 31). So you could be forgiven for thinking, especially from the particular evidence of the family/weepie/soap nexus in the field of melodrama, that melodrama fetishizes the family; certainly, that partly accounts for why the Lacanian inflection of Althusserian – Marxist theory in the 1970s was drawn toward melodrama.

But as Gledhill (1988, 31) points out, after Brooks, "For melodrama, working less towards the release of individual repression than towards the public enactment of socially unacknowledged states, the family is a means, not an end."

This insight helps to restore to the picture those tracts of melodrama that lie in action films of various kinds – space opera, westerns or horse operas, science fiction, detective and crime film – where the perverse grain of melodrama is often felt in the setting up of a double trajectory of meaning. The most satisfying examples allow the floor to fall through at the crisis of outward meaning in the text, revealing the other, hidden, psychic dimension of all the outward action. Minelli's *Home from the Hill* is a kind of 1950s example of family melodrama straining to be action film and one quite favored by 1970s criticism; Kazan's *East of Eden,* another. Male melodramas, or melodramas of paternity. But I am pointing to the "pure" action film that yet offers an inner pleasure organized by the melodrama of psychology. Gradually, for example, this element has built through the *Star Wars* cycle; sequels seem to demand new acts of elaboration, complexity, depth, and so the engagement with the evil empire gradually becomes a search for a father and for the true identity of the fallen angel, Darth Vader, and a flirtatious avoidance of the incest taboo at the level of the love interest.

Or take *Chinatown,* where the floor of meaning falls through to reveal that the whole public scandal of who is prepared to pervert a public good like the water supply, for private profit, is built over the rot of father–daughter incest. Or *Alien/Aliens,* with the elaborate probing in those films of chronic ambivalence toward "the mother." In the first film, it is played out in the untrustworthiness of the central computer ("Mother"), who is the relay of the corrupt morality of the Company, and it is, of course, implicit in the "primal scenes" of "conception" and "birth" of the monster through the face and stomach of the host, as well as in the "abortion" that finally rids the heroine of the alien when she ejects it into deep space. In the second, which follows the first move for move, but with a new, ever higher ante, one "mother" fights the big Mother of them all, this time, finally over the child – "You take your hands off her, you bitch!"

And remembering the action melodrama, in turn, provokes a new acknowledgment that the true register of melodrama includes not just tears but terror – that it is the register of nightmare, where nothing is understood, all is overstated, for the sake of the joy of a full, emotional indulgence. That it taps into the hunger to glimpse the wild and the gigantic, and to revel in absurdity on purpose. That it invites us in as children and dreamers – and neurotics and savages too. Oedipal drama and family romance are some of its staples, in a hundred different guises, but the moral occult (the struggle to drag evil forces out from cover and denounce, if not defeat them) is as fundamental to it as the psychic occult (of the struggle to drag the unconscious into the light of day and to name, if not to control it).

A nineteenth-century register of nightmare

This is the feeling for melodrama that I want to restore – a more nineteenth-century feeling, perhaps, for a fundamentally nineteenth-century form. The form has, of course, survived and adapted well into twentieth-century film and television conditions, because of particular circumstances that are worth following through, so that both the lineage and the important modifications or transmogrifications can be acknowledged and not swept from sight in an elevation of one variant of melodrama to stand for the original whole. Gledhill makes an interesting case for why melodrama was able to make the shift from legitimate theater to the new medium of film, and especially silent film, and flourish (Gledhill 1988, 14–38). And then, especially if you accept the Frankfurt School–inspired notion of the essential (despised) "femininity" of television, the relatively easy translation and modification of family melodrama across to television melodrama, usually taken to mean oedipal soap opera, is also understandable.[9]

The other way to restore a nineteenth-century feel for melodrama, so that the register of nightmare, when it appears, can be better understood, is to turn to a source like Bram Dijkstra's (1986) study of how late nineteenth-century European painting, literature, and "scientific" writing on biology, sexuality, and sociology unconsciously proposed itself as a melodrama of male versus female, dissolved into good versus evil. An extraordinarily rich picture emerges of the only lightly buried archaeology of twentieth-century horror and fantasy culture and politics emerges, much as it does in the more specialized study by Klaus Theweleit (1987) of the ethos of fascism in the German *freikorps*.

The merciless punishment of the feminine that runs as undercurrent through so much of melodramatic culture comes to light in a hundred subspecies of refinement here. The angel in the house, that extremely good object, turns so readily (in Kleinian terms) into any number of extremely bad objects. The cult of invalidism (the most beautiful woman is a near-dead one who can make no demands), the drowning woman (the countless Ophelias, Elaines, and Ladies of Shalot), the weightless woman, the nymph(omaniac), the sirens of death, the maenads, the clinging vines of degeneracy, the bestial women, the daughters of Dracula, the whores of Babylon, the women who require just one little thing – the severed head of the man. Dijkstra presents a bestiary of nineteenth-century femaleness, ones that not just titillated in a repressed age but were hung openly on the walls of good bourgeois households.

At one point he makes clear that there is a kind of loop of eternal return in this feast of psychoanalytical insights. He points out that it is wrong to smile and wonder at the simple naiveté about sexual symbolism displayed by the artists and writers of the period, which made them expose their repressed sexual desires in images that, post-Freud, may finally be read for what they are. Instead, it must be acknowledged how much the writers and artists, in consort with

the prurient speculations and suggestive lucubrations of the scientists of the period...planted a full-grown tree of sexual imagery in the minds of the psychoanalysts, who had grown up with these ideas and images all around them, and who now sought to prove the archetypal nature of these images by pointing to the unconscious symbolism of the very generation which had, to a large extent, quite consciously created that imagery. (Dijkstra 1986, 318–19)

The "healthy" side of melodrama, and its source of great fascination and importance, is the way it is prepared to dive in deep with repressed material, to delve into both psychic and moral occults wherever it can invent or discover them. It is admirable, always, for its power to stir a sense of the marvelous, from its most trashy and pulpy absurdity to its veritable sublime, always just a short leap away. But the marvels it can arouse are always limited to a juvenile, or even infantile sense of how reality may be negotiated.

And built into the very form itself is a kind of repetition compulsion that seems to me, in Brooks's terms of the "impossible" quest for the sacred in the postsacred world of melodrama's making, to breed in the eternal inadequacy of the form to its own quest. It has endless drive but no psychological means, finally, to reach any kind of grail. It is as large and vivid and full of the wished-for as romance, but can never dissolve through to a glimpse of the lack that structures it. It can engineer the most dazzling and desperate feats of delayed gratification, and then when, like *Pamela*, it cannot hold out against revelation another minute, it offers deprivation in the very same move. It satisfies only the perverse desire never to be satisfied.

So it's like rubbing the wound (the wound that it embellishes, if it does not create it from scratch). All that it can ever do is toss you back and forth between its own extreme terms. This may give a sort of feeling of taming, of dealing with the agonizing affect that gets produced by living within extreme contradiction. But finally it is more like an aggravation, an inflammation, an action insatiable, an analysis interminable.

II

When I look at the scene of Australian feature film production in its most recent incarnation, since the resurrection of the industry in the early 1970s, I begin to want to depart from Brooks in at least one respect.[10] Melodrama no longer looks like the most pervasive form of our times. Sure, melodramatic effects still litter the scene for miles in all directions, but they are like the debris in the tail of a comet, now almost passed from sight.

I offer as a serious joke the notion that the state of a nation's railway system may be a test for the melodramatic propensity of its culture. Looking at Australian film since the earliest years of the century, the decline of that nineteenth-century form, melodrama, coincides closely with the first signs of decay and abandonment in that other great nineteenth-century form, transportation by train. The gradual (and accelerating) loss of such an altruistic and dutiful institution of *communitas* as a well-maintained railway network is paralleled by marked decline in government support for other great nineteenth-century instruments of benign paternalism, such as government schools and hospitals – all in a state of shock since the hard-faced 1980s removed from them all sense of *natural* authority and loyalty. If a culture is industrially reorganized beyond the point of real reliance on its trains, it almost certainly is no longer truly moved by the register of melodrama, as I have defined it.

In the asynchrony that is to be expected of history, the nineteenth century is finally dying away with the last decades of the twentieth, and the episteme of melodrama is wavering with it. As new forms of electronically mediated reality replace or refine the age of mechanical reproduction, and as politically active religious fundamentalism(s) replaces or refines the imagined community of nationalism, melodrama is feeling out of date.

Looking at the case of Australia, I would argue that melodrama has been the episteme of the nineteenth century, and constellated under the sign of nationalism rising. Certainly for Australian film, with a social imaginary infused with an anxiety about identifiable Australianness, melodrama has been associated with the most potent and popular attempts to define this imagined community against the odds. Consider *Heritage* (1935), *Forty Thousand Horsemen* (1940), *Sons of Matthew* (1949), *Breaker Morant* (1980), *Gallipoli* (1981), *The Man from Snowy River* (1984) – all action melodramas, in fact, almost all horse operas, with oedipal trajectories and unashamed chauvinist sentiment about (male) Australianness. The *Crocodile Dundee* films, after 1986, mark the end of simple chauvinism in its late, late afterglow by the ironic, parodic (though still affectionate, very affectionate) overrating of the mythical character of male Australianness.

If a full-scale embrace of nightmare, and a desire for the terrors of the marvelous, are accepted as the real dimension of melodrama, its true imaginative scale, then there is little in Australian film and television culture that answers to it. About all you would mention are the *Mad Max/Road Warrior* films, *Ghosts ... of the Civil Dead, Shirley Thompson Versus the Aliens,* parts of *The Night of the Prowler,* and *Bliss.* On a more existential level, heavily qualified by a kind of structural antagonism to the romance form, except in its most inverted and negative state, you might consider *Wrong World* and *Sweetie.* There are plenty of unthrilling "thrillers," but, strikingly, no real horror films at all.

And certainly there are plenty of middle-class "personal-relations" films, fondly hoping to tap the market for the woman's picture, no doubt, but without any real sense of the drama of masochism, the feminine unconscious, and the family. The notable exceptions to this are the film and television adaptations of a number of strong family-melodrama novels by Sumner Locke Elliott, as I shall discuss. Otherwise, the strongest moments of outright family melodrama are to be found in the occasional television miniseries – some stretches of *Vietnam,* a fair bit of *Return to Eden,* most of *Dirtwater Dynasty* (with an increasingly high score on an imaginary Richter register of melodramatic).

But little else reaches this pitch. Most of the melodramatic effects are muted down to the most petty kind of domestic melodrama; at this level, they are *everywhere,* throughout most television drama and a great deal of small-scale, mainstream film. Perhaps this is why Australian audiences since the mid–1980s, in theaters and at the video shop, have largely deserted Australian movies in favor of the product of the American cinema, the quintessential modern cinema of violence and nightmare – although it must be admitted that they have remained largely entranced by Australian melodrama on the small screen in the form of that unique genre, and recent successful export, the Aussie soap opera.

Melodrama as it (dis)appears in Australian film

Up until the mid-1980s, the kind of Australian film best known overseas was a subgenre that has had a central, if not prolific, place in Australian cinema, the melodrama of male bonding. The founders of this subgenre are *Gallipoli* and *Breaker Morant.*[11] Two things are striking about these films. One is that they are largely so flatly naturalistic in style; the other, that the male characters in them are so eternally boyish. They seem to exist in some kind of latency period before full sexuality, before the need to come to terms properly with the feminine or the maternal. It seems that what is being played out is some endless melodrama of the innocence and eternal youth of the new country against the decadence of the old, corrupt parent country, Britain.

Perhaps the emblematic examples of the male melodrama in Australian cinema, although not male-ensemble films, are the *Man from Snowy River* films, explored in considerable detail elsewhere (Dermody and Jacka 1988a, 179–88; 1988b, 86). The first of these achieved box-office records (since eclipsed by the first *Crocodile Dundee*, which may, I think, fairly be said to have nothing to do with melodrama) because of its ability to ride a wave of overt nationalism in a reasonably well-crafted, old-fashioned action melodrama that boldly declared itself as melodrama. The second came in a moment when such simple, nationalist pieties were no longer so acceptable, and so the form did not work with very much power. It seems plain enough that fairly fundamental, conservative "verities" of feeling and affiliation have to be "in the air," in a latent form at least, for a melodrama of (orphaned) manhood and initiation – with symbolic patterns of high versus low country, unbridled horses and headstrong women, manhood and stallionhood, freedom versus duty – to begin to convince us.

Another version is that small group of films in which father–son conflict is played out – films like *The Irishman* (Dermody and Jacka 1988a, 32, 36) or *Coolangatta Gold*, thin and feeble echoes of *Home from the Hill*, or *East of Eden*. Again, the eternal boyishness even of the father figure seems to overwhelm the potential of the drama and diminish the sense of the inexorable law that the father represents, whose inevitability and symbolic force supplies the true strength of this kind of melodrama (witness Wotan in Wagner's Ring Cycle, now there's a father for you!).

Another quite prolific strand in Australian filmmaking, though less well-known internationally, is also a muted form of melodrama – of the domestic or "personal relations" variety (Dermody and Jacka 1988a, 52–58; 1988b, 111–5). Films about the struggles of the well-off, but troubled, to keep the full nightmare register of melodrama out of their lives, to secure the small bulwark of family and friends against the anarchy, violence, and anomie of the world, from an anxious, middle-class perspective. Films about midlife crisis or, more exactly, male menopause (*Going Sane, Fantasy Man, I Can't Get Started, The Perfectionist, Boulevarde of Broken Dreams* – why do they all star John Waters?); films about marital breakdown and infidelity *(Remember Me, My First Wife, Jilted, Double Sculls, Perhaps Love)*. Films about last chances to have babies *(Times Raging, A Matter of*

Convenience, Unfinished Business). Films about the separation of parents and children *(Jenny Kissed Me, High Tide, The Top-Enders),* about oedipal trauma *(The Boy Who Had Everything, The Lizard King, The Place at the Coast).* A few rare examples that deal with excessive love *(Warm Nights on a Slow-Moving Train, Candy Regentag).* Even films about old age *(Travelling North)* and death *(Olive),* though not many.

In this long list there is no sign at all of any deviation from a white, middle-class heterosexual Australia steeped in midlife crisis and suburban angst, but far removed from the exigencies of unemployment, poverty, and racial prejudice. Many of them are well-crafted tele-movies, with the scale and sensibility of small pieces for the small screen. Because they match so closely to the general class composition, age, social milieu, and sexual preference of Australian script-writers, there is a richness and psychological detail in many of them that makes them rewarding enough – as long as their distant, blurred relationship to melodrama doesn't remind you of how remote they are from the visionary, excessive, oneiric or marvelous – remote even from the ocean of tears.[12]

It seems surprising, given the strength of feminist filmmaking here since 1970, that representations of a threatening or excessive female desire, let alone the monstrous-feminine, make virtually no appearance in the mainstream. The exceptions crop up sparsely in the "Australian gothic" and more eccentric[13] reaches of filmmaking, where a clutch of rich and memorable dark feminist tragicomedies – *Shirley Thompson Versus the Aliens, The Night of the Prowler, Starstruck* (Dermody and Jacka 1988a, 82–4, 128–9, 196–8), and most recently, *Cella* and *Sweetie* – turn the tables on the tiredly familiar regime of male desire and begin to show the lineaments of a feminine imaginary, even if the royal road to it lies somewhere near madness.

If we have no horror tradition, outside of the car-crash movie in the vein of *Mad Max,* neither do we have more than a glimpse of the over-wrought family melodramas identified and discussed by Elsaesser, Mulvey, and others. What we have instead is a much blander Mills and Boon or *Women's Weekly* version of the "women's film," films like *The Winds of Jarrah* or *An Indecent Obsession,* the familiar tame romance in which everyone is pretty well-bred and everything turns out pretty okay at the end, without much hair of any kind getting ruffled. This is not to take a position of lofty disdain towards the weepie – if only the Australian examples could really make you weep in the intended way![14]

It seems that the only exceptions to this pattern of falling short are in works derived from novels by Summer Locke Elliott, not particularly well known overseas or held in the very highest regard in Australia, in spite of the fact that he is examining territory close to that of Patrick White, though with less of the symbolic and metaphysical baggage. *Careful, He Might Hear You* does succeed as a kind of powerful, high-camp Minnelliesque melodrama of family sexuality and identity, organized around a hysterical ice-maiden, with a 1940s period setting (Dermody and Jacka 1988a, 210–14). And *Eden's Lost,* a recent television miniseries, provided a rich piece of art television, flirting on the edges of *Brideshead Revisited* and *Dynasty* in its elaboration of three variations of female hysteria, in one family (Jacka 1989, 20–4).

The television miniseries was a prominent form in the profile of the Australian industry in the 1980s. It was for a while the easiest kind of project to get funded and presold through the generous 10BA taxation provisions of the first half of the decade.[15] Of the hundreds developed in this period, the majority were in some way or other mythologizing accounts of Australia's political and cultural history, and it is in no way accidental that most of these were melodramas.[16] The exceptions to the historical/political rule tended to be variants of the personal relations film, and of these, the most spectacularly successful were outrageously melodramatic, like *Return to Eden.*[17] Until only a couple of years ago, they still found a great deal of favor with Australian audiences. Production values were high (shot on film, with familiar film, rather than television, industry actors and crew); (eventual) narrative closure marked out a cinematic, rather than television soap, inflection of melodramatic form, and yet the story could sprawl (all over your leisure time, in fact) and prolong the sense of immersion even while promising a very tight sense of an ending.

The majority of the miniseries are descendants of a blend of "AFC-genre"[18] and the male-ensemble film referred to earlier. While their shape is often melodramatic, they rarely toy with the exaggeration and excess of true melodrama. Partly this seems due to the way that an overwhelming television naturalism strangles such possibilities, but perhaps the more significant underlying reason is that these respectful stories of a nation cannot countenance anything that moves away from official mythologizing into the messy underworld that is the domain of melodrama. The only exceptions tend to be the miniseries from the Kennedy–Miller[19] stable, especially *Dirtwater Dynasty* and *Bangkok Hilton.* But their political dramas, *The Dismissal* (reopening the wound of the sacking of the Whitlam government in 1975) and *Vietnam* (another set of wounds, explored brilliantly through family dynamics) are heavily influenced by melodramatic effects, both in their explicit narrative concerns and in their stylistic flourishes, especially their oracular narration, use of mise-en-scéne, and music.[20]

The other large, organizing grouping of Australian film where melodramatic effects, if not melodrama proper, play their part, is the social realist film, which has been explored in detail elsewhere (Dermody and Jacka 1988a, 39–43; 1988b, 90–7). This group has been the conscientious pole of the industry, not quite prominent or prestigious, but very numerous. It formed a bridge to the independent area of filmmaking and to documentary, concentrating on plain, dramatized documentary treatment of either "social problem" as it is defined by the media and other discourses, or else socially oppressed or marginalized individuals or groups – migrants, blacks, youth, derelicts, prisoners, women. The further away they manage to position themselves from a middle-class, "social work" perspective on their subject, the more likely they are to tap into genre and playful generic mix, on one hand, and more full-blown melodramatic effects, on the other—as in *Backroads, Wrong Side of the Road, Backlash,* and *Short Changed* (all dealing with race relations), or *Fran, The Pursuit of Happiness,* and *Shame* (all quite different, but all feminist in inflection and bold in their play with melodrama and genre).

Finally, it would be impossible to survey the field of recent Australian film melodrama without mentioning the important position of those errant road-movie car-crash films, those heroic explorations of "the monstrous-masculine," perhaps, *Mad Max, Mad Max 2 (The Road Warrior),* and *Mad Max: Beyond Thunderdome* (Dermody and Jacka 1988a, 137–40, 173–8, 238–43). These were avatars of eccentricity, bred out of the submerged but never quite exhausted spring of Australian gothic. Their images are large, nightmarish, fully melodramatic, and as the road-movie formwork gave way to revenge "Western" and sci-fi, crossed with samurai and ninja films, so did the sense of melodramatic plottedness, even with traces of oedipal drama and pastoral romance, steadily increase. They managed to remain marginal in flavor even as their mainstream popularity grew; their imitators, like *Running on Empty, Midnite Spares, Razorback, Roadgames,* all have a certain power (despite their various failures) stemming from the subterranean zones in which they at least partly move.

And their marginality aligns them with other, offbeat and eccentric delights to be found at the far edges of the Australian industry – often films whose power derives precisely from having full control of the register of melodrama at the level of imagery and unconscious power, while avoiding it like the devil at the level of plot and structure – films such as *Wrong World, Dogs in Space, The Navigator, The Tale of Ruby Rose, Sweetie, Ghosts . . . of the Living Dead.* But that's another story, largely already told elsewhere (Dermody and Jacka 1988b, 131–55).

We're now down to the small handful of films that truly answer to the lament expressed toward the end of *The Screening of Australia,* volume 2 (pp. 239–41), with which I shall close this brief survey, coming full circle:

For a start, melodrama is a curiously stunted branch of film. . . . Australian cinema shows a curious inability to deal with passion, dream, the marvellous, the play of extremes that belong to Romance and its mongrel offspring, melodrama. Outside the "gothic" and eccentric films . . . there has been a marked unwillingness to join the games of popular culture and engage with such close accomplices of surrealism as pulp literature, horror comics, fairytales, true romance confessions, popular science, the unconscious, rituals and dreams. Few Australian filmmakers appear to understand Raymond Chandler's remark, "It probably started in poetry, almost everything does." Where in Australian film is the appetite and readiness for the marvellous, the appeal to exaltation, impatience with the sham of official public culture, insistence on emotions and ideas experienced to the hilt?

Notes

1. In Australia, at least. See especially Barbara Creed's work on the "monstrous feminine" in, for example, Creed (1987).
2. In the sense of Julia Kristeva's use of this term in "Approaching Abjection" in Kristeva (1982).
3. For example, Gary Kildea's *Trobriand Cricket.*
4. For example, Ian and Judith Macdougall's *Joe Leahy's Neighbours.*
5. Bentley goes on to say (p. 218) that in tragedy, the reality principle is not flouted, one's guilt is axiomatic, one is not the sole reality to be respected, other people may or may not be threats or monsters, and the ending is usually *un*-happy. But that there is a melodrama in every tragedy, just as there is a child in every adult.
6. Compare Elsaesser (1967): "the aesthetic qualities of this type of cinema depend on the way 'melos' is given to 'drama' by means of lighting, montage, visual rhythm, decor, style of acting and music—, that is, on the ways mise-en-scène translates character into action, and action into gesture and dynamic space (cf. nineteenth century opera and ballet)."
7. However, as Brooks (1976) explores in chapter 3, "The Text of Muteness," in its extreme moments the melodramatic text has recourse to muteness, to non-verbal means of expression, pantomime, gesture, tableau, decor, lighting. Muteness is the particular deprivation of melodrama, as blindness is to tragedy and deafness to comedy. Muteness is the register of extreme hyperbole, perhaps.
8. Such as auteur-structuralism, "'70's neo-Marxism," the psychoanalytical inflection of that, feminist film criticism.
9. See, for example, Joyrich (1988, 129–51). Joyrich tends to lean unproblematically on the assumption that family/weepie soap is melodrama, and her desire to defend melodrama is stronger and clearer than her sense of how it survives and operates in postmodern conditions of culture.

10. Part II of this article was written in collaboration with Elizabeth Jacka.

11. See Dermody and Jacka (1988a), especially pages 58–62 and 151–67, on "male-ensemble" films and these in particular. Other examples would include *Stork, Don's Party, The Journalist, The Last of the Knucklemen, The Club, Phar Lap, Buddies,* and miniseries such as *The Dismissal, Waterfront, Bodyline, The Last Bastion, Cowra Breakout, Anzacs, The Light Horsemen, The Great Bookie Robbery,* and *The True Believers.*

12. With the possible exception of the ones in which the landscape figures as wilderness, a mystical place where the rules are overturned and the normal relations of time and space do not apply: *The Lizard King,* the much earlier *Walkabout,* and in other categories, *Burke and Wills* or *The Last Wave.* See Dermody and Jacka (1988b, 113–15) for a discussion of the very interesting *Lizard King,* a French coproduction written by Louis Nowra with Marie-Christine Barrault and John Hargreaves.

13. See a fairly full discussion of "Australian gothic" in Dermody and Jacka (1988a, 49–52, 128–9, 237–9). On eccentric filmmaking, see Dermody and Jacka (1988a, 71–4; 1988b, 131–55).

14. Two other films in this area had high hopes attached to them for their full-blooded melodramatic potential, but each was disappointing—*The Umbrella Woman* and *For Love Alone,* from the novel by Chistina Stead. See Dermody and Jacka (1988b, 83–5).

15. "10BA" refers to an amendment to the Taxation Act of Australia, introduced in 1980, to provide an incentive to investment in Australian film. Originally, it offered 150 percent write-off of the investment, for taxation purposes, and 50 percent write-off of profit earnings. In 1983, this extremely generous incentive was reduced to 133/33 percent and in 1985 to 120/20 percent. For a full discussion of its history and subsequent replacement by a film-finance bank under government sponsorship, see Dermody and Jacka (1988b, 7–21).

16. The lead example is *The Dismissal;* others would include many already mentioned—*Bodyline, Cowra Breakout, Vietnam, The Last Bastion, The True Believers, Captain James Cook.*

17. The plot: A woman who is being betrayed by her wealthy husband has a boating "accident" in crocodile-infested waters and is mauled to the very threshold of death, especially her once-plain face. She is believed to be dead. Plastic surgery and other medical miracles provide her with a beautiful new face and body, which is soon famous throughout the land, but unrecognizable to her treacherous husband and his new wife. She returns in her new guise to Eden, the rich cattle-station property of her former husband, who begins falling in love with her and edging toward betraying his new wife. I'll leave it there.

18. "AFC-genre" is a term we coined in Dermody and Jacka (1986; 1988a) to describe the period films most favored, for a time, by the main investment body, the Australian Film Commission. See especially Dermody and Jacka (1988a, 28–38).

19. For a full discussion of this interesting entity in the Australian industry and its miniseries output, see Cunningham (1988).

20. For further discussion of these films, see Dermody and Jacka (1988a): pp. 193–6, on *Dirtwater Dynasty;* pp. 184–7, on *The Dismissal;* and pp. 191–3, on *Vietnam.*

References

Bentley, Eric (1967). *The Life of Melodrama*. New York: Atheneum.

Brooks, Peter (1976). *The Melodramatic Imagination: Balzac, Henry James, Melodrama, and the Mode of Excess*. New Haven: Yale University Press.

Clement, Catherine (1989). *Opera, or the Undoing of Women*. Trans. Betsey Wing. London: Virago.

Creed, Barbara (1987). "Horror and the Monstrous-Feminine: An Imaginary Abjection." *Screen* 27, 2:47–67.

Cunningham, Stuart (1988). "Kennedy-Miller: House Style in Australian Television." In *The Imaginary Industry: Australian Film in the Late 80s*, ed. Susan Dermody and Elizabeth Jacka, 177–200. Sydney: Australian Film, Television and Radio School.

—(1990). *Featuring Australia: The Cinemas of Charles Chauvel*. Sydney: Allen and Unwin.

Dermody, Susan, and Elizabeth Jacka (1986). *The Screening of Australia*. Vol. 1, *Anatomy of a Film Industry*. Sydney: Currency Press.

—(1988a). *The Screening of Australia*. Vol. 2, *Anatomy of a National Cinema*. Sydney: Currency Press.

—(1988b). *The Imaginary Industry: Australian Film in the Late 80s*. Sydney: Australian Film, Television and Radio School.

Dijkstra, Bram (1986). *Idols of Perversity: Fantasies of Feminine Evil in Fin-de-siècle Culture*. New York: Oxford University Press.

Elsaesser, Thomas (1972). "Tales of Sound and Fury: Observations on the Family Melodrama." *Monogram* 4:2–15. Reprinted in *Movies and Methods: An Anthology*, vol. 2, ed. Bill Nichols. Berkeley: University of California Press.

Gledhill, Christine (1988). "The Melodramatic Field: An Investigation." In *Home Is Where the Heart Is: Studies in Melodrama and the Woman's Film*, ed. Christine Gledhill, 5–39. London: BFI Publishing.

Holman, C. Hugh (1972). *A Handbook to Literature*. 3d ed. New York: Odyssey Press.

Jacka, Elizabeth (1989). "Feast of Edens." *Cinema Papers* 75:20–4.

Joyrich, Lynne (1988). "All That Television Allows: TV Melodrama, Postmodernism and Consumer Culture." *Camera Obscura* 16:129–51.

Kristeva, Julia (1982). "Approaching Abjection." In *Powers of Horror: An Essay on Abjection*. New York: Columbia University Press.

Theweleit, Klaus (1987). *Male Fantasies*. Vol. 1, *Women, Floods, Bodies, History*. Theory and History of Literature Series. Minneapolis: University of Minnesota Press.

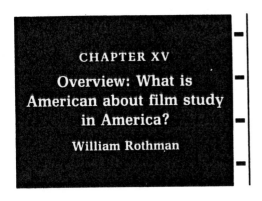

For over a decade, the Hawaii International Film Festival has been the
world's premier showcase for significant new films from Asia, and for
American films that, in whatever ways, contribute meaningfully to the
enrichment of mutual understanding between Asia and America. Of all
the exemplary features of the Hawaii Festival – all screenings are free
to the public, for example – none has proved worthier than the symposium organized by the East–West Center each fall in conjunction
with the event.

This symposium brings together Asian and American (and some
European) film historians, critics, and theorists to present and discuss
papers that address a theme of common interest even as they are sharing the heady experience of the festival itself – viewing extraordinary
films and conversing with filmmakers and each other.

All the papers collected in this volume were first presented at the
Hawaii Symposium. Most were written for the 1989 session, whose
theme was "Melodrama East and West." The rest were written for the
1988 session.

Since its inception in 1981, Wimal Dissanayake has been the symposium's coordinator and, I might add, its prime inspiration and guiding force. I think of this book as representing, almost above all, a
tribute to the shrewdness, imagination, and good humor with which
Dr. Dissanayake has each year put together a diverse cast of characters who always seem to come up with illuminating and provocative
papers, and who, with a few deft nudges, always prove ready to plunge
into rewarding conversations that lead to long-term friendships in the
spirit of the festival's goal of furthering understanding between "East"
and "West."

I have had the pleasure and privilege of participating in three of
these events. There is no way I can exaggerate their importance to my
own education in Asian cinema (this also means my education in cinema, because every Asian nation, like every Western one, has partici-

pated significantly in the international history of film, and has experienced that history in its own ways and in its own terms).

The first was in 1985. At that time, I possessed little special knowledge of Asian films, or the conditions of their production, beyond what any conscientious American professor of film study might have been expected to possess. This was more than we were expected to know about Martian cinema, but not much more.

Apart from the *Apu* trilogy and perhaps one or two other films by Satyajit Ray, few among us, in 1985, knew the work of any "serious" Indian directors, or were familiar, except by hearsay, with the vast subcontinent of the Indian commercial cinema. Other than martial arts films, few of us had seen a single film from Hong Kong, Taiwan, or mainland China. And it goes without saying that the cinema of Korea, the Phillipines, Indonesia, and Southeast Asia was completely unknown to us. There were excellent books on Japanese cinema in English, preeminently by Donald Richie, and a volume of brilliant essays by Sato Tadao, then hot off the press in English translation, was available under the title *Patterns of Japanese Cinema* (I was not to obtain this book until I returned from the symposium).[1] But firsthand knowledge of Japanese cinema was largely restricted to a handful of postwar films (all great works, to be sure) by Kurosawa, Mizoguchi, and Ozu.

The paper I presented at the 1985 symposium acknowledged a wish for an education in Asian cinema I did not possess, and declared an eagerness to participate in serious conversations about the relationship of film and culture.[2] It was, and is, my conviction that thinking seriously about film and culture does not mean applying a grand system of thought, what the field of film study calls a "theory." It means addressing this relationship concretely, as it works itself out in specific historical cases. And it means reflecting philosophically on the ways these cases illuminate each other, the ways they may be viewed as connected.

To this end, my paper posed the question, What is American about American cinema? I understood this to be at once a question about history and a question about philosophy. Following up a number of remarks in Stanley Cavell's *Pursuits of Happiness,* then relatively recently published, the paper offered at least part of an answer: The Americanness of American cinema cannot be separated from the ways American movie genres have taken up and revised, made their own, the American tradition of philosophy founded by Emerson and Thoreau, an American way of thinking philosophically that it has also been an American tradition to repress (as the voices of Emerson and Thoreau have been repressed within the academic field of philosophy in America, and as Cavell's voice has been repressed within film study in America).[3]

In claiming this connection between American philosophy and American cinema, in claiming that American cinema had itself claimed this connection, I was also claiming the connection between my own way of thinking (e.g., in entering that claim, and also *this* one) and this American tradition of philosophical thought. I was making a claim as to who I, an American philosopher, am. And I was claiming the authority to enter such claims, to make such connections, not by appeal to a "higher authority," but by appeal to my own experience, the way I actually find myself thinking. On philosophical principle, I was speaking in my own voice, and that is what *is* American about my way of thinking.

At Hawaii, among the most thought-provoking developments for me was discovering the harmonious attunement between my American way of thinking and Sato Tadao's very Japanese way. Sato too, in his critical writing and conversation about a film, characteristically makes a point of staking out a connection between the film and his way of thinking about the film, about the film's own way of thinking. And he, too, characteristically makes this connection by appealing to who he is, by speaking in his own voice, not by appealing to a higher authority.

I am not denying that Sato and I think very differently. His way of thinking, as I have said, is as characteristically – not typically – Japanese as mine is American. Yet there can be no real conversation between voices that are not separate, different from each other. But neither can there be conversation if there is no common ground.

It helps in surveying the common ground between Sato and myself to keep in mind that he was a young man during the years of Japan's postwar occupation by America. And it helps to keep in mind as well that while the Japanese films I knew were few, they had profoundly moved me. To be moved means for one's position, one's way of thinking, at least one's perspective on one's way of thinking, to be changed. Yet the Japanese films whose experience had changed my perspective, works such as *Ikiru, Ugetsu Monogatari,* and *Tokyo Story*, were themselves creations of the period of the American Occupation or its immediate aftermath.

Like Sato's writing and conversation, films such as *Ikiru, Ugetsu Monogatari,* and *Tokyo Story* affirm ways of thinking that may appear to be specifically American, as when they suggest that human beings deny their humanity when they bow to society's pressures to conform. Yet in no sense are these films examples of cultural domination or equally pernicious cultural assimilation. For even as each film is embracing a way of thinking with which Americans find themselves able to make connection, it is claiming, reclaiming, a specifically Japanese identity, recovering its own Japanese voice.

In their Japanese ways, these films are thinking for themselves. But thinking for oneself, speaking in a voice of one's own, what Emerson called "self-reliance," *is* the American philosophy, the form Emerson and Thoreau envisioned philosophy in America taking. As Cavell has taught us, their affirmation of "self-reliance" did not mean that Emerson and Thoreau were "relying" on a preconstituted thing called a "self." It meant that they were calling upon philosophy – in their writing, philosophy was calling upon itself – to attain a new perspective on itself, to take a stand on its own identity. It was by working out, philosophically, the conditions that constitute philosophical thought that American philosophy declared its own existence, its independence from the European philosophical tradition, and America at last accounted philosophically for the fact that it had secured its political independence from Europe.[4]

Emerson and Thoreau were known as transcendentalists. This meant that they acknowledged their solidarity with the Kantians whose "Copernican Revolution" had begun to transform the European philosophy from within. But Emerson and Thoreau no more simply inherited Kant's philosophical system than they inherited the systems Kant's philosophy had overturned. The new philosophy they aspired to found in America called for a fundamental reinterpretation of Kant's guiding intuitions that reason has limits and that knowledge of the world is possible because what things "objectively" are cannot be separated from the forms of our subjectivity. What Emerson and Thoreau were proposing and exemplifying was not a competing philosophical system, but a radically different understanding of what it means to think philosophically – an alternative practice of philosophy that breaks fundamentally with the European philosophical tradition, a tradition that predominantly equates philosophy with system building. (Through Nietzsche, a close follower of Emerson's thought, this radical alternative made its first decisive intervention within European philosophy itself.)

For Emerson and Thoreau, Western philosophy could only be defined by the dominant and dominating European tradition of philosophical system building. Thus they envisioned their way of thinking philosophically as, in a sense, specifically non-Western. As we know, Emerson and Thoreau were avid readers of the spiritual texts of Asia, eagerly awaiting each new translation. In their reading of every page, they felt confirmed in their conviction that their way of thinking, which called for them to break with European philosophy, was attuned to Asia's teaching. In turn, Emerson and Thoreau were read sympathetically in Asia, to world-historical effect. In India, for example, Tagore was a great reader of Emerson, and Gandhi was a devoted student of Thoreau's thought (as, coming full circle, Martin Luther King was a student of Gandhi's).

All peoples on earth stand on common ground. All human cultures are connected. But every human culture is also separate, different from every other. We cannot assume that the question of what is Indian about Indian cinema, the question of what is Chinese about Chinese cinema, or Japanese about Japanese cinema (or, for that matter, what is French about French cinema or German about German cinema) are questions that call for answers of a single form.

To the question of what is American about American cinema, I had offered an American form of answer. Then what forms of answer, specific to each culture (i.e., acknowledging a way of thinking internal to that culture, making its connection with that way of thinking) might these questions call for?

When I returned from Hawaii, bursting with eagerness to pursue such thoughts, I embarked on a crash course in Asian cinema. In retrospect, it is clear that I had chosen a uniquely privileged moment to do so.

Had I attempted even one year earlier to begin in earnest my education in Asian cinema, I would have lacked access, in America, to too many films that are crucial to view. But in the spring of 1986, "Film Utsav" traveled to Los Angeles, where I was spending the year. This was a major exhibition, unprecedented in scope, focusing on the work of five directors (V. Shantaram, Raj Kapoor, Guru Dutt, Ritwik Ghatak, Mrinal Sen) virtually unknown in America. That spring, too, Chen Mei and Professor Chiang Jihua were for the first time conducting their legendary UCLA seminar surveying the history of Chinese film. And Chen Xiaolin, the woman newly appointed head of the China Film Import and Export Company in America, graciously lent me cassettes of the latest films from China.

And had I begun one year later, I would have missed out on a decisive historical moment. For 1985 was the year the so-called Fifth Generation of Chinese filmmakers made its initial spectacular impact on America and Europe. At the 1985 Hawaii Festival, *Yellow Earth* was on the program, and Chen Kaige and Zhang Yimou were both in attendance. *Yellow Earth* turned out to be the sensation of the festival, as it was to be at film festivals all over the world. And it was followed, in the next several years, by a succession of stunning Fifth Generation films, each transgressing boundaries previously inviolable, each daring to push the limits further.

From 1986 to 1989, I was director of the International Honors Program on Film, Television and Social Change in Asia. It was my responsibility to fashion a curriculum, put together a small faculty, and personally lead groups of American college students on semester-long programs of study and travel in India, Hong Kong, China, and Japan (and sometimes Thailand). During the three years I was involved with the International Honors Program, America's attention was being drawn ever more compellingly to Asia, to China above all. And in China, film was not only "writing history with lightning," as Woodrow Wilson is said to have said about *The Birth of a Nation,* it was making – and unmaking – history. What was most remarkable about the Fifth Generation films, what riveted the attention of Americans who took an interest in them, cannot be separated from the breathtaking assurance with which these films claimed a leading role in the events of world-historical magnitude that were sweeping China. Film had not been in the vanguard like this, had not "manned the barricades," at least since the legendary events in Paris now known simply as "May '68" – and, to be truthful, not even then.

Americans studying Chinese film in this period found themselves swept up in these events and, indeed, called upon to play a role. Bearing witness to the Fifth Generation's struggle against villainous forces of repression, we were championing the films, taking their side. No doubt, the Fifth Generation filmmakers, shrewdly guided by Wu Tianming, their sage mentor, were counting on us to arouse the conscience of the world should they find themselves silenced.

In any case, as I mean my choice of words to suggest, like all Americans and like the Chinese themselves, we Americans studying Chinese cinema in those years found ourselves envisioning the events sweeping China as a grand historical melodrama (that these events constituted such a melodrama is a central intuition in Wang Yuejin's brilliant essay in this volume).[5] And we envisioned film in China, and ourselves, as champions of Chinese cinema, as playing roles in this melodrama. Historically, the appeal of being swept up in a grand melodramatic struggle between virtue and villainy was inseparable from the appeal, for Americans, of studying Chinese cinema during this period (to varying degrees, this was true of studying the cinemas of other Asian nations as well). And part of this appeal was that, swept up in such a melodrama, everything takes on cosmic significance. Nothing is merely academic. Not even film study (which by then had otherwise become, in America, all but completely "academicized").

By the fall of 1989, when I attended my third and most recent Hawaii Symposium, the grand melodrama had turned into a tragedy. At Hawaii, the still recent massacre in Tiananmen Square was fresh in everyone's mind. China had failed in its struggle to free itself from its tragic past. The Fifth Generation had failed. Film itself had failed to fulfill the heroic role it had assumed.

As I am writing these words, in the summer of 1991, it seems all too clear that a gloriously hopeful period in the history of Asian cinema has now definitively come to an end. In China, Zhang Yimou's despairing *Ju Dou,* released last year in the West but never released in China, was the ultimate, and the last, Fifth Generation masterpiece.

And while I have been dwelling on the example of China, what was a momentous historical period for cinema in other Asian countries, too, has likewise now ended. Among the events that mark the passing of this period, I am thinking of the deaths last spring of two great and irreplaceable artists, Lino Brocka in the Philippines and G. Aravindan in India. (Aravindan's death was especially heartbreaking to me because my wife and I had enjoyed the once-in-a-lifetime opportunity to collaborate with him on *Unni,* a feature film he directed from our script, which was based on experiences of our students in India, whom he had met and in whom he had taken an interest.)

And it is equally clear, looking back to the fall of 1989, that a formative period in the history of the study of Asian cinema, too, was then nearing its end. The study of Asian cinema, once marginal, has now become fully accepted by academic film study in America as an integral part of the field.

At the 1985 session of the Hawaii Symposium, most of the papers and discussions barely paid even lip service to the theoretical frameworks and historiographical methodologies that were already paradigms for academic film study in America. Most of the participants were either Asian film critics with distinguished professional careers in their own countries but who were not based in the academic world – Sato Tadao and Chidananda Dasgupta, for example; "cultural interpretors" and champions of Asian cinema such as Donald Richie and Tony Rayns, who were likewise not academics; and Americans like myself who were indeed university teachers, but who had come to Hawaii to take off our academic hats (caps?) and immerse ourselves in films and conversations solely for the sake of our own educations – we had not packed our academic axes, happy to be in a place where we didn't have to grind them. (No doubt, viewed from the perspective of the academic field of film study, we were simply on vacation.)

At the 1989 session, there was no one like Sato Tadao, no one like Chidananda Dasgupta, no one like Donald Richie, no one like Tony Rayns – and no one like me as I was in 1985, no one all but completely lacking an education in Asian cinema. In 1989, the participating Americans, including myself, were academic film scholars who listed Asian cinema among our areas of professional specialization. And most of the Americans' papers – here I do exclude myself – paid more than lip service to the dominant paradigms of academic film study in America. Most of the participants from Asia were also academic film scholars. They had received their professional training in American film study programs, and their papers, too, conformed to the paradigms of the field of film study in America, and were clearly conceived as contributions to this field.

I am not denying that there is cause for celebration in the recent acceptance of Asian cinema by the field of film study in America. But this development also has sobering implications we would do well to ponder.

A quarter of a century ago, when the case for the academic study of film was originally made to American university administrations and faculties, film study predominantly envisioned itself as a new field of criticism. The works to be studied were to encompass, but not be limited to, ordinary movies, in particular American movies of what the field has since come to call the "classical" period. And the new field of film study predicated its claim for recognition on the conviction that the achievements of cinema, importantly but not exclusively including the achievements of American classical cinema, called for serious critical acknowledgment, and on the corollary conviction that no existing academic field was capable of the kind of criticism film called for. And just as Asian cinema's first large-scale acceptance within the field of film study coincided with the definitive ending of the exhilarating period, all too brief, in which Asian cinema had captured the imagination of the world, cinema's first large-scale acceptance within the American university coincided with the definitive ending of the classical period of the American cinema.

This intriguing parallel makes it tempting to envision Asian cinema's acceptance by film study as recapitulating film's own acceptance by the American university a quarter of a century ago, and to envision both as comparable victories in comparable struggles. But there are two reasons to resist this temptation.

First, Asian cinema did not *win* the acceptance of the field; there was no significant opposition – no struggle, hence no victory. It is closer to the truth to say that the field of film study in America simply annexed Asian cinema, as if it were its manifest destiny to do so.

Thus, for example, the Society for Cinema Studies, the major professional organization of the field in America, interprets the recent surge of interest in Asian cinema, which it sees as part of a broader concern with "issues of multi-culturalism," as having been generated by considerations internal to the field's own priorities and agenda. This is clear from the language of the call for panel proposals that the society mailed to its membership in advance of its most recent annual conference.

In the past several years, the Society for Cinema Studies has encouraged attention to issues of race, ethnicity, class, gender, sexual orientation and national origin. Thus it seems appropriate to ask in a more intense way critical, philosophical and historical questions about the notion of multi-culturalism in relation to the traditional areas of research in film ... studies.

Why does it now "seem appropriate" to ask these (unspecified) questions? The statement implies that, given the steps the field has already taken, this is simply the logical next step. At no point does the statement reiterate what it takes to have justified the field in having taken those steps, nor does it justify the present step beyond saying, in effect, "This simply *is* the agenda of the field of film study in America, these *are* the field's priorities, *this* is the way we in the field do things."

No doubt, it adds to the greater glory of film study in America to recognize the study of Asian cinema as a new branch of the field – on the condition that the procedures of this new branch conform to the field's existing priorities and agenda. But to accept the study of Asian cinema on such terms is to reject out of hand the possibility that Asian films may call for fundamentally different ways of thinking, Asian ways of thinking, for example, if the films' own different ways of thinking are to be acknowledged. For film study in America to accept Asian cinema only as an object to be studied in accordance with already established procedures and doctrines is for the field to deny to Asian films, and to Asians, the status of subjects, subjects capable of thinking for themselves. It is to silence Asian voices, voices that are different from American voices, to suppress conversation between and among Americans and Asians.

For Asians wishing to study Asian cinema, the field of film study, insofar as the Society for Cinema Studies speaks for it, envisions no option but to subordinate their own diverse ways of thinking to procedures and doctrines that it is assumed Asian films must yield to, not confront or challenge. But, in truth, Americans studying Asian films are likewise offered no option but to subordinate our experience, too, to these procedures and doctrines. And it has long been one of the field's leading doctrines that American films, and American ways of thinking, must also yield to procedures and doctrines that themselves have been "authorized" by what the field recognizes as a higher authority.

And this brings us to the second reason for resisting the temptation to envision film study's acceptance of Asian cinema and the American university's acceptance of film as comparable victories in comparable struggles. Namely, the fact that the field of film study has never definitively won its struggle to secure its intellectual identity.

As I have said, in the late 1960s, film study was waging a struggle against powerful forces within the American university – I played my modest part in this struggle – to win recognition that films were worthy of serious critical acknowledgment, and to win recognition as well that no existing academic field was capable of performing that acknowledgment. Film study's original struggle, as I understood it then and now, was at once to win recognition for film as an object of study and to win recognition for the study of film as an independent academic field.

No existing field was capable of studying film seriously, we were claiming, because the medium of film was different. Films were different in ways that called for the creation of new terms of criticism, new ways of thinking that acknowledged what was different about film's own different ways of thinking. Thus to back up its claim to exist as a field in its own right, the discipline of film study we were envisioning would have to encompass a philosophical investigation of the ontology of the medium and the art of film, an investigation that would proceed, not by adopting a preexisting theoretical system whose authority the field accepted as given, but by reflecting on the testimony of the films themselves, the testimony of critics' experience of films.

But academic criticism in America, in departments of literature above all, was in the throes of radical transformation. One does not have to be a weatherman to know that, in the past two and a half decades, academic criticism in America has been swept by a succession of winds from the east – by structuralism, semiology, Althusserian Marxism, Lacanian psychoanalysis, Derridean deconstruction, and so on. Despite their mutual incompatibilities, and largely in disregard of the particularities of the French cultural contexts that motivated their original emergence, these theoretical systems became more or less collapsed, in America, into the single entity, origins unknown, usually called simply "Theory."

When film study in America embraced Theory, it envisioned itself as thereby acquiring the authority, the certainty, of a science. But by taking this fateful step, a field that had aspired to its own way of thinking denied its own authority and the authority of the films it studied, and ceded its claim to intellectual independence.

As I have said, film study in America had staked its claim to independence on the conviction that the field's mandate was to develop new terms of criticism capable of acknowledging film's own ways of thinking, as importantly – but not exclusively – exemplified by classical American cinema. Theory underwrites a conflicting claim: Classical cinema does not exemplify ways of thinking that call for forms of critical acknowledgment unique to film, classical cinema is only a repressive ideological system, a system thoroughly implicated in the dominant social order.

Under the regime of Theory, the field takes itself to be authorized to endorse this doctrine that classical films exemplify ways of not thinking, not ways of thinking, the doctrine that classical cinema is, indeed, a system for repressing thought. According to Theory, all there is about classical cinema for film study *to* study is the detailed workings, semiologically and historically, of this system. This "study" is envisioned as a joint task for deconstructive readings and what the field calls "historiography." Theory dictates not only the agenda but the results of this "study," whose mandate is not to paint an original portrait of the history of cinema, as it were, but to fill in the outline Theory provides, to colorize Theory's picture.

The surest way for the field to test the doctrines of Theory would be by attending to the testimony of the films themselves, that is, by performing acts of criticism accountable to the critic's experience, and by reflecting on the implications of the readings that emerge from those critical acts. But Theory peremptorily dismisses all such testimony. Theory authorizes film study to deny a priori – for the field, Theory *is* this systematic denial of the authority of experience – even the possibility that a classical film, or, for that matter, a critic testifying from her or his own experience, could be capable of "speaking" anything but ideology, could be capable of providing what would count – what Theory would count – as testimony.

A detailed historical account of the stages by which film study in America came to deny the authority of experience – to deny its own authority and that of the films it was its original aspiration to acknowledge – would cite the reception of a familiar litany of French texts. But I think of the decisive moment, historically, as the appearance in 1971 of Cavell's *The World Viewed.*[6]

What made the publication of Cavell's brilliant little book of philosophy so decisive was not its subsequent influence on film study in America, its reception by the field, but its all but complete nonreception, the silence with which the field responded to the book. Historically, the moment film study in America turned to European theoretical systems in search of a higher authority was also the moment it turned away from Cavell's American way of thinking philosophically, a way of thinking that denies the necessity, and the possibility, of any authority higher than experience, a way of thinking that had been embraced by Nietzsche, had profoundly influenced Heidegger, and thus played a central role, historically, in the emergence of Theory itself. In Cavell's book, film study in America, which had already declared itself a separate field, had at last accounted, philosophically and historically, for its existence, its capacity to think for itself, had found a voice it could call its own. By bowing down to Theory, film study in America betrayed its capacity to think for itself, and submitted to the suppression of its own voice.

To begin to understand how such a thing could possibly have taken place, it is helpful to think about what Americans least wish to think about, which is America's experience of the late 1960s, an experience that had opened, or reopened, deep wounds, wounds that have not since healed, but have festered. I think of America in those years as torn, I think of every American as torn – agonizingly, ecstatically – between thinking and repressing thought. I take it that, when American academics turned to French thought at that traumatic historical moment, it was less to think more deeply about their own experience than to stop thinking about it, to pull back from their own experience as if from a terrifying precipice.

In the aftermath of May 1968, French intellectuals, reflecting on their failure to effect a second French Revolution, had turned to Marx, to Nietzsche, to Freud, to Heidegger, at the same time turning their ways of thinking, not originally French, into philosophical systems that at once denied and, through the authority of that denial, reasserted the centrality of French culture. This is not the place for me to speculate as to whether these philosophical systems, within the French cultural context, primarily represented new French ways of thinking or new French ways of not thinking. But this is the place for me to point out that when Americans turned to these new French philosophical systems, they primarily turned them not into new American ways of thinking, but into new American ways of not thinking – new ways of not thinking about the way America has been torn since its creation, new ways of not thinking about the implications of the fact that America's Constitution declared the nation free while Americans were keeping slaves, new ways of not thinking about what was changing and what was unchanging in the relationships of men and women in America, new ways of not thinking about America's history of thinking and repressing thought. It was in quest of denying the necessity of thinking about itself, and the necessity of thinking for itself, I take it, that the field embraced the still dominant myth about its own origin – the myth that envisions film study in America as born, or born again, through its transfiguring faith in Theory. Within this myth, May 1968, a historical moment America never experienced, becomes the decisive moment of the field's creation. This myth is a disavowal of America's own experience, a denial that the American experience was formative for film study in America.

Following the advent of Theory, film study in America felt authorized to dismiss American ways of thinking – for example, about democracy, individual rights and freedom, but also about the conditions of the medium and the art of film – as having been completely discredited, unmasked as "dominant ideology," exposed as a system for repressing thought, as no way of thinking at all. That, within the field of film study in America, Theory itself was a system for repressing thought, was no way of thinking at all, was "dominant ideology," became comically clear the moment American academics, in wholesale numbers, suddenly began, in their professional capacity, to speak like committed Marxist/Leninists or even Maoists even as they continued securing tenure, keeping their eye on mortgage rates, and, in general, taking for granted the privileges of membership in the American academic world.

Nonetheless, when China found itself swept up in the death throes of Maoism, indeed the annihilation, the self-immolation, of Marxism as an intellectually defensible position, all Americans who took an interest in Chinese cinema rejoiced, even those who in theory were Maoists. In China at this time, only the villainous forces of repression viewed Americans as villains. The forces of virtue felt they shared common ground with us, with the American way of thinking. If Theory really held sway over their lives the way it does according to Theory, most Americans studying Chinese cinema would have found themselves on the side of the villains in China, not the heroes and heroines of the Fifth Generation.

The kind of melodrama – is it one kind? – I am invoking here hinges on a cosmic struggle between good and evil. That innumerable melodramas revolving around such cosmic struggles have been produced in every country of Asia as well as in America and Europe is one obvious justification for a symposium on the theme "Melodrama East and West." A subtler justification is that, as I have suggested, the appeal of studying Asian cinema for Americans has been, historically, inseparable from the way, when swept up in such a melodrama, all actions, even the study of film, take on cosmic significance.

Of course, within film study in America, the word "melodrama" is often used to refer to the so-called woman's picture. Characteristically, there is no villain in such a melodrama, hence no cosmic struggle. In a woman's picture, the central struggle is a human one, a woman's human struggle for selfhood, her struggle to speak in her own voice within a world in which no one knows her the way we do. That innumerable melodramas of this kind, too, have been made in Asia, as they have been made in America and Europe, is another obvious justification for a symposium on "Melodrama East and West." And it is another subtle justification that, historically, the experience of studying Asian cinema for Americans has had the appeal of the woman's picture. Swept up in the events of this kind of melodrama, too, everything is fateful, nothing merely academic – not because events take on cosmic significance, but because they assume a human dimension.

My experience of a particular Asian film – any film, for that matter – is a meeting, an exchange, between what I bring to the film (who I am, the way I think) and what I take from the film (what the film teaches me, how its way of thinking changes the way I think). And my experience of an Asian film cannot be separated from what that film means to me as I experience it, my understanding of what the film means, that is, my understanding of how the film understands its own meaning. And that understanding, my understanding of the film's own understanding, is something I create in collaboration with the film itself and with all the people who have helped me, in whatever ways, to be the human being I am. The moral to be drawn from this is that there can be, for Americans, no meaningful study of Asian cinema – and, indeed, no meaningful study of cinema – that does not have a human dimension, that is not collaborative, dependent on conversations between flesh-and-blood human beings, on human contacts that bridge the gulfs that separate every human being, and every human culture, from every other.

When I reflect on the human dimension of my own education in Asian cinema, Gayatri Chatterjee is a person who springs immediately to mind. In India, this woman helped select films for me to view, interpreted moments of these films for me, answered countless small and large questions about their cultural and social contexts, explained innumerable matters to me, and so on. But she also facilitated my education in ways that went beyond anything she did by way of instructing me. Simply by being there for me, by being herself – which means, at times, by masking herself – in my presence, by telling me anecdotes from her life story, by letting me in on her thoughts and hence her ways of thinking, by becoming my friend and letting me be her friend, she enabled me to get to know two or three things about who she is, what type of human being, to gain glimpses of her subjectivity, the way she views the world – in short, to get to know her from the "inside" as well as the "outside," to know her the way Gayatri has gotten to know me, as a subject as well as an object, the way we know the "unknown woman" in a woman's picture.

Whatever else Gayatri has become to me, in India she served me as a human reference point, an exemplar of the humanity of India, who enabled me to make connection with Indian films, to be open to their human dimension in a way that would not otherwise have been possible. And the Indian films her example helped opened to me also helped open her to me as a human being, helped me appreciate her Indian way of being human, helped to render her form of life intelligible to me, yet also unknowable – not unknowable because she is alien, but because she is human, as I am. Human beings are not unknowable because there is something about them we cannot know, some particular piece of knowledge we lack but can imagine possessing. Human beings are unknowable only in that they can never be possessed by what we call "knowledge." Human beings need to be acknowledged, not merely known. And what it is about human beings that needs to be acknowledged, acknowledged separately in every case, is that human beings cannot be possessed at all.

In China, Chen Mei similarly served as an exemplar of humanity for me. Becoming humanly attached to this witty, strong, passionate woman, who emerged from the nightmare of the Cultural Revolution unshakably committed to being her own person, helped me to experience China, and cinema in China, in ways that would otherwise not have been possible for me. Viewed from the perspective my relationship with Chen Mei enabled me to attain, the cosmic struggle between virtue and villainy sweeping China was a backdrop to the struggles for selfhood of individual human beings. From this perspective, the fate of Chen Mei's quest meant more to me, was more momentous, than any merely cosmic struggle. It is not possible to attain this perspective, which is the perspective of the woman's picture, without being attached to other human beings, and without acknowledging that we could not be so bound to others unless we were not also separate, different, unknowable by other human beings and by ourselves.

Clearly, the woman's picture is different, generically, from melodramas that revolve around cosmic struggles between virtue and villainy. The latter seem obviously to derive from the kind of nineteenth-century theatrical melodramas that are the focus of Peter Brooks's seminal study, *The Melodramatic Imagination,* a book that has wielded a powerful influence over studies of film melodramas.[7]

Brooks's book is heavily indebted to the new French thought, Lacanian psychoanalysis in particular. And it does, in the spirit of French thought, envision everything worthy of the name "melodrama" as originating in Paris, and only then crossing the Channel to England and the ocean to America. In Brooks's account of melodrama's origin, it is the French Revolution, not the American one, that is formative, even for melodrama in America. No doubt, this conviction that the French experience was central, the American experience marginal, no less than Brooks's erudition and flashes of brilliance, helped *The Melodramatic Imagination* to attain the prestige it enjoys within the field of film study in America. Typically, studies of film melodrama, including a number of the essays in the present volume, not only unquestioningly endorse Brooks's claims about the emergence and history of theatrical melodrama but extend these claims as they stand to film melodramas as well.

For example, in "Melodrama/subjectivity/ideology," her essay for this volume, E. Ann Kaplan poses the question of how we can justify calling contemporary Chinese films "melodramas" when European and American melodrama "arose at a time when the bourgeois class needed to differentiate itself from the working and aristocratic classes" whereas the Chinese films "emerge within a nation dominated by the Communist Party's ideology of classlessness."[8] However, although the bourgeoisie's wish to differentiate itself from the aristocracy as well as the working class may or may not plausibly explain the rise of theatrical melodrama in France, it is no part of an explanation in the American case, since America had no aristocracy when it embraced melodramatic theater. And it is also no explanation at all for the emergence of *film* melodramas in the twentieth century – unless one assumes that stage and screen melodramas are one and the same form. The fact is, the relationship of the classical American woman's picture to what Brooks takes to be the historically specific theatrical form that is the focus of his study is no less obscure than is the relationship of nineteenth-century theatrical melodrama to recent Chinese film melodramas.

Brooks does not deny the obvious fact that forms sharing crucial features with the theatrical melodramas he is studying have emerged in very different cultures at very different times. Yet by encouraging us to restrict the term "melodrama" to what he takes to be one historically specific theatrical form, Brooks is discouraging us from comparing other forms of melodrama with that form, or with each other. I take it that Brooks means to discourage such comparative studies out of respect for the principle of historical specificity. But what is specific about a historical moment cannot be separated from how that moment is specified. The moment at which theatrical melodrama emerged in postrevolutionary France is also a moment in the historical relationship between Europe and India, for example. Brooks does not choose to specify what he takes to be the moment of melodrama's emergence in Paris by making a connection between Europe and India in this way, presumably because he assumes that no such connection is relevant. Yet on what grounds can he dismiss out of hand the possibility that there is a historical connection as well as a formal relationship between, say, ancient or modern Indian melodramatic forms and the one theatrical form – if we assume it is one form – he is prepared to call "melodrama"? (The celebrated theatrical production directed by Peter Brook, Peter Brooks's near namesake, makes such a link seem tangible. Is this an illusion?) To rule out such a possibility a priori is to consign India and Europe to two completely separate worlds, as if they shared no common ground, hence were not capable of conversation.

To assume that theatrical melodrama and film melodrama constitute one and the same form is to deny that film and theater are separate, hence to deny as well that there could be a conversation between *them*. Film and theater are, in truth, fundamentally different, and the nature of their difference has been, historically, one of film's central concerns.[9] But this means that the relationship between stage and screen melodramas is not knowable a priori, even in cases in which both hinge on cosmic struggles between virtue and villainy. Brooks's book has actively inhibited film study from reflecting seriously on the relationship between theater and film as it works itself out in particular historical cases. And it has inhibited film study from meditating on the diversity of melodramatic forms in cinema, the diversity of their sources, the diversity of relationships these diverse forms of melodrama bear to one another. And these relationships cannot be separated from the historical specificity of each.

For example, in the case of the relationship of woman's pictures and film melodramas that revolve around cosmic struggles of virtue and villainy, it is by no means clear how these melodramatic forms are related to each other, generically or historically. Thus Cavell argues that the genre he calls the "melodrama of the unknown woman" (the examples he has studied in a series of extraordinary essays are *Stella Dallas, Gaslight, Now Voyager,* and *Letter from an Unknown Woman*) derive directly from the remarriage comedy, a contemporaneous American film genre whose relationship to the theatrical melodramas Brooks writes about is far from direct.[10] In *Pursuits of Happiness,* Cavell suggests that Shakespearean romance is a central theatrical source for remarriage comedy, although the genre also has an important source in nineteenth-century theater, namely, Ibsen.[11] And if we look to the nineteenth century for a source of the "unknown woman" melodrama, it would seem far more promising to turn first to Italian opera, rather than to French theatrical melodrama. And in working out the genre's connections with Italian opera, it is necessary to reflect on the ontological conditions of opera, as well as film. It is necessary to keep in mind, for example, that, although opera is performed on stage before live audiences, the medium of opera is fundamentally different from the medium of theater, as different as song is from speech, as different as both opera and theater are from the medium of film.

Of all the essays in the present volume, Maureen Turim's "Psyches, ideologies, and melodrama: The United States and Japan" presents the most detailed demonstration of the fruitfulness of tracing the intricately criss-crossing historical lineages of the diverse forms of stage and screen melodramas in cultures as different as those of America and Japan.[12] Yet when Turim claims that Japanese and American film melodramas have both had to assimilate – or, rather, translate into their own cultural terms and thus transfigure – an essentially French melodramatic tradition, even she allows the diversity of melodramatic forms, and the diversity of their sources, both of which she has taken such pains to elaborate, to collapse into a single form, a single source. In this collapse, the principle of historical specificity is one casualty. Another is the principle that the serious study of film cannot be separated from the task of acknowledging and addressing the ontological conditions of the film medium. Necessarily, to deny the latter principle is to deny the former. It is an unfortunate fact that the latter principle has been, since the advent of Theory, routinely denied by film study in America.

The woman's picture is the leading concern of Turim's essay, as it is of most of the essays in this volume. Virtually every one invokes the impressive body of work on the American woman's picture that has been a central legacy of the powerful impact of the feminist movement on film study in America. The emergence of feminist criticism within the field, beginning with the publication of Laura Mulvey's "Visual Pleasure and Narrative Cinema" fifteen years ago, and its subsequent rise to ascendancy, has surely been the most significant development since the advent of Theory – and the most encouraging.[13]

Feminism cannot be viewed simply as the latest in a succession of imported theoretical systems that American film study has incorporated into what the field calls "Theory." For one thing, although there are European feminists such as Julia Kristeva, Helene Cixous, and Luce Irigaray who are figures to reckon with in the Parisian intellectual world, feminist film criticism in America has not primarily been concerned with applying their theoretical systems, or "translating" their work into the American context. Feminist film critics in America have made a massive investment in French thought, as has virtually everyone in the field. But their primary allegiance and debt has been to feminism itself, not to Theory. And feminism is, primarily, an American movement. Its aspiration is to find its own voice, to think for itself.

Indeed, feminist film criticism in America has always been conscious that there is something problematic in its dependence on Theory. Already in "Visual Pleasure and Narrative Cinema," Mulvey recognized that feminism could not simply accept Lacanian psychoanalysis, say, because the Lacanian system envisions language, hence thought, hence psychoanalysis itself as thoroughly implicated in the patriarchal system that feminism is struggling to overcome. Yet although feminist film criticism has recognized from the outset that Theory is patriarchal, the greater its investment in French thought, the greater its resistance to writing off this investment.

Among feminist film critics, Mulvey's claims that all classical films are enunciated from the position of patriarchy, and that the classical "codes" allowed for no resistance to patriarchal ideology, were almost immediately felt to be too extreme. Every leading feminist film critic, including Mulvey herself, has since tried a hand at revising this position. However, none of these attempts to negotiate a compromise between feminism and the rigid doctrines of Theory has engendered a response remotely comparable with the widespread excitement aroused by Mulvey's original formulation. Nor has any of these revisions achieved anything approaching large-scale acceptance. What has made it impossible for feminist film critics to arrive at a consensus as to how to revise Mulvey's original position, I take it, is that there is no possible compromise that *could* satisfy both the conditions of feminism and the conditions of Theory. Once Theory starts entering into compromises, once it acknowledges that it is fallible, its standing as a "higher authority" is lost. Then it has no authority at all.

Feminist film critics in America have never found themselves able simply to believe in Theory, because Theory gives no answer or the wrong answer to feminism's most urgent questions. But if feminist film criticism has resisted Theory, it has never abandoned Theory completely, as if it were afraid of being abandoned by Theory. Thus feminist film criticism has never developed a comparably powerful system of thought it could call its own. Theory has its way of accounting for the unwillingness or inability of feminism to develop an alternative theoretical system, an account that envisions it as *impossible* for feminism to think for itself, to be anything but dependent on patriarchal systems of thought if it is not to be excluded from the realm of thought altogether. The feminist movement in America, committed to thinking for itself, has never actually credited Theory's account. But nor has feminism ever decisively challenged it, ever acknowledged that it has a viable alternative to remaining dependent on Theory.

In reality, the moment feminist film critics started considering exceptions to Mulvey's original position, the moment they started making distinctions, they found themselves turning for instruction to the films themselves, to the ways women experience them. The fact is, feminist film critics have been reading films without at every point depending on Theory. But they have still not looked down and discovered that the safety net of Theory is gone.

This, then, is feminist film criticism's alternative to remaining dependent on Theory: to acknowledge, on the basis of its own experience, that it is not necessary to possess a system of thought in order to be able to think seriously about film. The alternative, in other words, is to claim connection with the way of thinking philosophically founded in America by Emerson and Thoreau.

As I have suggested, the other face of film study's embrace of Theory has been the field's repression of this alternative to the dominant and dominating Western tradition of philosophical system building. Thus Cavell's work, which claims connection with this alternative philosophical tradition, remains repressed within the field of film study in America. This is evidenced, for example, by the fact that, although virtually every essay in the present volume, when summing up the work about melodrama that has already been done in the field, quite appropriately refers to the body of feminist criticism about the American woman's picture, virtually none refers to the radically different way of thinking articulated in the readings of *Letter from an Unknown Woman, Gaslight, Now Voyager,* and *Stella Dallas* that Cavell has published in recent years. It is as if Cavell's writing simply did not exist, or, at least, as if the field had presented legitimate arguments for excluding it. In fact, no such arguments have ever been articulated within the field. In particular, the field has presented no grounds for rejecting Cavell's leading claim that the "melodrama of the unknown woman," like the remarriage comedy that was the subject of *Pursuits of Happiness,* itself inherits, meaningfully participates in, the alternative tradition of philosophy to which Cavell's own writing claims connection. (That film study in America is so constituted as to be able to dismiss philosophical alternatives without argument is part of what I mean by saying that the field has not yet secured its intellectual identity.)

In their aversion to the system building of Western philosophy, Emerson and Thoreau envisioned their alternative way of thinking as specifically non-European, hence non-Western, as I have said. By envisioning philosophy as the enterprise of constructing philosophical systems, Western philosophy has predominantly envisioned itself as a paradigmatically male activity, hence has understood itself as speaking, as needing to speak, only in a masculine voice. One of Cavell's guiding insights is that the dominant tradition of Western philosophy has excluded the feminine voice from philosophy, has disavowed – denied, suppressed – what is feminine in philosophy's own voice. As Cavell reads them, Emerson and Thoreau understood it to be a central aspiration of the new philosophy they were founding in America to be the recovery of the feminine aspect of the human voice, apart from which it was not possible for philosophy in America to find a voice of its own with which to speak. By understanding the genres of American film that he has studied as aligning themselves with the philosophy of Emerson and Thoreau, Cavell understands these genres, as he understands his own writing, to be attuned to the goals of feminism.

There is an unbridgeable gulf between Cavell's way of thinking philosophically, which is repressed within film study in America as presently constituted, and the doctrines of Theory that claim to authorize this repression. But there is no gulf at all between Cavell's aspirations and the political aspirations of the feminist movement. Then why have feminist film critics never acknowledged or addressed Cavell's writing, why has feminism participated in film study's repression of Cavell's work?

In a letter to the editors of *Critical Inquiry,* Tania Modleski expresses outrage at Cavell's essay on *Letter from an Unknown Woman,* which had appeared in a recent issue, and accuses Cavell of being unscholarly for not responding in detail to the dialogues and debates about the woman's picture among feminist film critics.[14] Cavell's reply, published along with the letter, refuses to accept this charge. To be sure, he does not, beyond the specific debts he acknowledges in his essay, take instruction from the extensive body of feminist literature about the genre of melodrama he is writing about. But, as he points out, his interest in these melodramas, and his way of thinking about the genre, go back to *The World Viewed,* and, indeed, to even earlier writing he had published almost thirty years ago.[15] If there is a question of scholarly propriety, in other words, the question is not why Cavell has not systematically referred to feminist film criticism, but why feminist film criticism has not referred to Cavell's writing. Feminist film critics have not only not offered detailed responses to Cavell's work, but have not even acknowledged its existence, not acknowledged that it is *possible* to think about these films, about film, the way he does.

From Cavell's perspective, feminist film criticism's dependence on Theory has enabled it to remain fixated on doctrines that cannot be reconciled with the ontological conditions of film as he worked them out philosophically in *The World Viewed* – for example, the doctrine that in classical cinema the viewer's relationship to the film image can be adequately characterized by the psychoanalytic concept of the fetish. And its dependence on Theory has helped enable feminist criticism to remain fixated on the denial, likewise irreconcilable with Cavell's way of thinking, that classical American film melodramas, written and directed by men, produced under patriarchy, constructed in accordance with "codes" that are systematically implicated in dominant patriarchal ideology, could possibly be capable of thinking about the subjectivity of women in a way feminism could find acceptable.

A conversation between Modleski and Cavell is possible, a conversation that acknowledges and addresses the differences that separate them, only if Modleski acknowledges the common ground on which she and Cavell stand. It is not my concern whether Modleski, personally, is willing or able to enter into conversation with Cavell. But it is my concern whether feminism and philosophy in America will prove willing and able to converse with each other. This is, for both, a fateful question. And the fate of film study in America, too, is at stake.

The field of film study in America cannot be a sisterhood any more than it can be a men's club. I wish a say in its agenda. I wish a say in whether the field acknowledges women's voices, and men's voices, and Asians' voices, and whether the field acknowledges *my* voice. And I wish a say in whether film study in America goes on envisioning itself as nothing apart from Theory, or whether it acknowledges the voices it has repressed, revises its understanding of its own origin and history, and recognizes that there is a philosophical alternative to theoretical systematizing.

I seem to be proposing that film study in America replace one myth of origin (a myth about May 1968, about the advent of Theory) with another (a myth about late 1960s' America, about denying the authority of experience). In any case, I do not believe that it was only at one historical moment, safely in the past, that the field submitted to the silencing of its own voice. What I believe is what the dominant myth precisely denies, that film study in America came into being at a moment America was torn, and that the field has always been torn between thinking and repressing thought, between acknowledging and denying film's capacity, and its own, to think for itself.

I find it quite characteristic of writing in the field, even writing that conforms to the doctrines of Theory, that there are moments of resistance, moments when an attentive reader may sense a question about to be raised, a voice about to break its silence before it submits to silence yet again. I have this sense quite strongly with a number of the essays in this book.

In general, I find nearly all the foregoing essays to be most illuminating when they are attending to the Asian films they are addressing; less illuminating when they are summing up what they take the field to have learned from its extensive studies of American melodramas; and least illuminating when they are invoking, as if they were authoritative, the field's doctrines, especially about American films.

Nonetheless, all the essays in this volume contain a wealth of thought-provoking observations. Every one, read thoughtfully, provides examples of how we might fruitfully go on, at this fateful juncture in the history of film study in America, in pursuing our studies of melodrama and Asian cinema. A number of these essays also contain examples, likewise useful to thoughtful readers, that might caution us as to how not to go on.

Read thoughtfully, in other words, these essays can play a constructive role in helping the field of film study in America to free itself from the repressive regime of Theory. What could be more fitting than for the field to "find itself" in part through encounters with Asian cinema, and with Asians?

Paul Willemen warns against the danger, when reading "alien texts," of becoming "cultural ventriloquists," that is, believing we are allowing films to speak for themselves while it is really our own voices we are hearing. But for Americans, needing reassurance that we *have* voices of our own, it is an almost irresistible attraction of Theory that it appears to invest its practitioners with the marvelous power to cast our voices into the mouths of others. In America, the problem with

Theory is not that it leads us to drown out the voices of others while believing we are having a real conversation, but that it leads us to imagine we are speaking in our own voices when we are really only moving our lips. Entranced by Theory, Americans do not become ventriloquists. They become dummies.

For film study in America to awaken from its trance of Theory, to recover its own voice, all that is required is for the field to attain a new perspective, which is also an old perspective, on its own identity. Conversations about Asian cinema and about the diverse ways Asians have thought about cinema, conversations between and among Asians and Americans, can play a leading role in enabling the field to attain this transfiguring perspective.

From this perspective, it may be recognized not only that Asians and Americans, like women and men, are separate, different, but also that they stand on common ground, that conversation is possible.

And, from this perspective, it may be recognized as well that American culture and film study have become all but completely estranged. Yet conversation is possible between them, too. They, too, stand on common ground.

Notes

1. Sato Tadao, *Currents in Japanese Cinema,* trans. by Gregory Barrett (Tokyo: Kodansha International, 1982).

2. William Rothman, "Hollywood Reconsidered: Reflections on the Classical American Cinema," *East–West Film Journal* 1, 1 (December 1986): 36–47; reprinted in William Rothman, *The "I" of the Camera* (Cambridge: Cambridge University Press, 1988), pp. 1–12.

3. Stanley Cavell, *Pursuits of Happiness* (Cambridge, Mass.: Harvard University Press, 1981).

4. Cf. Stanley Cavell, *The Senses of Walden,* expanded ed. (San Francisco: North Point Press, 1981); *Themes Out of School* (San Francisco: North Point Press, 1984); *In Quest of the Ordinary: Lines of Scepticism and Romanticism* (Chicago: University of Chicago Press, 1988); and *This New Yet Unapproachable America: Lectures after Emerson and Wittgenstein* (Albuquerque: Living Batch Press, 1989).

5. Wang Yuejin, "History and Its Discontent: Melodrama as Historical Understanding" (Chapter 5 in the present volume).

6. Stanley Cavell, *The World Viewed: Reflections on the Ontology of Film,* enlarged ed. (Cambridge, Mass.: Harvard University Press, 1979).

7. Peter Brooks, *The Melodramatic Imagination: Balzac, Henry James, Melodrama and the Mode of Excess* (New Haven: Yale University Press, 1976).

8. E. Ann Kaplan, "Melodrama/Subjectivity/Ideology: Western Melodrama Theories and Their Relevance to Recent Chinese Cinema" (Chapter 2 in the present volume, pp. 9–28).

9. This is a central theme of the essays that compose my book *The "I" of the Camera.*

10. Cf. Stanley Cavell, "Psychoanalysis and Cinema: The Melodrama of the Unknown Woman," in *Images in Our Souls: Cavell, Psychoanalysis, Cinema,* ed. Joseph Smith and William Kerrigan (Baltimore: Johns Hopkins University Press, 1987), pp. 11–43; "Ugly Duckling, Funny Butterfly: Bette Davis and *Now Voyager"* and "Postscript (1989): To Whom It May Concern," *Critical Inquiry* 16 (Winter 1990): 213–89.

11. Cavell, *Pursuits of Happiness,* pp. 1, 20–4, 34, 47–51, 66–70, 103–4, 141–5, 153–60, 223, 260.

12. Maureen Turim, "Psyche, Ideologies and Melodrama: The United States and Japan" (Chapter 9 in the present volume).

13. Laura Mulvey, "Visual Pleasure and Narrative Cinema," *Screen* 16, 3 (1975): 6–18.

14. Tania Modleski, "Editorial Notes," *Critical Inquiry* 16 (Autumn 1990): 237–8.

15. Stanley Cavell, "Editorial Notes," *Critical Inquiry* 16 (Autumn 1990): 238–44.

Index

Printed in the United Kingdom
by Lightning Source UK Ltd.
106063UKS00002B/197